Organizational
Evolution

*To my wife, Marlies, for, above all,
patience and understanding.*

Organizational Evolution
New Directions

edited by
Jitendra V. Singh

Withdrawn

SAGE PUBLICATIONS
The International Professional Publishers
Newbury Park   London   New Delhi

For information address:

SAGE Publications, Inc.
2111 West Hillcrest Drive
Newbury Park, California 91320

SAGE Publications Ltd.
28 Banner Street
London EC1Y 8QE
England

SAGE Publications India Pvt. Ltd.
M-32 Market
Greater Kailash I
New Delhi 110 048 India

Printed in the United States of America

Library of Congress Cataloging-in-Publication Data

Main entry under title:

Organizational evolution : new directions / Jitendra V. Singh.
     p.   cm.
     Papers from a conference held Dec. 1988, sponsored by the Reginald
H. Jones Center for Management Policy, Strategy, and Organization.
     Includes bibliographical references.
     ISBN 0-8039-3658-3. -- ISBN 0-8039-3659-1 (pbk.)
     1. Organizational change--Congresses.   I. Singh, Jitendra, 1954-
. II. Reginald H. Jones Center for Management Policy, Strategy, and
Organization.
HD58.8.0735   1990
658.4'063--dc20
                                    90-33468
                                         CIP

FIRST PRINTING, 1990

Sage Production Editor: Diane S. Foster

Contents

Foreword

The Reginald H. Jones Center for Management Policy, Strategy and Organization is pleased to be able to present this book, the final results of a conference that was held in December 1988 at the Sinkler Estate outside of Philadelphia. This congenial setting, part of the University of Pennsylvania, enabled us to hold a pleasant two-day conference during which several original papers were presented. This book is mainly a compilation of those papers.

The Jones Center has been fortunate in being able to sponsor three academic workshops and three executive workshops within the past year. The academic workshops have dealt with organizational evolution, resulting in this book; management science theory and methodology applied to corporate strategy, which will result in a special issue of *Management Science*; and an exploration by young faculty of the leading edge in corporate strategy, which should subsequently result in a book.

The three executive workshops, composed of 15 to 20 corporate executives and half a dozen Wharton faculty, used a panel format to explore information systems for competitive advantage, international organization structure and process issues, and technology innovation and imitation challenges. The Reginald H. Jones Center is especially appreciative of its industry sponsors, which support and encourage these activities.

We not only use these workshops as a platform to describe the ongoing research activities of the Center, we are able to support a dozen or more active research projects in any given year as the ground from which these workshops spring. The research falls under three broad areas — policy analysis, corporate strategy, and organization behavior — and is undertaken by regular university faculty with the aid of their graduate students.

The Jones Center is an integral part of the Wharton School of the University of Pennsylvania, the oldest collegiate business school in the United States, founded in 1881. The Wharton School has historically been a center of research both to support the industrial community and to enlighten our academic colleagues.

The material in this ground-breaking book was explored in a conference that brought together leading scholars in organizational evolution, a topic area of academic endeavor that should have broad impact on the way we think about organizations. Jitendra Singh has been a very effective convener of this conference and we are appreciative of his efforts, as well as of the fine labors of the individual authors.

— Edward H. Bowman
Director,
Reginald Jones Center for Management
Policy, Strategy and Organization

Acknowledgments

There are many debts that I owe to people who helped make this edited volume possible. First and foremost is Ned Bowman, whose faith in my idea of organizing a conference on organizational evolution was backed with significant financial support. Second, thanks to all the authors who took the time to write their contributions to this volume. Third, special thanks to Bob House, John Kimberly, Hans Pennings, and Marshall Meyer, who helped organize the conference. Finally, least visible but perhaps most critical was the editorial and typing assistance of John Rutter; without him, this volume would not have been possible.

— Jitendra V. Singh

1

Introduction

JITENDRA V. SINGH

ORGANIZATIONAL ECOLOGY AND ORGANIZATIONAL EVOLUTION

Until about a decade and a half ago, the prominent approach in organization theory emphasized adaptive change in organizations. Thus, as environments changed, leaders or dominant coalitions in organizations modified the appropriate organizational features so as to increase their fit with environmental conditions. Since then, a selection approach to studying organizational change that was introduced at about that time (Aldrich, 1979; Hannan & Freeman, 1977) has become increasingly influential. Several recent key texts (Carroll, 1987, 1988; Hannan & Freeman, 1989) and reviews (Carroll, 1984b; Singh & Lumsden, 1990) attest to this growing importance of organizational ecology.

The central theoretical thrust of organizational ecology is the investigation of how social environments shape rates of creation and death of organizational forms, rates of organizational founding and mortality, and rates of change in organizational forms. With some exceptions, however, empirical research in organizational ecology has focused more on differential foundings and mortality of organizations. Thus changes in organizational populations are largely attributable to how environmental conditions influence the demographic processes of entry and exit in populations (Singh & Lumsden, 1990).

This book emphasizes organizational evolution, a broader theme. In the biological literature, ecology and evolution are treated distinctly. Whereas ecology focuses on the relative demographic abundances of forms in relation to environmental conditions, evolutionary arguments are more interested in the dynamics of change in forms over time, especially how core structural properties of organisms influence their adaptation to changing environmental conditions. Ecological and evolutionary arguments ask complementary questions about the same historical processes.

The various chapters in this book are addressed to issues of organizational evolution and collectively have several distinctive features. First, this book presents some of the latest thinking on approaches to organizational evolution by leading thinkers in the area, and several chapters break new ground. Second, the overarching framework is to examine population change as it is constituted by rates of creation and death of organizational forms and organizations, and rates of change in organizational forms. Third, the collection is multidisciplinary in spirit. Thus, in addition to chapters from organizational ecology, several chapters are rooted in strategy, evolutionary economics, organizational change, sociocultural evolution, mathematical sociology, and technological change. The unifying theme, however, is that each chapter is motivated by an interest in some aspect of organizational evolution. This edited volume is based primarily on papers presented at the Wharton Conference on Organizational Evolution held in Philadelphia during December 1988. But two chapters — one by Barnett and Amburgey and the other by Levinthal — both centrally relevant to the theme of the book, augment the collection. The objective of this conference was to bring together a group of leading scholars of organizational evolution from a variety of disciplinary backgrounds to present original work in an effort to examine where theory and research in the area stand and what questions are useful to ask in the future. This book is the culmination of that rapprochement between their different approaches.

PLAN OF THE BOOK

This book was conceived to stimulate new thinking in organizational evolution by presenting research by some key figures. It is not the intent here to provide a coherent synthesis of their collective thinking. Rather, the ideas are presented with all their differences of focus and content, with a view to encouraging debate and discussion among scholars.

The volume is divided into two parts. Part I, consisting of four chapters, is made up of chapters that focus on founding and mortality processes in organizational populations. Even though some novel ideas are discussed, the emphasis of these chapters coincides with the usual emphasis in organizational ecology. The section concludes with a critical commentary on the four chapters. Part II consists of seven chapters that focus on some new directions in which various authors have moved and that depart from the usual concern of organizational ecology with foundings and disbandings. Whereas some chapters examine processes of change in individual organizations, others explore creation of new forms, size distributions in organizational populations, or the implications of adaptation and selection processes for organizational survival patterns at the population level. This section also concludes with a critical commentary, and is followed by a brief concluding statement that outlines some problems that show promise for the future.

The first chapter in Part I, by Aldrich, Staber, Zimmer, and Beggs, is these authors' first major empirical study from their ongoing research on U.S. trade associations. In this chapter, they present results for disbanding patterns in this population during the period 1900-1983. The authors argue that trade associations face pressures based on the logic of membership, the need to manage internal diversity, and the logic of influence, the need to manage relations with other associations. They treat trade associations as minimalist organizations that have low start-up and maintenance costs, have extensive reserve infrastructures as a population, are adaptive and normatively flexible, and have overt norms against direct competition. Among other findings, Aldrich et al.'s results suggest that the age dependence of mortality rates is curvilinear, unlike many other populations, but that density, the number of organizations alive, has the predicted curvilinear effect on mortality rate.

The next chapter, by Freeman, though similar in spirit to the Aldrich et al. study because exits by semiconductor firms from the industry are studied, also brings in an interest in the role of technological change in population dynamics. Instead of disbanding, the exit rate is studied because of an interest in the market and technology, and because many of these are diversified organizations that simultaneously operate in multiple markets. Exit rate is studied as a function of, among others, organizational age, density (the number of organizations alive), business conditions, and competition between subsidiary and independent forms of organization. The results support the predicted liability of newness, the negative age dependence of mortality rate, a curvilinear density dependence as predicted, and asymmetric competition between independent and subsidiary firms, with density of subsidiary firms influencing exit rate of independent firms, but not vice versa.

In Chapter 4, Barnett and Amburgey tackle directly one important criticism of arguments for density dependence of founding and mortality rates in organizational populations. Such arguments implicitly assume each organization to have an equal competitive impact in the population, regardless of size. Barnett and Amburgey propose an alternative mass dependence argument in which larger organizations generate stronger competitive effects. Both density and mass dependence arguments are modeled simultaneously in an early telephone company population. The results show that after controlling for mass dependence, the effects of density on founding and mortality rates are still significant, although not fully, as predicted by the theoretical models.

The final chapter in Part I, by Carroll and Hannan, suggests that the persistent positive effect of density at founding on mortality rate may explain why organizational populations usually decline in size after reaching a peak. Higher density at founding leads to a liability of scarcity, which interferes with organization building for newly formed organizations. It also leads to tighter niche packing, as new entrants find themselves pushed to the margins of the resource space by established competitors. Data from five populations show strong support for this density delay argument, after the effects of contemporaneous density are controlled.

Baum and House, in a commentary on these four chapters, review the contributions made and highlight the inattention to changes associated with aging of organizational populations. They discuss the potential of three such changes — population maturation, technological change, and institutionalization — in integrating current organizational ecology research with notions of aging of organizational populations and in refining organizational ecology.

In Chapter 6, the first chapter in Part II, Lumsden and Singh address organizational speciation, the creation of the first organization of a new form, an unanswered question to which critics of organizational ecology have repeatedly pointed (Astley, 1985; Young, 1988). New organizational forms are treated as products of entrepreneurial thinking, and their creation is influenced by the emergence of new interconcept linkages in knowledge structures in the minds of entrepreneurs. Lumsden and Singh propose a multilevel schematic model that builds on recent work on the creative process, linking entrepreneurial creative thinking, the sociocultural environment, and organizational speciation. They develop a formal quantitative model of the speciation process that gives some insight into how that process may be managed better through altering key parameters.

The next chapter, by Burgelman, focuses on an intraorganizational question: Where do strategies come from? Organizations are viewed as contrived internal ecologies in which both induced and autonomous strategic processes occur. Induced strategic processes correspond to the traditional conception of strategy as it emanates from top management interventions, and are a form of variation-reducing mechanism. However, autonomous strategic processes that are variation enhancing occur without management intervention and are based in grass-roots autonomous action in organizations. These autonomous strategic processes allow fundamental renewals and reorientations to take place in organizations. Burgelman illuminates the evolution of Intel Corporation's corporate strategy using this intraorganizational ecology perspective.

The Tucker, Singh, and Meinhard chapter also has an intraorganizational focus, and addresses the question of imprinting in organizations. Although the concept of imprinting is frequently invoked by researchers in theorical arguments, it is not researched as frequently. The usual approach taken is to show that organizational characteristics at founding persist over time, and most evidence for imprinting is anecdotal. Tucker et al. examine imprinting by studying the effects of founding environmental conditions and organizational characteristics on rates of change in organizational features in a population of voluntary organizations. The results of their exploratory analysis suggest some support for the effects of founding conditions on rates of change, despite controlling for changes in environmental conditions over time.

In Chapter 9, Levinthal develops a simple analytical model to explore the implications of adaptation, selection, and random models of organizational change for the pattern of survival in organizational populations. His simulations are based on the premise that appropriate organizational choices increase wealth, inappropriate organizational choices decrease wealth, and, when the wealth level falls to zero, the organization dies. The results show that in populations of both adaptive and inert organizations the mortality rate is a declining function of organizational age. In fact, this negative duration dependence can be expected to occur even in the case of random organizational change, provided that early success buffers an organization from selection. Levinthal introduces the concept of a refined risk set with respect to which, he argues, the predictions for adaptation, selection, and random action models are quite different.

In Chapter 10, McPherson deals with how communities of voluntary organizations evolve over time. Instead of focusing on organizational traits, he argues for an emphasis on changes in the niches of organizations. Voluntary organizations compete with each other for members, a valuable resource. This competition is at the center of McPherson's ecological models of community organization, and selection of members drives niche movement. In comparing the members' characteristics with population characteristics, exploitation curves emerge that indicate over- and underexploited regions of the population. Since new members resemble existing members, those organizations closest to underexploited regions of the space can most readily take advantage of new members. This model generates hypotheses about change and stability in organizational niches and the growth, decline, origin, and death of voluntary groups.

Hannan, Ranger-Moore, and Banaszak-Holl's chapter addresses organizational growth, another important topic in organizational evolution, and asks how organizational size distributions evolve over time in an ecological context. These researchers' ecological formulation introduces a carrying capacity and entries and exits into classical models of size distributions. An important feature of the ecological model is size-localized competition; that is, competition is strongest between like-sized organizations. A special version of this model produces size distributions that depart significantly from the usual lognormal, with a depression at the center of the distribution. The plausibility of such a model is reinforced by empirical historical data from New York City banks and insurance companies in New York State.

The final chapter in Part II is Winter's essay on evolutionary economics, which goes significantly beyond and extends his earlier work (Nelson & Winter, 1982). Here again, as in the earlier chapters by Burgelman and Tucker et al., the focus is intraorganizational. Winter argues that the appropriate unit of analysis in studying organizations is the routine or comp (McKelvey, 1982). Routines that are successful — that is, appropriate to the environmental conditions — get replicated, whereas unsuccessful routines get selected out. Unlike biotic organisms, organizations grow through successful replication, either by vertical integration or by diversification. Winter also relates the concerns of evolutionary economics with organizational ecology and identifies issues for future research.

Meyer's commentary on the chapters in Part II takes the form of an initial statement that classifies research on organizational evolution based on a cross-classification of change in organizations and change in environments, and its implications for organizational mortality. This is followed by critical commentary on each of the seven chapters, in the order of their degree of departure from orthodox organizational ecology. Meyer concludes with a call for research on the conditions under which pure ecological or evolutionary arguments may hold.

The last chapter of this volume discusses some important questions related to organizational evolution that are currently outstanding and hold promise for the future. Imprinting in organizations and the underlying processes, individual organizational change, the convergence of ecological and institutional ideas, community ecology, organizational classification and taxonomy, organizational speciation, and the nature of organizational evolution are some of the questions highlighted.

REFERENCES

Aldrich, H. E. (1979). *Organizations and environments*. Englewood Cliffs, NJ: Prentice-Hall.

Astley, W. G. (1985). The two ecologies: Population and community perspectives on organizational evolution. *Administrative Science Quarterly, 30*(2), 224-241.

Carroll, G. R. (1984a). Dynamics of publisher succession in newspaper organizations. *Administrative Science Quarterly, 29*(1), 93-113.

Carroll, G. R. (1984b). Organizational ecology. *Annual Review of Sociology, 10*, 71-93.

Carroll, G. R. (1987). *Publish and perish: The organizational ecology of newspaper industries*. Greenwich, CT: JAI.

Carroll, G. R. (Ed.). (1988). *Ecological models of organization*. Cambridge, MA: Ballinger.

Hannan, M. T., & Freeman, J. (1977). The population ecology of organizations. *American Journal of Sociology, 82*, 929-964.

Hannan, M. T., & Freeman, J. (1989). *Organizational ecology*. Cambridge, MA: Harvard University Press.

McKelvey, B. (1982). *Organizational systematics: Taxonomy, evolution, classification*. Berkeley: University of California Press.

Nelson, R. R., & Winter, S. G. (1982). *An evolutionary theory of economic change*. Cambridge, MA: Harvard University Press.

Singh, J. V., & Lumsden, C. J. (1990). Theory and research in organizational ecology. *Annual Review of Sociology, 16*: 161-195.

Young, R. C. (1988). Is population ecology a useful paradigm for the study of organizations? *American Journal of Sociology, 94*(1), 1-24.

PART ONE

Founding and Mortality Processes

2

Minimalism and Organizational Mortality: Patterns of Disbanding Among U.S. Trade Associations, 1900-1983

HOWARD ALDRICH
UDO STABER
CATHERINE ZIMMER
JOHN J. BEGGS

Trade associations are organizations created to represent business interests within specific domains, mobilizing firms within their domain so that collective action can be taken on common problems. Political economists are beginning to pay more systematic attention to business interest groups (Schmitter & Streeck, 1981), and recent research has focused on interest mobilization and interest group foundings (Schmitter & Brand, 1979; Walker, 1983). Surprisingly, however, virtually no information is available on the organizational stability of trade associations and the conditions under which associations sustain member support.

There is no necessary relationship between the formation of formal collective action and a group's ability to maintain itself under changing circum-

Authors' Note: The following people helped us collect and organize the data: Sharon Byrd, Jeanne Hurlbert, Jane Morrow, Maureen O'Connor, Jane Salk, Jane Scott, and Leslie Wasson. Jan Bryant and Mal-Soon Min were the primary research assistants on our project, and saved us from serious errors on more than one occasion. Comments and criticisms from the following people helped immensely in our revisions: Avner Ben-Ner, Kenneth Bollen, John Campbell, Glenn Carroll, Jacques Delacroix, Paul DiMaggio, Terence Halliday, Dawn Kelly, Jeffrey Leiter, Duncan Macrae, Jr., Mark Mizruchi, Michael Powell, Jitendra Singh, Donald Tomaskovic-Devey, Michael Useem, and Frans Van Waarden.

stances. Studying the survival chances of trade associations has clear implications for understanding the role and stability of interest intermediation in modern industrial society (Schmitter & Lehmbruch, 1979). Studies have shown that business interests in the United States frequently organize ad hoc groups to deal with issues as they arise (Lynn & McKeown, 1988), rather than, as in more corporatist regimes, using existing associations to develop common positions. Interest mobilization is probably easier and more effective in regimes with stable association populations than in systems where businesses need to organize from scratch each time they perceive threats to their interests. The U.S. system of business interest representation is usually described in terms of a population of numerous, specialized, competitive, and fragile business associations (Salisbury, 1979). This depiction, however, is generally based on impressionistic, anecdotal, and small sample observations. Our objective in this chapter is to put the study of trade associations on a more solid empirical footing by examining the rate of disbandings in the entire population of national trade associations in the United States between 1900 and 1983.

Following Schmitter and Streeck (1981), we have organized our analysis around two central pressures facing trade associations: the logic of membership and the logic of influence. Together, these two pressures present associations with dilemmas that have no easy resolutions.

The *logic of membership* compels trade associations to minister to the needs of member firms, creating a governance structure to manage the diversity of members' interests. The greater their internal diversity, the greater the centrifugal pressure on associations and the greater the pressures toward costly administrative structures to manage diversity. More diverse associations also face the danger that more narrowly focused single-interest associations or coalitions may outcompete them for members' energies. On the other hand, internal diversity may also create opportunities if diversity implies a broad resource base that buffers associations from changes in the membership. From an ecological perspective, diversity may improve the capacity of groups to survive changing conditions.

The *logic of influence* compels associations to manage competition with other associations and relations with the state to meet their substantive goals. For example, a primary focus of trade associations is lobbying the federal government, responding to attempted regulation, or mitigating the negative effects of legislation. Dealing with external relations requires attention to domain definition and various forms of interorganizational relations, all of which may drain resources that could otherwise be directed toward members' demands for special services. Our research attempts to capture these two themes in associative action, insofar as this is possible with data from historical records, and to show the consequences that the pursuit of each logic has for associations' fates.

WHAT ARE TRADE ASSOCIATIONS?

Trade associations can be defined as business interest organizations that represent their members' political and economic preferences, although at times they also act as vehicles for governments to implement public policies (Coleman, 1988).[1] Trade associations differ in several important respects from many previously studied populations of organizations: They are voluntary associations that depend upon survival of their constituents for their own existence, they represent segments of the most politically privileged sector in capitalist countries, they strive for a monopoly position within their domain, and they restrict their prospects of changing domains by making substantial investments in their claimed domains. In these respects, they resemble most closely the state bar associations studied by Halliday, Powell, and Granfors (1987), but also have much in common with the trade unions studied by Hannan and Freeman (1988), the voluntary social service sector organizations studied by Singh, House, and Tucker (1986), and the cooperatives studied by Staber (1989b).

As interest associations, trade associations are subject to the collective rationality problem (Olson, 1965). They resemble labor unions in that their survival depends not only on how well they represent membership interests but also on how effective they are in aggregating the parochial preferences of their members. Unlike bar associations, trade associations attempt not only to represent the political interests of members but also to stabilize relations between members. Some associations represent specific industries, whereas others cut across what are commonly thought of as "industry" boundaries, linking groups of firms horizontally or vertically in different product or service lines. As second-order organizations, their survival chances are inextricably tied to the fates of their member organizations, irrespective of the effectiveness of interest representation and aggregation. Trade associations are also minimalist organizations that can survive on very low overhead expenses and supportive services, and thus may be subject to selection pressures that are different from those of other populations of organizations.

Halliday et al. (1987) identify five core dimensions of minimalist organizations: (a) low initial costs in labor commitments and capital; (b) low maintenance costs, allowing them to survive in fairly poor resource environments; (c) reserve infrastructures, which minimalist organizations can fall back on in times of hardship, such as by borrowing resources from members; (d) high adaptiveness, which allows minimalist organizations to adapt more readily to environmental changes than organizations with higher sunk costs in their existing structures; and (e) high normative flexibility, which allows minimalist organizations to alter the definition of their mission as circumstances require (p. 457).

Trade associations display most of these characteristics, but differ from bar associations in that they have never achieved government sanction as the sole representatives for their domains (except in times of national emergency). During their early years, many trade associations operate out of the offices of a member firm, with firms taking turns subsidizing much of the administrative overhead required to sustain the association. Since the 1960s, some associations have turned to association management firms, often based in Washington, D.C., New York, or Chicago, to carry out the routine activities of associations between annual meetings.

Trade associations are remarkably lean organizations, administratively, but they are *not* trivial organizations. For example, although average paid staff size hardly increased at all from 1976 to 1983, going from 14.2 to 14.5 employees, average budgets jumped from $297,000 to $623,000. The average number of member firms increased from 913 to 951 over this same period.[2] The figures for budget size may be compared to those of U.S. trade unions to gain some idea of their relative size. In 1982, 47.1% of U.S. trade unions had annual incomes of under $1 million, compared to 83.5% of U.S. trade associations. Unfortunately, data on staff size for the U.S. trade union population are not readily available. Comparisons of unions and trade associations on membership size are not particularly revealing, as union membership is often obligatory, whereas trade associations are legally prevented from requiring membership of firms in their industries.

STUDY DESIGN

We distinguish trade associations from professional societies (e.g., the American Bar Association), from trade unions (e.g., the United Auto Workers), and from various for-profit organizations that sometimes have the word *association* in their titles.[3] We include only associations that are national in scope and that are engaged in the promotion or defense of business interests, although 62 regional associations that were predecessors to national associations, or that are otherwise linked to national associations, are included. We excluded local associations because it would have been virtually impossible to compile information on the entire population and because local associations are of little substantive interest in the present analysis. Although there may be instances where local business associations compete with national associations or were predecessors to national organizations, such cases are probably rare. Most of our sample is in the manufacturing sector, reflecting that sector's higher level of collective activities.

Descriptive information about the associations was collected from two comprehensive listings of national trade associations, published annually since 1965 and intermittently in earlier years: the *Encyclopedia of Associations* (various years) and the *Directory of National and Professional Associations in the U.S.* (Colgate, 1966-1984). A third source, *Trade and Professional Associations of the U.S.* (Judkins, 1942, 1949), proved very valuable for the 1940s. (Judkins also published a list of trade associations in 1956 for the Commerce Department, but the list did not contain founding dates or historical detail.) For associations born in the nineteenth and early twentieth centuries, we consulted various Department of Commerce publications, research monographs, business history journals, newsletters, and other historical sources. For more information about the sources of data, see Aldrich and Staber (1988).[4] Our sample is as close to a complete listing of all trade associations ever founded as is possible, given our sources. For the purpose of analyzing associations' disbandings, we focus on the period 1900 to 1983, as data on trade association life cycles improved considerably from the nineteenth century to the twentieth.

HYPOTHESES AND MEASURES

The event of interest to us is the disbanding of a national trade association — an association ceases operating as an active organization, without merging or being absorbed into another association and without being transformed into a different association. Of the 3,339 associations with known founding dates ever active during the twentieth century, 2,248 were still active in 1983, 355 disbanded, 77 changed their forms so significantly they were classified as transformed, 460 merged with or were absorbed by other associations, and 199 were lost at some point in the historical record. All terminating events other than disbandings were treated as censoring the history of a trade association with respect to the risk of disbanding.[5]

The Logic of Membership

Interest Diversity

We assessed internal interest diversity in four ways: (a) a count of the number of discrete 4-digit Standard Industrial Classification (SIC) codes represented by an association; (b) a measure of whether the association included members from more than one link in the chain of production involving an industry, such as wholesalers and retailers of a manufactured product; (c) a measure of whether the association represented a specific industry/set of industries or was a cross-industry general-interest association that firms from any industry could join; and (d) whether the association was under the umbrella of another association. The latter three variables were measured with three time-constant dummy variables.

Number of SIC codes represented. A large majority of associations covered only one or two 4-digit SIC codes (62%), but 9% represented ten or more. Because this measure was highly skewed, we used the natural logarithm version of it in our analyses. Successive cohorts of associations have shown a slight tendency to become more internally diverse over this century, as measured by the number of 4-digit SIC codes covered (the correlation between year of birth and the natural log of the number of SIC codes represented is .07). There are at least two reasons for this trend. First, the professionalization of association administration — eventually institutionalized in the founding of the American Society of Association Executives — produced administrators who could manage the greater diversity induced by more heterogeneous associations. Second, mergers between associations created new associations that quite often contained firms from different 4-digit SIC codes. For example, in 1978 the American Hardboard Association (SIC 2499) merged with the Acoustical and Insulating Materials Association (SIC 3296), forming the American Board Products Association.

Previous research has suggested that trade associations representing a small number of product groups and industries are less likely to experience governance problems and internal conflict than are large and structurally heterogeneous associations (Staber, 1987). Internal conflict is particularly destabilizing in voluntary interest organizations, such as trade associations, whose survival depends on the continued support of their (major) members.

- *Hypothesis 1a:* The greater the number of 4-digit SIC codes an association represents, the greater its odds of disbanding.

Vertical linkages. About 29% of the associations included not only firms from a primary industry — the focal point of the association — but also firms that do business, upstream or downstream, with the primary firms. For example, the American Butter Institute, founded in 1908, includes not only butter manufacturers but also packagers and distributors of butter. The Metal Building Components Manufacturers' Association represents firms manufacturing and firms selling metal building components for architectural, commercial, industrial, and agricultural use.

Associations that include firms from more than one link in the chain of production tend to represent more 4-digit SIC codes: The correlation between the natural log of the number of SIC codes presented and the dummy variable for vertical linkages is .34 ($p < .01$). Of those associations with no vertical linkages, 56% covered only one 4-digit SIC, whereas of those with vertical linkages, only 15% covered just one 4-digit SIC, and trade associations with vertical linkages averaged about three and a half more SIC codes than those without vertical linkages. We expect vertical linkages to raise interest diversity and thus increase governance problems, making associations vulnerable to dissolution via internal conflict.

- *Hypothesis 1b:* Trade associations representing firms from more than one stage in the chain of production have higher disbanding rates than do horizontal associations.

General-interest associations. The number of business-oriented associations organizing across industry boundaries increased from 4 in 1900 to 35 in 1980. These associations, such as the Coalition for Common Sense in Government Procurement or the Convention Liaison Coalition, have claimed domains that are broad enough to encompass firms from a wide range of industries. Many conform closely to the classic definition of action sets: organizations created to achieve a limited set of goals within a short period of time (Aldrich & Whetten, 1981). The combination of their diverse membership and short-term time horizon should raise the disbanding rates for such associations.

- *Hypothesis 1c:* General-interest associations have higher disbanding rates than other trade associations.

Divisionalization. About 3% of the associations in our sample were divisions, institutes, or committees under the umbrellas of other associations. Such ties might be seen as protective for associations because they allow the

associations to specialize and perhaps use some of the administrative resources of the other associations. However, divisions must deal with two
kinds of pressures not found in independent associations: the potential of
having their mandate absorbed by the other associations, and the problem of
reconciling divergent policies between associations.

- *Hypothesis 1d:* Being a division of another business interest association raises
  the odds of a trade association's disbanding.

Minimalism

As minimalist organizations, trade associations have many characteristics
in common with state bar associations and cooperatives, which require
minimal resources for founding and sustenance. We assessed the importance
of minimalism in two ways: (a) a measure of age, in years, since year of
founding; and (b) two measures of possible disruption in an association's life
cycle — name changes and acquisitions of other associations.

Minimalism and the liability of adolescence. Fichman and Levinthal
(1988) have argued that many types of organizations and organizational
relationships face not a liability of newness but a "liability of adolescence,"
in which disbandings and terminations are low early in an organization's life
cycle and then rise as the participants' enthusiasm and commitments are
exhausted. We expect that trade associations are relatively protected from
early disbanding for two reasons.

First, like other products of collective action, they are sustained in their
early years by the enthusiasm and commitment of their founding members.
As minimalist organizations, trade associations resemble worker cooperatives, for example, which generally survive their first few years of existence
(Ben-Ner, 1988), benefiting from low setup costs and a high degree of
member commitment (Staber, 1989a). Worker cooperatives are most vulnerable during adolescence, when members rethink their commitment to the
organization and the original entrepreneurs evaluate the joint enterprise in
light of changing conditions.

Second, unlike newspapers or semiconductor firms, trade associations
need not meet an early test of profitability to survive. Many of the objectives
associations pursue (such as improving an industry's public image and
lobbying government agents) require several years before any results are
apparent. Their (larger) members probably take a wait-and-see attitude
before evaluating whether or not their continued support is worthwhile.

The age at which an association's members begin to question their commitment to collective efforts is an empirical question, but we expect the peak in disbanding rates to occur later in the life of trade associations than it does in other organizations. Unlike bar associations, voluntary social service organizations, and cooperatives, trade associations are made up of business firms, rather than individuals, and so we would expect more stability or inertia in their membership. The decision to support a trade association is made within the firm's organizational context and, like other strategic decisions, it is limited by bureaucratic and political considerations that raise the level of commitment to joint efforts once the decision to support an association is made. From the association's perspective, inertia-induced member commitment increases the duration of the "honeymoon" period (Fichman & Levinthal, 1988).

We expect that disbandings fall again after an adolescent peak, as the hardier associations have survived the crisis of falling esprit de corps. This reasoning suggests a curvilinear relationship between age and disbanding rates, modeled with a linear and a squared term for age in our equations.

- *Hypothesis 2a:* Disbanding rates increase with association age and then decline, as the association matures.

Changes: adaptive versus disruptive. In arguing that structural inertia characterizes most organizations, Hannan and Freeman (1984, pp. 156-157) suggest that changes in the peripheral features of organizations are more likely than changes in core features. They hypothesize that core changes are more disruptive than peripheral changes, with major changes resetting the liability of newness clock back to zero and hence raising disbanding rates. Singh, House, and Tucker (1986) tested this prediction on their sample of Toronto voluntary social service organizations. They found that of the six types of change they examined, goal and structural change had no effect on disbandings, chief executive and location changes early in the population's history lowered disbanding rates, and only two types of change actually raised disbanding rates — domain change early in the population's history and sponsorship change late in its history. Core changes, such as goal change and change in chief executive, were more, rather than less, frequent than more peripheral changes, such as domain and client change. This finding is not consistent with Hannan and Freeman's (1984) proposition but fits well with the depiction of minimalist organizations as adaptable, flexible, and capable of transforming even their core features.

We examined two types of changes relevant to trade associations' membership, given data availability: *changes in names* and *acquisitions of other trade associations*. A name change is often undertaken when an association's leaders wish to realign public perceptions of the association and convey more accurately the domain that it claims. For example, in 1959 the Wallpaper Wholesalers Association changed its name to the Wallcovering Wholesalers Association, reflecting the fact that other types of wall coverings were a significant portion of their distributed products, and then made another minor name change in 1979, to the Wallcovering Distributors Association. In the twentieth century, about 30% of associations have changed their names at least once: 22% changed once, 6% changed twice, and 2% changed three times or more.

Because we believe that name changes are made after changes in association membership, we hypothesize that they are relatively peripheral changes that have little or no effect on association mortality. By contrast, acquisitions of other associations bring new members into an association that must be absorbed, and we expect them to be somewhat more disruptive than name changes, although they are probably still not *core* changes in that they typically do not involve authority or goal changes.[6] For example, in 1965 the manufacturing members of the National Warm Air Heating & Air Conditioning Association were absorbed into the Air Conditioning and Refrigeration Institute, followed by the acquisition of the Air Filter Institute (formerly the National Association of Air Filter Manufacturers) in 1967. In the twentieth century, 4% of the associations were involved in at least one acquisition: Of the 141 associations making at least one acquisition, 115 made only one, 18 made two, and 8 made three or more acquisitions. Because they are somewhat more disruptive than name changes, we expect to find a stronger positive effect of acquisitions on disbanding rates.

- *Hypothesis 2b:* Acquisitions have a stronger positive effect on disbanding rates than do name changes.

The Logic of Influence

Acquiring legitimacy and protecting or enlarging their sphere of influence compels trade associations to manage competition with other associations. Additionally, many other environmental actors and forces confront trade associations with the need for action: the federal government's legislative and regulatory bodies, economic and social changes, and so forth. For this chapter, we focus only on the dynamics of legitimation and competition within the trade association population.[7] We assessed the logic of influence model by measuring (a) density — the total number of associations active in any given year, (b) the presence of competitor associations, and (c) the formation of interorganizational relations with other associations.

Density Dependence in Disbanding Rates

In recent papers, Hannan and Freeman (1988) and Carroll and Hannan (Chapter 5, this volume) have investigated the density dependence of organizational dissolution. They have found that dissolution rates begin at high levels with low densities, then, as density (ordinarily measured by the number of organizations in the population) increases, dissolution rates gradually decline and then gradually rise again. Carroll, Freeman, and Hannan interpret this U-shaped relationship between increasing density and dissolution rates as the net effect of two different processes: legitimation and competition.

First, with respect to legitimation, early in a population's history, organizations must fight for social and political legitimacy (Aldrich & Stern, 1983; Carroll, 1987; Hannan & Freeman, 1988). Also, early in the history of a population, potential founders lack information about effective internal organizational arrangements, and have few models to copy (Staber, 1989b). Lack of legitimacy, lack of information, and lack of effective models are expected to raise the dissolution rate when the population is small. As density increases — the number of organizations grows over time — the social and political legitimacy of the population may become better accepted, even institutionalized (Zucker, 1986). The organizations that survive the turbulent and dangerous early years of the population now present potential entrepreneurs with effective organizational models, which they can copy. Thus dissolution rates begin to drop.

Second, opposed to the increasing legitimacy of the population is the effect of competitive pressures. Early in a population's history, its domain is underpopulated and first movers have access to almost unlimited resources. As the population begins to grow, however, competitive pressures increase. So, whereas early in a population's history the effect of the lack of legitimacy dominated, causing high dissolution rates, in the middle years of the population, legitimacy has been achieved and density is not yet high enough to raise dissolution rates substantially. Then, even though the effect of legitimacy would produce lower dissolution rates, the effect of competition increasingly dominates the legitimacy effect and the net effect is rising dissolution rates.

Evidence of this relationship comes from research on a variety of organizational populations, including labor unions (Hannan & Freeman, 1988), newspapers, and breweries (Carroll & Hannan, Chapter 5, this volume). Delacroix, Swaminathan, and Solt (1989), however, found no significant relationship between density and the failings of California wineries. Finally, the estimated relationship between density and disbandings found by Tucker, Singh, Meinhard, and House (1988) for voluntary social service organizations was in the opposite direction; that is, disbanding rates first increased and then declined with population growth.

We are not certain whether Hannan and Freeman's formulation of density dependence in disbanding rates is limited to certain populations, whether some of the studies cited above covered truncated histories of populations, or whether other processes confound the estimated effects of density. Delacroix et al. (1989) argue that density dependence obscures processes of foundings and failings. Barnett and Amburgey (Chapter 4, this volume) show for a sample population of the early American telephone industry that the pattern of density dependence is affected by the size of organizations in the population. Specifically, modeling the effects of competitor average size eliminates the mutualistic effect and highlights the competitive effect of density. Unfortunately, because we have incomplete information on association size, we cannot replicate this finding.

Figure 2.1 shows the pattern of long-term change in the trade association population after 1900. Foundings, dissolutions, and transformations in the twentieth century produced a trade association population that grew rapidly from the turn of the century until the late 1950s. Elsewhere, we have shown that the slowdown in population growth after 1960 was the result of the gradual convergence of founding and dissolution rates (Aldrich & Staber, 1988).[8]

The major battles over the legitimacy of trade associations as an organizational form of business collective action took place in the late nineteenth century, when their forerunners — cartels and trusts — were established by firms attempting to regulate competition (Galambos, 1988). Even today, however, trade associations enjoy a precarious standing as legitimate participants in the marketplace. Antitrust law in the United States "recognizes the individual firms as the fundamental unit of production and legitimates the trade association as an industry wide representative only in so far as it serves the individual competitor" (Schmitter & Brand, 1979, p. 71). Hence we believe that our analysis, although restricted to the twentieth century, will still detect the legitimation effects of low density.

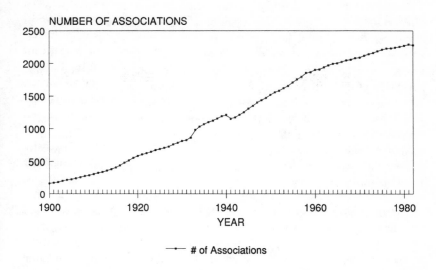

Figure 2.1. Number of trade associations, 1900-1980. All types of associations are included.

Density dependence should produce increasing disbanding rates for associations as the population grows toward carrying capacity in the late twentieth century. Consider three effects of increased density: (a) competition for skilled professional association administrators increases, assuming their supply is relatively fixed or lags behind association growth because educational institutions adapt slowly to the increase; (b) associations find their domains increasingly circumscribed and possible expansion constrained; and (c) the set of potential association memberships among U.S. firms, especially the large ones that subsidize association budgets, is increasingly saturated.[9] Staber (1987) found that in 1981, all but one of the 71 associations he studied included as members all of the four largest firms in their domains. We measure population density, $N(t)$, as the number of associations alive in a given year, regardless of when they were born. To model the curvilinear effects of population density, we also include the quadratic term $N^2(t)/1,000$.

- *Hypothesis 3a:* Disbanding rates decline with increasing population density to a point beyond which disbanding rates increase.

Density at the time of founding has been hypothesized to have a lasting effect on the life chances of organizations, and research has found such an effect in four different populations (Carroll & Hannan, Chapter 5, this volume; Tucker, Singh, & Meinhard, in press). Organizations founded in lean times, when competition for resources is fierce, may be pushed to the periphery of their niche and find themselves recruiting less able members, adopting cheaper and inferior technologies, and so forth. Such organizations would have elevated disbanding rates throughout their lifetimes. Similarly, organizations founded in affluent times have the luxury of perfecting their structures and processes, experimenting with innovations, and otherwise gaining the extra strength that will see them through periods that spell doom for weaker organizations.

- *Hypothesis 3b:* Associations founded in times of high population density have higher disbanding rates than associations founded in times of low density.

We tested this hypothesis by including a term for the size of the population at the time of an association's founding: population density at birth. We also included disbandings in the previous year, following Hannan and Freeman's (1988, p. 32) suggestion, on the assumption that a wave of disbandings might signal ominous times ahead for other associations and encourage them to disband.

Minimalist Organizations and Norms of Competition

The density dependence described above is associated with growth in the total population of trade associations, but there is another set of associations with an even more direct competitive effect on associations' fates: associations organizing firms in the same industry. Associations in the same niche can have at leave two potential effects on disbanding rates: a facilitative effect of predecessors on subsequent associations, and a competitive effect of coexisting associations seeking to organize the same domain.

First, predecessor associations in the same industry may smooth the way for future organizing attempts, showing the feasibility of an association, providing trained leaders, and creating a climate of cooperation. Such effects should decrease the vulnerability of subsequent associations and thus lower disbanding rates. We assume that the facilitative effects of predecessor associations would dissipate within a few years of an association's founding. Imitation and legitimation effects from predecessors ought to lower disbanding rates for a time, but then associations are on their own. We attempted to capture this effect by creating a term that took its maximum value the year an association was founded and then quickly dropped to a small value within a few years:

$$\text{predecessors} = 1/(\text{age} + 1)^2 * \ln(\text{number of predecessors} + 1) \quad [1]$$

For example, for an association with two predecessors (the median number in our sample), values of this variable would drop from 1.09 in the first year (when age is 0) to .07 in the fourth year (when age is 3) to .02 in the eighth year (when age is 7).

- *Hypothesis 4a:* Increases in the number of predecessor associations reduce the disbanding rates of subsequent associations, and this effect declines with association age.

Second, predecessors that survive become competitors for new associations in the same industry, possibly leading to domain conflict and raising disbanding rates. However, we expect the level of direct competition among trade associations organizing firms in the same industry to be minimal. Halliday et al. (1987) argue that, unlike organizations that inhabit overlapping or poorly defined niches, many minimalist associations "have well-defined niches and segmented competitive environments that require minimal defense" (p. 457). They had bar associations in mind, which eventually — 40 to 50 years after the first founding wave — achieved state-mandated monopolies, a standing generally not granted to trade associations. These authors also argue that norms against overt competition with similar associations often exist in populations of minimalist organizations, discouraging conflict over domains or members. Staber (1982) found evidence for such norms during intensive interviews with the heads of 71 trade associations in New York and Washington, D.C. Association officers explicitly discounted the possibility of overt competition with other associations in the same industry, arguing instead that "mutual accommodation" was more likely.

Figure 2.2 shows the mean number of competitors that the average trade association faced at its founding over the twentieth century. We have not presented a plot of the average number of predecessors because they are extremely similar — the correlation between the two time series is .95. We capture direct competition between associations by counting the number of other associations active in the same year that organize the same 4-digit SIC code. Because the variable was highly skewed, we used its natural logarithm in all analyses.

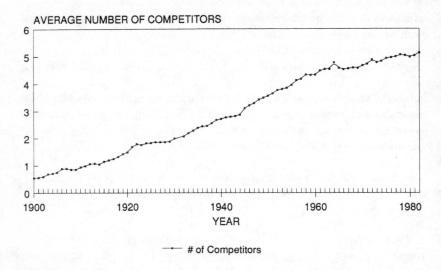

Figure 2.2. Average number of competitors, 1900-1980. Peak/general associations are excluded.

- *Hypothesis 4b:* The number of associations in the same industry has no effect on disbanding rates.

Interorganizational Relations

Trade associations, as minimalists, can attempt to increase their influence by attaching themselves to larger associations at little or no cost to the host association (Aldrich & Auster, 1986). Forming a tie to another association increases external sources of information (and possible resources) for associations, and may give associations greater visibility for their activities. Barnett and Amburgey (Chapter 4, this volume) found that small telephone companies could increase their survival chances by affiliating with a large firm in the industry. The benefits of linkages were not limited to direct partnerships, but included also diffuse ties to geographically removed companies. Singh, Tucker, and House (1986) found that external linkages to important sources of legitimacy lowered the disbanding rates of voluntary social service organizations.

We measured several types of interorganizational ties: being loosely affiliated in a coalition, working group, or other arms-length relationship with one or more associations, or being a member of a peak association.[10] All ties were collapsed into a single dummy variable, indicating whether an association had any interorganizational relations — slightly less than 7% had some form of external linkage. We expected that such interorganizational relations would reduce disbanding rates for associations, because of resources and other supports made available through such ties. However, we noted that Hannan and Freeman (1988) had found no significant effect of membership in national federations on the disbanding rates of unions.

- *Hypothesis 5:* External affiliations reduce disbanding rates.

Other Factors

Other possible influences on association disbanding are (a) type of founding, (b) whether the association is a peak association, and (c) societal-level changes.

Type of founding. Associations that are founded through mergers, transformations, or spin-offs involving previous associations should have a survival advantage over associations founded without predecessors. They can draw on the organizational experiences of members and administrators from their component associations to avoid the common mistakes that totally new foundings make. Merged associations are also larger than their predecessors, and this makes them more credible players of the logic of influence. Hannan and Freeman (1988), for example, found that unions without an immediate predecessor union had higher disbanding rates than those unions with immediate predecessors. We include dummy variables for three founding types in the analysis: merger, transformation, and spin-offs, with *de novo* foundings the omitted category.

- *Hypothesis 6:* Associations founded through mergers, transformations, or spin-offs from previous associations have lower disbanding rates than associations founded *de novo.*

Peak associations. Peak associations are associations made up of other associations, and as such might be more stable, as their membership base is spread over more firms than is typical of a trade association. Offsetting this advantage, however, is the inherent instability of collective actors that are more than one step removed from the ostensible beneficiaries of their actions. This variable is measured as a dummy.

- *Hypothesis 7:* Peak associations have higher disbanding rates than lower-level associations.

Societal-level changes. In their analysis of trade union disbandings, Hannan and Freeman (1988) examined eleven environmental covariates to account for changes in the social, economic, and political environments facing unions. They used time series on economic catastrophes and more moderate swings in the economy as independent variables, and found that the effects of most covariates were not significant. Of those that were significant, the effects were slight. We considered using their measures in this analysis, but did not for the following reason. The theoretical link between aggregate economic conditions and association disbandings is an indirect one. We posit that national economic conditions would affect population density, which, in turn, would affect association disbandings. This argument is supported by the high positive correlations between density and any measure of economic expansion that increased over this century, such as capital investment or GNP per capita.[11] Therefore, the correct specification of our model includes density, through which aggregate economic conditions affect disbandings.

EVENT HISTORY ANALYSIS

The Model

Event history analysis has two specifications, one used when events occur at discrete intervals, as in regime transitions after regular elections or when the timing of events has been measured grossly, and the other used when time has been measured finely enough to be treated as exact and continuous. Our data were collected by years and form partial event histories because we know whether an event occurred between two years but not exactly when in that period the event occurred. Therefore, for the purposes of this study, we assume the timing of an event to be at midyear and we use discrete event history analysis (Allison, 1982, 1984).

The dependent quantity we are modeling is the discrete-time hazard rate, $P(t)$, which is the probability that an event will occur at a particular time to a particular association, given that the association is at risk at the time. In our case, $P(t)$ is the probability that an association will disband within a particular year, given that the association exists in that year. Let t be any date between 1900 and 1983 when events could be recorded. Because $P(t)$ is a probability, it has a limited range of 0 to 1, which makes ordinary least squares regression an inappropriate estimation technique. We chose the log-odds or logit transformation and we use logistic regression to estimate the effects of explanatory variables. The model is as follows:

$$\log(P(t)/[1 - P(t)]) = a + \Sigma b_i x_i + \Sigma c_j x_j(t) \qquad [2]$$

where b_i is the set of coefficients for explanatory variables, x_i, that do not change over time, such as founding type (e.g., merger), and c_j is the set of coefficients for explanatory variables, $x_j(t)$, that do change over time, such as age and density, and a is the constant.

Event history analysis accounts for right censored cases and time-varying explanatory variables through a unique data structure. We created one record of data for each year an association was in existence. A dummy variable for each record indicates whether a dissolution actually occurred at the end of the time period. The unit of analysis is thus the association-year, rather than the association. This data structure allows use of information up to the time of censoring for those associations that do not disband. In addition, values of time-varying independent variables are assigned to associations by year.

The initial sample consisted of 3,339 trade associations. After cases with missing data on particular variables were deleted for analysis, the sample size was 3,147 associations. The final event history data set, then, had one record for each year an association was active, with associations added to the file when they were founded and dropped when they experienced a terminating event other than disbandings: merger, transformation, becoming inactive, or becoming lost due to lack of information. Over the period 1900 to 1983, there are a total of 105,171 association-years (spells).[12]

Table 2.1 reports coefficients from logistic regressions for the effects of our independent variables on the log-odds of association disbanding. To aid in interpretation, we transformed the log-odds to the odds by exponentiating the log-odds regression coefficients, and they are reported next to the log-odds coefficients. Negative log-odds coefficients become fractions on the odds scale, a log-odds coefficient of 0 becomes an odds of 1, and positive log-odds coefficients become odds coefficients greater than 1.

We estimate four models. The first two models test the hypotheses derived from the logic of membership and the logic of influence arguments separately. The model χ^2 values for Models 1 and 2 are statistically significant at

TABLE 2.1: Models of Trade Association Disbandings, 1900-1983

Independent Variable	1 Log-Odds	1 Odds	2 Log-Odds	2 Odds	3 Log-Odds	3 Odds	4 Log-Odds	4 Odds
Age	.0442***	1.0452***	.0191*	1.0193*	.0176*	1.0178*	.0153	1.0154
Age^2	-.0006***	.9994***	-.0005***	.9995***	-.0004***	.9996***	-.0004***	.9996***
Vertical links	-.3553***	.7010***	—	—	-.5038***	.6042***	-.5224***	.5931***
General interest association	.5677	1.7642	—	—	.6146	1.8489	.6229	1.8643
Division of an association	.4306*	1.5382*	—	—	.0488	1.0500	.0244	1.0247
Log number of SIC codes	-.1611*	.8512*	—	—	-.1751**	.8394**	-.1448	.8652
Density—$N(t)$	—	—	-.0031***	.9969***	-.0031***	.9969***	-.0031***	.9969***
$N^2(t)/1,000$	—	—	.0019***	1.0019***	.0020***	1.0020***	.0020***	1.0020***
Density at birth	—	—	-.0001	.9999	-.0002	.9998	-.0002*	.9998*
Previous disbandings $(t-1)$	—	—	.0135*	1.0136*	.0138*	1.0139*	.0142*	1.0143*
Log number of competitors (t)	—	—	.0382	1.0389	-.0153	.9848	-.0263	.9740
Predecessors	—	—	-2.5473**	.0783**	-2.5515***	.0780**	-2.5275**	.0799**
Affiliated with an association	—	—	-.8205***	.4402***	-.8196***	.4406***	-.8089***	.4453***
Merger	—	—	—	—	—	—	-.9762***	.3767***
Transformation	—	—	—	—	—	—	-.2433	.7840
Spin-off	—	—	—	—	—	—	.0474	1.0485
Peak association	—	—	—	—	—	—	-.2350	.7906
Intercept	-5.9625***	.0026***	-7.3581***	.0006***	-6.9893***	.0009***	-6.9563***	.0010***
Number of association-years	105,171		105,171		105,171		105,171	
Number of disbandings	352		352		352		352	
Model χ^2	47.59***		486.55***		515.55***		525.10***	
Degrees of freedom	6		9		13		17	

NOTE: Coefficients are effects of independent variables on log-odds and odds of disbanding.
$*p < .10$; $**p < .05$; $***p < .01$.

40

47.59, with 6 degrees of freedom, and 486.55, with 9 degrees of freedom, respectively. Both logics appear to affect the disbanding process. Therefore, in Model 3 we combine the variables from Models 1 and 2, and the model is a statistically significant improvement over the previous two. The χ^2 difference between nested Models 1 and 3 is 467.96, with 7 degrees of freedom, significant at $p < .01$. Similarly, the χ^2 difference between Models 2 and 3 is 29, with 4 degrees of freedom, significant at $p < .01$. The logic of influence hypotheses contribute much more to the χ^2 for Model 3 than do the logic of membership hypotheses. Together, the logics produce a statistically significant model of trade association disbandings. Finally, we add the additional explanatory variables to the fourth model in Table 2.1. As a group, the added variables increase the χ^2 by 9.55, with 4 degrees of freedom ($p < .10$). Model 4 is the most fully specified model, and therefore we interpret the coefficients for it, noting any differences between the results for Model 4 and the results for previous models.

Testing the Logic of Membership Hypotheses

We first examine the hypotheses derived from the logic of membership model, which posits increases in disbandings with increasing internal diversity and a liability of adolescence rather than newness. The disbanding rate of trade associations is extremely low, with the observed marginal odds of an association disbanding over the entire study period at about .0033 to 1. This figure serves as a point of reference for interpreting the effects of changes in the independent variables on the odds of disbanding in Table 2.1. In addition, we can compare it to the odds of dissolution observed in other organizational populations. This rate is much lower than that for unions (Hannan & Freeman, 1988) or the hazard rates estimated for worker cooperatives (Ben-Ner, 1988; Staber, 1989a), but is difficult to compare to bar associations because their rates are so contingent on historical period (Halliday et al., 1987, p. 469).

As shown in Model 4 of Table 2.1, only one of our four indicators of internal diversity produced the effects we had expected. Contradicting Hypothesis 1a, the log of the number of SIC codes does not affect the odds of disbanding significantly. In Models 1 and 3, the effect of the log of the number of SIC codes was statistically significant, but not in the hypothesized direction. Over the three models, the magnitude of the effect changes very little.

Associations that are divisions, institutes, or committees of other associations have odds of disbanding not significantly different from those of other associations, which does not support Hypothesis 1d. In Model 1, the effect on the odds of disbanding of an association being a division was strongly positive. The effect falls from 1.5382 in Model 1 to 1.0500 in Model 3 to 1.0247 in Model 4. Once the model is fully specified, that is, controlling for other important variables, status as a division is not an important determinant of associations' disbanding. Being a general-interest association does not affect the odds of disbanding, contrary to Hypothesis 1c.

Our final measure of diversity — whether an association had vertical links to firms in other industries — does significantly *lower* the odds of disbanding, rejecting Hypothesis 1b. Vertical linkages may be a form of domain defense and a way of achieving greater domain consensus. Vertical links among the membership may be instrumental for information sharing and strategic pooling of resources. Economically, manufacturers in an association may co-opt wholesalers and retailers, solidifying the position of their industry. Politically, vertical ties may force members to develop a common position on policy or regulatory issues that affect industries downstream and/or upstream. They extend the scope of an association's domain in ways that may strengthen its ability to implement policies. To the extent that such links are carefully chosen and fit in the overall strategy of member firms, the governance problems associated with internal diversity may be reduced.

The estimated coefficients for age and age^2 support Hypothesis 2a in showing there is *no* liability of newness in this population. Instead, the odds of disbanding *increase* with age 0 to 19 in Model 4, but very little, after which the odds of disbanding begin declining slowly. For practical purposes, age has no effect on the odds of disbanding until associations have been in existence for 50 years. Our model suggests a benefit of extreme longevity, and it would be stretching matters to label our findings a "liability of adolescence." They are more compatible with the notion that disbanding rates are very low at the start, and aging brings no additional gains in experience to lower them further until quite late in the life cycle of an association.

We hypothesized that acquisitions are more disruptive than name changes and thus would have a stronger positive effect on the odds of disbanding (Hypothesis 2b). Neither variable is included in the models of Table 2.1 because an inspection of the joint occurrence of the two changes and disbandings revealed very few instances of a change being followed by a disbanding (lagged up to five years). Including such variables in the models, under such conditions, caused convergence problems in the regressions due to marginal zeros because acquisitions, name changes, and disbandings are fairly rare events. Instead, we present the cross-tabulation of changes and disbandings in Table 2.2. The number of cases included varies over the five lagged years because some associations are lost to censoring events.

TABLE 2.2: Relationship Between Organizational Changes and Trade
            Association Survival: Number of Disbandings and Number
            of Events

| Event | Number of Disbandings: Lag in years | | | | |
	1	2	3	4	5
Name change	2 (1,149)	1 (1,097)	6 (1,061)	3 (1,014)	5 (970)
Acquisition of another association	0 (167)	1 (159)	0 (154)	0 (150)	1 (140)

NOTE: Total N at risk (number of associations) in years after the event is given in parentheses.

Clearly, neither name changes nor acquisitions pose major problems for trade associations. Of 1,149 instances in which name changes occurred, only 2 were followed by disbanding within one year, and the number of disbandings occurring in each subsequent year was also very small (1, 6, 3, and 5). Of 167 acquisitions of another association, none was followed by a disbanding within a year, and only 2 disbandings occurred within the span of five years after the acquisitions.

Testing the Logic of Influence Hypotheses

Next we examine hypotheses derived from the logic of influence model. As shown in Model 4 of Table 2.1, density has the predicted (Hypothesis 3a) quadratic effect on disbanding—the first-order term is negative and the second is positive. The effect on the odds of disbanding is negative when the population is small. As associations are added to the population, the odds of disbanding go down, until density reaches approximately 775 associations, where the effect of additional associations is zero. Then, the effect of increases in density on the odds of disbanding becomes positive, implying that disbanding rates increase with additional associations. At a population of approximately 1,550, the odds of disbanding reach the same level as those predicted with a population of 0, all other variables held constant. At the maximum population density we observed, 2,292 in 1981, the odds of disbanding are about 20 times higher than those predicted for a population of 0, all other variables held constant.

Density at the time of an association's founding has a very weak negative effect on its odds of disbanding, contradicting Hypothesis 3b. The effect is significant only in Model 4. Similarly, previous disbandings are significantly associated with subsequent disbandings. The coefficient is positive, as expected, but the main effect is small.

Our finding of high density at birth having facilitative effects on trade associations supports the argument that organizations often enter into networks with other members of the population to benefit from mutualistic relationships. Barnett and Carroll (1987) found evidence of mutualism, but only at the level of diffuse competition. An alternative explanation for the estimated negative effect of density at birth on the odds of association disbanding is that associations founded during lean times—when density is high—are forced to allocate their resources carefully to maximize their survival chances. By contrast, associations formed in times when resources are plentiful may squander their resources (e.g., recruit marginal members, attempt wasteful activities) rather than make the most of the good times and perfect their structures.

Hypotheses derived from the theory of minimalist organizations suggest that having predecessors in the same industry should reduce the chances of disbanding, and our results *strongly* confirm this prediction (Hypothesis 4a). In its first year after founding, an association with one predecessor substantially reduces its odds of disbanding, by a factor of .17, compared to an association with no predecessors. By the time the association reaches its fifth year after founding, the protective effect of one predecessor reduces the odds of disbanding only by a factor of .93, and by the eighth year, the protective effect has worn off completely.[13]

The minimalist argument also implies that direct competition among associations should be minimal, unlike a more resource-driven ecological model, which implies that competition should raise disbandings. Our measure of density indicating diffuse mutualism and diffuse competition (Barnett & Carroll, 1987) includes all associations, regardless of their claimed domains, whereas our measure of direct competition measures only the number of associations alive in each year recruiting firms from the same industry (sharing the same 4-digit SIC code). The coefficient for the log of the number of competitors in Model 4 is extremely small and statistically insignificant, supporting the minimalist argument about the lack of direct competition among associations (Hypothesis 4b).

To ensure that the possible effects of direct competition were not being overshadowed by the effects of density, we estimated an equation (not shown here) that included only age, age^2, the log of the number of competitors, and the log of the number of competitors squared. Neither term for competitors was significant in the regression, giving us added confidence in our results for competitors in Model 4.

As predicted (Hypothesis 5), affiliation with another association sharply lowers the odds of disbanding, reducing the odds by a factor of .4453. This effect strongly supports the strategic wisdom of associations' establishing ties to others as a protective measure. Our results thus differ from those of Hannan and Freeman (1988), who found that affiliation with a national federation was not effective in lowering trade unions' disbanding rates.

Adding Other Explanatory Variables

In Model 4, we added four variables to Model 3: founding type and whether an association was a peak association. Associations founded via mergers have significantly lower odds of disbanding than those founded on their own. Transformations also have lower odds of disbanding, but the relationship is not statistically significant. The coefficient for spin-offs is positive, but it is small and not statistically significant. Thus Hypothesis 6 is partially supported. The coefficient for peak associations is not statistically significant. We thus cannot reject the hypothesis that peak associations have about the same odds of disbanding as ordinary associations, a somewhat surprising finding. We had expected higher odds of disbanding for peak associations (Hypothesis 7), given the much broader and more diverse scope of interests represented by them.

DISCUSSION

We examined two models of trade association disbandings: a logic of membership model and a logic of influence model. Each captures some aspects of the organizational and environmental constraints facing associations — the need to manage internal diversity and the need to manage relations with other associations — but the logic of influence model seems more compelling in its power to explain association disbandings. Our understanding of these constraints was aided immensely by the conception of trade associations as minimalist organizations: Their start-up and maintenance costs are low, as a population they have an extensive reserve infrastructure, they are highly adaptive and normatively flexible, and they have institutionalized norms against overt direct competition. All minimalist organizations are not alike, however, and our findings differ in some respects from previous studies of bar associations, trade unions, voluntary social service organizations, and cooperatives.

Age. Bar associations display a liability of newness for the population, but not individual associations, as once the form was institutionalized, no further disbandings occurred. Unions display a strong liability of newness, similar to business organizations. The voluntary social service organizations of Toronto and worker cooperatives followed a liability of adolescence pattern, with disbandings peaking a few years after founding. We found no liability of newness, but rather found that disbandings rose very slightly — at a decreasing rate — with age well into the life cycle of trade associations.

Internal diversity. The studies of unions, worker cooperatives, and bar associations included no specific measures of internal diversity, although perhaps the types of workers organized by unions could be treated as an indicator of potential diversity (it was not a significant predictor of union disbandings). In our final model, none of our four indicators of internal diversity had the anticipated effect, which was that higher diversity would cause higher odds of disbanding. Perhaps minimalist organizations can tolerate a greater level of diversity than can other forms of organization.

Interorganizational ties. Affiliation with other associations strongly reduced the odds of disbanding. This goes against Hannan and Freeman's (1988) finding for national unions, where membership in federations had no effect on disbanding rates, but it supports Singh, Tucker, and House's (1986) conclusion for voluntary social service organizations, whose disbanding rates were lowered by various institutional supports.

Density dependence and competition. Our results highlight the importance of distinguishing between diffuse and direct competition, at least for minimalist organizations. Just as with studies of unions, newspapers, and breweries, we find density dependence in disbanding rates, with the odds of disbanding following a U-shaped pattern. We find no effect, however, of direct competition between associations, thus supporting Staber's (1982) finding that trade associations have institutionalized norms against overt competition. The increasing number of associations in the United States poses diffuse, rather than direct, competitive pressures for any one particular association.[14] We strongly suggest that future ecological studies distinguish between diffuse and direct competition, and attempt to specify the relevant domain within which direct competition occurs.

Predecessors. Halliday et al. (1987) stress the reductions in disbanding rates that occur through the diffusion of organizational learning, as they found that successive cohorts of bar associations apparently avoided the mistakes of early cohorts. Their argument is similar to the legitimation portion of the density dependence model, which emphasizes the gains early in a population's life from increasing legitimation, which could include the diffusion of knowledge about effective forms. We found a strong effect for organizational predecessors, as they reduced the odds of disbanding in the first few years of an association's life. Future studies should give more attention to historical and organizational precedents for specific forms.

Founding types. We found that associations created via mergers had lower odds of disbanding, thus replicating Hannan and Freeman's (1988) finding that unions founded via mergers and successions have lower disbanding rates. Our replication suggests that the effect of beginning with prior organizational experience is a pervasive advantage among minimalist organizations.

CONCLUSION

Trade associations, along with other forms of business interest representation, are enjoying renewed attention as business-oriented policies have been implemented at the state and national levels (Vogel, 1988). As minimalist organizations, they may achieve a great deal on a remarkably lean structure, and our results suggest they are highly adaptive, perhaps even opportunistic. Trade associations were found to be rather long-lived organizations, and they were especially protected from early demise. Business associations are evidently not seriously hampered by problems of collective rationality (Olson, 1965), at least not during their early years of existence.

Trade associations do very well during their infancy years, and membership maintenance is not a problem, but eventually they show a tendency to destabilize and dissolve. Further research should inquire into the sources of the initial "honeymoon" period. For example, we found organizational predecessors to be important for newly established associations as a source of experience and knowledge about effective forms of collective action. Consistent with the idea of prior organizational experience is our finding that formation via merger lowers the odds of disbanding.

The finding of curvilinear age dependence in disbanding rates raises the question of whether minimalism itself is an age-dependent variable. Perhaps associations become less minimalist as they mature (developing complex bureaucratic structures, relaxing norms against direct competition, and so on), or perhaps minimalism is not always sufficient to buffer associations from environmental change.

Another direction for further research concerns our finding of internal diversity lowering, or at least not increasing, the odds of disbanding. Interest diversity may not only confer an adaptive advantage by broadening the resource base, it may also force member firms into adopting collective structures and processes that help the association overcome centrifugal tendencies in the membership. In other words, an association that forms *despite* high levels of interest diversity may be a stronger — and more long-lived — organization than one that is formed only because interest diversity is not a problem. This proposition may hold especially for associations created in times of economic and political stress, when firms are driven into collective action and are forced to set their parochial preferences aside.

Further research might also consider outcome variables of business "associability" other than association survival, such as changes in organization structures, activities, and memberships. The role and stability of interest intermediation in society is affected not only by the longevity of associations but also by changes in their internal characteristics, especially membership structure. A business association that continues to represent the majority of its domain has effects in the political arena very different from those of an association that is small and nonrepresentative, and that does not speak for the interests of the largest firms in an industry.

In conclusion, our findings are generally consistent with the depiction of trade associations as minimalist organizations. They have low start-up and maintenance costs, they are highly adaptive and flexible, they have institutionalized norms against direct competition, and their members are carefully chosen to avoid interassociation competition and to maximize internal homogeneity. Where internal interest diversity exists, it tends to be managed successfully with appropriate organizational structures (Staber, 1987). The outcome is a remarkably low probability of organizational dissolution.

The high degree of stability in the population of national trade associations suggests the possibility that, together with the rise of expert lobbyists and umbrella groups, business is today considerably more active and better organized than during the previous history of the association movement. The evolution of this status was an extended process, spanning at least a hundred years. Association stability may be the basis for effective coalitional strategies among groups that wish to pool their scarce resources for concerted action. Ties between associations not only lower the probability of organizational dissolution, but may also facilitate the aggregation of narrow interests into more comprehensive bodies (a characteristic of corporatism) capable of authoritative participation in government policymaking and implementation. The jury is still out on the question of whether narrow trade associations stalemate liberal democracy (Olson, 1982) or overcome interest fragmentation through effective coalition building.

NOTES

1. We define trade associations as business interest organizations, and we recognize the need to consider other ways through which business interests can be expressed. For example, Vogel (1988) has identified a variety of ways in which business responded to what it perceived as a challenge to its influence in the 1970s, and Clawson, Neustadtl, and Bearden (1986) examined corporate political contributions to congressional elections. Useem (1984) studied the direct participation of corporations in government decision making, and Mizruchi (in press) examined Political Action Committees (PACs). We focus only on trade associations because an analysis of business PACs, single-issue coalitions, and other forms of business interest articulation is beyond the scope of our research.

2. Unfortunately, reasonably complete data on associations' staff and membership size became available only in the early 1950s, and thus including such measures in the present analysis would reduce the size of our sample by almost three-fourths. We plan to include these variables in further analyses.

3. In the sources we used, we discovered a number of for-profit associations that had apparently crept in because of misleading names or descriptions of purpose, such as insurance rating bureaus, wholesale buying cooperatives, and franchise businesses. Indeed, the two standard references on associations (the *Encyclopedia of Associations* and the *Directory of National and Professional Associations in the U.S.*) must be used with a great deal of caution.

4. Coding and processing this information in preparation for analysis took over three years, as it is a time-consuming and tedious task. Discrepancies between sources were investigated, and hundreds of letters were written to associations, followed up by hundreds of phone calls, asking them about their predecessors.

5. Most association disbandings were clearly indicated in the historical record. Some associations, however, were listed as becoming "inactive." If an inactive association did not appear in subsequent records as active, it was coded as a disbanding.

6. By definition, acquisitions are unlikely to be core changes, for they involve a dominant association absorbing or acquiring a subordinate association, without changing the association's authority structure. When two associations joined on equal terms, we classified it as a merger, which is a censoring event for this analysis.

7. As we wish to analyze the trade association population over the entire twentieth century, and detailed Census Bureau information — at the 2- or 3-digit level — became available only in 1947, we do not use business census information in this chapter. Our source for trends in federal regulation is the Federal Register, which has been available only since 1937. Therefore, our analysis also excludes federal regulations, as they are available for only about half the period under investigation. In any case, we think the major effect of federal regulations has been on association foundings and changes in association activities (increases in lobbying and the like).

8. Our data are extremely reliable for the past four decades — since about 1940 — and thus we are confident that the observed equilibrium has indeed been reached. Claims about an increasing association population are undoubtedly valid if all types of associations, and not just trade associations, are counted. Also, existing associations have become increasingly active, perhaps giving the impression of an expanding trade association population.

9. Two subpopulations of trade associations that posed increased competitive pressures for all associations grew in parallel with the total association population: peak associations (associations in which members are other associations, not firms) and single-issue cross-industry

associations (coalitions). The sizes of these two subpopulations are almost perfectly correlated with the total association population (correlations of .96 and .93), and so they are not included in our analysis.

10. Our sources provided reasonably complete information for most associations on their formal affiliations with others, but we are less certain about the more autonomous relationships among associations. In particular, we undoubtedly undercounted memberships in peak associations and thus may have underestimated the extent to which affiliations reduce disbanding rates.

11. For example, GNP per capita, real wages, and capital investments are correlated .93, .98, and .81, respectively, with density. We thank John Freeman and Michael Hannan for making their time-series data available to us.

12. Means, standard deviations, and correlations of the independent variables are available from the authors upon request.

13. Note that age and age^2 are included in Model 2, because age is also a component of our measure of the effect of predecessors. To obtain a proper estimate of the effect of age, all three terms are needed. Our computations show that the effect of age is changed very little (from Model 1) by the introduction of the predecessor variable.

14. Hannan and Freeman (1988, p. 49) found negative effects of craft union density on industrial union survival, but they did not examine the microecology of this competition, that is, the question of whether any unions were actually competing for the same members.

REFERENCES

Aldrich, H., & Auster, E. (1986). Even dwarfs started small: Liabilities of size and age and their strategic implications. In B. Staw & L. L. Cummings (Eds.), *Research in organizational behavior* (Vol. 8, pp. 165-198). Greenwich, CT: JAI.

Aldrich, H., & Staber, U. (1988). Organizing business interests: Patterns of trade association foundings, transformation, and deaths. In G. Carroll (Ed.), *Ecological models of organizations* (pp. 111-126). Cambridge, MA: Ballinger.

Aldrich, H., & Stern, R. N. (1983). Resource mobilization and the creation of U.S. producers' cooperatives, 1835-1935. *Economic and Industrial Democracy, 3*, 371-406.

Aldrich, H., & Whetten, D. (1981). Organization sets, action sets, and networks: Making the most of simplicity. In P. Nystrom & W. Starbuck (Eds.), *Handbook of organizational design* (pp. 385-408). New York: Oxford University Press.

Allison, P. (1982). Discrete-time methods for the analysis of event histories. In S. Leinhardt (Ed.), *Sociological methodology 1982* (pp. 61-98). San Francisco: Jossey-Bass.

Allison, P. (1984). *Event history analysis: Regression for longitudinal event data.* Beverly Hills, CA: Sage.

Barnett, W., & Carroll, G. (1987). Competition and mutualism among early telephone companies. *Administrative Science Quarterly, 32*, 400-421.

Ben-Ner, A. (1988). Comparative empirical observations on worker-owned and capitalist firms. *International Journal of Industrial Organization, 6*, 7-31.

Carroll, G. (1987). *Publish and perish: The organizational ecology of newspaper industries.* Greenwich, CT: JAI.

Clawson, D., Neustadtl, A., & Bearden J. (1986). The logic of business unity: Corporate contributions to the 1980 congressional elections. *American Sociological Review, 51*, 797-811.

Coleman, W. (1988). *Business and politics: A study of collective action.* Kingston, Ontario: McGill-Queens University Press.

Colgate, C., Jr. (Ed.). (1966-1984). *Directory of national and professional associations in the U.S.* Washington, DC: Columbia.

Delacroix, J., Swaminathan, A., & Solt, M. (1989). Density dependence versus population dynamics: An ecological study of failings in the California wine industry. *American Sociological Review, 54,* 245-262.

Encyclopedia of associations. (1956-1984). Detroit: Gale.

Fichman, M., & Levinthal, D. A. (1988). *Honeymoons and the liability of adolescence: A new perspective on duration dependence in social and organizational relationships.* Paper presented at the annual meetings of the Academy of Management, Anaheim, CA.

Galambos, L. (1988). The American trade association movement revisited. In H. Yamazaki & M. Miyamoto (Eds.), *Trade associations in business history* (pp. 121-135). Tokyo: University of Tokyo.

Halliday, T., Powell, M., & Granfors M. (1987). Minimalist organizations: Vital events in state bar associations, 1870-1930. *American Sociological Review, 52,* 456-471.

Hannan, M., & Freeman, J. H. (1984). Structural inertia and organizational change. *American Sociological Review, 49,* 149-164.

Hannan, M., & Freeman, J. H. (1988). The ecology of organizational mortality: American labor unions, 1836-1985. *American Journal of Sociology, 94,* 25-52.

Judkins, C. J. (Ed.). (1942). *Trade and professional associations of the U.S.* Washington, DC: Government Printing Office.

Judkins, C. J. (Ed.). (1949). *Trade and professional associations of the U.S.* Washington, DC: Government Printing Office.

Lynn, L., & McKeown, T. (1988). *Organizing business: Trade associations in America and Japan.* Washington, DC: American Enterprise Institute for Public Policy.

Mizruchi, M. S. (in press). Similarity of political behavior among large American corporations. *American Journal of Sociology.*

Olson, M. (1965). *The logic of collective action.* Cambridge, MA: Harvard University Press.

Olson, M. (1982). *The rise and decline of nations.* New Haven, CT: Yale University Press.

Salisbury, R. (1979). Why no corporatism in America? In P. Schmitter & G. Lehmbruch (Eds.), *Trends toward corporatist intermediation* (pp. 213-230). Beverly Hills, CA: Sage.

Schmitter, P., & Brand, D. (1979). *Organizing capitalists in the United States: The advantages and disadvantages of exceptionalism.* Paper presented at the annual meetings of the American Political Science Association.

Schmitter, P., & Lehmbruch, G. (Eds.). (1979). *Trends toward corporatist intermediation.* Beverly Hills, CA: Sage.

Schmitter, P., & Streeck, W. (1981). *The organization of business interests.* Unpublished manuscript, International Institute of Management, Wissenschaftzentrum, Berlin.

Singh, J. V., House, R. J., & Tucker, D. J. (1986). Organizational change and organizational mortality. *Administrative Science Quarterly, 31,* 587-611.

Singh, J. V., Tucker, D. J., & House, R. J. (1986). Organizational legitimacy and the liability of newness. *Administrative Science Quarterly, 31,* 171-193.

Staber, U. (1982). *The organizational properties of trade associations.* Unpublished doctoral dissertation, Cornell University.

Staber, U. (1987). Corporatism and the governance structure of American trade associations. *Political Studies, 35,* 278-288.

Staber, U. (1989a). Age-dependence and historical effects on the failure rates of worker cooperatives: An event-history analysis. *Economic and Industrial Democracy, 10*, 59-80.

Staber, U. (1989b). Organizational foundings in the cooperative sector in Atlantic Canada: An ecological perspective. *Organization Studies, 10*, 383-405.

Tucker, D., Singh, J., & Meinhard, A. (in press). Organizational form, population dynamics, and institutional change: A study of founding patterns of voluntary organizations. *Academy of Management Journal.*

Tucker, D., Singh, J., Meinhard, A., & House R. (1988). Ecological and institutional sources of change in organizational populations. In G. Carroll (Ed.), *Ecological models of organizations* (pp. 127-151). Cambridge, MA: Ballinger.

Useem, M. (1984). *The inner circle: Large corporations and the rise of business political activity in the U.S. and U.K.* New York: Oxford University Press.

Vogel, D. (1988). *The resurgence of business political power in America: An explanation* (Business and Public Policy Working Paper No. BPP-36). Berkeley: University of California, Business School.

Walker, J. (1983). The origins and maintenance of interest groups in America. *American Political Science Review, 77*, 390-406.

Zucker, L. (1986). The production of trust: Institutional sources of economic structure, 1840-1920. In B. Staw & L. L. Cummings (Eds.), *Research in organizational behavior* (Vol. 8, pp. 53-112). Greenwich, CT: JAI.

3

Ecological Analysis of Semiconductor Firm Mortality

JOHN FREEMAN

Changes in technology are often salient events for organizations because they disrupt markets, change the relative importance of various resources, challenge the learning capacities of individuals and organizations, and make suspect previously accepted claims to legitimacy. In consequence, they break up patterns of social relationships in organizations. Because the resource bases of organizations are changed, and the importance of one resource rises or falls relative to others, the power distribution among organizational units and individuals changes. Because various kinds of expertise become more or less important, people with particular knowledge and skills become more or less numerous. Tushman and Anderson (1986) have shown how innovations themselves vary with regard to their effects on such processes, particularly as they build on or make obsolete preexisting organizational competencies.

Technical innovation generates opportunities for the creation of new organizations when it occurs rapidly or erratically in the context of expanding resources. It also imposes uncertainties and risks on existing organizations. It opens the door to new competition, challenges the usefulness of existing allocations of capital and human effort, and threatens accumulated experi-

Author's Note: The research reported here was conducted collaboratively with Michael T. Hannan and supported by National Science Foundation grants SES-8510277 and SES-8811489. Jack Brittain assisted in the design and data gathering. Computations supporting this research were performed on the Cornell Production Supercomputer Facility, which is supported by the National Science Foundation, New York State, and the IBM Corporation.

53

ence with obsolescence. In short, it generates turmoil in organizational populations (Brittain & Freeman, 1980). This chapter reports research on such turbulence in the semiconductor industry. It links competitive processes among the firms active in that industry with environmental conditions and shows how both affect the dynamics of firm mortality, defined in terms of the cessation of operations in the semiconductor business.

TECHNOLOGY AND ORGANIZATION

In the 1940s and 1950s, research in the human relations tradition focused on psychological and interpersonal reactions to work conditions. Technology figured prominently as a factor influencing those work conditions. Since the sociology of organizations had not yet emerged as a specialized field of research, much of this work is more properly categorized as sociology of work. Such pioneering studies as W. Fred Cottrell's *The Railroader* (1940), Trist and Bamforth's "Social and Psychological Consequences of the Longwall Method of Coal-Getting" (1951), and Ely Chinoy's *Automobile Workers and the American Dream* (1955) drew attention to the effects of technology on workplace organization. Each concentrated on the effects of a single major branch of technology on organizations. These authors did not conceptualize technology in terms of continua, distributed across a sample of organizations, but as systems subject to discontinuous changes taking the form of innovations, or as constraints channeling the development of both informal and formal organization.

In time, this approach gave way to studies attempting to measure specific variables describing manufacturing technology in cross-sectional designs. This research tradition began with Woodward's studies reported in *Industrial Organization: Theory and Practice* (1965). It continued in a series of papers written by David Hickson, Derek Pugh, and their associates in the so-called Aston school (for a review, see Pugh, 1981). This line of work was highly successful in drawing attention to technology as a set of exogenous variables having effects on both the structure of organizations and the processes through which they operate. Woodward's efforts were mainly inductive. Her conceptual development of technology and the variables describing it fed directly into the subsequent theoretical efforts of the Aston researchers. Their work provided the strongest empirical support for the entire corpus of contingency theory and persuaded most researchers that what the organization produces and how it produces it has much to do with how it is organized.

In so doing, it laid the groundwork for the currently popular marriage of strategic analysis and organizational analysis. It was also successful in demonstrating the usefulness of careful measurement and sampling in organization research.

Research on technology seems to have gone out of fashion when the Aston studies became bogged down in a fruitless debate over whether size or technology was the dominant cause of variation in the organization characteristics of interest (Aldrich, 1972). Ironically, weaknesses in operationalization, the hallmark of this research style, formed the basis of later criticism (Starbuck, 1981).

Other trends in organizational research drew attention away from technology in the early 1970s. Examples are Blau's work on size and structure (Blau & Schoenherr, 1971), research based on theories of quasi-rational choice processes (March & Olsen, 1976), and the study of resource dependencies and political processes in organizations (Pfeffer & Salancik, 1978). These developments often addressed organizational issues of greatest interest outside the realm of manufacturing, so technology is less obviously important. They also seem more relevant to structures and processes located at higher levels in organizations than in those located on the shop floor.

Contemporary research on technology and organizations is concerned fundamentally with organizational antecedents and consequences of technical innovation. The time path of technological development, not the overall structure of sociotechnical systems, is the issue of greatest relevance. This approach grew out of Chandler's (1977) influential treatment of the effects of technology and other changing environmental conditions on the structure of corporations, and through that structure on the rise of the managerial class in America. Chandler's work considered technology and organization from a long-term time perspective. Lawrence and Dyer (1983) examined the histories of seven industries in the United States to serve as an empirical basis for developing a theory of "readaptation," which means adjusting structure and operational processes to balance efficiency against innovation in the context of changing technology. Barley's (1986) research on CT scanners in radiology departments is based on a more specific technical development and its impact on social processes in a work setting. For him, organization is process, and changes in technology give occasion to processes that lead to destruction of prior patterns of interaction and the emergence of new patterns (i.e., "structuration"). One industry that is notable for its repeated technological revolutions, and for the impact of those innovations on the society surrounding it, is the semiconductor industry.

THE SEMICONDUCTOR INDUSTRY

The word *semiconductor* refers to the electrical properties of silicon and a few other substances that, when exposed to heat, light, or certain impurities, turn an insulator (through which electricity will not pass) into a conductor of electricity. Silicon devices are the building blocks of modern microelectronics. Transistors and integrated circuits (chips) such as microprocessors and random access memory circuits are semiconductor devices.

History of the Industry

Semiconductor devices were manufactured in the 1930s, but the industry's birth date is usually considered to be December 23, 1947, when the transistor was invented by a research team at the Bell Telephone Laboratories Division of American Telephone and Telegraph (Braun & MacDonald, 1978, p. 38). Scientific interest in semiconductors developed rapidly in the early 1950s, but commercial application came slowly. The manufacturing technology necessary to produce silicon transistors had not yet been developed, and germanium was the most widely used semiconducting material. But germanium could not tolerate fluctuations in heat, and it is a rather rare and expensive material. To make matters worse, the production process was expensive and unreliable. All of these factors severely limited interest in commercial development of the technology. By 1952, about 100 transistors per month were being produced by the Western Electric division of AT&T. Raytheon, RCA, and General Electric were among the seven other companies producing prototypes (Braun & MacDonald, 1978, p. 62). In the mid-1950s several developments in product design and production technology made commercial production more feasible. In 1956, AT&T entered into a consent decree that caused it to surrender its patents on the transistor. The door to new entrants was thus opened.

A competition between two forms of organization ensued. Large established subsidiaries of firms such as RCA, Westinghouse, and General Electric dominated production and invested the bulk of research and development effort in the technology. New, specialized producers also entered the industry. These organizations were distinguished by their small initial size, their entrepreneurial form of entry, and their functional organizational structure. Perhaps most important, they were run by technically sophisticated people whose commercial interests grew out of their knowledge and experience in physics, chemistry, and engineering. In contrast, the people running the subsidiary corporations were less knowledgeable about and less committed to the technology itself.

Subsidiary firms have obvious advantages in this sort of competition. Their diverse economic base and large size provide easier access to financing through the parent firm's superior credit rating (compared with entrepreneurial firms) and visibility in the securities markets. The parent firm buffers the semiconductor division(s) from fluctuations in other environmental conditions as well (e.g., supplies of crucial kinds of labor, legal protection, rare or expensive raw materials). The parent firm can provide research capabilities that small firms have to build slowly. Finally, the parent firm's management is likely to be more sophisticated across the full range of business functions, and this carries over to the semiconductor division. Sophisticated planning, financial controls, and carefully designed reporting relationships make for higher efficiency.

The independent entrepreneurial firm has advantages as well. Its managers are very likely to be technically sophisticated and, therefore, can better understand developments in the fundamental technology. Where the general manager sees risks, the scientist-entrepreneur sees opportunities. Because such firms are quite small, managers maintain close contact with the scientists and engineers working on development. They usually enter the business in part because they are committed to the technology and its future. Indeed, entrepreneurial activity is itself committing in a way that assignment to work on a new technology within an existing diverse corporate structure is not. Most important, small entrepreneurial firms can change their technology much more quickly than subsidiary firms. Their managers do not have to justify their actions to their superiors. The very discipline that gives the larger subsidiary firm so much of its power of action also makes it relatively inert (Hannan & Freeman, 1989).

Subsidiary firms were often forced to back away from semiconductor technology because they were involved in a competing technology — vacuum tube technology — for which risks were much lower. This technology was still highly profitable in the 1960s, so it represented an approach to the market with known profitability and apparently low risk.

A second problem for the subsidiary companies of the 1950s was the organization of their semiconductor development efforts. Their managers surveyed the corporation for a place to house the scientists and engineers who were so good at spending money and so bad at making it. A logical place to put them was in the division producing vacuum tubes. Transistors are, after all, replacements for vacuum tubes; but vacuum tube production was the epitome of large-batch mass manufacturing. It was bureaucratized, as Burns and Stalker (1961) would have predicted. The rigid structure in which semiconductor development was carried out stifled innovation, and most of these early subsidiary firms backed off from investment in semiconductors just as the entrepreneurial firms took off.[1]

Technology Dynamics

Developments in semiconductor technology over the industry's 30-year history occurred at a breathtaking pace. More and more electronic functions can be performed on a single chip of silicon each year. Miniaturization in design is limited primarily by manufacturing technology. As miniaturization proceeds, more complexity can be designed into an integrated semiconductor device. One expression of this trend is "Moore's law." Gordon Moore, the president of Intel Corporation, predicted in 1965 that function density would double yearly. This prediction was approximately accurate for 15 years (Wilson, Ashton, & Egan, 1980, p. 35).

The price paid for miniaturization is increasing loss of reliability in manufacturing due to inadvertent depositing of impurities on the wafer from which chips are cut. A speck of dust can render a chip useless. Minute specks of dust that would not cause failures in chips with large feature sizes can destroy more highly miniaturized chips. As feature sizes shrink, the ability to tolerate variations in the thickness of the silicon wafer or flatness of the surface declines.

The pattern of innovation driving ever finer miniaturization and ever more complex circuitry is not a smooth one. In each branch of the technology, scientists and engineers have substantial knowledge about the next step forward, but they do not know which company will solve the puzzle required to take that step, nor do they know when it will occur. Once adopted by customers, each innovation is likely to set an industry standard to which other producers will have to adjust. So falling behind in these sprints tends to accumulate deficiencies that are hard to make up. While the long-term trend is a dependable exponential increase in the capabilities of devices, the short-term pattern is erratic change. Consequently, uncertainty is extreme (Brittain & Freeman, 1980).

The product life cycle in semiconductors tends to be short. It is characterized by a pronounced learning curve that is driven by rising "yields." The yield is the proportion of chips manufactured in each production run that work well enough to be sold. A prototype design may yield only a single functioning chip from a wafer that contains more than 400 chips. As more chips are produced, the firm learns how to modify the production process and the chip's design so as to increase the yield. In so doing, the cost per unit is lowered. This drop in prices is often more than 90%. As one would expect, falling prices lead to rising demand.

Market Dynamics

The market shows a pattern of change very similar to that displayed by the technology. Long-term growth in sales has been astonishing. Worldwide semiconductor sales increased from $5.4 billion in 1974 to $18.6 billion in 1983, for a compound annual rate of 14.8%. Integrated circuit sales increased at a compound annual rate of 21.2%. Of course, inflation accounts for some of this increase, but integrated circuit unit sales increased over this same period at a compound annual rate of 22.4%. A relatively new branch of the technology, MOS integrated circuits, increased unit sales at an annual rate of 39.6%. Even the oldest branch, transistors, grew at a rate of 11.2%, measured in terms of units shipped (Dataquest, 1984b). Detrending the time series of dollar sales reveals a second pattern in the data, an accentuated business cycle.

The semiconductor industry is famous for its tendency to magnify the worldwide business cycle. This pattern results from several factors. First, semiconductor devices are used as components in bigger electronic systems. They are expensive parts, and maintaining inventories of them is costly. They also have a rather short shelf life, not because they cease to operate but because the technology changes so fast that they become obsolete quickly. Finally, the reliable tendency for prices to drop over time encourages customers to keep inventories small. So when a user of semiconductors experiences a drop in demand for its own products, it seeks to economize on inventories by cutting back more than proportionately on orders for semiconductors. When demand begins to rise again, that customer is likely to fear a potential shortage in supply of crucial semiconductor components and so increases its orders by an amount more than proportionate to the forecasted sales of its own product.

So the market and technology both show patterns of long-term accelerating growth and short-term uncertainty generated by an erratic pace of change. This dual pattern generates volatility in the populations of firms producing semiconductor devices. Given such volatility, which firms disappear and under what circumstances is this likely?

THEORY

Answering this question involves three tasks. The first is to build a baseline model that reflects the life-cycle characteristics of the firms and competitive processes within populations of organizations. Then this specification must be elaborated to reflect the changes in market and technology that seem most pertinent. Finally, differences in organizational form that lead to population growth or contraction must be studied. In particular, competition between subsidiary and independent forms is analyzed.

Exits and Mortality

An interest in the intersection of organizational population dynamics and the dynamics of technology raises a problem that should be addressed before the theory is developed. This problem is that using technology to date life events is sometimes difficult. Some semiconductor firms begin with an entrepreneurial founding and end with bankruptcy and disbanding. Others, however, get into the industry when an existing organization builds or acquires a semiconductor facility. The problem is deciding when such organizations are "born" and when they "die." Deciding on such an operationalization is tantamount to defining the organization itself.

Semiconductor manufacturing makes heavy demands on the organization. It requires a very special and unusual set of technical and managerial skills. The equipment required to produce such devices is expensive and highly specialized in application. Consequently, semiconductor manufacturing tends to be organized as a specialized endeavor even when the firm is involved in other technologies as well. So one approach to the problem would be to take the corporate division producing semiconductors as the unit of analysis and to define starting and ending dates in terms of these units. This is not a good solution because subunit boundaries for corporations are often quite malleable. Divisions are collapsed or split easily. A huge firm might have five semiconductor divisions today and three tomorrow, with little actual change in the operations.

Since the focus here is on participation in the technology and market, the appropriate definitions of starting and ending dates are the dates of entry and exit from the market — when they start and stop selling semiconductors. To help keep this fact in mind, the terms *entries* and *exits* are used below, rather than *births* and *deaths*.

Baseline Model

Fortunately, previously developed theory and research provides grounding on which to build the model. Hannan and Freeman (1989) present a detailed account of research on mortality processes in a wide variety of organizations. We begin with the most general properties of such mortality processes, and then add increasing specificity as we focus on the semiconductor industry. The dependent variable, $\mu(t)$, is the rate of exiting at time t.

Age dependence. Many different kinds of organizations have been shown to exhibit a *liability of newness.* Stinchcombe (1965) notes that in any population new organizations are more likely to die than older organizations and, at any age, organizations of a new form are more likely to die than organizations of an old form. Stinchcombe's reasoning can be described in terms of an "inside logic" and an "outside logic." The inside logic is that new organizations have to design themselves as they function. Role relationships have to be worked out in the process. People learn to trust each other through interaction. Controls develop as mistakes are made. Yet it is exactly in the earliest times that organizations usually have the least slack with which to compensate for errors. New organizations using an established form have models to imitate. The more a new form of organization innovates, the less it can learn from previous experience.

The outside logic is that new organizations struggle to build relationships with people and organizations supplying resources. All of the problems of resource dependency (Pfeffer & Salancik, 1978) are exacerbated by youth. The issue of legitimacy is particularly salient in Stinchcombe's treatment. New organizations are likely to be more suspect than existing organizations with known track records. New organizations of a new form are particularly suspect. The line between innovation and eccentricity is always a perilous one.

Freeman, Carroll, and Hannan (1983) report analyses of age dependence in populations of national labor unions, newspapers, and semiconductor firms (in an early analysis of some of the data under study here). Carroll (1983, 1984) analyzed age dependence for a wide variety of organizations. Singh, Tucker, and House (1986) studied the phenomenon for voluntary social service organizations, but this study produced findings differing from the others in that an initial rise in the mortality rate is followed by the same decline predicted by Stinchcombe and found by the others. In this book, Aldrich, Staber, Zimmer, and Beggs (Chapter 2) term this a "liability of adolescence" and model it using arguments of waning founder enthusiasm.

Since previous analysis of these data has shown such age dependence, and its presence has been found in many different organizational populations, it is an appropriate first component in our model. We expect the rate of exit to be a monotonically decreasing function of age. Although the existence of age dependence is not at issue here, an important question is whether or not it persists as the model is elaborated.

Density dependence. Age dependence addresses only part of Stinchcombe's arguments. It builds into the model the idea that older organizations are less likely to die than younger organizations. It says nothing, however, about the newness of the form.

In research on national labor unions, Hannan and Freeman (1987, 1988) note that the 150 years of history of such organizations in the United States is a history of early repression and violence followed by the rise of "business unionism" in which unions and the collective bargaining process became institutionalized (Ulman, 1955). Legitimacy developed around the idea that unions bargain over concrete issues of wages, benefits, and work rules. As time passed and unions became more numerous, they gained acceptance as routine participants in the social organization of economic life. This supports the prediction that the *number* of unions, the density of the population, serves as both a measure of and a cause of legitimacy.

Applying this line of reasoning to semiconductor manufacturing organizations poses some problems that provoke extensions to the model. It is convenient to address these problems by considering the two elements of the theory: the population growth rate accelerator and the growth rate decelerator.

The growth rate accelerator posits rising legitimacy as a function of population size. When organizations of a given form are rare, institutional mechanisms that give the form a taken-for-granted status do not exist. Over time, founding rates accelerate and mortality rates decelerate because challenges to legitimacy are more difficult to mount. This argument fits the case of labor unions well because resistance to them was so widespread when the form was new. In fact, they were often treated as downright subversive.

Semiconductor manufacturers face different problems. When they were new, denial of legitimacy in the strict sense was probably rare. Semiconductor firms were, after all, a specialized kind of electronics company that was well established; but there certainly was plenty of doubt that such companies would prove viable. The market for semiconductor devices was limited by the fact that applications for the technology had not yet been invented. The processes by which semiconductors were manufactured were as new as the devices themselves. So links to other organizations were difficult to establish, not because semiconductor firms were lacking normative support, but because relationships of support were missing for other reasons. In other words, *legitimacy is a necessary but not sufficient condition for the development of ties among organizations that sustain them.* Other factors leading to population growth rate acceleration include mimicry, the establishment of protective alliances, and lowering transaction costs.

DiMaggio and Powell (1983) discuss mimicry as one of the mechanisms leading to isomorphism among organizations. For them, this is most often a process of adaptive change. However, it seems obvious that mimicry also operates when organizations are founded. People with experience in an organization manifesting a particular form carry their experience with them. Starting new organizations is less risky and more efficient when previous learning by doing can be transferred to the new organization. The larger the pool of such experienced individuals, the faster the population can grow. That is, birthrates rise because new organizational entrants do not have to discover the routines necessary to implement the form, and mortality rates drop because resources are being used more efficiently and also because organizations can grow through critical stages by acquiring experienced people to fill key roles. Notice that such processes are greatly facilitated by legitimacy; but they will provide bases of accelerating population growth even when legitimacy is well established.

A "protective alliance" is created when a focal organization establishes a long-term relationship with some other organization that is designed to allow that focal organization to ride out temporary shortages of crucial resources. An obvious kind of protective alliance is a line of credit provided by a bank. Long-term sales agreements have the same capability of turning short-term transactions into continuing relationships that lower risks attending the ebb and flow of business. However, such alliances are not confined to market exchanges. Labor unions often band together at the local level to support each other when strikes and other job actions are called and to bargain together with employers. Such alliances are easier to establish when legitimacy of the form is high. However, the alliances themselves have legitimacy properties. They are easier to establish when other alliances already exist. So contractual relationships among actors can be structured in ways that make them enforceable even when the social actors negotiating them are not themselves legitimate in the taken-for-granted sense mentioned here. Similarly, two organizations with common, legitimate forms may establish relationships that are not themselves supported by large, codified bodies of norms. This commonly occurs when some third actor demands a protective alliance between two organizations as a means of defraying the risks involved in establishing relationships with either of them. Banks require cosigners for loans when borrowers do not have established credit, for example.

In the semiconductor industry, customers usually demand that innovators license their technology to a "second source." The risks inherent in the manufacturing process are magnified by the fact that customers often invest much more in the design of their systems around new semiconductor components than the semiconductor firm invests in the component design. So a failure to raise yields to commercially acceptable levels can cost both the semiconductor manufacturer and the customer dearly. Furthermore, technical innovation creates the potential for opportunism (Williamson, 1975). Once the customer has invested in redesigning the system, a sole-source semiconductor supplier can coerce high prices from the customer. So the customer demands that suppliers develop alliances to reduce the customer's risk.

As the population grows, establishing such protective alliances becomes easier and easier. Such patterns of ties between organizations lower mortality rates and raise birthrates. They are, then, population growth accelerators.

Finally, growing population density lowers transaction costs as the number of organizations engaged in a particular kind of transaction leads to the evolution of a common set of standards and practices. Of course, such standards for transactions may serve as barriers to entry. So they can serve as both population growth accelerators and decelerators. The analysis of such standards is a subject eclipsing the scope of the present discussion. The point here is that small organizational populations often grow at accelerating rates because the modes of transacting exchanges become more efficient and easier for neophytes to adopt, and this effect of growing population size goes beyond the legitimacy of the form.

These various accelerators operate at different levels of analysis. Some pertain to markets that transcend national boundaries. Legitimacy arguments operate through commonly accepted norms and thus have a societal referent. Mimicry operates at the level of individuals. So subpopulations may grow at widely varying rates because the movements of people are likely to be predominantly local. In semiconductors, for example, concentrations of firms in California, Texas, and Massachusetts grew at different points in history and at different rates.

Turning to growth rate decelerators, a similar observation is warranted. The model calls for eventual deceleration of population growth as the population approaches an environmental carrying capacity. Intraform competition rises as the carrying capacity is approached. However, such competitive processes are formed by the providers of resources. If those resource providers operate within localized boundaries, the competitive processes generating deceleration also will be local.

The problem here is that the model combines accelerators and decelerators in the same expression. So while legitimacy issues may be national in scope, markets may be local. When great disjunctures between appropriate units of observation occur, expected density dependence may not occur.

For example, Delacroix, Swaminathan, and Solt (1989) use a national legal event, the repeal of Prohibition, to define the start of "legitimate" production of wine in California. Clearly, legitimacy in the sense of taking the kind of organization for granted predates repeal. The large number of wineries before Prohibition, and the large number of European immigrants in California wine country, would suggest that the form of organization was legitimate in our sense, though illegal during Prohibition.

Carroll, Preisendoerfer, Swaminathan, and Wiedenmayer (1989) compare density dependence in two populations of breweries: Germany and the United States. In both cases, brewing was primarily a local business in the early years, but in the United States it became a national or at least regional business after World War II. In Germany it has remained a business localized at the city level. In Germany there is simply no question that issues of legitimacy were resolved centuries ago. In the United States, such issues may have actually been more local. The point here is that such differences may make operationalization in identical ways across units of comparison inappropriate.

Fortunately for present concerns, it seems likely that for semiconductor firms, both legitimacy and resource boundaries were national for most of the time under study. We expect that mortality rates will be high initially but will decline as the number of firms in the population grows. But as the population grows, this decline should eventually bottom out and the exit rate will rise again. We expect this nonmonotonic function to characterize density dependence because, as the population approaches the limits of resources available, population expansion eventually generates competition.

When density is low and organizations of the form under study are rare, accelerators operate at low levels: Legitimacy is likely to be lacking, the pool of people with knowledge of routines used to operate organizations manifesting the form in question is small, protective alliances are difficult to set up, and transactions are time-consuming and costly to effect. Raising population density, by increasing these accelerators, lowers the rate of exiting.[2] As the population grows, mortality rates fall, only to rise again as the carrying capacity is approached. Both accelerating factors and competition increase with density, but competition increases more rapidly. We assume that the exit rate, $\mu(t)$, is proportional to the level of competition, C_t, and inversely proportional to the growth accelerators of the population, G_t:

$$\mu(t) = a(t) \cdot (C_t/G_t) \qquad [1]$$

If we assume that

$$C_t = \alpha \cdot \exp(\beta N_t^2), \ \alpha > 0, \ \beta > 0 \qquad [1a]$$

and

$$G_t = \gamma \cdot \exp(\theta N_t), \ \theta > 0 \qquad [1b]$$

the exit rate equals

$$\mu(t) = \psi(t) \cdot \exp(-\theta N_t + \beta N_t^2) \qquad [2]$$

where $\psi(t) = a(t) \cdot \alpha/\gamma$.

Rate dependence. The viability of organizations in a population is variable at any point in time. Some members of the population are strong while others are on the brink of failing. It is plausible to assume that the decision to accept what seems to be inevitable or to press on in adversity will rest on how other similar organizations are doing. A recent upswing in failures may trigger additional failures until all the vulnerable organizations have surrendered. If this is what happens, waves of failures should be observed. Previous research on foundings has shown such waves (Delacroix & Carroll, 1983; Hannan & Freeman, 1987). By building such a process into the model, we can see whether such rate dependence persists when other variables of interest are controlled. This can be done by counting the number of exits in the previous year and adding it to the model along with its square. The effects of the squared term should be negative, showing the exhaustion of the wave.

Business conditions. Finally, two variables describing business conditions should be added to the model. First, it seeming obvious that the volume of semiconductor sales should have an effect on the exit rate. When sales are unusually high, exit rates should be lower. A second relevant business condition is the cost of capital. Semiconductor manufacturing is very capital intensive and, given the long-term growth pattern and heavy research and development expenditures involved, capital is a particularly crucial resource.

If this were a study of the details of financing semiconductor firms, a great deal of attention would have to be given to specifying such models. The goal here is more modest, however. It is to control the effects of cost of capital to see if the organizational hypotheses continue to receive empirical support. Consequently, the industrial bond interest rate is added to the model.

Our baseline model, then, is as follows:

$$\mu_p(t) = A^{p-1} \cdot \exp(\beta_1 N_t + \beta_2 N_t^2) \cdot \exp(\pi' x_t + \phi_p) \qquad [3]$$

where A is the number of years since entry, N is the size of the population in the year prior to t, x_t represents a vector of independent variables measured in year t, and ϕ_p is a series of period effects. The hypothesis of *age dependence* is represented in this model with the prediction that $p - 1 < 0$. *Density dependence* is present and operating as predicted if $\beta_1 < 0$ and $\beta_2 > 0$. The variables in x_t are as follows:

variable	prediction
entries	no prediction
entries squared	no prediction
exits	$\pi > 0$
exits squared	$\pi < 0$
total sales	$\pi < 0$
interest sales	$\pi > 0$
size of firm	$\pi < 0$

The analysis estimates effects of being in three time periods, one of which is suppressed. We make no predictions about which of these time periods should show the highest rates of exiting.

Competition Between Forms

Competition within an organizational population intensifies as density rises. Competition among organizational forms also rises. When two populations occupy similar niches, the density of one imposes constraints on the demography of the other. In particular, the mortality of population rises as the density of the other rises.

Previously we noted that the history of the semiconductor industry can be seen as a struggle between subsidiary and independent forms of organization. The superior performance of the independent form under conditions of high risk and high growth rates has been noted. The larger, subsidiary organizations backed off and let the newer, more entrepreneurial firms take the lead.

Companies like Texas Instruments and Fairchild Semiconductor, and later National Semiconductor and Intel, became glamorous examples of the success of the entrepreneurial firm. More recently, however, Japanese firms have entered the world market. Their success is the subject of much consternation in the United States. They are subsidiary in form and, indeed, look much like the American firms that previously lost dominance in the industry to the independent organizations. Subsidiary status should lower the exiting rate of semiconductor firms.

Competition between subsidiary and independent forms is analyzed here by positing slightly simplified versions of the baseline model for each population as simultaneous equations, and adding terms for the density of the other population.

$$\mu_{pi}(t) = A^{p_i-1} \cdot \exp(\beta_{1i}N_{it} + \beta_{2i}N_{it}^2 + \beta_{3s}N_{st} + \beta_{4s}N_{st}^2 \cdot \exp(\pi_i'x_t + \phi_{pi})$$

[4a]

$$\mu_{ps}(t) = A^{p_2-1} \cdot \exp(\beta_{1s}N_{st} + \beta_{2s}N_{st}^2 + \beta_{3i}N_{it} + \beta_{4i}N_{it}^2 \cdot \exp(\pi_2'x_t + \phi_{ps})$$

[4b]

where the subscripts s and i refer to subsidiary and independent forms, respectively.

Populations of independent and subsidiary organizations use the same resources, and their rates of exiting ought to show competition. However, one of the important differences between subsidiary and independent firms is that the former are buffered from many competitive processes by their parent firms. Independent firms have no such protection. Consequently, we expect to find a positive effect of density of subsidiary firms on exiting rates of independent firms, but not the reverse. That is, number of independent firms should not have a negative effect on the exit rate of subsidiary firms, or at least the effect should be weaker.

DESIGN AND ESTIMATION

To estimate the models presented in the previous section, two kinds of data are required. First, we need data on the entire population of firms. We need to know when they enter the semiconductor business and when they leave it, if ever. We also need to know about the products they make and when they start and stop making them. Second, we need to know about the markets for semiconductor devices and the cost of the capital.

We obtained the first kind of data from the *Electronics Buyer's Guide*. This is a sourcebook used by industrial purchasers of electronics components that lists various products and the firms manufacturing them. It is published yearly. We coded a three-dimensional array: firms by devices by years. We defined a firm's entry date as the first year in which it sold any semiconductor device. The exit date was the last year it offered any semiconductor for sale.

Some firms appeared erratically. In order to avoid inflating the number of short spells, we developed a procedure for ignoring temporary absences. On the other hand, we could not ignore long absences from the market, particularly when there was a lone observation at the beginning or end of a lengthy hiatus. Our procedure was to ignore any single-year hiatus. We treated a hiatus of two or more years as an exit followed by a new entry. A lone observation, separated from two or more observations by two or more years was ignored. In this situation the date of entry was the start of the longer contiguous string of observations. We found 1,197 firms active in the U.S. semiconductor industry between 1946 and 1984. There were 302 still operating in 1984, which means that 895 firms exited. The peak year for exits was 1972, when there were 110 exits. Some 85 product categories appeared in the *Guide* at one time or another. The subsidiary or independent form of organization was measured by noting the name of the firm, as represented in the *Guide*, and by noting the presence of more than one entry for a given corporation. Finally, we supplemented information from the *Guide* with other standard sources (e.g., annual reports).

The second kind of data came primarily from Dataquest (1984a, 1984b), a market research firm that tracks the semiconductor industry. Dataquest provided yearly dollar volume of sales data for the industry as a whole (TOTSLS is North American sales) and for nine separate product families. We measured the cost of capital (BINT) using the average rate for Triple A Rated Corporate Bonds (Federal Reserve Bulletin). Both TOTSLS and BINT vary yearly, but not across firms within a year.

Our last measure was the number of employees in the organization. Data were gleaned from several sources: the *Electronics News Financial Fact Book*, and the *Manufacturer's Directory* from Arizona, California, New York, and the New England states. When a missing observation occurred in a time series, we interpolated. In spite of this, our sample falls by one-third.

We estimated models in which various period effects were controlled. In particular, we used dummy variables to control whether the observation in question occurred in one of the following periods:

(1) 1946-1959
(2) 1960-1969 (We broke at 1960, which was the approximate time in which the
     planar process was introduced, followed shortly by the integrated circuit.)
(3) 1970-1984 (A number of important innovations in both production process
     and product design occurred in 1970 and 1971; especially important was the
     introduction of the microprocessor in 1971.)[3]

Following Tuma and Hannan (1984, chap. 7), we allowed regressors to
change over time by splitting the spells of time between entry and exit into
yearly subspells, each of which was right censored except when an exit
actually occurred. This generated 6,856 spells for analysis.

We estimate the models described in the previous section with Cox's
partial likelihood estimator. Partial likelihood assumes that some "noise"
process affects the exit probability for each firm in the same way in a given
year, but that rate changes variably over time. PL treats time nonparametric-
ally. That is, it assumes that observations can be ranked in time. This fits our
situation well because we do not know when, within a year, an exit or entry
occurred, only that it occurred sometime during the year. The same is true of
the independent variables. To avoid confounding the entry or exit of the firm
with the counts of firms in the density measure and counts of prior exits, these
life event counts were lagged one year. The variables describing the market
for semiconductors were not lagged. That is, we tried to predict increases in
the rate of exiting in a given year by variables measured in that year, such as
total sales of semiconductor devices.

RESULTS

Our baseline model begins with hypotheses asserting the expectation that
density dependence will characterize mortality processes in this industry. The
key prediction here is that as density rises from low levels, exit rates will first
drop and then rise. Early gains in viability due to rising legitimacy and other
factors are eventually overwhelmed by rising competition as the carrying
capacity is approached.

The first column of Table 3.1 shows the predicted effects.[4] $N(t)$ has a
negative effect and $N(t)^2$ has a positive effect.

When age dependence is introduced through the addition of time since
entry, the expected negative effect is observed. The rate dependence is strong.
The estimate (−.115) is about 19 times its standard error (.006). The likelihood ratio test, by which hierarchically nested models can be compared, is
also significant. The difference in log-likelihoods reported at the bottom of

TABLE 3.1: PL Estimates of Semiconductor Firm Exits, 1946-1984

	1	2	3	4	5	6
Regressors						
$N(t)$	-.011***	-.036***	-.037***	-.001	-.041***	-.042***
	(.004)	(.005)	(.005)	(.007)	(.009)	(.009)
$N^2(t)/1{,}000$	.029***	.094***	.097***	.013	.120***	.120***
	(.009)	(.012)	(.012)	(.016)	(.022)	(.022)
Log of time since entry	-.115***	-.116***	-.110***	-.126***	-.128***	-.125***
	(.006)	(.006)	(.006)	(.022)	(.023)	(.023)
Exits (t)	.—	.030***	.031***	—	.034***	.034***
		(.007)	(.007)		(.009)	(.009)
Exits$^2(t)/1{,}000$	—	-.333***	-.337***	—	-.402	-.403***
		(.054)	(.054)		(.071)	(.071)
Entries (t)	—	.047***	.046***	—	.020	.020
		(.015)	(.015)		(.025)	(.025)
Entries$^2(t)/1{,}000$	—	-.063***	-.647***	—	-.400	-.396
		(.182)	(.183)		(.239)	(.239)
Subsidiary	—	—	-.605***	—	-.563***	-.516***
			(.092)		(.123)	(.126)
Period 2 (1960-1984)	.480	1.080***	1.101***	.798	2.712***	2.700***
	(.311)	(.348)	(.349)	(.663)	(.516)	(.815)
Period 3 (1970-1984)	-.670***	-.666***	-.683***	-.735	-.876***	-.880***
	(.135)	(.128)	(.128)	(.176)	(.188)	(.188)
Aggregate sales (billions $)	-.259***	-.357***	-.360***	-.252***	-.321***	-.320***
	(.038)	(.047)	(.047)	(.075)	(.102)	(.102)
Interest rate	.267***	.303***	.303***	.243***	.245***	.243***
	(.040)	(.050)	(.050)	(.070)	(.094)	(.094)
Employees (thousands)	—	—	—	-.007*	—	-.003
				(.005)		(.003)
Log-likelihood	-7,549.3	-7,498.7	-7,474.2	-3,665.5	-3,616.9	-3,615.6
Number of spells	6,856	6,856	6,856	4,318	4,318	4,318
Number of events	895	895	895	448	448	448
Degrees of freedom	7	11	12	8	13	14

NOTE: Figures in parentheses are asymptotic standard errors.
*$p < .10$; **$p < .05$; ***$p < .01$.

Models 1 and 2 is distributed as χ^2 with 1 degree of freedom. This means that the addition of age dependence to the model significantly improves its fit (χ^2 declines by 51.6). The shift between periods shows strong effects. Other variables in the model, interacting with period (because the model is log-linear), have stronger effects in the second period than in the first or third.

As expected, the volume of sales (TOTSLS) lowers the exit rate. When semiconductor devices are selling well and environments are, therefore, munificent, mortality rates are lower. When the cost of the capital (BINT) is high, semiconductor firms have trouble obtaining the capital necessary for expansion. As a result, their mortality rates are high.

A more elaborate specification of the baseline model is reported in Model 2. In this model, rate dependence is introduced. The effect of prior exits is positive at low levels of exits and negative at high levels. If there is a signaling effect, with an exhaustion process involved (in which the marginal firms are weeded out), this pattern of rate dependence is what one would expect.

The effect of prior entries was not predicted. It shows the same wavelike pattern produced by prior exits. Perhaps in times when entry rates are high, a larger number of weak firms enter the industry, only to fail later. It is interesting that it persists under controls for sales volume and cost of capital. Model 2 improves the fit significantly according to the likelihood ratio test.

The addition of a binary variable for subsidiary form (Model 3) has the expected negative effect on the exit rate. That is, subsidiaries of bigger diversified corporations have lower exiting rates than do independents. Again, because the model as specified is log-linear, the proper interpretation is that the other variables in the model have weaker effects when the organization in question is a subsidiary. We look at this more closely below.

The density dependence prediction requires a more careful examination because one cannot tell from the signs of the coefficients alone whether the nonmonotonic function predicted by the theory is actually observed in the data. Perhaps the negative effect of N^2 is too small to overwhelm the positive effect of N except at unrealistically high levels of N. The effects of density, then, are correctly interpreted in terms of their multiplicative effect over the range of variation of density in the data. In fact, this multiplicative effect first drops and then rises with density over the range of data observed here.

The addition of number of employees has the expected negative effect. Bigger organizations are slightly less likely to exit than are small organizations. However, the effect is not significant in Model 6, the fully specified model. So our model works well under such controls in spite of the loss of a part of the sample.

TABLE 3.2: PL Estimates of Exit Rates of Subsidiary and Independent Semiconductor Firms, 1946-1984

Independent Firms		Subsidiary Firms	
$N_I(t)$	-.086***	$N_S(t)$	.053
	(.014)		(.100)
$N_S^2(t)$	.291***	$N_S^2(t)/1000$	-.209
	(.039)		(.664)
Log time since entry	-.109***	Log time since entry	-.108
	(.007)		(.016)
Exits	.033***	Exits	-.156
	(.008)		(.117)
Exits^2/1,000	-.505***	Exits^2/1,000	6.470
	(.077)		(6.921)
Entries	.061***	Entries	.144
	(.022)		(.160)
Entries^2/1,000	-1.209***	Entries^2/1,000	-13.229
	(.318)		(10.986)
$N_S(t)$	.110***	$N_I(t)$	-.045
	(.035)		(.035)
$N_S^2(t)/1,000$	-.833***	$N_I^2(t)/1,000$	.137
	(.241)		(.095)
Period 2	.759***	Period 2	2.084**
(1960-1984)	(.348)	(1960-1984)	(1.048)
Period 3	-.297	Period 3	-.734
(1970-1984)	(.222)	(1970-1984)	(.534)
Aggregate sales	-.472***	Aggregate sales	-.306**
(billions $)	(.065)	(billions $)	(.129)
Interest rate	.352***	Interest rate	.335***
	(.061)		(.121)
Log-likelihood	-6,015.3		-1,038.2
Number of spells	5,000		1,856
Number of events	750		145
Degrees of freedom	13		13

NOTE: Figures in parentheses are asymptotic standard errors.
*$p < .10$; **$p < .05$; ***$p < .01$.

The second model elaborates the baseline model by considering the competitive relations between two organizational populations: subsidiary and independent organizations. There are two kinds of subsidiary firms. In one, the semiconductor division is part of a bigger, more diversified organization. Such divisions are buffered from competition (and many other sources of uncertainty) by their parent firms. The second kind is a semiconductor company with several operating divisions. Since these are collapsed into a single organization in the coding process, the subsidiary structure probably signals large size and internal diversity. The important point is that for both kinds of subsidiary organization, competition from the independent form should be muted. For independent firms, however, competition from firms with the subsidiary form should be a serious matter indeed. We would, then, expect the effect of subsidiary density on independent exit rates to be strong. The coefficients should mirror the intraform competition in the previous density dependence analysis. The effects of independent firm population density on subsidiary exit rates should be much weaker.

This prediction is strongly supported. The models in Table 3.2 (based on equations 4a and 4b, above) are modified to reflect the simultaneous equation specification of competition. This model fits the data for independent firms better than it fits the data for subsidiary firms. For subsidiaries, several of the coefficients are insignificant. This is partly because the number of observations is much smaller. However, it is consistent with the general view developed earlier in this chapter about the competitive advantages of subsidiary firms. This should not be confused with the advantages or disadvantages of the subsidiary *form*. Independent organizations may well be cheaper and easier to set up than subsidiary firms. While exit rates may be higher and more subject to competitive effects, it may be that entry rates compensate. So the form may be quite viable. High rates of exiting do not suggest that the independent form is less efficient or effective. In fact, higher rates of entry and exit for such a population may offer competitive advantages for American society. Social Darwinist conclusions are not justified.

The controls for number of employees were not significant for either model, nor did such controls disrupt the previously described pattern of differences between subsidiary and independent firms, so they are not reported here.

CONCLUSIONS

As technologies develop and markets expand, populations of organizations grow. But even in a rapidly expanding industry, competition occurs among the organizations in a population. As the number of organizations grows from the industry's inception, initial legitimacy problems are overcome, and eventually the population starts to push against the available resources used in building and maintaining organizations. This carrying capacity imposes constraints on population growth and, with them, constraints on the management and operations of the organizations in that population. But even when legitimacy problems do not plague the population, accelerating population growth is to be expected.

When more than one form of organization exists in an industry, processes of population growth lead to competition between populations. Such competitive processes are revealed in the effects of one population's density on the rate of mortality of the other. In this study, subsidiary firms appear to be almost impervious to the competitive effects of density of the competing way of organizing — independent organizations. The latter are less protected from such competitive effects.

Finally, this research supports previous studies showing that specialized organizations outcompete organizations with a more generalized approach to the industry when environments are shifting frequently. In this study the shifts were business cycle changes.

When organizational researchers focus on single organizations, the efforts of individuals sometimes assume heroic proportions. The analysis of organizational populations shows that some modes of organizing impose risks, manifested in higher mortality rates, that pose challenges to those struggling to make organizations work.

Technologies change in ways that overwhelm the individual organization. Studies at the population level provide theoretical and methodological tools that can help researchers understand the organizational implications of such societal-level changes.

NOTES

1. This information came from Lester Hogan in a person communication. See also Braun and MacDonald (1978, pp. 120-145).

2. The density dependence model presented here was first developed by Hannan (1986). It is further developed and estimated in a series of studies summarized in Hannan and Freeman (1989).

3. See Wilson et al. (1980, chap. 3) for a discussion of the record of innovation in semiconductors.

4. The significance levels are for two-tailed tests because in some models we include variables whose effects are not predicted. However, for those variables whose signs are predicted, the probability values can be cut in half.

REFERENCES

Aldrich, H. E. (1972). Technology and organizational structure: A reexamination of the findings of the Aston Group. *Administrative Science Quarterly, 17*, 26-43.

Barley, S. R. (1986). Technology as an occasion for structuring: Evidence from observations of CT scanners and the social order of radiology departments. *Administrative Science Quarterly, 31*, 78-108.

Blau, P. M., & Schoenherr, R. A. (1971). *The structure of organizations.* New York: Basic Books.

Braun, E., & MacDonald, S. (1978). *Revolution in miniature: The history and impact of semiconductor electronics.* Cambridge: Cambridge University Press.

Brittain, J. W., & Freeman, J. (1980). Organizational proliferation and density-dependent selection: Organizational evolution in the semiconductor industry. In J. R. Kimberly & R. H. Miles (Eds.), *The organizational life cycle* (pp. 291-338). San Francisco: Jossey-Bass.

Burns, T., & Stalker, G. M. (1961). *The management of innovation.* London: Tavistock.

Carroll, G. R. (1983). A stochastic model of organizational mortality: Review and reanalysis. *Social Science Research, 12*, 303-329.

Carroll, G. R. (1984). Organizational ecology. *Annual Review of Sociology, 10*, 71-93.

Carroll, G. R., Preisendoerfer, P., Swaminathan, A., & Wiedenmayer, G. (1989, July). *Brewery and brauerei: The comparative organizational ecology of American and German brewing industries.* Paper presented at the EGOS Colloquium, Berlin.

Chandler, A. D., Jr. (1977). *The visible hand: The managerial revolution in American business.* Cambridge, MA: Belknap.

Chinoy, E. (1955). *Automobile workers and the American dream.* Garden City, NY: Doubleday.

Cottrell, W. F. (1940). *The railroader.* Stanford, CA: Stanford University Press.

Dataquest. (1984a). *Consumption and factory shipments.*

Dataquest. (1984b). *Preliminary market share estimates.*

Delacroix, J., & Carroll, G. R. (1983). Organizational foundings: An ecological study of the newspaper industries of Argentina and Ireland. *Administrative Science Quarterly, 28*, 274-291.

Delacroix, J., Swaminathan, A., & Solt, M. E. (1989). Density dependence versus population dynamics: An ecological study of failings in the California wine industry. *American Sociological Review, 54*, 245-262.

DiMaggio, P. J., & Powell, W. W. (1983). The iron cage revisited: Institutional isomorphism and collective rationality in organizational fields. *American Sociological Review, 48*, 147-160.

Freeman, J., Carroll, G. R., & Hannan, M. T. (1983). The liability of newness: Age dependence in organizational death rates. *American Sociological Review, 48*, 692-710.

Freeman, J., & Hannan, M. T. (1983). Niche width and the dynamics of organizational populations. *American Journal of Sociology, 88*, 1116-1145.

Hannan, M. T. (1986). *Competitive and institutional processes in organizational ecology* (Technical Report 86-13). Ithaca, NY: Cornell University, Department of Sociology.

Hannan, M. T., & Freeman, J. (1987). The ecology of organizational founding: American labor unions, 1836-1985. *American Journal of Sociology, 92*, 910-943.

Hannan, M. T., & Freeman, J. (1988). The ecology of organizational mortality: American labor unions, 1836-1985. *American Journal of Sociology, 94*, 25-52.

Hannan, M. T., & Freeman, J. (1989). *Organizational ecology.* Cambridge, MA: Harvard University Press.

Lawrence, P. R., & Dyer, D. (1983). *Renewing American industry.* New York: Free Press.

March, J. G., & Olsen, J. P. (1976). *Ambiguity and choice in organizations.* Bergen, Norway; Universitetsforlaget.

Pfeffer, J., & Salancik, G. (1978). *The external control of organizations: A resource dependence perspective.* New York: Harper & Row.

Pugh, D. S. (1981). The Aston program of research: Retrospect and prospect. In A. H. Van de Ven & W. F. Joyce (Eds.), *Perspectives on organization design and behavior* (pp. 135-166). New York: John Wiley.

Singh, J., Tucker, D. J., & House, R. J. (1986). Organizational legitimacy and the liability of newness. *Administrative Science Quarterly, 31,* 171-193.

Starbuck, W. (1981). A trip to view the elephants and rattlesnakes in the garden of Aston. In A. H. Van de Ven & W. F. Joyce (Eds.), *Perspectives on organization design and behavior* (pp. 168-198). New York: John Wiley.

Stinchcombe, A. L. (1965). Social structure and organizations. In J. G. March (Ed.), *Handbook of organizations* (pp. 142-193). Chicago: Rand McNally.

Trist, E. L., & Bamforth, K. W. (1951). Social and psychological consequences of the longwall method of coal-getting. *Human Relations, 4,* 3-28.

Tuma, N. B., & Hannan, M. T. (1984). *Social dynamics: Models and methods.* New York: Academic Press.

Tushman, M. L., & Anderson, P. (1986). Technological discontinuities and organizational environments. *Administrative Science Quarterly, 31,* 439-465.

Ulman, L. (1955). *The rise of the national trade union.* Cambridge, MA: Harvard University Press.

Williamson, O. E. (1975). *Markets and hierarchies: Analysis and antitrust implications.* New York: Free Press.

Wilson, R. W., Ashton, P. K., & Egan, T. P. (1980). *Innovation, competition, and government policy in the semiconductor industry.* Lexington, MA: D. C. Heath.

Woodward, J. (1965). *Industrial organization: Theory and practice.* New York: Oxford University Press.

4

Do Larger Organizations
Generate Stronger Competition?

WILLIAM P. BARNETT
TERRY L. AMBURGEY

Organizational ecology is regarded by many to be a theory of small organizations. Perrow (1986) observes that most organizations are small, so most variation and selection are among small organizations. Furthermore, large organizations are seen to be less susceptible to selection pressures, since they are capable of altering their environments (Scott, 1987). For these reasons, it is thought that ecological models can be applied to large numbers of small organizations, but cannot inform our understanding of individually large firms. As Winter concludes elsewhere in this volume: "population ecology models may be particularly relevant when opportunities or incentives for organizational growth are absent. In such cases one would not expect to see the highly skewed size distributions characteristic of business firms, and numbers of organizations should be a good proxy for the burden placed on the carrying capacity of the environment" (Chapter 12).

If correct, this conclusion represents a serious shortcoming of ecological research. Large organizations wield great political and economic power, and

Authors' Note: This research received support from the AT&T Fellowship in Telephone History and from a grant from the Chancellor's Patent Fund of the University of California, Berkeley. We appreciate the valuable advice provided by Glenn Carroll, Claude Fischer, and Charles O'Reilly throughout this project. We are also grateful for suggestions from Howard Aldrich, Jonathan Leonard, Anne Miner, Will Mitchell, and Jitendra Singh. A number of people deserve thanks for assisting with data collection: Gerry Barrett of the Telephony Publishing Company and Robert Lewis, Robert Garnet, and Mildred Ettlinger of the AT&T Historical Archives.

so many of the richest aspects of collective behavior would be outside the domain of ecological analysis (Perrow, 1986). Instead, approaches such as resource dependence theory or institutional theory would be more appropriate for the study of large, powerful organizations (Scott, 1987). However, this assessment attends only to the organization-level significance of size and power. At that level, the focus is on the ability of individual large organizations to avert the *effects* of selection pressures. By contrast, we investigate whether large organizations are an especially important *cause* of competitive pressure. Indeed, large organizations may play a central role in the ecology of organizations not because they are affected individually by selection pressures, but because they affect the evolution of entire organizational populations. Generally, such a finding would demonstrate that observers have been too quick to confine the domain of ecological research. Specifically, it would mean that those who disregard ecological analysis in order to focus on individual powerful organizations are limiting themselves, ironically, to an incomplete understanding of the role such organizations play.

In this study, we discuss why larger organizations may generate stronger competition, or why competition may depend on the number of organizations, regardless of their sizes. We then report empirical evidence of the effects of organizational size and numbers on founding and failure rates in the early American telephone industry.

THE COMPETITIVE STRENGTH
OF LARGE ORGANIZATIONS

To assess the competitive strength of large organizations, we adopt the broad ecological definition of interdependence. In ecological terms, organizations compete when their life chances are negatively related. This definition includes both direct competition among interacting organizations and diffuse competition among noninteracting organizations (Hannan & Freeman, 1989). Conversely, organizations are said to be "mutualistic" when their life chances are positively related. Again, this relation may be either direct or diffuse (Barnett & Carroll, 1987).

In terms of direct competition, the strength of large organizations is often noted in the context of economic price rivalry (Edwards, 1955). Large organizations sometimes can exploit absolute economies of scale in production that allow them to price below the levels possible for smaller organizations. Furthermore, large organizations can better endure unprofitable periods, and so can use predatory pricing tactics to undercut smaller firms. These strengths may also apply to direct economic competition in factor markets (Khandwalla, 1981). For example, larger organizations often outcompete small organizations for quality labor (Aldrich & Auster, 1986).

However, from an ecological perspective the competitive strength of large organizations need not be limited to market environments. More broadly, this strength may extend to the many other contexts that fit Simmel's (1908/1955) definition of competition: a situation in which two parties vie for the sanction of a third. For example, large organizations are seen as stronger opponents in Key's (1942) theory of competition among political parties over the allegiance of voters. From an ecological view, the market context of economic price rivalry is only a subset of the environments in which large organizations may be especially powerful direct competitors (see also McPherson & Smith-Lovin, 1988).

Large organizations are also likely to generate stronger diffuse competition. Such competition occurs when organizations reduce one another's viability by depleting a limited common supply of resources (Hannan & Freeman, 1989). A larger organization exploits a greater quantity of resources than does a smaller organization; it meets more of the available demands, transacts with more suppliers, hires more labor, and attracts more capital. In these ways, as an organization grows in size it increasingly depletes available resources, and so increasingly harms the viability of other organizations that also depend on those resources.

Overall, a good case can be made that larger organizations generate stronger competition. If correct, this view has important evolutionary implications: Over time, the size of the individual large organization may displace, through competition, its population's size in numbers (Winter, Chapter 12, this volume). This would result in highly concentrated size distributions of organizations as observed, for example, by Ijiri and Simon (1977). However, this concentration would not be primarily the result of large firms growing in size, as argued by many (including Ijiri and Simon). Instead, it would result primarily from large organizations reducing the founding rate and increasing the failure rates of their competitors.

However, there is still some question about whether large competitors are in fact more threatening. This is because the nature of competition depends not only on the characteristics of the competing organizations, but also on the technical and institutional characteristics of the environment (Hannan & Freeman, 1977). Next, we ask whether the structure of the resource environment segregates organizations from the power of large competitors.

COMPETITION IN A SEGREGATED NICHE

Hannan and Freeman (1977) have observed that although we often think of environmental niches as distinct and internally homogeneous, they are so only in a relative sense (see also Duncan, 1959). For example, Carroll (1985) found that the (relatively distinct) newspaper industry has become partitioned between generalist and specialist market segments. In turn, these niches — while relatively homogeneous — are also likely to be partitioned by even lower-order distinctions, such as the idiosyncratic differences among specialist newspaper organizations.

The more heterogeneous the niche, the more organizations are segregated from the strength of large competitors. The segmented environment rewards organizations for tailoring differentiated strategies. But to compete at once with a set of differentiated specialists, a large organization must simultaneously duplicate all of the specialists' varied competencies — a rare ability (Hannan & Freeman, 1977). Instead, a large organization is more likely to tailor its strategy, focusing on a domain that can sustain large-scale operations. In this way, niche segmentation narrows the competitive range of any one large organization.

This idea implies a fundamental trade-off between competition from size and competition from numbers. In a homogeneous environment, the competitive strength of a large organization is felt throughout the population, and the organization's size can displace the population's numbers. However, in the heterogeneous niche, each organization's competitive effect is localized to its segment of operations — even if the organization is large. In this case, competition is a function of the number of organizations — regardless of size — that vie for a limited number of domains.

This raises the question, How heterogeneous are organizational environments? Hannan and Freeman (1986) propose that five types of "segregating processes" lead to a good deal of heterogeneity. First, technological discontinuities segregate markets, so that technologically differentiated organizations operate in distinct segments (Brittain & Freeman, 1980). Second, the costs associated with organizing vary according to transaction characteristics in different parts of an industry, leading to distinct subfields appropriate for different strategies (Mitchell, 1989). Third, organizations are embedded in limited networks of social relations, which constrain the segments of the environment in which they operate (Granovetter, 1985). Fourth, through collective associations, organizations constrain the range of activities open to both member and nonmember organizations (Aldrich & Staber, 1988). Finally, several types of institutional constraints limit the range of possible organizational activities, leading to distinct segments in which organizations can obtain resources (Carroll, Delacroix, & Goodstein, 1988).

In fact, organizations themselves are often responsible for segregating their environments through their own strategic moves. As Hawley (1950, pp. 202-203) explains, competition among homogeneous units eventually leads to differentiation, since entrepreneurs seek out distinct functions in which they hold a competitive advantage. This logic also underlies Chamberlin's (1950) theory of monopolistic competition, in which competitive industries are predicted to become increasingly differentiated. Recently, these ideas received empirical support from Delacroix, Swaminathan, and Solt (1989), who found that strategic differentiation occurred in response to competition in the California wine industry.

Altogether, it can be argued that organizational environments either are very segmented or are destined to become so through competitive dynamics. If this view is correct, then competition depends less on the sizes of competing organizations and more on the number that compete over a limited number of domains. Ultimately, the question requires an empirical resolution. To permit this, we next frame the discussion in terms of alternative operational constructs.

DENSITY- VERSUS MASS-DEPENDENT SELECTION

Operationally, the question of whether competition depends on the number or the collective size of organizations can be addressed using alternative models of organizational founding and failure. Reflecting the view that competition depends on numbers, Hannan and Freeman (1977, 1989) have developed the "density-dependent" selection model. Their formulation assumes that the intensity of competition depends on the number of organizations in a population, irrespective of their sizes, as illustrated by the so-called Lotka-Volterra equation:

$$dN/dt = rN[(K - N)/K]$$

In this equation, N is population density, or the number of organizations in the population, K denotes the carrying capacity for the population, defined as the number of organizations in the population that can survive at a given level of resource availability, and r represents the population's intrinsic rate of growth in number. When resources are munificent relative to population density, the birth rate exceeds failure rates. In the equation, such munificence is represented by $[(K - N)/K]$ approaching unity and results in a population growth rate of rN. However, when resources are scarce relative to N, the population growth rate is slowed as both direct and diffuse competition increase failure rates and decrease the birth rate. So at a given level of resource availability, the intensity of competition is a function only of the number of organizations in the population.

Based on this framework, Hannan and Freeman (1987, 1988) empirically modeled density-dependent founding and failure among national labor unions without allowing for stronger competition from larger unions. They found that at low levels, increasing population density actually increased the founding rate and decreased failure rates among unions. They attributed this mutualism to an increase in the legitimacy of labor unions as they became more numerous. In contrast, competition occurred at high density levels, apparently because of crowding in the niche as predicted by the Lotka-Volterra equation. Following Hannan and Freeman, a number of other researchers are using density-dependent models to study competition and mutualism, still with little attention paid to whether or not larger organizations are stronger competitors.[1]

However, if larger organizations are stronger competitors, than the density-dependent model is incorrect. Instead, researchers should describe the population using a measure that reflects the greater significance of larger organizations. One way to do this is to model the effects of population "mass," which can be thought of as population density with each organization weighted by its size. Mass dependence can be represented by reformulating the Lotka-Volterra equation:

$$dN/dt = rN[(K_M - M)/K_M]$$

where K_M reflects the population mass that can be supported in the niche with the level of resources held constant, and where M is a measure of the population's mass at a given time. In the absence of resource constraints, the population's growth in numbers is rN, as in the original Lotka-Volterra equation. However, that rate can be slowed by either of two competitive processes: when many small organizations proliferate in number or when individual organizations grow to be large in size. But by either process, competition depends on population mass rather than density.

Operationally, mass dependence can be modeled using the same approach now used to estimate density dependence. Population mass and population density can both be included in models of organizational founding and failure, with mass measured by the sum of the sizes of all organizations in the population. If larger organizations generate stronger competition, then population mass should increase death rates and lower the founding rate. Population density, meanwhile, should not significantly affect foundings or failures once mass is included in the model.

In this study, we estimated both density- and mass-dependent models of organizational founding and failure using a sample population from the early American telephone industry. Because of technical characteristics, larger telephone companies probably generated stronger competition. However, the industry originated in a highly segmented environment, suggesting that competition resulted instead from the number of organizations, regardless of their sizes. For these reasons, this sample was well suited to a strong test of both arguments.

SIZE, SEGMENTATION, AND THE EVOLUTION OF THE TELEPHONE INDUSTRY

It is widely believed that the telephone industry, perhaps more than any other, has been shaped by the competitive strength of organizational size. Thompson (1967) refers to the industry in his discussion of the "mediating" technology: systems that connect people to people. From his view, a large organization holds a competitive advantage in this industry since it can best ensure the standardization and extensiveness of the system.

Similar arguments appear in neoclassical economics. Baumol, Panzar, and Willig (1982) argue that the telephone industry is a "natural monopoly," because its mediating nature leads to an ever declining average cost curve for a single telephone company. Larger companies should gain a competitive price advantage from this practically limitless economy of scale. Using a network externality argument, Artle and Averous (1975) reach a similar conclusion. They observe that the utility of subscribing to a company's network is a positive function of the number of other subscribers. As a result, larger telephone companies are seen to have a competitive advantage due to their ability to attract new subscribers.

These arguments suggest that the telephone industry developed under particularly strong competition from large companies, especially from the Bell System. In fact, this conclusion has been accepted as a truism by a number of industry histories (see, especially, Brock, 1981; Brooks, 1976; Danielian, 1939). In terms of the ecological model, it implies that organizational selection in the industry was mass dependent, with the competition generated by each organization a function of its size.

However, there is also evidence that before 1933, when the FCC began effective regulation, the industry evolved in a highly segregated environment. In fact, the early telephone industry was affected by several of the segregating processes described by Hannan and Freeman. For this reason, conventional telephone histories may overstate the competitive importance of size. Instead, it is possible that the industry developed through density-dependent selection, with competition highest when the largest number of organizations existed to compete for a limited number of domains. To understand this, it is necessary to consider each of the segregating processes that operated in the early telephone industry.

One process was technological fragmentation. A large number of often incompatible telephone designs became commercially viable in the late nineteenth century (Dunsheath, 1962). As a result, when the Bell patents expired in 1896, new telephone companies proliferated across the country, numbering about 9,000 by 1902 (U.S. Bureau of the Census, 1906). These companies managed an explosive growth in the number of telephones, and controlled more of the national market than Bell by 1903 (Brooks, 1976). But because they often used incompatible technologies, they were sometimes unable to connect their systems. In this way, the new industry began as a collection of fragmented telephone networks (Barnett & Carroll, 1987). Technological segmentation also resulted from the high unit costs of rural telephone service. Many of the largest commercial companies refused to enter the rural markets, leaving them to mutually operated cooperative companies (Fischer, 1987).

But the fragmentation of the industry was not only caused by technical factors. Especially in rural areas, the telephone — and thus the local company — was valued for its social uses (Fischer, 1988). Presumably, this would have reduced the incentive to extend the local network much beyond the relevant geographic community. Institutional factors also segmented the industry. MacMeal (1934) explains that a large number of regional telephone company associations were formed after the turn of the century. In most cases, these associations increased coordination among their member companies. However, MacMeal notes that divisions often developed between rival associations, increasing fragmentation in some parts of the industry. Finally, political institutions also fragmented the industry, establishing legal barriers to direct competition and increasing the numbers of distinct companies (Barnett & Carroll, 1989).

Altogether, the telephone industry developed in an extremely heterogeneous environment. As a result, we find it plausible that competition among telephone companies may have been density dependent, with greater numbers of companies crowding the industry's limited number of segregated domains. However, a strong case also was made for the competitive strength of large telephone companies, implying that selection was mass dependent. So our strategy was to search for evidence of each process in the development of our sample population.

SAMPLE

The sample includes the life histories of all 707 telephone companies that operated in Pennsylvania at any time from the invention of the telephone in 1877 until FCC regulation began in 1933. Three sources were used to trace these life histories. The *Annual Report* of the Pennsylvania State Department of Internal Affairs, published from 1874 until 1917, was exhaustive and included the smallest of companies. This source provided the founding date and annual size information for each company. The *Industrial Directory of the Commonwealth of Pennsylvania* included a complete census of telephone companies. It was published with varying periodicity between 1914 and 1935 (Pennsylvania State Department of Internal Affairs, various years). Finally, *Telephony's Directory*, an industry directory published annually over most of the period, contained detailed size and technology information (Independent Telephone Association, Inc., various years).

The distribution of these companies over time is shown in Figure 4.1. Reflecting the national pattern, the population increased until 1915, when it abruptly dropped in number through the end of the sample period.

As shown in Figure 4.2, the total size of the industry (population mass) developed more steadily than did population density, declining in numbers only during the Great Depression.[2] This exponential diffusion process mirrored the national pattern (Fischer & Carroll, 1988). However, unlike much of the rest of the nation, in Pennsylvania this increased industry size was not concentrated mainly in the Bell System. In fact, of the more urbanized states, Pennsylvania had the least concentrated telephone industry during these years (see Independent Telephone Association, Inc., various years). Throughout the sample period, it had between 30 and 40 companies of over 1,000 subscribers, and over 100 firms with more than 250 subscribers. So the increase in average organizational size in Pennsylvania during this period resulted from the growth in size of a number of large organizations.

Beneath these overall trends were sporadic waves of organizational foundings and failures, illustrated in Figure 4.3. These waves may have been the result of exogenous factors, such as periods of economic prosperity or decline

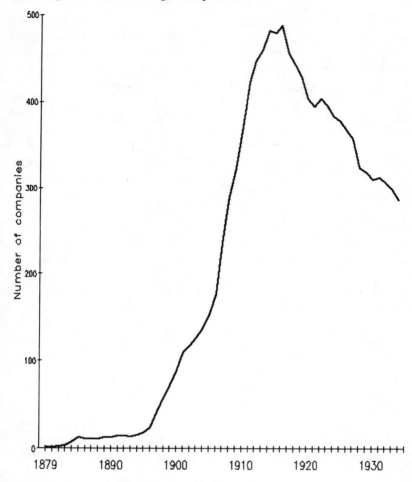

Figure 4.1. Operating telephone companies in Pennsylvania.

(MacMeal, 1934). And in many cases the failures may have been the result of organization-level factors, such as the failure of poorly managed rural companies (Fischer, 1987). Our concern, however, is whether these patterns were the systematic result of competition within the industry. Specifically, we looked for evidence of density- and mass-dependent competition while controlling for exogenous and organizational variables.

Operationally, this required that we collect information on these variables over the entire period. Several organizational variables were recorded: organ-

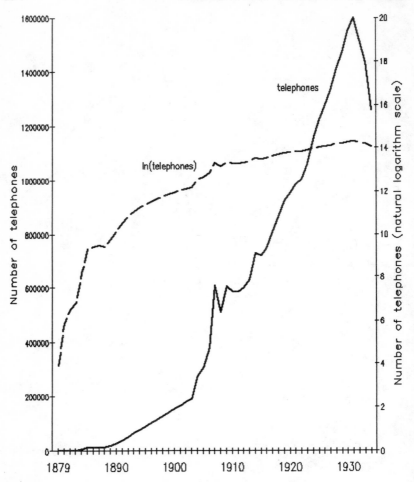

Figure 4.2. The diffusion of the telephone in Pennsylvania.

izational age (measured in years), organizational size measured by the number of subscribers,[3] form of ownership (mutual versus commercial), and whether the company had primitive or advanced power and transmission technologies.

To control for the carrying capacity of the environment, eight exogenous variables were recorded: population, the number of manufacturing establishments, the average size of manufacturing establishments, the number of electrical equipment manufacturers, the indexed average wage, the number

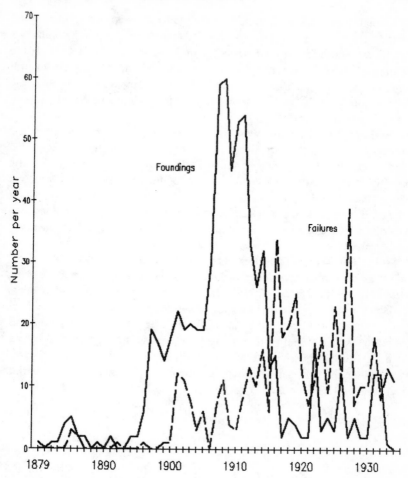

Figure 4.3. Foundings and failures of telephone companies in Pennsylvania.

of farms (divided by 1,000), the average farm acreage, and the indexed average farm value. Each of these variables was measured at the state level and was taken from the decennial census. Their values were interpolated linearly for intervening years.

Population density was measured as the total number of telephone companies in existence in any given year. To allow for a nonmonotonic effect, density was modeled as a quadratic by including both density and density squared, with the squared term divided by 1,000 for rescaling.

Population mass was measured by the total number of subscribers of all existing companies in a given year. For the failure analysis, each company's system was subtracted from this total, so the mass variable reflected only the number of subscribers held by *other* companies. In all models, the natural logarithm of mass was used in order to reduce the skewness of the variable's distribution. As with density, a scaled squared term was also included to allow for a nonmonotonic effect.

Different data structures were needed for each analysis. The founding process occurred at the population level, with the sample region "experiencing" the creation of new organizations (Delacroix & Carroll, 1983). Ideally, we would have constructed an event history of the region, including the exact time of each founding. However, only the year of founding was known over the entire sample, so we constructed an annual event count of the number of foundings. All explanatory variables were then lagged one year to avoid simultaneity.

For the failure process the unit of analysis was the individual organization, and the operational dependent variable was the waiting time until failure. Ordinarily, the analysis of such an event history does not permit independent variables to vary over an organization's lifetime, since each organization has but one spell of a duration equal to its waiting time. We overcame this limitation by dividing the lifetime of each company into one-year segments, with the waiting time incremented from segment to segment. This allowed us to update the values of all independent variables annually, so each varied over time as a step function.

METHODS

We modeled both the founding and failure processes in terms of the instantaneous transition rate:

$$r_j(t) = \frac{\lim}{\Delta t -> 0}[q_j(t, t + \Delta t)/\Delta t]$$

where q is the discrete probability of an event occurring for unit j. For the founding process, the probability is unconditional. The unit of analysis is the population, and the events are repeatable. For the failure process, this is a conditional probability. Since the unit of analysis is the organization, failure is a nonrepeatable event and the rate is conditional upon the event not having occurred earlier.

Since both founding and failure are continuous-time processes, they are most appropriately modeled using this continuous-time construct. Furthermore, available methods for estimating the rate permit the analysis of risks when not all units experience the event by the end of the sample period. This problem, known as "right censoring," has been shown to lead to biased and inefficient estimates if not taken into account (Tuma & Hannan, 1984). Since 39% of the sample population does not fail by the end of the sample period, it is especially important that we accommodate right censoring in the failure analysis. For the founding analysis, right censoring is not an issue.

A considerable body of research indicates that organizational failure rates are age dependent (Hannan & Freeman, 1989). For this reason, we modeled the failure rate as an explicit function of age using a generalized Gompertz specification. The original Gompertz model assumes that the probability of failure changes exponentially over time in the same fashion for all members of the population. So we used the generalized version, since it allows for heterogeneity in terms of the effects of the independent variables. For the generalized Gompertz, the hazard rate is given by:

$$r(t) = \exp[\beta'X(\tau)]\exp[\gamma t]$$

where Υ captures the effects of age, $X(\tau)$ are the covariates (permitted to vary over historical time, τ), and β are their coefficients to be estimated. We used the statistical software RATE to estimate the model using the method of maximum likelihood (Tuma, 1979).

We modeled organizational founding as a Poisson process, a model appropriate for relatively rare events (Coleman, 1981). The basic Poisson model for event count data is a single parameter distribution where the probability of a given number of events is given by:

$$\text{Prob}(N_t = n) = \exp[-rt][(rt)^n/n!]$$

where r is the (constant) rate parameter. However, the basic Poisson process assumes that there is no heterogeneity within the sample. For this reason, we allowed the parameter r to be an exponential function of the independent variables: $r = \exp(\beta'X)$. This relation implies the compound Poisson process, which illustrates the relationship between the observed annual number of foundings and the observed independent variables:

$$\text{Prob}(N_t = n) = \exp[-te^{\beta'X}][(te^{\beta'X})^n/n!]$$

This is a useful relation, since it can be solved using the method of maximum likelihood (Amburgey & Carroll, 1984). In this study, we estimated the model using the statistical software LIMDEP (Greene, 1988).

RESULTS

Table 4.1 reports the estimated parameters of the founding rate models. The quadratic density specification in Model 1 replicates the findings of Hannan and Freeman (1987): At low levels of density, an increase in density increased the founding rate, but at high levels the effect became competitive as the squared term dominated.

Model 2 shows that this effect was robust when lagged foundings and failures were controlled. Lagged foundings were positively and significantly related to the founding rate, probably evidence of first-order autocorrelation. Lagged failures were negatively related to foundings. This may also have been the result of autocorrelation if unobserved factors that increased failure rates also depressed the founding rate. In any case, there was no evidence of a renewal process through which failures generated foundings.

In Model 3, various environmental characteristics were added.[4] Including these variables reversed the effects of population density. The main effect of density became negative, indicating competition. And although the squared term was positive, the net density effect remained competitive throughout its observed range. So the positive squared term dampened the competitive density effect, but did not reverse it.

In Model 4, a log-quadratic specification of population mass was added, but neither term was statistically significant. However, dropping the squared term in Model 5 revealed an unexpected *positive* and significant relationship between population mass and the founding rate. With the number of organizations controlled, this indicated that the larger the size of existing organizations, the greater the founding rate for new organizations.

This mutualistic effect was powerful. Figure 4.4 shows the predicted annual probability of organizational founding over the period according to the estimates of Model 5, compared to the model's prediction with the size of each existing organization reduced by 90%.[5] As the figure demonstrates, larger organizations dramatically increased the founding rate of new organizations.

Furthermore, the effect was especially pronounced during years when the founding rate was higher. Note that before 1876 and after 1917, when the

TABLE 4.1: Poisson Regression Estimates of Organizational Founding Rate Models: The Effects of Population Density and Mass

Independent Variables	Models				
	1	2	3	4	5
Constant	1.544**	1.502**	–22108**	–24461**	–24466**
	(.0989)	(.1004)	(5271)	(5430)	(5445)
Population			.5608**	.6196**	.6199**
			(.1381)	(.1422)	(.1426)
Number of manufacturing establishments			–.1813**	–.2007**	–.2008**
			(.0437)	(.0451)	(.0452)
Average size of manufacturing establishments			–240.2**	–266.0**	–266.1**
			(58.34)	(60.10)	(60.26)
Number of electrical equipment manufacturers			7.795**	8.629**	8.631**
			(1.857)	(1.913)	(1.918)
Indexed average wage			471.6**	521.9**	522.1**
			(113.4)	(116.9)	(117.2)
Average farm acreage			223.1**	247.1**	247.2**
			(53.50)	(55.12)	(55.26)
Indexed average farm value			12.88**	14.12**	14.11**
			(2.902)	(2.986)	(2.994)
Lagged founding of telephone companies		.0355**	.0298**	.0313**	.0311**
		(.0022)	(.0061)	(.0063)	(.0062)
Lagged failures of telephone companies		–.0383**	–.0327**	–.0354**	–.0353**
		(.0085)	(.0094)	(.0094)	(.0094)
Density	.0136**	.0070**	–.0158**	–.0128*	–.0118*
	(.0010)	(.0012)	(.0065)	(.0069)	(.0067)
Density^2/1,000	–.0271**	–.1287**	.0164**	.0174**	.0168**
	(.0021)	(.0023)	(.0080)	(.0082)	(.0081)
ln(Mass)				1.548	1.020**
				(1.040)	(.2694)
ln(Mass)^2				–.0257	
				(.0482)	
χ^2	697.13	276.23	106.27	92.949	93.330
Degrees of freedom	2	4	11	13	12

NOTE: N = 55 years. Standard errors are in parentheses. All independent variables are lagged one year.
*$p < .10$; **$p < .05$.

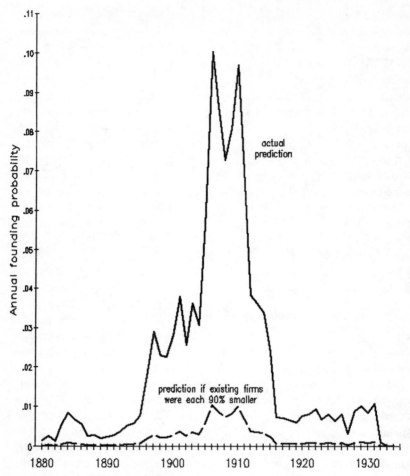

Figure 4.4. Estimated annual probability of organizational founding.

estimated annual founding probability was below .01, the founding probability was not very sensitive to reducing population mass. However, in the
intervening period when the founding probability was higher, its sensitivity
to the mass effect was substantial. This suggests that mutualism from large
organizations was most fruitful when other factors also encouraged the
building of new organizations.

Model 5 also shows that population density continued to have a strictly
competitive effect on the founding rate even after population mass was

controlled for. This finding supports the density-dependent selection model. Competition resulted from an increase in the population's size in numbers, irrespective of the organizations' sizes.

A similar model-building strategy was followed for the analysis of organizational failure, except that organization-level characteristics were also included in all models. Table 4.2 reports the estimated parameters of these models. In Models 6 and 7, a quadratic specification of population density was estimated with and without controls for environmental factors.[6] Both models supported the findings of Hannan and Freeman (1988). At low levels of density, increasing density reduced failure rates. But at high levels, the positive squared term overwhelmed the main effect, resulting in competition as increases in density increased failure rates.

Model 8 is a reestimate of Model 7, including a log-quadratic specification of population mass. Neither mass term was significant, but including the terms had a dramatic influence on the density effect. The main effect of density was nearly eliminated, changing from –.0075 in Model 7 to –.0010 in Model 8. Similarly, the squared density term was reduced by half. As a result, neither density term was significant, so we reestimated the equation without the squared density term. As Model 9 shows, this resulted in a statistically significant positive density effect, indicating competition. As was the case for the founding models, competition with respect to organizational failure was density dependent, increasing as the number of organizations increased, regardless of their sizes.

Because both mass terms were nonsignificant in Model 9, we excluded the squared term and reestimated the equation in Model 10. This resulted in a statistically significant negative effect of population mass on the failure rates. Again, like the founding models, the failure models show a mutualistic mass effect. With the number of organizations controlled, this means that as the size of an organization's "competitors" increased, its failure rate decreased.

Figure 4.5 illustrates how important this mutualism was. It compares the predicted annual failure probability according to Model 10 to a prediction with the sizes of each organization's "competitors" reduced by 90%.[7] Over most of the period, the predicted annual failure probability was below .025. However, with competitor sizes reduced by 90%, the prediction increased dramatically to the neighborhood of .10. And similar to the founding analysis, the magnitude of this effect was pronounced in years when the failure probability was already higher. For example, 1901 was an exceptionally hazardous year, with a predicted average failure probability of about 5%. But if each organization's competitors had been 90% smaller, then about 30% of the population probably would have failed in that year alone.

TABLE 4.2: Maximum-Likelihood Estimates of Organizational Failure Rates: Gompertz Models of the Effects of Population Density and Mass

Independent Variables	Models				
	6	7	8	9	10
Constant	-2.675**	-.9681	2.467	1.310	3.081
	(.2581)	(3.139)	(4.188)	(4.031)	(2.763)
Organizational age	.0432**	.0477**	.0474**	.0478**	.0479**
	(.0069)	(.0086)	(.0086)	(.0086)	(.0086)
Organizational size	-.0012	-.0014	-.0014	-.0014	-.0014
	(.0013)	(.0013)	(.0013)	(.0013)	(.0013)
Multi-exchange	-.2890**	-.2814**	-.2861**	-.2863**	-.2897**
	(.1103)	(.1103)	(.1105)	(.1104)	(.1103)
Common battery	-.1611	-.1875	-.1868	-.1895	-.1884
	(.1628)	(.1626)	(.1627)	(.1626)	(.1626)
Calendar year		-.1132*	-.0578	-.0037	-.0457
		(.0588)	(.0675)	(.0655)	(.0649)
Number of farms/1,000		.0084	.0114*	.0120**	.0113*
		(.0061)	(.0062)	(.0061)	(.0060)
Number of manufacturing establishments		-.00012**	-.00009	-.00008	-.00008
		(.00006)	(.00006)	(.00006)	(.00006)
Number of electrical equipment manufacturers		.0325**	.0296**	.0286**	.0282**
		(.0110)	(.0111)	(.0115)	(.0117)
Density	-.0067**	-.0075**	-.0010	.0047**	.0045**
	(.0020)	(.0036)	(.0056)	(.0012)	(.0011)
Density^2/1,000	.0110**	.0168**	.0082		
	(.0034)	(.0055)	(.0080)		
ln(Mass)			-.5770	-.2913	-.7471**
			(.7923)	(.7325)	(.1753)
ln(Mass)^2			-.0006	-.0261	
			(.0474)	(.0399)	
χ^2	57.37	82.05	86.54	85.49	85.05
Degrees of freedom	7	11	13	12	11

NOTE: 431 deaths, 276 censored cases, 11,842 total one-year spells. Standard errors are in parentheses.
*$p < .10$; **$p < .05$.

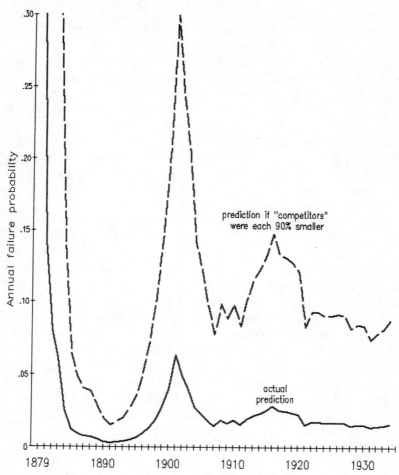

Figure 4.5. Estimated annual probability of organizational failure.

DISCUSSION AND CONCLUSION

We found a consistent but unexpected pattern of results in both the founding and failure analyses. First, as predicted by the niche heterogeneity argument, increases in population density depressed the founding rate and increased the failure rates. Furthermore, these effects were robust when population mass was controlled. Greater competition was generated by greater numbers of organizations, regardless of their sizes. We interpret this as evidence that the segregating processes operating in the early telephone industry — technical, economic, social, and institutional — effectively isolated organizations from the competitive force of large firms.

This finding makes us more confident in the density-dependent competition model, even when some organizations are considerably larger then others. However, we also find reason for caution. Initially, our models supported those of Hannan and Freeman (1987, 1988), who showed population density to be mutualistic at low levels and competitive at high levels. However, when the models included control variables the effects of density changed direction, becoming strictly competitive. If these results are an indication, density-dependent models may be very sensitive to specification error. This may help to explain the inconsistent findings across different studies of density dependence (see Delacroix et al., 1989).

The results for mass-dependent selection were surprising. Population mass had a mutualistic effect on both founding and failure rates. With the number of organizations controlled, this means that the larger the size of those organizations, the higher the founding rate and the lower the failure rates. Not only did larger organizations not generate stronger competition, they actually increased the viability of other organizations.

How can this be explained? We note that because these companies operated in segregated market segments, they often worked together by connecting their lines (Atwood, 1984). Our findings suggest that larger organizations made better partners in such arrangements. By connecting to a large firm, a company could expand its reach to thousands of new customers and in some cases to regional or national networks (Fischer, 1987). Furthermore, an otherwise weak organization could gain many of the other strengths of the large firm, such as political clout, by becoming affiliated with one. In this way, it appears that when these organizations worked together, the strengths that might have made a large firm dangerous instead made it a valuable ally.

Although it is helpful to think in terms of partners, our findings are not limited to direct mutualism between pairs of organizations. The estimates of mass dependence show that as any organization in the sample grew in size, it increased the viability of other organizations throughout the region. So large organizations also generated *diffuse* mutualism, improving the viability of geographically removed organizations.

This result may seem puzzling, since these companies could connect only when they were geographically proximate. However, we see the finding as the understandable outcome of community-level interdependence. By connecting to a system of other organizations, a company linked its viability to the viability of that entire system taken as a whole (Barnett & Carroll, 1987). As a result, each individual company benefited when another organization anywhere in its system grew larger in size. From the community-level perspective, diffuse mutualism is to be expected.

Of course, the telephone industry is an extreme example of network interdependence. Nonetheless, we caution against viewing this result as idiosyncratic to network technology industries. On the contrary, as Fombrun (1988) explains, organizations are commonly nested in higher-order collectivities in which large organizations play a leading role. For example, he points out that each of the leading American automobile manufacturers is embedded in "loosely coordinated suppliers, dealers, parts manufacturers, assemblers, data processors, advertising agencies, designers, and labor unions" (p. 233). Our findings imply that where such interdependencies arise, the viability of each constituent organization strongly depends on the growth and survival of the larger organizations in the community.

We are intrigued by the evolutionary implications of this idea. In particular, we note that large firms affected the evolution of their communities through two processes. First, as Figure 4.4 illustrates, mutualism from large firms was especially strong when conditions were already favorable for the creation of new organizations. This implies that the large firm promoted its interests — and so the interests of its community — by facilitating the process of organization building. Second, as shown in Figure 4.5, we found that a large organization protected its community from exogenous shocks. Apparently, the large firm used its resources to maintain the viability of its community as a whole during periods that would otherwise have been especially hazardous.

More generally, we speculate that whenever these two processes operate, the concentrated organizational community will have a selection advantage. It will expand in numbers at a greater rate than other communities, since its dominant members will facilitate new foundings. Furthermore, it will better endure exogenous hazards to survival, again drawing on the strengths of its dominant organizations.

To conclude, we challenge those who are primarily interested in large, powerful organizations to broaden their view of organizational ecology. By doing so, they may join in our attempt to understand the evolutionary significance of large organizations. This would result in a greater understanding of both large organizations and, more generally, the dynamics of organizational communities.

NOTES

1. Researchers have very quickly adopted the density-dependent model in studies of a variety of populations: medical diagnostic imaging producers (Mitchell, 1989), telephone companies (Barnett & Carroll, 1987), semiconductor companies (Hannan & Freeman, 1989), voluntary social service organizations (Tucker, Singh, Meinhard, & House, 1988), wine producers (Delacroix et al., 1989), and newspaper publishers (Carroll & Hannan, 1989). The results of these studies are not consistent, with opposing patterns of competition and mutualism appearing across the different populations (see Delacroix et al., 1989, for a review).

2. As proposed by Hannan and Freeman (1989, p. 140), population mass was measured by the total number of subscribers of all existing companies in a sample region in a given year. This measure was most relevant to these companies because they were known to compete mostly over subscribers, especially in the early years (Brooks, 1976). Furthermore, most other size measures — such as financial assets or number of employees — may have varied because of technological differences even when the number of subscribers was constant.

3. There was a small amount of missing information on size (455 of the 11,411 observations). In these cases size was estimated by linear interpolation and the estimates were included in the analysis.

4. In models not shown, neither a calendar time trend nor the number of farms is statistically significant when included alone or with the other environmental variables. However, each variable introduces collinearity, reducing the efficiency of the model. As a result, these variables are not included in the analysis.

5. The annual event probability for a constant rate Poisson model is easily obtained from the predicted instantaneous transition rate (see Tuma & Hannan, 1984). We calculated each year's predicted probability using the relation $q = 1 - (\exp[-r])$, where q is the annual founding probability and r is the instantaneous founding rate estimated for each calendar year using the values of all covariates for that year.

6. In models not shown, average farm size, indexed average farm value, population, the average size of manufacturing establishments, and the indexed average wage were each nonsignificant either alone or when modeled with the other environmental variables and organization-level characteristics. For this reason, none of these variables was included in the analysis.

7. The predicted failure probability was calculated using the average value for each organization-level characteristic for each year. Note that for the years before 1896, the prediction has little statistical power because very few organizations were in operation.

REFERENCES

Aldrich, H., & Auster, E. (1986). Even dwarfs started small: Liabilities of size and age and their strategic implications. In B. Staw & L. L. Cummings (Eds.), *Research in organizational behavior* (Vol. 8, pp. 165-198). Greenwich, CT: JAI.

Aldrich, H., & Staber, U. (1988). Organizational business interests: Patterns of trade association foundings, transformation, and deaths. In G. Carroll (Ed.), *Ecological models of organizations* (pp. 111-126). Cambridge, MA: Ballinger.

Amburgey, T. L., & Carroll, G. R. (1984). Time series models for event counts. *Social Science Research, 13*, 38-54.

Artle, R., & Averous, C. (1975). The telephone system as public good: Static and dynamic aspects. *Bell Journal of Economics, 4,* 89-100.

Atwood, R. (1984). *Telephony and its cultural meanings in southeastern Iowa, 1900-1917.* Unpublished doctoral dissertation, University of Iowa.

Barnett, W. P., & Carroll, G. R. (1987). Competition and mutualism among early telephone companies. *Administrative Science Quarterly, 32,* 400-421.

Barnett, W. P., & Carroll, G. R. (1989). *How institutional constraints shaped and changed competition in the early American telephone industry: An ecological analysis* (Working Paper 4-89-6). Madison: University of Wisconsin, School of Business.

Baumol, W. J., Panzar, J. C., & Willig, R. D. (1982). *Contestable markets and the theory of industry structure.* New York: Harcourt Brace Jovanovich.

Brittain, J. W., & Freeman, J. (1980). Organizational proliferation and density-dependent selection: Organizational evolution in the semiconductor industry. In J. R. Kimberly & R. H. Miles (Eds.), *The organizational life cycle* (pp. 291-338). San Francisco: Jossey-Bass.

Brock, G. W. (1981). *The telecommunications industry: The dynamics of market structure.* Cambridge, MA: Harvard University Press.

Brooks, J. (1976). *Telephone: The first hundred years.* New York: Harper & Row.

Carroll, G. R. (1985). Concentration and specialization: Dynamics of niche width in populations of organizations. *American Journal of Sociology, 90,* 1262-1283.

Carroll, G. R., Delacroix, J., & Goodstein, F. (1988). The political environments of organizations: An ecological view. In B. Staw & L. L. Cummings (Eds.), *Research in organizational behavior* (Vol. 10, pp. 359-392). Greenwich, CT: JAI.

Carroll, G. R., & Hannan, M. T. (1989). Density dependence in the evolution of populations of newspaper organizations. *American Sociological Review, 54,* 524-541.

Chamberlin, E. (1950). *The theory of monopolistic competition* (5th ed.). Cambridge, MA: Harvard University Press.

Coleman, J. S. (1981). *Longitudinal data analysis.* New York: Basic Books.

Danielian, M. R. (1939). *AT&T: The story of industrial conquest.* New York: Vanguard.

Delacroix, J., & Carroll, G. R. (1983). Organizational foundings: An ecological study of the newspaper industries of Argentina and Ireland. *Administrative Science Quarterly, 28,* 274-291.

Delacroix, J., Swaminathan, A., & Solt, M. E. (1989). Density dependence versus population dynamics: An ecological study of failings in the California wine industry. *American Sociological Review, 54,* 245-262.

Duncan, O. D. (1959). Human ecology and population studies. In M. Hauser & O. D. Duncan (Eds.). *The study of population* (pp. 678-716). Chicago: University of Chicago Press.

Dunsheath, P. (1962). *A history of electrical engineering.* New York: Pitman.

Edwards, C. D. (1955). Conglomerate bigness as a source of power. In National Bureau of Economics Research, *Business concentration and price policy* (pp. 331-359). Princeton, NJ: Princeton University Press.

Fischer, C. S. (1987). The revolution in rural telephony. *Journal of Social History, 21,* 5-26.

Fischer, C. S. (1988). "Touch someone": The telephone industry discovers sociability. *Technology and Culture,* pp. 32-61.

Fischer, C. S., & Carroll, G. R. (1988). Telephone and automobile diffusion in the United States, 1902-1937. *American Journal of Sociology, 93,* 1153-1178.

Fombrun, C. J. (1988). Crafting an institutionally informed ecology of organizations. In G. R. Carroll (Ed.), *Ecological models of organizations* (pp. 223-239). Cambridge, MA: Ballinger.

Granovetter, M. S. (1985). Economic action and social structure: The problem of embeddedness. *American Journal of Sociology, 91*, 481-510.

Greene, W. (1988). *LIMDEP.* Unpublished manuscript.

Hannan, M. T., & Freeman, J. (1977). The population ecology of organizations. *American Journal of Sociology, 82*, 929-964.

Hannan, M. T., & Freeman, J. (1986). Where do organizational forms come from? *Sociological Forum, 1*, 50-72.

Hannan, M. T., & Freeman, J. (1987). The ecology of organizational founding: American labor unions, 1836-1985. *American Journal of Sociology, 92*, 910-943.

Hannan, M. T., & Freeman, J. (1988). The ecology of organizational mortality: American labor unions, 1836-1985. *American Journal of Sociology, 94*, 25-52.

Hannan, M. T., & Freeman, J. (1989). *Organizational ecology.* Cambridge, MA: Harvard University Press.

Hawley, A. H. (1950). *Human ecology: A theory of community structure.* New York: Ronald.

Ijiri, Y., & Simon, H. A. (1977). *Skew distributions and the sizes of business firms.* New York: North-Holland.

Independent Telephone Association, Inc. (various years). *Telephony's directory.* Chicago: Telephony Publishing Corp.

Key, V. O. (1942). *Politics, parties and pressure groups.* New York: Thomas Y. Crowell.

Khandwalla, P. N. (1981). Properties of competing organizations. In P. Nystrom & W. Starbuck (Eds.), *Handbook of organizational design* (pp. 409-432). New York: Oxford University Press.

MacMeal, H. B. (1934). *The story of independent telephony.* Chicago: Independent Pioneer Telephone Association.

McPherson, J. M., & Smith-Lovin, L. (1988). A comparative ecology of five nations. In G. R. Carroll (Ed.), *Ecological models of organizations* (pp. 85-110). Cambridge, MA: Ballinger.

Mitchell, W. (1989). Whether and when? Probability and timing of incumbent entry into emerging industrial subfields. *Administrative Science Quarterly, 34*, 208-230.

Pennsylvania State Department of Internal Affairs. (various years). *Industrial directory of the Commonwealth of Pennsylvania.* Harrisburg: Pennsylvania Bureau of Publications.

Pennsylvania State Department of Internal Affairs. (various years). *Annual report, part IV: Railroad, canal, navigation, telegraph, and telephone companies.* Harrisburg: Pennsylvania Bureau of Publications.

Perrow, C. (1986). *Complex organizations: A critical essay* (3rd ed.). Glenview, IL: Scott-Foresman.

Scott, W. R. (1987). *Organizations: Rational, natural, and open systems* (2nd ed.). Englewood Cliffs, NJ: Prentice-Hall.

Simmel, G. (1955). *Conflict.* Glencoe, IL: Free Press. (Original work published 1908)

Thompson, J. (1967). *Organizations in action.* New York: McGraw-Hill.

Tucker, D., Singh, J., Meinhard, A., & House, R. (1988). Ecological and institutional sources of change in organizational populations. In G. Carroll (Ed.), *Ecological models of organizations* (pp. 127-151). Cambridge, MA: Ballinger.

Tuma, N. B. (1979). *Invoking RATE* (2nd ed.). Menlo Park, CA: SRI International.

Tuma, N. B., & Hannan, M. T. (1984). *Social dynamics: Models and methods.* New York: Academic Press.

U.S. Bureau of the Census. (1906). *Census of electrical industries: Telephones.* Washington, DC: Government Printing Office.

5

Density Delay in the Evolution of Organizational Populations: A Model and Five Empirical Tests

GLENN R. CARROLL
MICHAEL T. HANNAN

Recent research has found that density (the number of organizations in a population) affects rates of organizational founding and mortality. This research has concentrated on the *contemporaneous* effects of density, how density at particular historical times affects the vital rates at those times. We seek to broaden the issues by proposing that density might also have a *delayed* effect on mortality rates. In particular, we suggest that density at time of founding affects the life chances of organizations, that organizations founded during periods of high density have persistently higher age-specific rates of mortality.

We pursue the issue of density delay for two reasons. First, distinguishing between contemporaneous and delayed effects of density helps clarify the processes by which density affects the evolution of organizational populations. Second, exploring this issue may also help to explain a puzzling feature of growth trajectories of diverse organizational populations: The number of organizations in a population typically grows slowly initially, then increases rapidly to a peak. Once the peak is reached, there is usually a sharp decline

Authors' Note: This research was supported by National Science Foundation grant SES-8809006 and by the Institute of Industrial Relations, University of California, Berkeley. An earlier version was presented at the Wharton Conference on Organizational Evolution, December 1988. We appreciate the research assistance of Anand Swaminathan and the comments of John Freeman, Dan Levinthal, and Jitendra Singh.

103

and sometimes stabilization. We are concerned here with the decline from the peak rather than with the stability of density beyond the peak. Recent theory and research in organizational ecology can account for the shape of the growth path to a peak (Hannan & Freeman, 1989). However, a general explanation for the decline from the peak has yet to appear. Processes involving density delay have promise for explaining such patterns. If density at founding has a positive effect on mortality rates, then mortality rates are especially high just after a population has reached its peak, and density declines from the peak. In fact, such a process may engender cyclic variations dampening to an equilibrium.

This chapter proposes a specific model of density delay in organizational mortality. It tests the implications of the model using data on five populations of organizations: American labor unions (1836-1985), Argentinean newspapers (1800-1900), Irish newspapers (1800-1970), newspaper publishers in the San Francisco region (1840-1975), and American breweries (1633-1988). These populations are especially useful for this analysis because data are available over long historical periods and because the set possesses diversity in terms of types of organization and national contexts. Thus these five populations provide an opportunity to evaluate whether the proposed effect is a general one. The model proposed here builds on an existing model of density dependence in vital rates of organizational populations. We merely sketch the model here because it has been discussed at length elsewhere (Hannan & Freeman, 1988a, 1989).

DENSITY DEPENDENCE
IN ORGANIZATIONAL POPULATIONS

The model of density dependence in rates of organizational founding and mortality that has motivated the research to date assumes that (a) processes of legitimation and competition shape rates of founding and mortality, and (b) processes of legitimation and competition depend on density. In particular, Hannan (1986) and Hannan and Freeman (1989) have argued that the founding rate is proportional to the legitimacy (L) of the organizational form and inversely proportional to the level of competition (C) within the population:

$$\gamma(t) = \alpha(t)(L_t/C_t) \qquad [1]$$

where $\gamma(t)$ denotes the founding rate at time t, and $\alpha(t)$ is a function summarizing time-varying environmental conditions. Reasoning that organizational density increases legitimacy at a decreasing rate and increases competition at an increasing rate, Hannan (1986) proposed the following parametric relationships with density (n):

$$L_t = n_t^\beta, \; 0 < \beta < 1 \qquad [2]$$

and

$$C_t = \exp(\gamma n_t^2), \; \gamma > 0 \qquad [3]$$

Combining equations 1-3 gives a model for the effect of density on the founding rate:

$$\gamma(t) = \alpha(t)n_t^\beta \exp(\gamma n_t^2) \qquad [4a]$$

with the restrictions

$$0 < \beta < 1; \gamma < 0 \qquad [4b]$$

According to this model, the founding rate has a *nonmonotonic* inverted U-shaped relationship with density: Initial growth in density increases the founding rate, but further increases eventually depress it.

Parallel arguments hold for the mortality rate, but with the rate proportional to C and inversely proportional to L. This assumption, along with those in equations 2 and 3, leads to models of density with the form of 4a but with the expected signs of the coefficients in 4b reversed. Because Hannan and Freeman (1988b) had difficulty in getting maximum likelihood programs to converge in estimating this model, they used a slightly different model, which has been adopted by subsequent researchers. The revised model has the following form:

$$\mu(a) = \zeta(a)\exp(\theta_1 n_a + \theta_2 n_a^2) \qquad [5a]$$

with the restrictions

$$\theta_1 < 0; \theta_2 > 0; |\theta_1| > |\theta_2| \qquad [5b]$$

Here $\mu(a)$ denotes an age-specific mortality rate, the rate of mortality of an organization at age a; n_a denotes the density of the population at the time that the organization in question attains age a; and $\zeta(a)$ summarizes the effects of environmental conditions operating at that time. There are two ways of motivating this alternative model. The first assumes that legitimation is an exponential function of density. The second assumes that legitimation is a log-quadratic function of density with a positive first-order effect and a negative second-order effect. Such a function implies that legitimation eventually declines at high densities, which is not consistent with Hannan's argument. However, if we restrict attention to the range over which the log-quadratic relationship is positive, this model gives a potentially useful approximation to the relationship assumed in equation 2. The second motivation seems to be a more useful one in the present context.

Hannan and Freeman (1987, 1988b) tested the model of density dependence in equations 4 and 5 using data on national labor unions in the United States over the entire history of the population, 1836-1985. Their findings strongly support the model. Since then, several other studies have replicated these results using data on different kinds of populations. Six studies have found patterns of density dependence that agree with the model: (a) Hannan and Freeman's (1989) analysis of rates of exit from the population of American semiconductor manufacturers (1945-1980), (b) Barnett and Carroll's (1987) analysis of rates of founding and mortality of independent local telephone companies in several Iowa counties (1900-1917), (c) Mitchell's (1987) study of rates of entry into the medical diagnostic imaging industry (1959-1986), (d) Carroll and Swaminathan's (1989a) investigation of foundings and mortality in the American brewing industry (1633-1988), (e) Carroll and Hannan's (1989) analysis of foundings and mortality in nine populations of newspapers (1800-1975), and (f) Aldrich, Staber, Zimmer, and Beggs's (Chapter 2, this volume) analysis of disbandings of American trade associations between 1900 and 1983.

Other studies have reported findings that do not support the model. Hannan and Freeman's (1989) analysis of rates of entry into the semiconductor manufacturing industry revealed that density had a monotonic positive effect on the rate. Delacroix, Swaminathan, and Solt's (1989) analysis of exits from the population of California wine producers (1940-1985) found no consistent evidence of density dependence. Tucker, Singh, Meinhard, and House (1988) report that density dependence in rates of mortality of voluntary social service organizations in Toronto (1970-1982) had a nonmonotonic pattern but with signs opposite to the predictions of the model in some analyses. At the same time, Tucker et al.'s (1988) analysis provides limited support. While these researchers report that the predicted pattern of density dependence does hold (Table 8-1, second equation), they conclude that this is the case only during times of increased public funding.

As Carroll and Hannan (1989) explain, these studies differ greatly in completeness of coverage of the populations' histories. Only the studies of national labor unions, semiconductor manufacturers, newspapers, and diagnostic imaging companies have information on the early history of the population. Excluding data on the formative period raises special problems for studying the legitimacy process because the model implies strong effects of density in the early period of low density. Ignoring the early period makes it difficult, if not impossible, to distinguish between the legitimating and competition-intensifying effects of rising density. The general pattern of results reported so far bears out this concern. Studies that include the entire history of a population have tended to find effects of density on vital rates consistent with the model in equations 4 and 5.

DENSITY DELAY AND THE TIME OF FOUNDING

Our interest in the delayed effects of density stems partly from an interest in learning why density typically declines from its peak rather than fluctuating in a narrow range around the peak. One type of answer focuses on the effects of environmental change and the obsolescence of organizational forms. If strong inertial forces hamper organizations' capacities to reorganize rapidly, then populations of organizations existing in uncertain and changing environments eventually become obsolete. Organizations with strategies and structures fashioned in distant eras presumably fare badly in competition for members and resources. Eventually such diminished competitiveness leads to heightened mortality and perhaps to the disappearance of the population and the organizational form.

Obsolescence processes undoubtedly have played a major role in shaping the world of organizations, and it is tempting to attribute the observed demographic pattern to them. In any concrete application, however, this type of explanation does little more than restate what can be observed in a historical trajectory of density. It does not account for the dynamics of the trajectories, the actual timing of the rise and fall in numbers.

As an alternative to ad hoc explanations based on obsolescence, we suggest that ecological dynamics might also explain the observed pattern. The relevant dynamics involve density dependence in mortality rates in a slightly broadened model, one with delayed as well as contemporaneous effects of density on mortality rates.

The model of density dependence described above assumes that the mortality of all organizations in a population responds to variations in density in the same way. An increase in density beyond a certain threshold (determined by the parameters of the model) increases the mortality rates of all organizations proportionately. That is, the mortality rate of any particular organization at a specific historical time is found by taking the rate implied by its age and other characteristics and multiplying it by the effect of the level of density that obtains at that time — the effect of density is contemporaneous.

Another possibility is that organizations may be particularly sensitive to density *at the time of founding*. This would be consistent with Stinchcombe's (1965) well-known argument about imprinting of conditions of founding; below, we discuss a number of reasons this argument might hold for effects of density at time of founding. Assuming for the moment that density at time of founding does affect later mortality, there are several implications. If the effect of density at time of founding persists, then organizations entering a population at high density have elevated rates of mortality for some time. As a consequence, the size of the population falls from the peak, unless the founding rate rises in compensation.[1]

A similar scenario has received attention in the literature on mathematical population biology. Leslie (1959) has proposed a model in which the mortality rate depends on contemporaneous density and conditions at time of birth. Citing research on human mortality, Leslie observes that "it appears that each generation of young tends to carry throughout life a relative degree of mortality peculiar to itself, and it is supposed that this characteristic mortality . . . represents the effect of environmental conditions experienced by each generation during the early years of its life in the population" (p. 152).

For present purposes, what is important is that Leslie showed that adding delayed density dependence (with an implicit interaction with age structure) produces dampened cycles in trajectories of growth even when the environment does not vary.[2] This kind of process can generate the type of trajectory commonly observed for organizational populations.

The appeal of Leslie's model leads us to ask whether density at time of founding might affect the mortality rate of "mature" organizations. We suggest that there are two related affirmative answers. The first concerns a *liability of resource scarcity*. Intense competition at time of founding (due to high density) creates conditions of resource scarcity. When resources are scarce, new organizations that cannot move quickly from organizing to full-scale operation face very strong selection pressures. Those that survive the initial period of organizing presumably do not have the luxury of devoting time, attention, and resources to creating formal structure and perfecting stable, reproducible routines for making decisions and taking collective action. In cohorts of organizations facing such circumstances, staff members have little motivation for investing heavily in acquiring organization-specific skills, which is an essential part of developing reproducible routines.

It might be difficult to recover fully from such deprived initial organizing. Inertial forces presumably operate in this context as well as others. That is, attempts at redesigning poorly fashioned structures may well encounter the risks identified by Hannan and Freeman (1984). If so, cohorts of organizations that experience high density at founding will tend to be inferior competitors at every age.

A second consequence of high density at time of founding concerns *tight niche packing.* When density is high, resources are subject to intense exploitation and few resources go unexploited. Since newly founded organizations can seldom compete head-to-head with established organizations, the new entrants tend to be pushed to the margins of resource distributions. Tight niche packing thus causes new organizations to attempt to exploit thinly spread and ephemeral resources. Even if they suceed at creating structures and routines for adapting successfully to the inferior regions of the resource space, in the course of doing so they commit themselves to persisting at the margins. The specialized learning of staff, the collective experience of the organization, and the organization's connections with the environment all become specialized to exploiting the inferior regions of the environment. Attempting to shift toward the richer center at some later time entails high risks of mortality during periods of reorganization. If reorganization is successful, it brings the organization into competition with others specialized in exploiting the center. In either case, these marginal organizations have higher-than-average mortality rates.

A reviewer has proposed a third possibility, namely, that there is a *trial by fire.* Suppose that each cohort of organizations has a distribution of unobserved frailty (to follow the terminology of Vaupel, Manton, & Stallard, 1979). Presumably, the most frail organizations are likely to fail early in their histories under almost any circumstance. Those with slightly less frailty may persist if founded in favorable environmental circumstances, but they will fail otherwise. Those with moderate frailty will tend to persist unless founding conditions are highly unfavorable, and so forth. Founding conditions affect population dynamics by altering the "posttrial" distributions of frailty by cohort rather than by elevating the mortality rates of individual organizations. In particular, cohorts founded in periods of high environmental stress, such as high density, have a lower mean frailty after the initial year than cohorts founded in favorable circumstances. As a consequence, they have lower mortality rates after the period of initial selection (Vaupel et al., 1979). In the imagery proposed by the reviewer, cohorts of organizations that survive the trial by fire have lower mortality rates than those that do not face the trial.

The trial-by-fire hypothesis leads to a different prediction from the arguments about liability of scarcity and tight niche packing. A trial by fire affects the postselection distribution of mortality rates in a population but does not elevate the rates for particular organizations. In other words, an organization that passes the trial has the same mortality rate it had before the trial. The arguments involving liability of scarcity and tight niche packing imply that mortality rates are elevated for all members of cohorts founded in periods of high density and that this increase persists over time.

In order to learn whether density at time of founding has persistent effects on mortality rates, we pursue a variant of Leslie's model. Our model holds that *density at time of founding* matters — not time of founding per se. The difference is that two cohorts founded in different periods when density happened to be at the same level have the same rate according to our argument but not according to Leslie's. The arguments about the liability of scarcity and tight niche packing suggest that the effect of density at founding is monotonic and positive. It seems likely to us that such an effect has the same *relative* effect at all ages, which means that the absolute effect is largest at young ages, since the rate is highest at those ages. So we propose a model of mortality with the following form:

$$\mu_i(a) = \exp(\theta_1 n_a + \theta_2 n_a^2 + n_{f_i}) \qquad [6a]$$

where n_a denotes density at age a, and n_{f_i} denotes density at time of founding of the ith organization. We continue to assume that contemporaneous density has the nonmonotonic pattern of effects (at all ages) discussed above. We hypothesize that *density at time of founding has a positive effect on the age-specific mortality rate and that this effect persists over time*. In terms of the model above, the hypotheses are that

$$\theta_1 < 0; \theta_2 > 0; \phi > 0 \qquad [6b]$$

The trial-by-fire hypothesis leads to a different prediction. In this view, high density at time of founding increases the mortality rate of new organizations (this is an effect of contemporaneous density) but does not affect mortality rates of individual organizations conditional on their level of frailty. However, we do not observe frailty. What does this hypothesis imply about the relationship between density and the unconditional mortality rate after the founding period? The claim that density at time of founding affects mortality rates at that time is an instance of an effect of contemporaneous density. Net of the effect of contemporaneous density, would founding density affect later mortality? The answer seems to depend on one's conception of the length of the period of a trial by fire. We presume here that this trial occurs during the year of founding. Since the trial-by-fire hypothesis assumes that high founding density causes mortalities over a broader range of frailty, one interpretation is that the unconditional mortality rate is lower after the founding year for cohorts founded in periods of high density. In terms of the model in equation 6, this means that the persisting effect of founding density on the mortality rate is *negative*: $\phi < 0$.

EMPIRICAL STUDIES

In view of the previous studies, we claim that separating the effects of delayed and contemporaneous density requires analyzing organizational populations for which complete histories can be coded over long periods. This section briefly reviews the designs that produced the data we use. Since the populations and their social contexts differ, we do not use exactly the same covariates in all analyses of rates of mortality. This section also describes the covariates we used to represent external conditions and secular trends.

Newspapers

Newspaper publication leaves behind dated material products that have been used extensively by historians and others. Consequently, there are many publishing histories. In addition, directories compiled for advertisers have been published yearly since about 1870. We analyzed data from studies that attempted to define and enumerate the complete historical populations of newspapers in Argentina, Ireland, and the San Francisco metropolitan area in the United States. For each locality, archival sources were used to record

Figure 5.1. Historical variations in density for the population of Irish newspapers.

life-history data on all identified members of the newspaper population. The cornerstones of this effort were compilations of library newspaper holdings prepared by councils of librarians and annual directories of advertising agencies. A complete discussion of these sources and their quality can be found in Carroll (1987).

Because some dates are precise only to the year, we measured density on an annual basis. It counts the number of newspapers recorded as existing at any time during the year as the density for that year. Figures 5.1-5.3 display fluctuations of density from 1800 to 1975 for Ireland and San Francisco and from 1800 to 1900 for Argentina. The Irish and San Francisco populations exhibit the patterns of growth and decline discussed at the outset. The Irish population grows to a peak level of 224 before declining by roughly half by 1975. In the San Francisco area, density grows to a peak level of 395 and then declines by about 40% by 1975. The history of the population in Argentina is censored by a lack of data at what would appear to be its approximate peak (the observed maximum is 125), assuming that it follows the general pattern.

Carroll and his collaborators coded the history of political turmoil in Argentina, Ireland, and San Francisco. They found that population turmoil

Figure 5.2. Historical variations in density for the population of San Francisco newspapers.

Figure 5.3. Historical variations in density for the population of Argentinean newspapers.

coincides with increased foundings and that papers founded in turmoil-ridden periods have higher mortality rates (Carroll & Delacroix, 1982; Carroll & Huo, 1986; Delacroix & Carroll, 1983). We thus included a dummy variable for years of political turmoil in models of the mortality of newspaper organizations.

We also used the number of foundings and the number of closures in the immediately preceding years as controls for short-run variations in environmental conditions. On the basis of previous findings (Carroll & Huo, 1986; Delacroix & Carroll, 1983), we used quadratic specifications of the effects of these variables. Models with these variables as covariates also allow the separation of the effects of transitory changes in density (due to foundings and closures in the prior year) from the effects of longer-term, presumably more systematic changes in density.

National Labor Unions

Unlike the other kinds of organizations under study, labor unions do not rely on commercial viability in the marketplace in order to survive, yet unions are historically very important organizations. The existence of unions and their actions have shaped American industrial structure and politics. Consequently, unions have attracted the attention of historians and other scholars, and their histories, too, can be reconstructed from archival sources. The data on national unions used here come from an effort to collect information about every national labor union that has existed, however briefly, in the United States during the period from 1836 (the year of the first national unions) to 1985. This coding began with lists of names and starting dates from reports published in various years that claimed to cover the population of unions. These publications yielded an initial master list. This set was extended by consulting standard histories of the labor movement, which were especially useful for the early period, 1830-1870. This procedure identified 621 national unions with usable histories. More detailed discussion of the design used in this study can be found in Hannan (1988b) and Hannan and Freeman (1989, chap. 7).

Figure 5.4 shows the trajectory of density over the 150-year period, beginning with the founding of the first national union. The number of national unions fluctuated near zero until the Civil War era, rose modestly until about 1881, and then grew explosively until 1905. From that point on, growth in the number of unions was slower and more erratic until the series reached its peak level of 211 in 1954. The last portion of the series shows

Figure 5.4. Historical variations in density for the population of American national labor unions.

consistent but modest contraction in the number of unions. This trajectory, like those for newspaper populations, fits the pattern discussed at the outset.

In analyzing mortality, we considered events of *disbanding*, by which we mean that a union ceased to operate as a national union without merging with another union. We concentrated on disbanding here rather than mortality due to all causes (including mergers) because earlier research reveals that the pattern of density dependence is quite different for the various forms of mortality in the population of national labor unions (Hannan, 1988a). Roughly one-third of the unions studied were disbanded (191). Because previous research indicates that rates of mortality have varied over time in response to changes in the legal standing of unions and major organizational changes in the national union movement (Hannan & Freeman, 1987, 1988b), we used a set of five period effects in the analysis reported below. The first period begins in 1836, the start of national unionization. The second begins in 1887, following the formation of the American Federation of Labor (AFL). The third begins in 1932 with the New Deal, when unions acquired substantial legal protection. The fourth begins in 1948, following passage of the Taft-Hartley Act, which eliminated some New Deal provisions. The fifth period begins in 1955, the year of the merger of the AFL and the CIO. We also included a dummy variable that distinguishes years of economic depression and a pair of dummy variables that indicate whether a union began with a founding or a secession from an existing union (the omitted category is "started by merger"). We did not include counts of prior foundings and disbandings in these analyses because earlier research revealed that such effects are negligible for the population of labor unions (Hannan & Freeman, 1989, chap. 11).

Brewing Firms

Beer brewing may be the oldest production industry, yet it remains an important activity in modern economies. As in most countries, the American brewing industry has experienced many transformations over its long history. The best known are the long-term decline in the number of firms in the industry and the attendant increase in the average size of the surviving firms. Today the American brewing industry shows fairly high levels of concentration, with strong economies of scale in production and advertising favoring the largest firms.

We used event history data on foundings and closures of beer producers from 1633 to 1988. Bull, Freidrich, and Gottschalk's (1984) compilation constitutes the primary source of data. This source claimed to have included information on all beer producers (excluding companies who sell beer produced under contract by others, so-called contract brewers). The preface to the volume remarks that "a tremendous amount of research has gone into compiling American Breweries. Experts in various areas of the country have contributed their knowledge which was coordinated by long-time brewery historian Robert Gottschalk" (p. 3). The data entries include the founding company name and address and the year the company went out of business or changed name or address. Several entries in Bull et al. (1984) were changed in the coding process for our analyses because one of the volume's authors indicated to us that new information had been uncovered and the printed volume had inadvertently omitted some brewers (R. Gottschalk, personal communication). Because the listings in this volume pertain to plants (breweries) rather than to firms, we aggregated the histories for all plants belonging to the same firm. We also extended the coverage up to the autumn of 1988. These tasks were accomplished with the aid of the *Modern Brewery Age Bluebooks* (Modern Brewery Age, various years), Tremblay and Tremblay (1988), and the *Microbrewers Resource Handbook* (Institute of

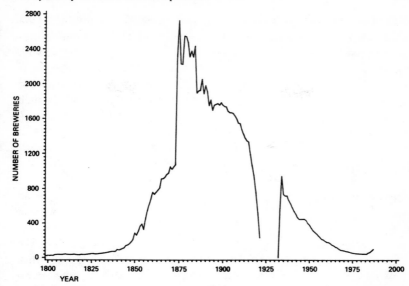

Figure 5.5. Historical variations in density for the population of American brewers.

Fermentation and Brewing Studies, various years). More details can be found in Carroll and Swaminathan (1989b).

Figure 5.5 shows the trajectory of density of firms in the American brewing industry from 1633 to 1988. The common pattern of slow initial growth, then rapid growth to a peak of about 2,700, followed by a very sharp decline to a seemingly stable equilibrium appears again. In this case, however, the decline phase is interrupted by the federal Prohibition (1920-1933). Remarkably, the population pattern resumes after Prohibition in what seems to be its natural trend.[3]

The study of brewing firms remains in its early stages, and we have yet to code and analyze environmental variables. We can at this point, however, use the life-history data to construct measures of population variables pertinent to the models of density dependence. We can also control for factors endogenous to the population's evolution that previous ecological research suggests will be important. For models of organizational mortality, these include the following: age of firm, number of foundings in the previous year, and number of closures in the previous year.

We also included a dummy variable to deal with the effects of state and federal prohibitions. This variable indicates the year before the start of a prohibition that affects the brewing firm in question (usually the year in which the prohibition was passed into law). The federal Prohibition begun by the Volstead Act, ratified on January 16, 1919, and beginning in 1920, affected all brewing firms in this population; therefore, all brewers receive a value of 1 on this variable for the year 1919. State prohibitions produce values of 1 on this variable for all brewers operating in the state in question. Since some of the breweries opening after Prohibition did not have permits, we included an indicator for operating without a permit. Finally, because an unusually large number of foundings was reported for 1874 and we suspect that this clumping might be an artifact in the original sources used by Bull et al. (R. Gottschalk, personal communication), we distinguished firms that were coded as beginning in that year.

FINDINGS

We analyzed effects of covariates on the mortality rates of organizations, using the histories of individual organizations (the unit of observation is the organization rather than the population). Following Carroll (1983), Freeman, Carroll, and Hannan (1983), and much subsequent research, we used the Gompertz specification of monotonic age dependence in analyzing newspapers and breweries. Because Hannan (1988a) found that the Weibull model of age dependence fits better than the Gompertz model for labor unions, we used the former in analyzing unions. In order to allow values of the covariates to vary over lifetimes, we broke each organization's history into a sequence of yearly spells, with all but the last spell treated as censored on the right (and the last spell is also censored on the right if the organization was still in existence at the end of the period of observation). The age of the organization and the values of density and other covariates were updated at the beginning of each year for each organization. This means that the mortality rate in any year was assumed to depend on the level of density in that year (which we call *contemporaneous density*) and on the levels of other covariates in that year. However, all covariates were treated as constant within years. This procedure assumes that the covariates change as step functions over time (Tuma & Hannan, 1984, chap. 7). Thus the models that we estimated have the following form:

$$\mu_{ia} = \exp(\theta_1 n_a + \theta_2 n_a^2 + \phi n_{f_i} + \pi' x_{ia} + \psi a), \ a = 0, 1, \ldots, A_i \quad [7a]$$

for newspapers and breweries, and

$$\mu_{ia} = \exp(\theta_1 n_a + \theta_2 n_a^2 + \phi n_{f_i} + \pi' x_{ia}) a^{\rho-1}, \, a = 0, 1, \ldots, A_i \quad [7b]$$

for labor unions. In each case a is a discreet clock that measures age in years, n_a denotes the density at the beginning of the calendar year in which the organization in question reached age a, x_{ia} is a vector of measures of organizational characteristics and environmental conditions at that time, and a_i is the maximum age observed for the organization. The term $\exp(\psi a)$ in equation 7a is a discrete approximation to the Gompertz model of age dependence. Likewise, $a^{\rho-1}$ in 7b is a discrete approximation to the Weibull model of age dependence. Because $a^\sigma = \exp(\sigma \log a)$, we can implement the Weibull model by using the logarithm of age at the beginning of a spell rather than simple age in the log-linear specification for the rate. We estimated the parameters of such models using the method of maximum likelihood (ML), which allows us to take right censoring into account. We report both point estimates and asymptotic standard errors.

Because we have reported and discussed the effects of aging, environmental conditions, and secular trends on the mortality rates of these populations elsewhere, we concentrated on the effects of contemporaneous density and density at founding here. Table 5.1 reports estimates of the effects of contemporaneous density from the model in 7 in which the effect of density at founding is constrained to be zero (the full set of estimates can be found in the Appendix to this chapter). The first-order effect of contemporaneous density is negative and the second-order effect is positive for all five populations, in agreement with the predictions in 6b. These point estimates imply that the mortality rate is a nonmonotonic, U-shaped function of density as predicted. That is, the mortality rate falls with increasing density to some point and then rises with further increases in density. Moreover, each point estimate in Table 5.1 differs significantly from zero at the .05 level (two-tailed test).

In considering the effect of density at time of founding, we used the models whose estimates appear in Table 5.1 as baselines. That is, we added density at time of founding to those models in order to learn whether it would have the predicted positive effect, net of the effects of contemporaneous density, age, and the other covariates. Table 5.2 reports the key results; again, the full set of estimates can be found in the Appendix. As arguments about a liability of scarcity and niche packing predict, density at time of founding has a positive effect on mortality rates in all five populations. The point estimates are significantly different from zero at the .05 level (two-tailed) for all but the population of Irish newspapers. Because the data on brewing firms before the nineteenth century may not be as reliable as those for the nineteenth and

TABLE 5.1: Effects of Contemporaneous Density on Rates of Organizational Mortality (ML estimates with asymptotic standard errors in parentheses)

Population	Contemporaneous Density	Contemporaneous Density^2
Labor unions[a]	−.027* (.013)	.011* × 10^{-2} (.005 × 10^{-2})
Breweries[b]	−.00017* (.00007)	.054* × 10^{-6} (.025 × 10^{-6})
San Francisco newspapers[c]	−.012* (.002)	.019* × 10^{-3} (.003 × 10^{-3})
Argentinean newspapers[c]	−.032* (.008)	.130* × 10^{-3} (.045 × 10^{-3})
Irish newspapers[c]	−.013* (.004)	.028* × 10^{-3} (.012 × 10^{-3})

a. Other covariates in the model include age of organization, a set of five period effects (see text), an indicator for depression years, and dummy variables that indicate that a union started by founding or by secession (rather than by merger, the excluded category).
b. Other covariates include age of organization, foundings in the prior year, a dummy variable for operating without a permit, closures in the prior year, a dummy variable for founded in 1874, and a dummy variable for years immediately before any federal or state prohibition (state prohibitions are considered only for brewers operating in the state).
c. Other covariates include age of organization, age of population, foundings in prior year and its square, disbandings in prior year and its square, and a dummy variable for years of political turmoil.
*$p < .05$.

twentieth, we also estimated the model for this population using data only for the period from 1800 to 1988. The point estimates were very similar to those in Table 5.2, but the standard errors were slightly larger (the three effects of density were still significantly different from zero at the .05 level, nonetheless). In all cases, the model with the effect of contemporaneous density improves the fit over the models in Table 5.1 at the .05 level, according to a likelihood ratio test. These results provide strong evidence supporting the use of this version of Leslie's model in analyzing organizational ecology.

The estimated effects of density at founding have striking substantive implications. Consider the predicted effect of the highest level observed for density at founding in each population. We express these effects as multipliers of a base rate implied by our estimates (reflecting the effect of age, contemporaneous density, and other covariates). These effects are huge

TABLE 5.2: Effects of Contemporaneous and Delayed Density on Rates of Organizational Mortality (ML estimates with asymptotic standard errors in parentheses)

Population	Contemporaneous Density	Contemporaneous Density^2	Founding Density
Labor unions[a]	−.045* (.014)	.013* × 10^{-2} (.005 × 10^{-2}	.014* (.003)
Breweries[b]	−.0012* (.0001)	.290* × 10^{-6} (.026 × 10^{-6}	.00051* (.00002)
San Francisco newspapers[c]	−.015* (.002)	.018* × 10^{-3} (.003 × 10^{-3}	.0037* (.0005)
Argentinean newspapers[c]	−.050* (.010)	.160* × 10^{-3} (.046 × 10^{-3}	.0145* (.0044)
Irish newspapers[c]	−.015* (.004)	.027* × 10^{-3} (.012 × 10^{-3}	.0024 (.0013)

a. Other covariates in the model include age of organization, a set of five period effects (see text), an indicator for depression years, and dummy variables that indicate that a union started by founding or by secession (rather than by merger, the excluded category).
b. Other covariates include age of organization, foundings in the prior year, a dummy variable for operating without a permit, closures in the prior year, a dummy variable for founded in 1874, and a dummy variable for years immediately before any federal or state prohibition (state prohibitions are considered only for brewers operating in the state).
c. Other covariates include age of organization, age of population, foundings in prior year and its square, disbandings in prior year and its square, and a dummy variable for years of political turmoil.
*$p < .05$.

relative to a baseline of zero density. For instance, the predicted age-specific mortality rate for San Francisco newspapers founded at the peak is 4.3 times higher than the rate for those founded in a population with no other organizations. The corresponding multipliers are 1.7 for Irish newspapers, 6.1 for Argentinean newspapers, 19.2 for national labor unions, and 4.0 for brewing firms. It is perhaps more interesting to use a baseline of half of the peak level in assessing the strength of the effect of density delay. Comparisons of the effects of density at founding using this baseline are made by taking the ratio of the predicted effect at the peak to the predicted effect at half of the peak. According to these calculations, the predicted age-specific mortality rate of organizations founded at the peak density is 31% higher at any age than those founded at half of the peak for Irish newspapers. For Argentinean newspapers, it is 147% higher; for San Francisco newspapers, 107% higher. In the case of national labor unions, this rate is 338% higher; for American brewers, it is 99% higher. Evidently, density at founding has strongly affected the life chances of organizations in each of these populations.

Finally, adding the effect of density at founding does not eliminate the nonmonotonic effect of contemporaneous density. That is, the first-order effect of contemporaneous density is negative and significant in Table 5.2 for all five populations, and the second-order effect is positive and significant for all five populations. It thus appears that both forms of density dependence have operated in each of these populations.

DISCUSSION AND CONCLUSION

We sought to learn whether density at time of founding affects mortality rates of organizations. In addressing this question, we advanced plausible sociological reasons for expecting that density at founding has enduring effects on mortality rates. These have to do with resource scarcity and niche packing. Analysis of data on five populations, covering three countries and involving both market and nonmarket organizations, shows strong support for our version of a model of density delay.

It remains to be seen whether the delayed effect of density at time of founding is best explained by resource scarcity or niche packing. While the two explanations do not conflict, research that distinguishes the two will clarify the fundamental dynamics. Such research requires the collection of life-history data on complete populations, as we have used here. But it also requires that the strategic orientations and resource endowments of individual organizations be determined. Organizations founded in high-density periods might, for instance, begin smaller in size, on the average, favoring the resource scarcity argument.[4] Alternatively, they might begin at moderate or even large size but attempt to develop new markets, favoring the niche packing argument.

Informal observation of the current, fairly low-density conditions for the populations studied here suggests that the arguments we have developed may need to be integrated with theories of resource partitioning (Carroll, 1985) and niche width (Freeman & Hannan, 1983). In American brewing and newspaper industries, recent entrants appear to exist predominantly in small, specialized niches on the fringes of central markets (Carroll, 1987; Carroll & Swaminathan, 1989a). This pattern appears to reflect an impact of high concentration in the central markets. And high concentration is a consequence of low density in the late stages of the evolution of an industry —

reductions in numbers of firms without reductions in the size of a market imply increases in concentration. There is an important difference between the low-density conditions in an infant industry and those in a mature one. In the period in which an industry takes shape and density is low, the markets are typically dispersed. No one firm or small group of firms typically dominates. In the late stages of the evolution of an industry, one or a few firms often dominate large segments of a connected set of markets. In the early low-density condition, entrants typically differ little from established organizations. In the late low-density condition, they appear to differ considerably in size and strategy as a consequence of high concentration. Clearly, we need to learn more about the interrelated dynamics of density and concentration in order to reach a deeper understanding of the issues raised in this chapter.

The fact that density at founding has a persistent positive effect on mortality rates implies that processes of density delay cause densities of these populations to decline from their peaks. But we do not yet know how much of the observed declines can be explained by density delay. Assessing whether the effects of density at founding can explain the observed declines in the size of organizational populations from their peaks requires that both founding rates and mortality rates be considered. Although we have not reported estimates of founding rates here, previous research using these five data sets has supported the basic model of nonmonotonic density dependence in founding rates—these rates are inverted U-shaped functions of density, according to our estimates. So what remains to be done is an analysis of the population-level implications of the complete model, which is a stochastic birth-death process. Such research is currently under way.

APPENDIX:
COMPLETE SETS OF ESTIMATES FOR
FULL MODEL OF ORGANIZATIONAL MORTALITY

TABLE 5A.1: Estimates of Full Models for Population of American Labor
Unions (ML estimates with asymptotic standard errors in
parentheses)

	1	2
Constant	-4.51*	-4.63*
	(.672)	(.672)
Log of age	-.314*	-.122*
	(.045)	(.059)
Density	-.027*	-.045*
	(.013)	(.014)
Density^2/100	.011*	.013*
	(.005)	(.005)
Density at founding		.014*
		(.003)
Period 1887+	.343	.667
	(.602)	(.606)
Period 1932+	-1.00*	-1.13*
	(.301)	(.302)
Period 1948+	-1.10*	-1.19*
	(.552)	(.552)
Period 1955+	1.13*	.775
	(.571)	(.580)
Economic depression	.434*	.452*
	(.164)	(.164)
Start = founding	2.03*	2.13*
	(.584)	(.584)
Start = secession	1.45*	1.48*
	(.633)	(.633)
Spells	17,797	17,797
Events	191	191
Log L	-1162.5	-1145.3
Degrees of freedom	11	12

*$p < .05$.

TABLE 5A.2: Estimates of Full Models for Population of American Brewers (ML estimates with asymptotic standard errors in parentheses)

	1	2
Constant	−2.63* (.042)	−2.60* (.041)
Age	−.018* (.001)	−.011* (.001)
Density/100	−.017* (.007)	−.120* (.008)
Density^2/100,000	.0054* (.0025)	.029* (.003)
Density at founding/100		.051* (.002)
Founded in 1874	.186* (.035)	−.160* (.037)
No permit	−3.22* (.083)	3.38* (.084)
Year before prohibition	−3.27* (.033)	3.09* (.034)
Prior foundings	.0009* (.0005)	.0011 (.0001)
Prior closures	−.0007* (.0001)	−.0009* (.0001)
Spells	112,734	112,734
Events	7,587	7,587
Log $\mathcal{L}$	−24,265	−23,994
Degrees of freedom	8	9

*$p < .05$.

TABLE 5A.3: Estimates of Full Models for Population of Newspapers (ML estimates with asymptotic standard errors in parentheses)

	Argentina		Ireland		San Francisco	
	1	2	3	4	5	6
Constant	.037	−.020	−3.07	−2.93*	−1.33*	−1.41*
	(.157)	(.159)	(.233)	(.243)	(.164)	(.164)
Age	−.214*	−.194*	−.029*	−.027*	−.029*	−.021*
	(.012)	(.013)	(.002)	(.002)	(.002)	(.002)
Density	−.032*	−.050*	−.013*	−.015*	−.012*	−.015*
	(.008)	(.010)	(.004)	(.004)	(.002)	(.002)
$Density^2/1,000$	.130*	.160*	.028*	.027*	.019*	.018*
	(.045)	(.046)	(.012)	(.012)	(.003)	(.003)
Density at founding		.0145*		.0024		.0037*
		(.0044)		(.0013)		(.0005)
Population age	.002	.002	.005*	.004*	.004*	−.001
	(.003)	(.004)	(.001)	(.002)	(.002)	(.002)
Founded in political turmoil	.013	−.063	.027	.030	.062	.111
	(.067)	(.071)	(.070)	(.070)	(.057)	(.059)
Prior foundings	−.011	.000	.025	.031	.004	.010
	(.024)	(.024)	(.028)	(.029)	(.010)	(.010)
$Prior\ foundings^2$	.0003	.0001	.0003	.0001	.0003	.0002
	(.0005)	(.0005)	(.0015)	(.0015)	(.0002)	(.0002)
Prior closures	.076*	.076*	.152*	.031	.040*	.040*
	(.023)	(.023)	(.029)	(.030)	(.011)	(.011)
$Prior\ closures^2$	−.0009	−.0008	−.0055*	−.0056*	−.0008*	−.0008*
	(.0005)	(.0005)	(.0016)	(.0016)	(.0003)	(.0003)
Spells	3,799	3,799	21,325	21,325	30,880	30,880
Events	1,345	1,345	889	889	1,859	1,859
Log L	−1,899	−1,893	−3,499	−3,497	−6,720	−6,692
Degrees of freedom	9	10	9	10	9	10

*p < .05.

NOTES

1. According to the model of density dependence, the founding rate does compensate in the sense that a decrease in density in the high range increases the founding rate, which tends to increase density. But this response takes time to unfold, and it actually adds a cyclic component to the population dynamics.

2. Much other theory and research has explored models in which the effect of density on mortality is lagged by some constant or averaged over time. These models, too, produce cyclic population growth in constant environments. Cushing (1977) provides a review of the mathematical structure of these models.

3. This pattern illustrates that one can be seriously misled by estimating models of density dependence with only partial histories of industries, as noted above. Delacroix et al. (1989) conducted such an analysis of the population of wineries in California after Prohibition and, not surprisingly, found inconsistent effects of density on mortality rates. Carroll and Swaminathan (1989a) report that the effect of density on rates of founding and mortality are strong and significant over the entire history of the American brewing population but that restricting analysis to the post-Prohibition period makes these effects small and statistically insignificant.

4. Inspection of the data on size at time of founding for national labor unions, the one case for which we currently have useful data on initial size, does not reveal any such pattern, however.

REFERENCES

Barnett, W. P., & Carroll, G. R. (1987). Competition and mutualism among early telephone companies. *Administrative Science Quarterly, 32*, 400-421.

Bull, D., Freidrich, M., & Gottschalk, R. (1984). *American breweries.* Trumball, CT: Bullworks.

Carroll, G. R. (1983). A stochastic model of organizational mortality: Review and reanalysis. *Social Science Research, 12*, 303-329.

Carroll, G. R. (1985). Concentration and specialization: Dynamics of niche width in populations or organizations. *American Journal of Sociology, 90*, 1262-1283.

Carroll, G. (1987). *Publish and perish: The organizational ecology of newspaper industries.* Greenwich, CT: JAI.

Carroll, G. R., & Delacroix, J. (1982). Organizational mortality in the newspaper industries of Argentina and Ireland: An ecological approach. *Administrative Science Quarterly, 27*, 169-198.

Carroll, G. R., & Hannan, M. T. (1989). Density dependence in the evolution of populations of newspaper organizations. *American Sociological Review, 54*, 524-541.

Carroll, G. R., & Huo, Y. P. (1986). Organizational task and institutional environments in evolutionary perspective: Findings from the local newspaper industry. *American Journal of Sociology, 91*, 838-873.

Carroll, G. R., & Swaminathan, A. (1989a). *Density dependent evolution in the American brewing industry from 1633 to 1988* (Tech. Rep. No. OBIR-35). Berkeley: University of California, Center for Research Management.

Carroll, G. R., & Swaminathan, A. (1989b). *Documentation for public-use data set on American brewers* (Tech. Rep. No. OBIR-37). Berkeley: University of California, Center for Research Management.

Cushing, J. M. (1977). *Integrodifferential equations and delay models in population dynamics.* Berlin: Springer-Verlag.

Delacroix, J., & Carroll, G. R. (1983). Organizational foundings: An ecological study of the newspaper industries of Argentina and Ireland. *Administrative Science Quarterly, 28,* 274-291.

Delacroix, J., Swaminathan, A., & Solt, M. E. (1989). Density dependence versus population dynamics: An ecological study of failings in the California wine industry. *American Sociological Review, 54,* 245-262.

Freeman, J., Carroll, G. R., & Hannan, M. T. (1983). The liability of newness: Age dependence in organizational death rates. *American Sociological Review, 48,* 692-710.

Freeman, J., & Hannan, M. T. (1983). Niche width and the dynamics of organizational populations. *American Journal of Sociology, 88,* 1116-1145.

Hannan, M. T. (1986). *Competitive and institutional processes in organizational ecology* (Tech. Rep. No. 86-13). Ithaca, NY: Cornell University, Department of Sociology.

Hannan, M. T. (1988a). Age dependence in the mortality of national labor unions: Comparisons of parametric models. *Journal of Mathematical Sociology, 14,* 1-30.

Hannan, M. T. (1988b). *Documentation of public-use data set: Ecology of labor unions study* (Tech. Rep. No. 88-2). Ithaca, NY: Cornell University, Sociology Department.

Hannan, M. T., & Freeman, J. (1984). Structural inertia and organizational change. *American Sociological Review, 49,* 149-164.

Hannan, M. T., & Freeman, J. (1987). The ecology of organizational founding: American labor unions, 1836-1985. *American Journal of Sociology, 92,* 910-943.

Hannan, M. T., & Freeman, J. (1988a). Density dependence in the growth of organizational populations. In G. R. Carroll (Ed.), *Ecological models of organizations* (pp. 7-32). Cambridge, MA: Ballinger.

Hannan, M. T., & Freeman, J. (1988b). The ecology of organizational mortality: American labor unions, 1836-1985. *American Journal of Sociology, 94,* 25-52.

Hannan, M. T., & Freeman, J. (1989). *Organizational ecology.* Cambridge, MA: Harvard University Press.

Institute of Fermentation and Brewing Studies. (various years). *Microbrewers resource handbook.* Boulder, CO: Author.

Leslie, P. H. (1959). The properties of a certain lag type of population growth and the influence of an external random factor on the number of such populations. *Physiological Zoölogy, 3,* 151-159.

Mitchell, W. G. (1987, May). *Dynamic tension: Theoretical and empirical analyses of entry into emerging industries.* Paper presented at the Stanford Asilomar Conference on Organizations, Asilomar, CA.

Modern Brewery Age. (various years). *Modern Brewery Age bluebook.* Norwalk, CT: Author.

Stinchcombe, A. L. (1965). Social structure and organizations. In J. G. March (Ed.), *Handbook of organizations* (pp. 142-193). Chicago: Rand McNally.

Tremblay, V. J., & Tremblay, C. H. (1988). The development of acquisition: Evidence from the U.S. brewing industry. *Journal of Industrial Economics, 37,* 21-46.

Tucker, D., Singh, J., Meinhard, A., & House, R. (1988). Ecological and institutional sources of change in organizational populations. In G. Carroll (Ed.), *Ecological models of organizations* (pp. 127-151). Cambridge, MA: Ballinger.

Tuma, N. B., & Hannan, M. T. (1984). *Social dynamics: Models and methods.* New York: Academic Press.

Vaupel, J. W., Manton, K. G., & Stallard, E. (1979). The impact of heterogeneity in individual frailty on the dynamics of mortality. *Demography, 6,* 439-454.

Commentary

On the Maturation and Aging of Organizational Populations

JOEL A. C. BAUM
ROBERT J. HOUSE

Over the past decade, ecological studies of founding and failure have made important contributions to understanding growth, persistence, and change processes in organizational populations. The preceding chapters continue in this tradition: They are thoughtful and analytically rigorous, and they investigate encyclopedic data bases covering long periods of organizational history. At the same time, they demonstrate the relative infancy of organizational ecology. The authors struggle with the operationalization of theoretical constructs, the explanation of empirical regularities in organizational populations, and the definition and description of organizational environments and even units of selection.

A common thread that links these chapters and, more generally, research in organizational ecology, is the study of dynamic processes affecting change in organizational populations over extended periods of time. This approach requires that attention be paid to the changing nature of organizational populations and their environments over time. Yet, for the most part, discussion of such change is absent from ecological theory and research. In reviewing the preceding chapters, our commentary will highlight three kinds of change relating to the aging of organizational populations: maturation processes, technological change, and institutionalization processes. We conclude that analysis of these processes of change may provide insight into the ecology of organizations and may have substantive implications for theorizing.

DENSITY DELAY IN THE
GROWTH OF ORGANIZATIONAL POPULATIONS

To explain the observation that the size of organizational populations commonly declines and stabilizes after reaching an initial peak, Carroll and Hannan propose that population density at the time of founding affects organizational mortality rates. Specifically, if organizations founded under conditions of high density experience higher failure rates, this may contribute to an explanation of the observed pattern of growth. Two reasons are advanced for expecting this relationship: (a) High density at founding creates conditions of resource scarcity, and (b) high density at founding forces organizations to exploit marginal resources in tightly packed niches. Conditions of resource scarcity and tight niche packing are proposed to "imprint" themselves on organizations and to affect their viability throughout their existence. Consequently, it is hypothesized that density at founding will have a positive effect on the failure rate.

Carroll and Hannan's findings provide support for the delayed effects of density on failure rates. Tucker, Singh, and Meinhard (1989) have also shown that density at founding has a positive effect on the mortality rate in a population of voluntary social service organizations. However, Aldrich, Staber, Zimmer, and Beggs (Chapter 2) found no support for the density delay hypothesis. Unfortunately, these mixed results for density at founding do not allow an assessment of the underlying resource scarcity and niche packing theses. While future research operationalizing resource scarcity and niche packing may be fruitful, there are reasons to expect that the logic behind Carroll and Hannan's explanation for the commonly observed growth pattern in organizational populations is oversimplified.

The density delay thesis overlooks three interrelated processes that may commonly affect organizational populations and their environments as they mature: (a) the transition from r to K selection associated with increasing population density (Brittain & Freeman, 1980; Zammuto, 1988), (b) the consolidation and concentration that occurs as populations reach carrying capacity (Carroll, 1984, 1985), and (c) the niche elaboration that accompanies competition at carrying capacity (Carroll, 1984, 1985; Pianka, 1978).

The r to K transition. In the ecological literature organizational populations are described as undergoing an r to K transition as increased population density alters the basis of competition (Brittain & Freeman, 1980). In emergent populations r-type firms compete by discovering new opportunities to exploit and by offering innovative goods and services (Kamien & Schwartz, 1982). Their dependence on first mover advantages makes them high-risk and, potentially, high-payoff organizations that thrive in temporarily rich and dispersed resource environments in which no firm or small group of firms dominates competition. As populations grow toward their carrying capacity, dispersed markets become connected. Organizations begin to make universal appeals to all potential customers in attempts to increase market share and maintain profitability in the low margin, mass markets such appeals engender. Competition centers on the exploitation of competitive advantages associated with the efficiency of standardized products and technologies and is oriented toward cost and price reduction. K-types are organizations structured to compete on the basis of efficiency in densely settled populations; r-types are effective only where the pattern of resource viability is highly uncertain and dispersed. Their success depends on the ability to exploit resources before competition makes survival problematic. Where resources become available with any certainty, r-types usually succumb to K-types, emphasizing competitive efficiency. Consequently, populations that have densities approaching carrying capacity should not have numerous r-types (Brittain & Freeman, 1980).

Consolidation, concentration, and niche elaboration. At carrying capacity, the resources available to a population become exhausted and shakeouts or waves of consolidation occur as K selection intensifies. This decreases population density, increases the average size of population members, and increases market concentration. Carroll (1984, 1985) suggests that concentration in central markets serves to partition resources and creates pockets of specialized demand. This is consistent with the idea that competition at carrying capacity leads to niche elaboration (Pianka, 1978). Thus as market concentration increases, distinct resource spaces favorable to r- and K-types may emerge. The ability of K-types to differentiate affects the level of concentration and resource partitioning: The greater the differentiation among K-types, the lower the consolidation and concentration of markets and the fewer the resource pockets available for r-types. Consequently, following the consolidation of populations, a second "K to r transition" may occur. Consistent with this transition is that K-types generally expand more slowly into emerging resource spaces than do r-types because structures generating competitive efficiency often preclude the rapid adjustments necessary to capture first mover advantages (Brittain & Freeman, 1980).[1]

Density delay and population maturation. The population maturation process has a number of implications for the density delay thesis. The differential fitness of r- and K-types under conditions of low and high density in young populations suggests that the effect of density at founding on mortality rates may depend on whether an organization is an r- or K-type. Similarly, the concentration and niche elaboration generated by competition at carrying capacity suggests that the effect of density at founding may continue to vary between r- and K-types in mature populations. Density of r-types in emergent markets may have the predicted effects on r-types, while low density of K-types in central markets (i.e., high concentration) may reduce life chances of K-types and increase those of r-types. Similarly, the effects of contemporaneous population density (Hannan & Freeman, 1988) may have distinct effects on the failure rates of r- and K-type firms in emergent and mature populations. This suggests the need to consider population maturation as an important moderator of the relationships between population density and organizational mortality. Clearly, we need to learn more about the interrelated dynamics of density and maturation in organizational populations.

Overall, the maturation process suggests an alternative explanation for the density delay effect: bad timing. Given the commonly observed population growth pattern, r-type organizations founded in high-density conditions are more likely to face the shift from r to K selection, and K-types to face the pressures of competition at carrying capacity. Moreover, the higher the level of density at the time of its founding, the more likely an organization is to suffer the liabilities of young age and small size during the r to K transition and competitive shakeout. Consequently, the relationship between density at founding and mortality rates may be an artifact of the maturation process. However, bad timing need not conflict with effects of resource scarcity and niche packing. Controlling for bad timing, measured as the time of founding relative to peak density or organizational age at peak density, while simultaneously assessing the effects of resource scarcity and niche packing may help to clarify the dynamics underlying the growth pattern commonly observed in organizational populations.

Both density delay and bad timing suggest that a great deal of "wasteful organizing" may occur around the time of peak population density as organizations with impoverished survival prospects are created. From a practical point of view, this suggests the need to develop predictive indicators of carrying capacity to assist entrepreneurs and society in avoiding wasteful endeavors and smoothing the maturation process in organizational populations.

MASS-DEPENDENT SELECTION AND THE ROLE OF LARGE ORGANIZATIONS

Barnett and Amburgey address the fundamental question of the role of large size in organizational ecology. They contend that the strength of competitive pressures generated by large organizations depends on niche characteristics. They propose that the more heterogeneous a niche, the more sheltered population members are from competition with large competitors: heterogeneity increases the benefits of differentiated specialism and makes it difficult for large generalists to compete, at once, with the set of differentiated specialists. Thus niche heterogeneity is proposed to localize the competitive impact of large organizations to particular segments within the niche. In a homogeneous niche, however, the competitive strength of large organizations is proposed to be felt throughout the relatively undifferentiated population of organizations. Thus density-dependent selection (Hannan & Freeman, 1987, 1988), which emphasizes the competitive effects of the number of organizations regardless of size, is proposed to describe competition in heterogeneous niches, while mass-dependent selection is proposed to describe competition in homogeneous niches.

The results of Barnett and Amburgey's investigation are intriguing. The larger the average size of organizations in the early telephone industry, the higher the rate of founding and the lower the rate of failure. While Barnett and Amburgey are careful to note that the mediating technology (Thompson, 1967) of the telephone industry may have contributed to the mutualistic nature of the findings, they urge us not to view the result as idiosyncratic, but rather as applicable to organizational communities where such network interdependencies arise and lead members to depend on the larger members of the community. If this is the case, then the effects of contemporaneous population density on founding and failure rates predicted by Hannan and Freeman (1987, 1988) may not hold for populations applying a mediating technology.

An alternative explanation of technological interdependence may be found in Carroll's (1984, 1985) resource partitioning model. In their description of the early telephone industry, Barnett and Amburgey report that the increase in average organizational size, while not centralized in the Bell System, did result to a disproportionate extent from the growth of 30 to 40 large organizations. Thus concentration likely increased more rapidly than average size following peak density. As concentration increased, the population's niche may have become elaborated and partitioned into central markets served by larger K-type organizations and peripheral markets served by smaller, specialized organizations. If such segmentation did occur, the emergence of large, mass-market K-types may have created partitioned environmental conditions favorable to the relatively large number of smaller, specialized firms during the postpeak density period.

Mass dependence and population maturation. The trajectories of population mass and density in the early telephone industry appear consistent with the maturation process outlined above: Population density increases to a peak in 1915 and then declines, while population mass increases throughout the observation period. In combination, these patterns indicate increasing levels of consolidation and market concentration under conditions of competition at carrying capacity. The average size of telephone organizations remained relatively stable (around 1,500 telephones) until 1915. After 1915, average size increased dramatically (to 2,500 by 1920 and to over 5,300 by 1930). Consequently, most of the variance in average population member size occurred after 1915. Thus the positive effect of population mass for founding and failure in the early telephone industry may have been most important in the period following peak density. This implies that the waves of founding and failure during the pre-1915 period may have been unrelated to population mass; rather, they may have been dependent primarily on environmental conditions and contemporaneous population density.

One way to investigate the possibility of period-based effects for population density and mass would be to estimate a model including a dummy variable reflecting the pre- and postpeak density periods, the main effects of population mass and density, and terms for the interaction of population mass and population density with the period dummy. Given the apparent commonality of population density and mass growth patterns in many maturing organizational populations, the possibility that population mass plays an important role in determining entry and exit rates following peak density merits further attention.

Niche heterogeneity and population maturation. An important question is whether such a period-based effect of population mass is consistent with Barnett and Amburgey's niche heterogeneity thesis. Consistent with the model is that younger organizational populations are typically associated with dispersed, heterogeneous niches in which it is proposed that density dependence will best reflect the competitive dynamic. However, the process of population maturation complicates niche shape and structure. As described earlier, the r to K transition and competition at carrying capacity result in a partitioning of resources that may segment the effects of density between r- and K-type firms competing in central and emergent markets. Does this partitioning of competition also segment the effects of population mass? If so, combining the niche heterogeneity and resource partitioning models, we might expect mass-dependent selection to operate in the homogeneous central market, density-dependent selection to occur among the peripheral segmented markets, and the relationship between central and peripheral markets to be explained by the resource partitioning model.

Future research clarifying the roles of and relationships among population density, population mass, niche structure, and population maturation may provide the basis for an elaboration and clarification of current ecological thinking by linking existing propositions to each other and with those related to fundamental changes that occur to populations as they age. Central to any attempt to investigate these relationships will be a focus on the changing competitive orientations (r and K) of the firms that make up populations and the form of interdependence among population members (Thompson, 1967).

TECHNOLOGY AND ENVIRONMENT

Freeman's chapter investigating the complementary roles of population density and environmental conditions extends recent research on technology and organizational environments (e.g., Tushman & Anderson, 1986; Tushman & Romanelli, 1985). Technology and technological change are important determinants of the environmental conditions of organizational populations. Technology affects the nature of required resources, technical and management skills and expertise, interdependencies with suppliers and buyers, and the opportunities available to existing organizations and entrepreneurs.

Tushman and his colleagues have shown that technology evolves through periods of stability punctuated by discontinuities (Tushman & Anderson, 1986; Tushman & Romanelli, 1985). These discontinuities have also been shown to have a significant impact on the environmental conditions and required competence for a variety of industries, including minicomputers, airlines, and cement. The dynamics of technological change affecting the semiconductor industry appear consistent with such a discontinuous pattern of change. Moreover, Freeman's results show that the shifts between environmental periods have strong and distinctive effects on exit rates from the semiconductor market, even when market and population dynamics are controlled.[2] This suggests that the technological changes identified by Freeman did affect the environmental conditions of the semiconductor industry.

Technological discontinuities and organizational evolution. Tushman and his colleagues have described two kinds of technological discontinuities: competence enhancing and competence destroying. Competence-enhancing discontinuities permit greater product class standardization and industry consolidation and increase order. Competence-destroying discontinuities open new product classes or represent the substitution of one product and/or process for another. Such changes render existing systems, procedures, and technical and workplace management competence obsolete. These discontinuous changes may have important effects on the shape of a population's niche and the distribution of strategic orientations and core technologies employed by population members.

By imposing a successful dominant design or process on a population and reinforcing the existing order of the population, competence-enhancing discontinuities result in increased product standardization and can result in shakeouts, increased barriers to entry, and concentration in central markets (Tushman & Anderson, 1986). In doing so, they may serve to open specialized opportunities for technologically differentiated r-types in a manner analogous to Carroll's resource partitioning model. Thus, following a competence-enhancing discontinuity, a consolidated group of K-types may continue to dominate a more concentrated, established portion of the niche that favors production efficiencies. At the same time, a wave of new r-types may find previously nonexistent opportunities in the emerging segments of the niche that favor their abilities.

By increasing uncertainty and disorder, decreasing barriers to entry, and creating new market and process possibilities, competence-destroying technological changes create new opportunities for technologically differentiated r-types. However, established K-types may be unable to adapt to a fundamentally new product design or process as a function of the level of investment in the technology of the previous order, the cost and time required to acquire the competence necessary to adopt the new technology, and structural inertia. Consequently, competence-destroying changes may also be associated with waves of withdrawal among established firms and waves of founding of r-types.

Freeman's analysis of rate dependence in the semiconductor industry indicates that exits from the semiconductor industry did take on a wavelike pattern. It is unclear, however, whether these waves of exits were associated with the technological discontinuities affecting the semiconductor industry and whether founding patterns also followed such a pattern. The association of these waves of entries and exits with the discontinuities would have important implications for the evolution of organizational populations. Each wave of exits would be associated with the demise of firms from the previously existing technological order. Each wave of entries would be "imprinted" (Stinchcombe, 1965) with a new, differentiated technological order. Consequently, each wave would possess distinctive sets of capital assets, technical and workplace management competencies, and resource requirements from earlier cohorts of population members, and may operate in distinctive segments of the population's niche. Each wave of entrants might, therefore, be conceived as representing a new form of organization (McKelvey, 1982).

It may be fruitful, therefore, to investigate the dynamics of each successive cohort individually and in interaction with survivors from prior technological cohorts. Do organizations from the new order compete or exist in distinct partitioned niches that do not interact (and speciate?), or are their interactions consistent with Carroll's resource partitioning model? Do cohort dynamics and interrelationships vary depending on the type of discontinuity generating the entry wave? For example, is the emergence of a new population operating in a distinct niche more likely following a competence-enhancing or a competence-destroying discontinuity? An investigation of these questions may provide insight into the process of succession among organizational forms, and may highlight the potential applicability of a punctuated versus gradualist approach to organizational evolution.

MINIMALIST ORGANIZATIONS
AND THE LOGIC OF INFLUENCE

Aldrich et al. describe trade associations as "minimalist organizations" that have low start-up costs and can survive on very low overhead expenses and support services. They suggest that the characteristics of minimalist organizations may result from their being subject to selection pressures distinct from those facing other kinds of organizations. The identification and description of such broad classes of organizations, which may assist in establishing the limits of generalizability of research hypotheses, is fundamental to the advancement of organizational science.

One important outcome of these researchers' interest in the minimalist class of organizations is their concern with age dependence in mortality rates. Most ecological research on organizational mortality has used Makeham or Gompertz specifications of hazard rates. Consistent with the liability of newness hypothesis, these models embody the assumption that mortality rates vary monotonically with age. Such a parametric approach to age dependence is valuable when substantive theory or previous empirical research suggests the form of age dependence in mortality rates. As Freeman, Carroll, and Hannan (1983) have noted, however, the disadvantage of a parametric approach "is that the estimates of the effects and test of hypotheses are only as good as the parametric assumptions. This is a potentially important problem in organizational research, because theory and previous research do not give good guidelines about model specification" (p. 697). The ability to specify appropriate models of age dependence depends on theory and research. Consequently, the conceptual and empirical exploration of age dependence and the identification of classes of organization for which alternative base-rate models of age dependence are appropriate must continue to be a focus of research.

Aldrich et al. contend that minimalist organizations do not face a liability of newness (Stinchcombe, 1965), but rather one of "adolescence" (Fichman & Levinthal, 1988). Minimalist organizations are proposed to be sustained during their initial years by the enthusiasm and commitment of their founding members. They become vulnerable during adolescence as initial commitments and prior positive beliefs are evaluated. In contrast to these expectations, the results of their analysis of trade associations indicate a "liability of maturity" in which the rate of disbanding rose at a decreasing rate, reaching a maximum well into the life cycle of trade associations. This liability of maturity appears consistent with Aldrich et al.'s definition of trade associations as "action sets" designed to exist only as long as it takes to manage problems facing the membership. In a test of a two-risk-period age-dependence model, Baum (1989a) found that disbanding rates in populations of day-care centers and nursery schools experienced both liabilities of adolescence and "obsolescence." The obsolescence risk period was proposed to result from the decreasing fit of aging organizations with their local environments (Stinchcombe, 1965). Perhaps the two-risk model is appropriate for trade associations, sheltered early in life by their minimalist form and later rendered obsolete by goal accomplishment.

Perhaps the greatest strength of the chapter is Aldrich et al.'s attempt to operationalize two theoretical models of associative action within the ecological framework. The results of their analysis indicate that a "logic of influence" model representative of the need to manage relationships with other associations and the broader institutional environment to achieve their goals provides a more powerful explanation of trade association disbanding than a "logic of membership" model that focuses on the need to manage internal diversity.

The institutionalization of organizational populations. Aldrich et al.'s support for the logic of influence model serves to highlight one further source of change in aging populations: institutionalization. New forms of organizations suffer from a lack of external legitimacy and stable exchange relationships with other organizational populations in their communities (Stinchcombe, 1965). However, as organizational populations age, they are likely to establish channels of exchange and relationships with other populations and become part of the power structure of the broader ecological communities in which they reside. Thus as populations age, they are more likely to have their actions and structures endorsed and legitimated by powerful collective actors. They are also likely to develop populational infrastructures that serve to stabilize relationships among population members through collective activities such as the establishment of industry associations. Older populations are therefore more likely to be institutionalized in at least three ways: (a) They develop populational infrastructures, (b) they become embedded within the institutional infrastructures of their ecological communities, and (c) they come to be viewed as legitimate by external constituents.

The collective actions, centrality, and legitimacy of mature populations can increase access to resources, reduce selection pressures, and increase survival chances for organizations and the populations they constitute. Consequently, the processes through which population members link themselves to the environment, stabilize internal relationships, and become embedded in and legitimated by their ecological communities are key to understanding survival and change in organizational populations—and ecological communities. Freeman's analysis of the semiconductor industry illustrates the importance of one such relationship for the fate of individual organizations: Subsidiary semiconductor firms were almost completely sheltered from selection pressures.

Organizational ecologists have tended to focus on aggregations of organizations related through their common dependence on the environment. As a result, ecological research has concentrated primarily on the roles of dynamic interactions among the members of an organizational population and between the population and its resource environment to the exclusion of collaborative relationships among populations in broader ecological communities (Astley, 1985). The increased institutional embeddedness associated with population aging suggests, however, that the investigation of the linkages among populations and hierarchically nested selection pressures within higher-order ecological collectivities may be an important area for future research. Given the apparent importance of large organizations in a network as indicated by their results, Barnett and Amburgey call for the ecological analysis of such organizational communities and the investigation of organizational populations as nested within higher-order collectivities. Barnett and Amburgey's results indicating that concentrated organizational communities may have a survival advantage serve to highlight the potential contribution of studying the emergence and roles of institutional structures at the community level of analysis. One factor that may contribute importantly to the survival advantage of concentrated communities is that highly concentrated environments are relatively certain. Concentrated communities may better endure exogenous threats to survival by drawing on the strengths of their dominant organizations.

Other recent research on interorganizational relationships has shown that the effects of interorganizational linkages may vary with organizational age (Baum & Oliver, 1989; Singh, Tucker, & House, 1986). Specifically, associative relationships appear to have their greatest impact on mortality rates for young organizations. This may also be the case for organizational populations. Collective strategies for stabilizing relationships within populations, increasing embeddedness and centrality in the ecological community, and obtaining the support of powerful collective actors may have their greatest impact on survival rates in emerging populations. In this regard, the liability of newness hypothesis has been applied to organizations in existing populations with little consideration of the institutional maturity of populations. However, to the extent that populations increase their levels of legitimacy and institutional embeddedness as they age, each successive cohort of entrants to the population should experience a weaker liability of newness (Carroll & Delacroix, 1982; Eylon, 1989).

CONCLUSION

Drawing heavily on insights from the scholars on whose work our discussion is based, we have speculated that a more explicit consideration of changes in the characteristics of organizational populations and their environments over time may provide new insights for future research in organizational ecology. In this regard we have suggested that attention be paid to the processes of population maturation and institutionalization and the dynamics of technological change. In particular, we have indicated the need to clarify the dynamic interrelationships between existing ecological hypotheses and the dynamic processes associated with the aging of organizational populations. Pursuing these interrelationships may afford a deeper understanding of the dynamics of organizational populations.

Characterizing the age-dependent dynamics of heterogeneity in organizational populations and their environments is central to the development of an understanding of these processes and their relationships with existing theory. A framework for characterizing variation in environmental heterogeneity, consistent with this discussion, is Hannan and Freeman's (1986) boundary process framework. Studying the dynamics of boundaries in organizational space by investigating the dynamics of technology, transaction cost characteristics, networks of social relationships, collective strategies, and institutional processes provides a basis on which to map out variation in environmental heterogeneity over time. In combination with a theory of organizational classification (e.g., McKelvey, 1982), understanding the boundaries in organizational space may provide insights into the emergence of diversity in organizational populations as they age and evolve (Baum, 1989b). It may also provide a basis on which to found a population perspective on organizations that encompasses taxonomy, classification, and evolution as well as population ecology.

NOTES

1. That technological change can result in similar alterations to niche structure is described below.

2. Freeman's use of market exit rates raises a fundamental question: What is the unit of selection? While discussion of this question is beyond the scope of this commentary, see McKelvey's (1982, chap. 7) discussion of "fundamental taxonomic units" (FTUs).

REFERENCES

Astley, W. G. (1985). The two ecologies: Population and community perspectives on organizational evolution. *Administrative Science Quarterly, 30*, 224-241.

Baum, J. A. C. (1989a). Liabilities of newness, adolescence and obsolescence: Exploring age dependence in the dissolution of organizational relationships and organizations. *Proceedings of the Administrative Sciences Association of Canada National Meetings*, Vol. 10, Part 5, 1-10. Unpublished manuscript, New York University.

Baum, J. A. C. (1989b). *A population perspective on organizations: A study of diversity and transformation in child care service organizations.* Unpublished doctoral dissertation, University of Toronto.

Baum, J. A. C., & Oliver, C. (1989). *Institutional linkages and organizational mortality.* Unpublished manuscript, New York University.

Brittain, J. W., & Freeman, J. H. (1980). Organizational proliferation and density dependent selection: Organizational evolution in the semiconductor industry. In J. R. Kimberly & R. H. Miles (Eds.), *The organizational life cycle* (pp. 291-338). San Francisco: Jossey-Bass.

Carroll, G. R. (1984). The specialist strategy. *California Management Review, 26*, 126-137.

Carroll, G. R. (1985). Concentration and specialism: Dynamics of niche width in populations or organizations. *American Journal of Sociology, 90*, 1262-1283.

Carroll, G. R., & Delacroix, J. (1982). Organizational mortality in the newspaper industries of Argentina and Ireland: An ecological approach. *Administrative Science Quarterly, 27*, 169-198.

Eylon, D. (1989). Form and environment: An institutional perspective on the liability of newness. *Proceedings of the Administrative Sciences Association of Canada National Meetings*, Vol. 10, Part 5, 138-146.

Fichman, M., & Levinthal, D. A. (1988). *Honeymoons and the liability of adolescence: A new perspective on duration dependence in social and organizational relationships.* Paper presented at the annual meetings of the Academy of Management, Anaheim, CA.

Freeman, J. H. (1982). Organizational life-cycles and natural selection processes. In B. M. Staw & L. L. Cummings (Eds.), *Research in organizational behavior* (Vol. 4, pp. 1-32). Greenwich, CT: JAI.

Freeman, J. H., Carroll, G. R., & Hannan, M. T. (1983). The liability of newness: Age dependence in organizational death rates. *American Sociological Review, 48*, 692-710.

Hannan, M. T., & Freeman, J. H. (1986). Where do organizational forms come from? *Sociological Forum, 1*, 50-72.

Hannan, M. T., & Freeman, J. H. (1987). The ecology of organizational founding: American labor unions, 1836-1985. *American Journal of Sociology, 92*, 910-943.

Hannan, M. T., & Freeman, J. H. (1988). The ecology of organizational failure: American labor unions, 1836-1985. *American Journal of Sociology, 94*, 25-52.

Kamien, M. I., & Schwartz, N. L. (1982). *Market structure and innovation.* New York: Cambridge University Press.

McKelvey, B. (1982). *Organizational systematics: Taxonomy, evolution, classification.* Berkeley: University of California Press.

Pianka, E. (1978). *Evolutionary ecology* (2nd ed.). New York: Harper & Row.

Singh, J. V., Tucker, D. J., & House, R. J. (1986). Organizational legitimacy and the liability of newness. *Administrative Science Quarterly, 31*, 171-193.

Stinchcombe, A. L. (1965). Social structure and organizations. In J. G. March (Ed.), *Handbook of organizations* (pp. 142-193). Chicago: Rand McNally.

Thompson, J. D. (1967). *Organizations in action.* New York: McGraw-Hill.

Tucker, D. J., Singh, J. V., & Meinhard, A. (1989). *Founding conditions, environmental change and organizational mortality.* Unpublished manuscript, McMaster University.

Tushman, M. L., & Anderson, P. (1986). Technological discontinuities and organizational environments. *Administrative Science Quarterly, 31*, 439-465.

Tushman, M. L., & Romanelli, E. (1985). Organizational evolution: A metamorphosis model of convergence and reorientation. In B. M. Staw & L. L. Cummings (Eds.), *Research in organizational behavior* (Vol. 7, pp. 171-222). Greenwich, CT: JAI.

Zammuto, R. F. (1988). Organizational adaptation: Some implications of organizational ecology for strategic choice. *Journal of Management Studies, 25*, 105-120.

PART TWO

New Directions

6

The Dynamics of
Organizational Speciation

CHARLES J. LUMSDEN
JITENDRA V. SINGH

The question of organizational creation has received attention in the organizational literature in diverse areas, although, of course, the specific focus in each has been different. Thus, to provide a few examples from these many literatures, a respected tradition in sociology has examined the emergence of special purpose organizations in modern society and the factors that led to their emergence (Coleman, 1944; Durkheim, 1893/1949; Stinchcombe, 1965; Weber, 1947). In the economic literature, the new institutional economics work (Arrow, 1974; Williamson, 1975, 1985) has taken a transactions cost view of how organizations are created. Under specific conditions, when the market mode fails due to the transaction costs being too high, organizations are seen as an efficient way of organizing transactions. The entrepreneurship literature has concentrated on factors that account for entrepreneurial success (see Low & MacMillan, 1988, for a comprehensive review), although entrepreneurial success is usually associated with the successful creation of an organization.

Some of the recent developments in organizational sociology have also addressed this question. Research in organizational ecology has addressed

Authors' Note: This research was supported in part by Population Biology Grant Number A0393 to the first author, by Crosby and Foggitt and Doris and Michael Goldberg Fellowships in Entrepreneurship awarded to the second author in 1987-88 and 1988-89, respectively, and by the Snider Entrepreneurial Center, The Wharton School, University of Pennsylvania. It is a pleasure to thank Ian MacMillan for discussions that helped lay the conceptual basis for the chapter.

questions of change in organizational populations by examining patterns of organizational founding and mortality (see Chapters 2-4 of this volume). More specifically related to organizational creations, researchers have directly studied how environmental factors, such as population density, influence patterns of organizational founding (Carroll & Huo, 1986; Delacroix & Carroll, 1983; Hannan & Freeman, 1987; Singh, Tucker, & Meinhard, in press; Tucker, Singh, & Meinhard, in press; Tucker, Singh, Meinhard, & House, 1988). Institutionalization theory research, however, has dealt with the question more indirectly. Institutional theorists point out that rationalized elements in modern societal environments encourage the creation of organizations (DiMaggio & Powell, 1983; Meyer & Rowan, 1977). Zucker (1983) adds that organizations have become so central to modern society that creating an organization to achieve a specific goal is an important way of symbolizing seriousness of purpose.

We think it is useful to parse the literature on organizational creation into at least three distinct questions. First, it is of great historical interest to ask how formal, special-purpose organizations emerged as a distinct organizational form and what other forms or arrangements they replaced (for an argument with this flavor, see, for example, Kieser, 1989). This question has been addressed by sociologists, among others. Another important question is how new organizations of a specific form get created; that is, what explains the founding of new members in an organizational population? Both the organizational ecology and entrepreneurship literature have addressed this question. A third approach is to ask how the first of a specific new form of organization is created, an occurrence that we will call the *speciation event.* In other words, how do new populations or organizations emerge? Although this question has been raised in the ecological literature in discussing how new opportunities are created through technological and demographic changes that result in new resource sets (Brittain & Freeman, 1980), the usual focus of research has been more on the creation of further new organizations once the speciation event has already taken place. Indeed, some critics of organizational ecology have suggested that this relative inattention to the creation of new organizational forms is a drawback of this research (Astley, 1985). In this chapter we attempt to build a model of the organizational speciation process, paying particular attention to speciation as a creative act on the part of innovating actors in the society. For convenience, we shall refer to these actors as entrepreneurs, and ask how entrepreneurial activity shapes organizational speciation.

THE SPECIATION PROCESS

Organizational speciation is the budding of cooperate cultures from those of preexisting firms. These nascent cultures exemplify ideational change, and one place to look for what stimulates this change is the mind of the entrepreneur. When the new corporate cultures take root, they may do so close by the parent, in which case the entrepreneurial leap is modest and the resulting product is similar to the motivating innovation. Once in a while the new firm may gather its culture around a radically new idea for a product or service, and the speciation event founds a "new breed" of enterprise, along with its correlative organizational form, in the most literal sense.

Just what is this thing called "culture," so important, in our view, to organizational speciation? The idea of culture as created product of the human mind has enjoyed at least three different broad usages among scholars. For sociologists and social anthropologists, the term *culture* commonly refers to the lifeways of a people, defined loosely as the assemblage of behavior patterns that fit the social group to its environment. In contrast, archaeologists emphasize the artifacts produced by these lifeways, with particular reference to the distribution of the objects through space and time. Although useful in many ways, these first two classes of definitions are not sufficient for studies of organizational speciation. The reason is that lifeways and artifacts are final products; underlying them are the ongoing mental processes of individual brains. Thus to uncover the essence of culture it is necessary to delve more deeply into human behavior.

With this requirement in mind, some cultural anthropologists have concentrated on culture as a shared system of meaning and symbolic representation (e.g., Geertz, 1973; Goodenough, 1979). This semantic approach parallels cognitive science and improves the well-known synthetic definition proposed by Kroeber and Kluckhohn in 1952. After reviewing 164 prior definitions, they conclude that "culture is a product; is historical; includes ideas, patterns, and values; is selective; is learned; is based upon symbols; and is an abstraction from behavior and the products of behavior." Kroeber (1948) also argues that it has a holistic quality and represents "an accommodation of discrete parts, largely inflowing parts, into a more or less workable fit" (p. 287).

Such characterizations of culture involve a semiotic perspective, with culture considered as a system of signs, signifiers, and symbols; a hermeneutic perspective, with culture considered as a system of interpretation; an ethological perspective, with culture considered as a system of communicative behaviors and embodied information; and a functional perspective, with culture considered as adaptive response to the environment. But irrespective of the particular vantage point, all approaches known to us share four central themes about culture and its relation to mind, namely, that (a) culture is characterizable, that is, it can be decomposed, for the purpose of analysis, into observable components (the sign, the symbol, the artifact, the belief, and so on); (b) these observables are present not only from the investigator's perspective, but also from the perspective of the cultural organism itself, in the sense that they are interpreted and acted upon; (c) culture is a system of information transmission, so that irrespective of whether information resides in the form of symbols, beliefs, rituals, knowledge, and so on, these things take on the status of cultural elements only when formalized within the context of an interpretive system to which more than one individual has access (so a single organism does not have culture, but a group of organisms may); and (d) culture is subject to change through the creative process.

Thus a *corporate culture* is a dynamic system of information, shared among managers and employees who have the capacity to interpret it, and potentially the capacity to modify and contribute to it. Put another way, the entrepreneur spends a good deal of time in an aggressively creative posture, reading the cultural text, annotating it, editing it, and adding footnotes, as the search for market opportunities takes place. How is this possible, and what are the implications for organizational dynamics?

SOME KEY TERMS

As we will be using the term here, *creative process* refers to the array of mental activities involved in the formulation of a specific problem in an initially ill-defined problem domain, in advancing a novel and appropriate solution to an extant problem, or both. We will use the term *creativity* to refer to the constellation of personality and intellectual traits shown by individuals who, when given a measure of free rein, spend significant amounts of time engaged in the creative process (see Perkins, 1981). A *problem* refers to some set of circumstances to which the organism is motivated to respond. A *problem domain* is that information initially perceived as relevant to specification of a problem or formulation of its solution. *Information* as used here refers to the organism's current knowledge of itself and its surroundings (see, for example, Newell & Simon, 1972).

We define *discovery* as the product of the creative process. Thus a discovery may be the statement of a new problem, a solution to a preexisting problem, or both. Thus discovery necessarily implies some element of creative thought. The creative process, on the other hand, need not manifest itself in discovery or, more specifically, in a discovery that is made apparent to an external observer or consciously apprehended by the creator.

An *innovation* is any discovery that attains some level of adoption in the society under consideration. To qualify as an innovation, a discovery must be transmitted, and thus must be transmissible. Discoveries are more or less novel, so nontransmissibility generally implies a high probability of extinction correlated (inversely) with the motivation or life expectancy of the discoverer. Thus a degree of transmissibility (transition rate for adoption by others) determines whether or not a discovery attains innovation status. Previous definitional emphasis on *technological* innovation has tended to encourage a purely demographic viewpoint and to obscure the underlying structure of the innovation process, particularly its intimate relationship to the creative process and discovery.

HETERARCHY AND THE CREATIVE PROCESS

In human societies the response of members to a problem is mediated by both biological and cultural information. A social group, for example, comprises (in part) biological individuals. But we cannot enumerate the properties of the group simply by enumerating the properties of its members and their interactions. Rather, we need also to refer to such properties as cultural context, within which the properties of individuals develop and are defined. Similarly, the biological organism contains cells, tissues, and the like. Yet the biological state of the organism is not elucidated solely by reference to these constituents, because their properties may be influenced by the properties of supraindividual effects, such as the overall temperature of a tissue or concentration of hormones in an organ. While for biocultural systems there are many conduits of causation, there is no ultimate level of causality and no primitive stratum of functional organization from which one can construct all higher levels. Such systems are called *heterarchies* (Hofstadter, 1979).

The data available to us suggest that entrepreneurs can be understood only within the matrix of heterarchical relationships constituting the corporate culture and, beyond that, culture as a whole. Creative activity is influenced by a wide variety of sociocultural factors (Simonton, 1984) such as teaching environment (reviewed by Amabile, 1983, chap. 8), a condition whose status at any time also reflects the accumulation of innovations in the teaching profession. Conversely, the entrepreneurial process is involved not only in discovery, but also in the transmission thereof through the new firm. This reasoning suggests that innovation arises from the heterarchical linkages of two interdependent subsystems operating at distinct levels of social organization. One subsystem is concerned with the mental properties and events underlying the entrepreneur's creative thinking. The other involves the mechanism whereby discoveries become innovations marketed by new firms. Since the former pertains to the state and propensities of individuals within the society, we refer to its constituents as components of the *cognitive phenotype*. This is a term referring to the functional structure of mental operations within the entrepreneur's mind, especially (in this case) those affecting the creative process. The latter, on the other hand, are properties of groups of individuals and will be referred to as components of the *sociocultural environment*.

An immediate task, we believe, is to ascertain the relevant factors and mechanisms involved in each of the two subsystems. We are of course in no position to adduce a comprehensive list, but a number of potential factors are identified in our approach. Key components of the cognitive phenotype include intelligence, imagery, memory, learning, personality, motivation, and affect. For the sociocultural environment, a number of more or less specific factors can be subsumed under the general headings of social and political organization, including spatial distribution of individuals, social stratification, education policies, and the distribution of power.

In the transition from discovery to innovation, transmission implies communication. The ability to communicate a discovery depends on a variety of aspects of the cognitive phenotype, including communicative ability, personality (e.g., degree of extroversion), and motivation, as well as such sociocultural variables as perceived status of the firm in the community. Similarly, background knowledge depends not only on the entrepreneur's capacity to learn and store information, but also on such macroscopic factors as the accessibility of sociocultural environments (Friedman, Raymond, & Feldhausen, 1978). Components of the sociocultural environment affect the entrepreneur through the tendency of the individual to make decisions based on the decisions of peers and competitors (Friedman et al., 1978; Lumsden & Wilson, 1981) or through formal education and legislation (Rosenthal & Zimmerman, 1978). Communication between entrepreneurs and society is also influenced by factors traditionally of interest to cultural anthropologists, including the spatial distribution of individuals (Hägerstrand, 1967), individual mobility, migration patterns (Menozzi, Piazza, & Cavalli-Sforza, 1978), and social stratification (Cavalli-Sforza & Feldman, 1981). There is, therefore, ample empirical evidence to indicate that the creative process, discovery, and innovation arise from a heterarchical interplay of causal elements.

Figure 6.1 illustrates a provisional scheme (see also Findlay & Lumsden, 1988) for mapping the innovation heterarchy into a circuit of interaction between the genetic information and the cultural information present in all human populations. The genetic and cultural information that guides brain development yields the cognitive phenotype, the complex array of cognitive functions of which entrepreneurial creativity is suggested to be one integral component. Transmissibility involves two components: (a) the ability of the discoverer to communicate the discovery to peers and/or customers, and (b) the tendency of competitors to capitalize on the discovery once exposed to it. The integrative step taken in Figure 6.1 suggests that the degree to which the ability to create, innovate, and modify corporate culture has evolved depends on the complexity of the problem faced by the entrepreneur, where, for example, complexity measures the number and predictability of problems confronted over time and the degree to which solutions to previously encountered problems are applicable. We will develop this point further below.

CREATIVITY AND THE PROCESS OF COEVOLUTION

Many investigators have attempted to understand how the creative process and discovery work. Despite persisting differences in interpretation, one theme recurs: The creative process involves the linking of previously dissociated elements of existing knowledge. This theme has appeared in many guises, including Campbell's (1960) theory of blind variation and selective retention, Mednick's (1962) concept of remote association, Koestler's (1964) bisociation, and Rothenberg's (1979) Janusian thinking. Several cultural anthropologists and sociologists have suggested that innovation arises from the "renetworking" of elements already present in the sociocultural environment (e.g., see Clarke, 1978). However, innovations as defined here do not exist at the cognitive level, since for us innovation implies some level of phenotypic expression. The cognitive analogue (indeed, the cognitive antecedent) is a discovery, which we take as plausibly modeled by the appearance of a new interconcept linkage in the mind. As indicated previously, discovery is not sufficient for innovation because the latter is defined only with reference to the extant knowledge structure of the society as a whole.

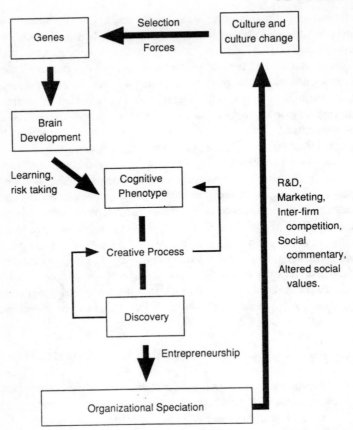

Figure 6.1. Entrepreneurship and organizational speciation are viewed as a manifestation of the cognitive phenotype, itself a product of an ongoing program of learning, risk-taking, and brain development processes that combine the effects of both genetic and environmental information. At the heart of the process is a system of innately determined algorithms (the "epigenetic rules") that modulate the person's response to both physical and sociocultural environments. These constraints are postulated to underlie both the creative process itself and the tendency of an entrepreneur to launch a discovery into a new organization dedicated to its dissemination. Entrepreneurial innovation and organizational speciation influence not only the sociocultural and physical environments, but ultimately also the genetic composition of the next generation through natural selection or various nonselective evolutionary processes, a mode of inheritance termed *gene-culture transmission* (Lumsden & Wilson, 1981). Temporal changes in the patterns of entrepreneurial innovation may eventually affect the underlying genetic structure of the population, which in turn influences discovery and innovation — an example of *gene-culture coevolution.*

On the basis of these studies, Findlay and Lumsden (1988) have advanced the thesis that there are particular characteristics — particular geometries — of the mind's knowledge structures that render it more prone to discovery (see also Figure 6.2 and further discussion in the next section). The production of these geometries is an activity of the innovation heterarchy. Differences among individuals with respect to creative activity in particular problem domains then relate in part to the differences in the relational configuration of relevant portions of their knowledge about the world. According to the hypothesis described here, such differences arise from a combination of genetic and experiential factors (see also Lumsden & Wilson, 1981). Moreover, since knowledge is a dynamic entity open to change, the strategies included in formulating it can vary over the course of a lifetime. Essential to each strategy are the processes by which knowledge is updated to assimilate both the discovery and the antecedent creative process.

Taking interconcept linking as a prominent component of the creative process gives a means of modeling discovery and the creative process as bioculturally evolved strategies, and relating these strategies quantitatively to the course of individual development, as well as to causal factors operating on other levels of the cultural heterarchy. Because linkage is specified in causal terms shaped by the semantic content of a person's knowledge and beliefs, it is possible to envisage formal models that predict the behavioral consequences — including those related to survival and reproduction — of different mechanisms for the creative process and innovation (Findlay & Lumsden, 1988). There are immediate consequences for a quantitative approach to organizational speciation.

A SPECIATION MODEL

We begin by considering a model of the simplest type involving the innovation heterarchy and the speciation process. We take a single dimension of S of organizational form, comprising a set C of N different forms for the firm (e.g., geared to manufacturing N different products), each coded as a conceptual schema $\theta_\kappa, k = 1, \ldots, N$ stored in long-term memory and indexed by an α-node α_κ. An α-node is an informational unit at higher levels of semantic organization within entrepreneurial thought, obtained from the distillation of information ("chunking") from subordinate concepts at lower levels of organization. Each entrepreneur in the society possesses various combinations of the α_ks. (For a review of basic terminology from cognitive psychology, see Lumsden & Wilson, 1981; Newell & Simon, 1972.)

The process of organizational speciation, insofar as it involves the creative process, depends on the production of a novel organizational schema (an entrepreneurial discovery) indexed by a new α-node. Here we consider the case that this new schema does not arise *de novo*, but rather is derived from the establishment of new links among previously existing ideas. For simplicity, each schema is taken as a set of subordinate cognitive units (primitive elements) and their associated links. Speciation in this system entails the activation of two or more α-nodes such that both are represented in working memory and a schema for a viable new organizational form results. A theoretically well-understood activation strategy is that of spreading activation, whereby activation of a particular concept's semantic node initiates a flow of activation to the semantic nodes linked to the activated node. The strength of a node is determined by its frequency of activation: Frequently activated nodes have a greater cognitive strength, and hence are more readily recalled in response to an attempt to retrieve information. Typically, the relative strength of a link between two nodes i and j is specified as $r_{ij} = s_j/\Sigma ks_k$ where s_j is the strength of node j and the summation is over all nodes (including j) connected to i (e.g., see Anderson, 1983, p. 27). According to spreading activation theory, relative strengths of associated linkages determine the relative amount of activation that spreads along each path, and hence the probability of recall of various associated elements. The strength of a node in turn determines not only its probability of activation via spread from other linked nodes, but also its ability to initiate activation in response to a direct memory probe.

To exemplify the type of model consistent with such assumptions, consider the simple node-link structure shown in Figure 6.2. Two organizational traits c_1 (e.g., direct marketing to private sector R&D personnel) and c_2 (e.g., the power of personal workstations) are represented by their respective schemata θ_1 and θ_2 and their associated α-nodes α_1 and α_2. If the *inter*schematic link ξ is weak relative to the *intra*schematic links, spread of activation from α_1 will for the most part be confined to θ_1. The same applies for α_2. Since a prerequisite of *discovery* is the activation of primitive elements from *different* schemata, the probability of a discovery under such conditions is relatively low (Figure 6.2a). However, an increase in the strength of ξ implies a greater interschemata spread of activation, with the activation of either α_1 or α_2 potentially leading to the simultaneous representation of primitive elements from both schemata in working memory. In Figure 6.2b, an initial locus of activation at α_1 may activate element 1 (e.g., "direct marketing") in θ_1 through spread of activation along link $r_{\alpha_1},1$ and element 2 (e.g., "workstations") in θ_2 via ξ and $r_{\alpha_2},2$, creating the opportunity for a new linkage

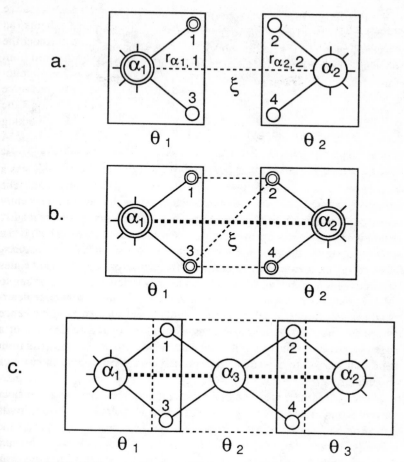

Figure 6.2. The linking model of the creative process. For details, see text.

between two previously unlinked units. Initially the link is rather weak, with strength increasing with subsequent activations of the relevant nodes. Strong interschemata connections allow for the activation of any number of elements in each schemata in response to successive activation events (e.g., 3 and 4) depending on the relative strengths of the intraschematic links (Figure 6.2b). Elements in θ_2 may also acquire connections with several different elements in θ_2 and vice versa (Figure 6.2b). As the strength and complexity of the derivative network of connections increase, a new schema arises, to which the process of vertical chunking assigns a new α-node (Figure 6.2c) (e.g., a high-tech start-up firm devoted to direct-to-user marketing of engineering workstations). This firm is the founder of a new organizational species.

According to this speciation model, there are structural characteristics of organizational birth tightly linked to the creative process. Suppose that in Figure 6.2, node α_1 is activated, and $r_{\alpha_1},1 > r_{\alpha_1},n$ for all $n = 2, \ldots, M$, where M is the number of links from α_1 to other associated nodes. Then each activation event invariably yields the same outcome, namely, a large flow of activation along $r_{\alpha_1},1$ and, consequently, a disproportionate representation of information from subnode 1 in working memory. If, on the other hand, all links r_{α_1},n are strong and have approximately the same relative strength, then for a finite number of activation events the expected number of different outcomes accumulated over the set of such events is maximized. This is so because the activation of node α_1 leads to the activation of all associated subordinate nodes with approximately equal frequency. Similarly, if α_1 is the node indexing θ_1, then the greater the number of interschematic linkages *involving* α_1, the greater the expected number of different outcomes to a finite set of activation events initiated at α_1. Once again, the expected number of different outcomes is maximized when all interschematic connections are strong on an absolute scale, but are of the same relative strength. This expected number of different outcomes is one measure of the entrepreneur's *creative potential* (i.e., the entrepreneur's ability to think up alternative possible responses to any situation or probable solutions to a problem), and we denote it at time τ by $\Psi(\tau)$. When the problem is that of designing an organization's form, a greater creative potential implies a greater number of conjectured alternatives for the form, and thus an increased probability of finding an appropriate organizational form for the new venture.

If $M(\tau)$ denotes the total number of different outcomes to an activation event occurring at time τ and $p_i(\tau)$ is the probability of the ith outcome being realized, $i = 1, \ldots, M(\tau)$, then the probabilities of the logarithm guarantee that the quantity

$$I(\tau) = -\sum_{i=1}^{M(\tau)} p_i(\tau) \log p_i(\tau) \qquad [1]$$

which measures the information entropy of the activation process, has the same increase-decrease dependence on the distribution of strengths among nodes expressed through $p_i(\tau)$ as described above for $\Psi(\tau)$. Thus

$$\Psi(\tau) = cI(\tau) \qquad [2]$$

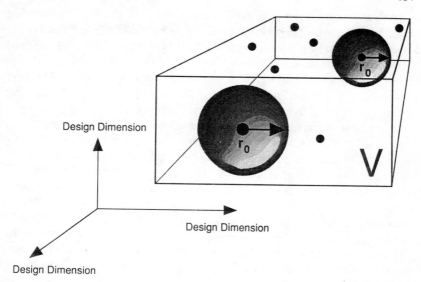

Figure 6.3. A speciation space for entrepreneurial start-up of new firms. Each dot positioned within the volume V corresponds to a design for a highly competitive new venture. The problem is to find these points. For details, see text.

where c is a constant of proportionality. By equation 2, entrepreneurial creative potential in a particular domain S is directly proportional to the information entropy associated with the relevant portions of the relevant semantic network.

Entrepreneurs are of course strategy as well as diversity oriented: Not all organizational forms, and therefore prospective new firms, are gauged equally viable. Entrepreneurial excellence is in part the ability to target high-viability opportunities, and to do so before anyone else. Consider therefore the N-dimensional *speciation space* in which the axes correspond to the properties or attributes of the organizations addressing such opportunities. Owing to the finite capacity of sensory and cognitive processing systems, the organizational forms that can be envisaged are contained in a finite volume of size V in the space. The information processing capacity of entrepreneurs is finite, so that two firms are perceived as essentially the same if the cognitive distance between them is r_0 or less (Figure 6.3).

For an entrepreneur of near maximal creative potential (high semantic information entropy), start-up ideas appear uniformly throughout V. In other words, if θ denotes a newly innovated start-up idea and v is any volume within

V, then the probability that θ lies in v is equal to v/V. But within the speciation space there exist some points corresponding to firms that are competitively neutral or noncompetitive in the marketplace and other points corresponding to firms that are highly competitive by measure of their market share, the rate at which they are imitated, and the like. When a newly innovated schema for start-up falls within r_0 of a competitively active point, the two are equated and a highly competitive new firm enters the society.

At any time a certain fraction of the schemata for potential new firms correspond to highly competitive designs. The waiting time to the first appearance of such a firm, which one wants to be short, is a function of both the size of this fraction and the innovation rate of the population of entrepreneurs, that is, the rate at which they are getting ideas about start-ups irrespective of their competitive viability. If during some time interval δt an innovation occurs, the probability that the organizational form is highly competitive is equal to the summed volume of all radius r_0 spheres centered on competitively active points, divided by the total accessible volume of the speciation space, V. The volume of an N-dimensional sphere of radius r_0 in the speciation space is

$$V_0 = \frac{\pi^{N/2} \, r_0^N}{\Gamma(\frac{N}{2} + 1)}$$

where $\gamma(N/2 + 1)$ is the gamma function; for any N, γ is a constant.

There exists a natural unit of length, $V^{1/N}$, associated with the speciation space, so that r_0 can be expressed as

$$r_0 = \beta V^{1/N} \qquad\qquad [3]$$

where β is a constant. If M points correspond to highly competitive start-ups in the space, the probability that an innovated firm will be identified with one of them is

$$p = \frac{M}{V} \, \frac{\pi^{N/2}}{\Gamma(\frac{N}{2} + 1)} \, (\beta V^{1/N})^N = \frac{M(\pi^{1/2}\beta)^N}{\Gamma(\frac{N}{2} + 1)} \qquad\qquad [4]$$

If n is the number of highly competitive firms started by time t, then $n = 0$ at $t = 0$ and there is a probability per unit time, λ, that such a firm will start and thus increase n by one. (We consider nothing more complex than $\lambda =$ constant here.) Since we are interested in the cumulative total of new species by time t, we set the speciation (not the *species*) extinction rate $\mu = 0$, and have

$$\text{Prob}\{n \to n + 1 \text{ in } (t, t + \delta t)\} = \lambda \delta t$$

$$\text{Prob}\{n \to n - 1 \text{ in } (t, t + \delta t)\} = \mu \lambda \delta t = 0 \qquad [5]$$

The course of cumulative speciation is a Poisson process with density

$$P(n,t) = \begin{cases} e^{-\lambda t}(\lambda t)^n / n!, & n \geq 0 \\ 0 & n < 0 \end{cases} \qquad [6]$$

and expected value

$$<n> = \lambda t \qquad [7]$$

of total firms started by time t. If $v = v(\Psi)$ is the average innovation rate per innovator, and I is the number of such individuals in the population, then

$$\lambda = vIp \qquad [8]$$

and we can write the *mean time to the first highly competitive start-up design* as

$$t = [vMI(\pi^{1/2}\beta)^N]^{-1}\Gamma(N/2 + 1) \qquad [9]$$

or

$$\log_{10} t = \log_{10}[\gamma(N/2 + 1)/vMI] - N\log_{10}(\pi^{1/2}\beta) \qquad [10]$$

In Figure 6.4 we illustrate the sensitivity of this waiting time to the parameters of the speciation model.

The most realistic conditions under which a short waiting time to highly competitive start-up is expected are the following:

(1) A low-speciation space dimension, N: This is important. Although archaeologists have distinguished twenty or more dimensions in statistical studies of artifacts, it is likely that "feature extraction" is important in creative thinking (Findlay & Lumsden, 1988). Thereby, perceptually important traits are extracted from the pattern while other information is discarded. Steps that reduce the complexity, not by simplifying the start-up conception but *by shortening*

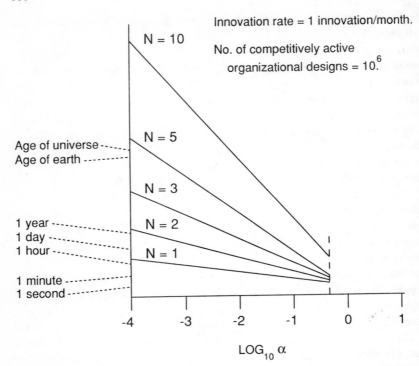

Figure 6.4. Waiting time to the appearance of a highly competitive new firm as affected by key parameters of entrepreneurial thinking.

the list of organizational parameters considered essential to the firm's structure, are pivotally important to achieving competitive speciation in short times.

(2) A large β, which means a large r_0 and hence few distinguishable organizational designs along any one axis: Since this blurs potentially critical distinctions among competing designs, smaller βs are to be preferred.

(3) A high M, or number of competitive start-up opportunities active in the selective process, the result expected if the economy is complex and heterogeneous.

In marketplaces that encourage competition through innovation, strategic planners need to know the parameter t. This number gives the expected time lapse until the occurrence of the first highly competitive start-up to appear in a situation when more than one entrepreneur (or innovation manager) is searching for new venture opportunities. The value of t defines the time horizon within which heavy investment in R&D makes sense: Before time t, all entrepreneurs are contending for leadership and dominant market share through innovation development; after t, a leader is present and managers must consider the rationality of maintaining their heavy R&D investment versus two alternatives — a low-cost imitation-innovation process based on minor changes to the new leader's product, or cutting their investment and switching the R&D effort to fresh opportunities in other markets. Enumerating t does not specify the optimal choice among these strategies. It does, however, provide a rough estimate of the time window during which innovation managers must discount the present value of R&D investments versus the likelihood of significant future returns.

Perhaps the most important lesson to be drawn from the form of t's dependence on its independent variables (recall Figure 6.4) is the exponential rate at which t increases as the list of design parameters (quantified in our equations by the symbol N) grows. Although more work on the problem remains to be done, we find the trends suggested by Figure 6.4 clear enough to warrant the provisional hypothesis that, all other things being equal, *optimal management of innovation, entrepreneurship, and organizational speciation seeks to minimize* N. *In terms of speciation space dimension, truly small is truly beautiful.*

Speciation waiting times (and their dependence on the creative process) are of course only a subset of the dynamic variables needed to begin treating rigorous models of organizational speciation. Within the grasp of methods from dynamics and mathematical evolutionary theory, but still largely open, are critical questions about the geometry of speciation space, about the distribution within it of attractor regions corresponding to highly competitive firms (which we have for simplicity modeled in this chapter as single points sprinkled around in the speciation space), and about the shape of the resulting trajectories populations of evolving organizations take through speciation space. We wish to suggest that answers to these questions will provide organizational ecologists with a new view of speciation among firms that live and die in environments where innovation-driven competition holds the key to success.

REFERENCES

Anderson, J. R. (1983). *The architecture of cognition*. Cambridge, MA: Harvard University Press.

Amabile, T. M. (1983). *The social psychology of creativity*. New York: Springer-Verlag.

Arrow, K. J. (1974). *The limits of organization.* New York: W. W. Norton.

Astley, W. G. (1985). The two ecologies: Population and community perspectives on organizational evolution. *Administrative Science Quarterly, 30,* 224-241.

Brittain, J. W., & Freeman, J. (1980). Organizational proliferation and density-dependent selection: Organizational evolution in the semiconductor industry. In J. R. Kimberly & R. H. Miles (Eds.), *The organizational life cycle* (pp. 291-338). San Francisco: Jossey-Bass.

Campbell, D. T. (1960). Blind variation and selective retention in creative thought as in other knowledge processes. *Psychological Review, 67,* 380-400.

Carroll, G. R., & Huo, Y. P. (1986). Organizational task and institutional environments in evolutionary perspective: Findings from the local newspaper industry. *American Journal of Sociology, 91,* 838-873.

Cavalli-Sforza, L. L., & Feldman, M. W. (1981). *Cultural transmission and evolution.* Princeton, NJ: Princeton University Press.

Clarke, D. L. (1978). *Analytical archaeology.* London: Methuen.

Coleman, J. S. (1974). *Power and the structure of society.* New York: W. W. Norton.

Delacroix, J., & Carroll, G. R. (1983). Organizational foundings: An ecological study of the newspaper industries of Argentina and Ireland. *Administrative Science Quarterly, 28,* 274-291.

DiMaggio, P. J., & Powell, W. W. (1983). The iron cage revisited: Institutional isomorphism and collective rationality in organizational fields. *American Sociological Review, 48,* 147-160.

Durkheim, E. (1949). *Division of labor in society.* Glencoe, IL: Free Press. (Original work published 1893)

Findlay, C. S., & Lumsden, C. J. (1988). *The creative mind: Toward an evolutionary theory of discovery and innovation.* London: Academic Press.

Friedman, F., Raymond, B. A., & Feldhausen, J. F. (1978). Effects of environmental scanning on creativity. *Gifted Child Quarterly, 22,* 248-251.

Geertz, C. (1973). *The interpretation of cultures.* New York: Basic Books.

Goodenough, W. (1979). *Description and comparison in cultural anthropology.* Chicago: Aldine.

Hägerstrand, T. (1967). *Innovation diffusion as a spatial process.* Chicago: University of Chicago Press.

Hannan, M. T., & Freeman, J. (1987). The ecology of organizational founding: American labor unions, 1836-1985. *American Journal of Sociology, 92,* 910-943.

Hofstadter, D. R. (1979). *Gödel, Escher, Bach: An eternal golden braid.* New York: Basic Books.

Kieser, A. (1989). *The medieval craft guild and the genesis of formal organizations.* Unpublished manuscript, Lehrstuhl fur Allgemeine Betriebswirtschaftslehre und Organization, Universität Mannheim, West Germany.

Koestler, A. (1964). *The act of creation.* London: Pan.

Kroeber, A. L. (1948). *Anthropology* (rev. ed.). New York: Harcourt, Brace & World.

Kroeber, A. L., & Kluckhohn, C. (1952). *Culture: A critical review of concepts and definitions.* New York: Random House.

Low, M. B., & MacMillan, I. C. (1988). Entrepreneurship: Past research and future challenges. *Journal of Management, 14,* 139-161.

Lumsden, C. J., & Wilson, E. O. (1981). *Genes, mind and culture: The coevolutionary process.* Cambridge, MA: Harvard University Press.

Mednick, S. A. (1962). The associative basis of the creative process. *Psychological Review, 69,* 220-232.

Menozzi, P., Piazza, A., & Cavalli-Sforza, L. L. (1978). Synthetic maps of human gene-frequencies in Europeans. *Science, 201*, 786-792.

Meyer, J. W., & Rowan, B. (1977). Institutionalized organizations: Formal structure as myth and ceremony. *American Journal of Sociology, 83*, 340-363.

Newell, A., & Simon, H. A. (1972). *Human problem solving*. Englewood Cliffs, NJ: Prentice-Hall.

Perkins, D. N. (1981). *The mind's best work*. Cambridge, MA: Harvard University Press.

Rosenthal, T. L., & Zimmerman, B. J. (1978). *Social learning and cognition*. New York: Academic Press.

Rothenberg, A. (1979). *The emerging goddess: The creative process in art, science and other fields*. Chicago: University of Chicago Press.

Simonton, D. K. (1984). *Genius, creativity and leadership: Historiometric inquiries*. Cambridge, MA: Harvard University Press.

Singh, J. V., Tucker, D. J., & Meinhard, A. G. (in press). Institutional change and ecological dynamics. In W. W. Powell & P. J. DiMaggio (Eds.), *The new institutionalism in organizational analysis*. Chicago: University of Chicago Press.

Stinchcombe, A. L. (1965). Social structure and organizations. In J. G. March (Ed.), *Handbook of organizations* (pp. 142-193). Chicago: Rand McNally.

Tucker, D. J., Singh, J. V., & Meinhard, A. G. (in press). Organizational form, population dynamics, and institutional change: A study of founding patterns of voluntary organizations. *Academy of Management Journal*.

Tucker, D. J., Singh, J. V., Meinhard, A. G., & House, R. J. (1988). Ecological and institutional sources of change in organizational populations. In G. Carroll (Ed.), *Ecological models of organizations* (pp. 127-151). Cambridge, MA: Ballinger.

Weber, M. (1947). *The theory of social and economic organization* (A. H. Henderson & T. Parsons, Eds.). Glencoe, IL: Free Press.

Williamson, O. E. (1975). *Markets and hierarchies: Analysis and antitrust implications*. New York: Free Press.

Williamson, O. E. (1985). *The economic institutions of capitalism*. New York: Free Press.

Zucker, L. G. (1983). Organizations as institutions. In S. B. Bacharach (Ed.), *Research in the sociology of organizations* (Vol. 2, pp. 1-47). Greenwich, CT: JAI.

7

Strategy-Making and Organizational Ecology: A Conceptual Integration

ROBERT A. BURGELMAN

The role of strategy making is central to two related but subtly different debates currently going on in organizational science. One debate centers on the issue of environmental determinism versus strategic choice (Astley & Van de Ven, 1983; Bourgeois, 1984; Child, 1972; Hrebiniak & Joyce, 1985). The second debate concerns the relative importance of selection versus adaptation in explaining organizational change and survival (Hannan & Freeman, 1984; Miles & Cameron, 1982; Singh, House, & Tucker, 1986). In the first debate, strategic choice is sometimes confused with adaptation; in the second, selection is sometimes mistaken for determinism.

This chapter intends to contribute to the second debate. Building on work positing a correspondence between organizing processes and evolutionary theory (Aldrich, 1979; Campbell, 1969; Weick, 1979), the question of where strategies come from is addressed, and the role of strategy making in relation to selection and adaptation is examined. The premise of this chapter is that strategy making in large, complex organizations can be usefully viewed as the outcome of *intra*organizational ecological processes that are themselves nested in multiple levels of ecological systems: organizations, populations, communities. Regularities exist at each of these levels (Aldrich & Auster,

Author's Note: Support from the Strategic Management Program of Stanford University's Graduate School of Business is gratefully acknowledged. Glenn Carroll, Jim March, Ann Miner, Brian Mittman, Dick Scott, and Jitendra Singh have provided comments along the way that have been helpful in shaping the arguments presented in this chapter.

1986; Astley, 1985; Carroll, 1984) and may also occur at the intraorganizational level. The main focus is on how strategic behavior is generated, how some behaviors are selected, and how they are retained within large, complex organizations. The perspective is ecological because it concerns itself with the emergence and demise of different types of strategic behaviors and views organizational-level strategy, in part, as the outcome of internal competition among types of strategic behavior. Such competition is viewed as governed by both internal resource constraints and institutional considerations.

The intraorganizational ecology of strategy making views organizational-level change, in part, as the outcome of internal variation, selection, and retention mechanisms. Strategy making at the level of large, complex organizations is viewed as a social learning process involving multiple levels of management. Allowing a role for social learning implies that cultural as well as biological evolutionary models may be useful for explaining intraorganizational and organizational-level phenomena (Boyd & Richerson, 1985). Cultural evolutionary processes can be orders of magnitude faster than biological evolution, can pass on learned traits directly to descendants (they are Lamarckian rather than Darwinian), and allow passing on of traits across lineages (Gould, 1987). For instance, effective management systems may be passed on directly to newly created internal corporate ventures, learning from one product family may be transferred to another product family, and all of this may be done within a relatively short period of time (see, e.g., Imai, Nonaka, & Takeuchi, 1985; Maidique & Zirger, 1985).

By elucidating the intraorganizational ecology of strategy making, this chapter purports to contribute to the synthesis of biological and cultural evolutionary models in organizational science (Langton, 1984). Other seeds for such a synthesis already exist. Economic evolutionists provide a detailed theoretical picture of the mechanisms of inheritance, selection, and survival (Nelson & Winter, 1982; Winter, Chapter 12, this volume). Recent work of organizational evolutionists augments ecological theory by studying the "imprinting" effects of founding characteristics of organizations on subsequent rates of organizational change (Tucker, Singh, & Meinhard, Chapter 8, this volume). These lines of work deal squarely with issues of intraorganizational change, and are important for the line of reasoning offered here.

The next section specifies variation, selection, and retention mechanisms encompassed by strategy-making processes in large, complex organizations. The third section examines relationships between strategy-making processes and modes of organizational adaptation. The final section discusses implications for further research.

INTRAORGANIZATIONAL ECOLOGY
OF STRATEGY MAKING

Strategy making in large, complex organizations may be conceptualized in terms of two processes: an induced process and an autonomous process (Burgelman, 1983b). This conceptualization is an outcropping of grounded theorizing encompassing field studies of different areas of substantive strategic action in large, related, diversified firms (Bower & Doz, 1979; Burgelman, 1983c). Together, the induced and autonomous strategic processes provide a parsimonious theoretical framework for integrating previous research findings. The autonomous process elucidates the emergence of new strategies and identifies the mechanisms through which they may become realized and may subsequently be transformed into intended strategy (Mintzberg, 1978; Mintzberg & McHugh, 1985). The induced strategic process sheds further light on the role of logical incrementalism (Quinn, 1982) in the ensemble of strategy-making processes in organizations.

Induced Strategic Process

Consider a newly founded and currently succeeding business organization. Whether success is the result of competence or luck, top management's role is to articulate a concept of strategy that will help secure continued survival. Such a concept of strategy may be viewed as a retention mechanism impounding top management's learning about the basis for the firm's past success. It encompasses technical and economic as well as symbolic and ideological factors (Beyer, 1981; Donaldson & Lorsch, 1983; March, 1981b; Pettigrew, 1979; Pfeffer, 1981; Weick, 1987), and serves to articulate the goals of the organization, to identify its distinctive competencies, and to delineate its action domain (McKelvey & Aldrich, 1983; Selznick, 1957). The concept of strategy may be expressed in substantive rules (March, 1981a; Nelson & Winter, 1982) guiding organizational-level strategic action and inducing strategic behavior at the individual level.[1] Through the application of these rules strategic decisions are joined over time (Freeman & Boeker, 1984) and distinct patterns of organizational-level strategy are realized (Miles & Snow, 1978; Miller & Friesen, 1984; Mintzberg, 1978).

Research suggests that the awareness of a firm's concept of strategy is likely to be concentrated at the top level of the organization (Hambrick, 1981) and that there may be less than full agreement on what the firm's distinctive competencies are (Snow & Hrebiniak, 1980; Stevenson, 1976). Also, as an organization grows in size, strategy making becomes increasingly differentiated over multiple levels of management (Williamson, 1970) and the concept of strategy can no longer be directly communicated in substantive detail to all levels of management. Participants differentially situated in the organization are likely to perceive different strategies as having the best potential for their and the organization's advancement. This provides an important source of internal variation. But, unless an organization is able to establish internal selection mechanisms, a gradual unraveling of the induced strategic process seems probable. Top management is expected, therefore, to establish a structural context encompassing administrative (Bower, 1970) and cultural (Ouchi, 1980) mechanisms. These serve to maintain coupling between strategic behavior at operational levels and the concept of strategy through shaping the participants' perceptions about which strategic behavior is likely to be supported by the organization. In this sense, the induced strategic process serves as a variation-reduction mechanism. Different forms of structural context provide more or less tight coupling (e.g., Chandler, 1962; Haspeslagh, 1983; Mintzberg, 1979; Rumelt, 1974; Williamson, 1970).

Autonomous Strategic Process

Autonomous strategic behavior is significantly different from induced behavior on such substantive dimensions as technology, customer functions, and customer groups (e.g., Abell, 1980). It is expected to derive from fungible organizational skills and capabilities (Penrose, 1968; Teece, 1982), that is, from new competencies that are not recognized as distinctive to the firm in its current concept of strategy. This sort of strategic behavior, which increases variation, has been documented in a number of studies of public organizations (Daft & Becker, 1978; Lewis, 1980) and private organizations (Burgelman, 1983c; Kanter, 1982; Mintzberg & McHugh, 1985; Shephard, 1967). It can originate at any level of management, but in large, complex organizations it would seem most likely to originate at a level where managers are directly in contact with new technological developments and changes in market conditions, and have some budgetary discretion. It is expected to emerge fortuitously and unpredictably, but not completely randomly, since it is rooted in and constrained by the evolving competence set of the organization (McKelvey & Aldrich, 1983).

At the time of its origination, the relation of autonomous strategic behavior to the firm's concept of strategy is indeterminate. To resolve the indeterminacy, strategic context determination processes can be activated (Burgelman, 1983c; Haspeslagh, 1983). These processes allow autonomous strategic behavior to be evaluated and selected internally, potentially leading to a change in the organization's concept of strategy. Strategic context determination involves the gradual development of a substantive strategy and associated administrative framework for new business activities. A study of internal corporate venturing suggests that the process evolves from creating a viable activity in a relatively narrow new business area by an entrepreneurial manager to establishing more broad-based new business activities under the impulse of a higher-level manager and concludes with the recognition on the part of top management that an amendment of the concept of strategy is warranted (Burgelman, 1983c, 1984). Such amendments lead to integrating the new activities with the induced strategic process.

Strategic context determination processes may be among the most elusive, volatile, and precarious decision processes in organizations. They deal with highly equivocal inputs and are therefore expected to involve relatively few rules but relatively many interlocked cycles for their assembly (Daft & Weick, 1984; Weick, 1979); that is, they require much iterative substantive interaction among managers from different levels in the organization. In contrast to the structural context that selects strategic behavior toward realizing an *ex ante* vision, strategic context determination processes select toward a vision that becomes articulated *ex post* (Burgelman, 1983a). They require that viability must be established, in both the internal and external environments, at each intermediate stage of the development of an autonomous activity before the final vision or purpose at the level of the organization can become completely articulated.[2]

Rationality in Strategy-Making Processes

The organizational learning impounded by the concept of strategy is likely to have been achieved at significant organizational and individual costs (Langton, 1984). Participants are expected to be aware of this and therefore motivated to pursue strategies through the induced strategic process. Such strategies allow them to take advantage of the available organizational learning rather than to incur the potentially high costs of new individually driven learning associated with pursuing strategies through the autonomous process.

The question then arises as to why managers would be willing to engage at all in autonomous strategic behavior. Their motivation may be rooted in an "obligatory logic" (March, 1988). Managers may engage in an autonomous course of action because it is congruent with their self-image, with who they are. Motivation may also be rooted in "consequential logic" (March,

1988). Managers may feel that they have capabilities and skills that make the envisaged autonomous course of action not really more risky than an induced one. Or, even if they perceive the autonomous process as more risky, managers may see it as an alternative avenue for making career progress if they consider their access to the induced process as limited (e.g., because of previous unfavorable performance outcomes, poor prospects of available activities in the induced process, and so on). Managers may also want to emulate colleagues who have received high internal rewards for pursuing autonomous courses of action or were able to obtain outside venture capital when internal support was not forthcoming.

From the perspective of the organization, the rationality of the induced strategic process seems clear. In this process, intentional strategy may serve the organization to leverage the existing learning and to exploit the opportunities associated with the current action domain. The organization may, within resource constraints, also rationally tolerate autonomous strategic behavior because it offers opportunities to explore and extend the boundaries of its capabilities set and to enact new environmental niches in which external selective pressures are as yet less strong (Astley, 1985; Burgelman, 1983a; Itami, 1983). In this process, myopically purposeful (McKelvey, 1982) individual strategic behavior may serve the organization to find out what its intentions could be. The possibilities for participants to engage in opportunistic behavior in the strategic processes (Bower, 1970; Rumelt, 1987; Williamson, 1970), however, highlights the importance of the structural and strategic contexts as internal selection mechanisms.

As noted earlier, the organization's concept of strategy is to a large extent based on retrospective rationality. However, this does not preclude prospective rationality that involves top management efforts to anticipate the state of the objective task environment. Earlier work has suggested how top management's perceptions about the prospects of reaching the organization's performance goals in the current task environment may increase or decrease the firmness with which they attempt to maintain the induced strategic process (Burgelman, 1983a).

Retrospective and prospective rationality involve processes of perception that can be more or less decoupled from the actual states of the environment. Close coupling is expected to increase an organization's chances to achieve performance targets. But even with complete decoupling between perceptions and reality, organizations may still survive over extended periods of time (March, 1981b). This seems to be an important reason that it is useful to distinguish strategic choice from adaptation.

STRATEGY MAKING AND
ORGANIZATIONAL ADAPTATION

The view of strategy making as an intraorganizational ecological process yields a new theoretical question: Under what conditions will internal selection be relatively more important than external selection for explaining continued organizational survival? This question, in turn, offers the opportunity to reconsider received arguments concerning organizational adaptation.

The Adaptation Paradox Revisited

Overcoming the liabilities of newness (Stinchcombe, 1965) requires organizations to develop a capacity for reliability and accountability in their transactions with the environment and to structure themselves so as to be legitimate. But doing so may result in structural inertia (Hannan & Freeman, 1984). Paradoxically, adaptation to existing environmental demands may reduce the organization's capacity to adapt to future changes in environmental parameters or to seek out new environments.

Empirical evidence suggests that organizational mortality is highest in young organizations, because of lack of external institutional support, and declines with age (see, e.g., Carroll & Delacroix, 1982; Freeman, Carroll, & Hannan, 1983; Singh, Tucker, & House, 1986). Hannan and Freeman (1984) have suggested that mortality declines with age in part because rates of change decline with age; that is, organizations become more rigid. But recent research does not fully support this "rigidity of aging" hypothesis, especially for peripheral features of organizations (Singh, Tucker, & Meinhard, 1988). In fact, the propensity to change may increase as organizations grow older, especially for peripheral features of organizations, suggesting support for a "fluidity of aging" hypothesis. The intraorganizational ecological perspective may shed further light on these seeming paradoxes associated with current ecological research.

Relative inertia and realignment. The view of an induced strategic process would seem to be consistent with both *relative inertia* (Hannan & Freeman, 1984) and *fluidity of aging* (Singh et al., 1988) arguments.

Inertial consequences of selection are likely to bear on the core features of an organization (Hannan & Freeman, 1984; Scott, 1981; Singh, House, & Tucker, 1986). From an evolutionary perspective, the concept of strategy seems most closely associated with the core features. Because the roots of an organization's concept of strategy are in organizational experience and learning, top managers are likely to be reluctant to make frequent changes in that concept. Research suggests that an organization's concept of strategy tends to remain in place for extended periods of time (see, e.g., Mintzberg & Waters, 1982). Recognizing that there may be differences between specialists and generalists (e.g., Freeman & Hannan, 1983) and between large and small organizations, it seems nevertheless plausible in many instances to expect the evolution of the concept of strategy to show a degree of inertia relative to the rate of change in the environment.

On the other hand, tendencies toward relative inertia of the concept of strategy do not preclude changes in more peripheral organizational features associated here with the structural context. In fact, based on organizational learning arguments (e.g., Levitt & March, 1988), one could expect that the frequency of these types of peripheral changes could be quite high and even increasing with age (Singh et al., 1988). Recent research suggests that some types of peripheral changes, such as top management succession, may enhance an organization's life chances (Singh, House, & Tucker, 1986). Such adaptive peripheral changes are called *realignment* here and are implemented through changes in the structural context. Organizational outcomes associated with realignment are expected to be to a large extent deliberate, reflecting different degrees of managerial discretion (Hambrick & Finkelstein, 1987) and providing important instances of nonrandom adaptation.

Relative inertia and realignment would seem to coexist in the induced strategic process. Relative inertia does not preclude realignment, and realignment may temporarily result in improved performance. In the long run, however, cumulative environmental selection pressures are expected to overwhelm realignment effected through the induced strategic process, and it seems likely that the concept of strategy itself will eventually have to change in major ways.

Transformation and strategic renewal. Empirical evidence suggests that changes in core features are governed by environmental selection processes (Singh, House, & Tucker, 1986). Tushman and Romanelli (1985), on the other hand, suggest that strategic "reorientations" — which imply here changes in the concept of strategy — are an integral part of a punctuated equilibrium model of firm evolution. Firms that do not reorient when major changes are necessary or reorient when the need for such changes is not compelling, they argue, will see their life chances reduced. The seeming contradiction between these two positions can be resolved in terms of the role of the autonomous strategic process, as explained below.

Major changes in the concept of strategy (reorientations or transformations) instigated by top management in response to chronic performance deficiencies would seem likely to upset the induced strategic process in fundamental ways. The necessity for these sorts of changes in core features suggests that external selective pressures have made the organization's capacity for realignment largely irrelevant. At first, threat-rigidity (Staw, Sandelands, & Dutton, 1981) may lead top management to reaffirm familiar approaches. Cooper and Schendel (1976), for instance, found that established firms confronted with the threat of radically new technologies were likely to increase their efforts to improve the existing technology rather than switch to the new technology even after the latter had passed the threshold of viability. Eventually, however, confronted with chronic low performance top management is susceptible to taking major risks (March, 1981b; Singh, 1986) and to attempting changes in the concept of strategy, potentially involving a complete change of domain.[3] To the extent that an organization finds itself in a precarious situation, transformation may be perceived by top management as necessary to maintain or regain viability (Miles & Cameron, 1982) and may be better than doing nothing. However, as March (1981b) has observed, organizations facing bad times and therefore following riskier and riskier strategies may simultaneously increase their chances of survival through the present crisis and reduce their life expectancy: "For those organizations that do not survive, efforts to survive will have speeded the process of failure" (p. 567).

Changes in the concept of strategy effected through the autonomous strategic process, however, need not be completely governed by external selection processes. Autonomous strategic behavior as conceptualized in an intraorganizational ecological perspective may provide early warning concerning impending radical external changes. To the extent that strategic context determination processes are effectively activated, the organization may learn new capabilities and skills in anticipation of making changes in the concept of strategy but without knowing in advance how it should be changed. Changes of this sort form the basis for "strategic renewal." Managing the strategic renewal process seems to be difficult for many companies.[4] The history of areas such as Silicon Valley indicates that autonomous strategic initiatives in established firms often result in the creation of new firms, rather than in strategic renewal of the firms where they originated. Many internal entrepreneurs seem to have left reluctantly because of lack of organizational support.[5] Anecdotal evidence suggests that even highly innovative firms are likely to try to keep the strategic behavior of their participants within the confines of the concept of strategy associated with the founders or their successors.[6] Yet, established companies may lose out severely if they fail to capitalize on autonomous strategic behavior.[7]

Transformation and strategic renewal are *not* expected to coexist in the autonomous strategic process. Consistent with the view of organizational ecology (Hannan & Freeman, 1984), environmental selection is expected to govern transformations. This is so because transformations seem fundamentally incompatible with strategy making as a social learning process. Transformations would inherently seem to involve "betting the organization" because they eliminate a good deal of its cumulative learning. Strategic renewal, on the other hand, seems to be the critical process through which an organization can indefinitely maintain an important role for the internal selection processes in organizational adaptation. A potentially interesting hypothesis may be that successful reorientations in the sense of Tushman and Romanelli (1985) are likely to be preceded by internal experimentation and selection processes effected through the autonomous strategic process.

Summary: The Role of Strategy-Making Processes

Organizations are both creators and prisoners of their environments (Miles & Cameron, 1982). Chances of organizational survival depend to a significant extent on the realignment and renewal capacities of strategy-making processes. Such strategy-making processes are an emergent property of organizations that may be differentially distributed within a population of organizations. Firms that overcome the liabilities of newness can draw on accumulated organizational learning and deliberate combining of competencies in the induced strategic process to create business activities capable of aligning and realigning themselves efficiently to specific environmental pressures. Realignment effected through the induced strategic process serves to stay in a given state of adaptation (Burgelman, 1983a; Chakravarty, 1982). The autonomous strategic process, on the other hand, serves organizations to appropriate and retain new individual learning. Strategic renewal through autonomous strategic behavior allows an organization to move to a new state of adaptation (Burgelman, 1983a; Chakravarty, 1982).

Combining induced and autonomous processes in their strategy making would seem to give organizations a chance to outsmart or outrun environmental selective pressures. An intriguing possibility suggested by the analysis is that organizations may have to keep both processes in play at all times, even though this means that the organization never completely maximizes its efforts in the current domain. At different times in an organization's development different emphases on the induced and autonomous strategic processes may be warranted, and there may not necessarily be a fixed series of stages in firm evolution, as some researchers seem to suggest (e.g., Kimberly & Miles, 1980; Miller & Friesen, 1984). Old firms may continue to be able to act like young ones, even though young ones may not equally be able to act like old ones. The renewal capacity associated with autonomous strategic behavior may allow organizations to negate the inevitability of aging and decline. By the same token, this may expose them again to some extent to the liabilities of newness (Hannan & Freeman, 1984).

IMPLICATIONS AND CONCLUSIONS

This chapter has offered an intraorganizational ecological perspective on strategy making and organizational adaptation. The framework posits balancing variation-reducing and variation-increasing mechanisms. It suggests that one process leads to relative inertia and incremental, peripheral adaptation while the other expands the firm's domain and thus renews the organization, countering inertia and serving some of the functions of a reorientation.

The proposed framework fits in an emergent effort attempting to integrate evolutionary views of strategy making and organization (Burgelman & Singh, 1987). These efforts recognize the importance of some forms of rationality and learning, and the need to go beyond biological evolutionary arguments. They reflect a belief that evolutionary theory may be useful for integrating insights from organizational ecology, rational adaptation, and random transformation perspectives (Hannan & Freeman, 1984). Presumably, a test of the fruitfulness of a conceptual integration like the one presented here lies in whether it raises novel theoretical questions and helps indicate new directions for research.

Implications for Theory and Research

One potentially important theoretical question concerns the conditions under which internal selection may be relatively more important than environmental selection. The possibilities to combine alignment and renewal processes effectively over time depend on top management's capacity to adjust the structural and strategic contexts in the organization. Discovering the determinants of such capacities and how the latter relate to rates of adjustment remains an important agenda for further research (Hannan & Freeman, 1984; March, 1981b). Here, the purpose has been limited to elucidating the behavioral mechanisms through which such capacities are likely to manifest themselves.

Structural and strategic contexts emerge as critical process design variables. In the induced strategic process top management's role is to ensure the pursuit of an intended strategy through mechanisms coupling operational-level strategic behavior with an organizational-level concept of strategy. Doing so makes it possible for the organization to exploit fully the opportunities associated with the current domain. In the autonomous strategic process, top management's role is strategic recognition rather than strategic planning (Burgelman, 1983a; Van de Ven, 1986). Top management needs strategic context determination processes to find out which of the spontaneously generated new opportunities outside the current domain deserve to be supported and to become part of the organizational-level concept of strategy. Rather than setting strategic direction and then structuring the organization for implementation, top management's role seems to be concerned with making sure that the induced and autonomous strategic processes work themselves out in a balanced way. This concern with managing strategic processes rather than with strategy (or "strategic choice") itself fits with a wide range of research findings — from field research (Bower & Doz, 1979) to formal analyses of garbage-can decision processes in a Weberian bureaucracy model (Padgett, 1980).

In order for internal selection mechanisms to be useful, organizations must be able to motivate strategic behavior on the part of their participants. As a result of internal selection, some participants may win big and others may lose big. But the genius of surviving organizations lies in how they benefit from both winning and losing individual strategic behaviors through their capacity for social learning. This suggests an organizational-level analogy to societal-level processes described by Rosenberg and Birdzell (1986). These authors show how Western capitalism has used decentralized entrepreneurialism: allowing innovators to bear the losses of failed experiments or to gain the profits of successful ones as much as they can capture, and benefiting from both in terms of growth.

It also suggests a link between strategy making and "foolishness" (March, 1981b). Organizations may use individual-level foolishness to enhance organizational-level survival in somewhat the same way as organizational-level foolishness may enhance the survival chances of a system of organizations. March views organizational foolishness as a form of altruism, but it might be possible to link such individual-level behavior to the idea that strategy making may be viewed as part of the organization's opportunity structure for career advancement. This, in turn, motivates interest in further examining how the Barnard-March-Simon theory of inducements and contributions may be realized. It raises, for instance, the issue of how the balance between inducements and contributions may be different in the induced and autonomous strategic processes and how shifting balances may affect organizational adaptation. It also directs attention to the effect of slack (e.g., Singh, 1986) on the frequency of induced and autonomous strategic behavior. These links would seem to open new directions for research.

Several other avenues for further research can be identified as well. Research could address the hypothesis that successful reorientations (Tushman & Romanelli, 1985) are likely to be preceded by internal experimentation and selection processes effected through the autonomous strategic process. Research could also address the hypothesis that there may be an optimal level of ambiguity in the concept of strategy (March, 1978) and an optimal degree of coupling in the structural context (Weick, 1976). This, in turn, may raise further questions about the relationships between strategy making and organization form, provide deeper insight into the distinction between core and peripheral features, and elucidate the mechanisms that determine structural features and their transformation, that is, organizational morphology. Finally, the intraorganizational ecology of strategy making would seem to constitute an important fourth level in the nested hierarchy of ecological systems encompassing organizations, populations, and communities (for example, Carroll, 1984). More work attempting to integrate the four levels in a new synthesis would seem useful. Such integration may suggest interesting interactions between selection and adaptation across levels of systems (Burgelman & Singh, 1987).

Several research approaches can be fruitfully employed. Longitudinal-processual (Pettigrew, 1979) and comparative-longitudinal (Romanelli & Tushman, 1986) research can reveal patterns of strategy making and organizational adaptation that may confirm, disconfirm, or refine the relationships posited in this chapter. Langton's (1984) study of Wedgewood Pottery presents an example, but additional efforts should seek to make use of primary rather than secondary data. Computer simulation methods may be useful for formalizing the conceptual framework into a model and tracing the dynamics implied by the model (e.g., Burgelman & Mittman, 1987).

One conclusion deriving from the integrative conceptual framework presented in this chapter seems reasonably certain: The opposite views of blind natural selection or prescient and comprehensive strategic planning as the basis for understanding organizational adaptation both seem too narrow. The pure external selection view misses the additional insight that can be obtained from considering internal selection. The pure strategic planning view misses the ecological components altogether. Rich behavioral phenomena are currently being documented in a variety of studies and will have to be accounted for by equally rich theories of organizations. An ecological perspective on strategy making seems likely to provide a useful input to organization theory. It also suggests the need to reconsider important precepts of received strategic management theory.

NOTES

1. An example of top management wanting to establish an induced strategic process based on the understanding of past success is provided by Patrick Haggerty (1981), one of the founders of Texas Instruments: "What organizational learning achieves is the building into the culture of the organization the process and the attitudes conceived by one or a few key individuals who fill a leadership role through a fraction of the overall lifetime of the institution and so extend the ideas and the processes and the attitudes of these key leaders beyond the span of either influence or time they could attain as individuals" (p. 98).

2. The power of selecting toward an existing vision is nicely illustrated by Dawkins's (1986) computer simulation models. Dawkins also develops the argument in biological evolution that intermediate forms must have survival value in order for the ultimate form or purpose to become realized. A discussion with Lou Pondy drew my attention to this literature.

3. Gould, Inc., for instance, has transformed itself from a relatively low-technology battery maker into a diversified high-tech company through acquisitions and divestments. For a while, the transformation seemed to work out well. However, Gould has recently been encountering problems, has had to scale back dramatically in size, and has been named as a potential takeover target (*Wall Street Journal*, October 3, 1984).

4. Few firms, such as 3M and Hewlett-Packard, are known for their capacity to manage strategic renewal consistently well.

5. For instance, Steve Wozniak (Apple) and Sam Eletr (Applied Biosystems) at Hewlett-Packard, Larry Boucher (Adaptec) at Shugart Associates, Rod Canion (Compaq) at Texas Instruments, and Bob Metcalfe (3Com) at Xerox.

6. Under Edwin Land, Polaroid was renowned for its creativity-nurturing culture. Scientists working in Polaroid's labs could pursue any research project they wanted, *provided* it was in the area of instant photography. In the early 1980s, Polaroid's growth and diversification may have been stunted because of the original vision.

7. Bendix Corporation may have missed a chance to become the world leader in automotive electronics. Electronic fuel injection was invented and fully patented by Bendix during the 1950s. The very first system was built by a Bendix engineer in the aerospace division who liked to be able to fly his airplane upside down. Bendix automotive group management did not want to pursue this technology. Rather, they licensed Bosch and gave .ʼ .m a chance to catch up and later surpass them. Today, Bosch is widely recognized as a world leader in automotive electronics. The point of this story is *not* that Bendix was poorly managed, but that the company may have missed the opportunity *because it was very well managed within the concept of strategy considered given at the time.* (See Bendix Corporation A 9-378-257, HBS Case Services, Harvard Business School, Boston.) (It seems also interesting to note that the framework presented in this chapter provides lenses for identifying the *internal* issues facing Bendix as a result of EFI development. The Harvard case was actually written to show the *external* issues associated with a highly uncertain industry development.)

REFERENCES

Abell, D. (1980). *Defining the business.* Englewood Cliffs, NJ: Prentice-Hall.

Aldrich, H. E. (1979). *Organizations and environments.* Englewood Cliffs, NJ: Prentice-Hall.

Aldrich, H., & Auster, E. (1986). Even dwarfs started small: Liabilities of size and age and their strategic implications. In B. Staw & L. L. Cummings (Eds.), *Research in organizational behavior* (Vol. 8, pp. 165-198). Greenwich, CT: JAI.

Astley, W. G. (1985). The two ecologies: Population and community perspectives on organizational evolution. *Administrative Science Quarterly, 30,* 224-241.

Astley, W. G., & Van de Ven, A. H. (1983). Central perspectives and debates in organization theory. *Administrative Science Quarterly, 28,* 245-273.

Beyer, J. M. (1981). Ideologies, values and decision making in organizations. In P. E. Nystrom & W. H. Starbuck (Eds.), *Handbook of organization design* (Vol. 2, pp. 166-202). New York: Oxford University Press.

Bourgeois, L. J., III. (1984). Strategic management and determinism. *Academy of Management Review, 9,* 586-596.

Bower, J. L. (1970). *Managing the resource allocation process.* Boston: Harvard University, Graduate School of Business Administration.

Bower, J. L., & Doz, I. (1979). Strategy formulation: A social and political process. In D. E. Schendel & C. W. Hofer (Eds.), *Strategic management* (pp. 152-166). Boston: Little, Brown.

Boyd, R., & Richerson, P. J. (1985). *Culture and the evolutionary process.* Chicago: University of Chicago Press.

Burgelman, R. A. (1983a). Corporate entrepreneurship and strategic management: Insights from a process study. *Management Science, 29,* 1349-1364.

Burgelman, R. A. (1983b). A model of the interaction of strategic behavior, corporate context, and the context of strategy. *Academy of Management Review, 8*(1), 61-70.

Burgelman, R. A. (1983c). A process model of internal corporate venturing in the diversified major firm. *Administrative Science Quarterly, 28,* 223-244.

Burgelman, R. A. (1984). On the interplay of process and content in internal corporate ventures: Action and cognition in strategy-making. *Academy of Management Proceedings,* pp. 2-6.

Burgelman, R. A., & Mittman, B. S. (1987, August). *Formalizing an evolutionary process perspective on strategy-making: Toward a strategic process simulation model.* Paper presented at the annual meetings of the Academy of Management, New Orleans.

Burgelman, R. A., & Singh, J. V. (1987, August). *Strategy and organization: An evolutionary approach.* Paper presented at the annual meetings of the Academy of Management, New Orleans.

Campbell, D. T. (1969). Variation and selective retention in sociocultural evolution. *General Systems, 14,* 69-85.

Carroll, G. R. (1984). Organizational ecology. *Annual Review of Sociology, 10,* 71-93.

Carroll, G. R., & Delacroix, J. (1982). Organizational mortality in the newspaper industries of Argentina and Ireland: An ecological approach. *Administrative Science Quarterly, 27,* 169-198.

Chakravarty, B. S. (1982). Adaptation: A promising metaphor for strategic management. *Academy of Management Review, 7*(1), 35-44.

Chandler, A. D. (1962). *Strategy and structure.* Cambridge: MIT Press.

Child, J. (1972). Organization structure, environment, and performance: The role of strategic choice. *Sociology, 6,* 1-22.

Cooper, A. C., & Schendel, D. E. (1976, February). Strategic responses to technological threats. *Business Horizons*, pp. 61-63.

Daft, R. L., & Becker, S. W. (1978). *The innovative organization.* New York: Elsevier.

Daft, R. L., & Weick, K. E. (1984). Toward a model of organizations as interpretation systems. *Academy of Management Review, 9,* 284-295.

Dawkins, R. (1986). *The blind watchmaker.* New York: W. W. Norton.

Donaldson, G., & Lorsch, J. W. (1983). *Decision making at the top.* New York: Basic Books.

Freeman, J. H., & Boeker, W. (1984, Spring). The ecological analysis of business strategy. *California Management Review, 26,* 73-86.

Freeman, J. H., Carroll, G. R., & Hannan, M. T. (1983). The liability of newness: Age dependence in organizational death rates. *American Sociological Review, 48,* 692-710.

Freeman, J. H., & Hannan, M. T. (1983). Niche width and the dynamics of organizational populations. *American Journal of Sociology, 88,* 1116-1145.

Gould, S. J. (1987, January). The panda's thumb of technology. *National History,* pp. 14-23.

Haggerty, P. E. (1981). The corporation and innovation. *Strategic Management Journal, 2,* 97-118.

Hambrick, D. C. (1981). Strategic awareness within top management teams. *Strategic Management Journal, 2,* 263-279.

Hambrick, D. C., & Finkelstein, S. (1987). Managerial discretion: A bridge between polar views of organizational outcomes. In L. L. Cummings & B. Staw (Eds.), *Research in organizational behavior* (Vol. 9, pp. 369-406). Greenwich, CT: JAI.

Hannan, M. T., & Freeman, J. (1984). Structural inertia and organizational change. *American Sociological Review, 49,* 149-164.

Haspeslagh, P. (1983). *Portfolio planning approaches and the strategic management process in diversified industrial companies.* Unpublished doctoral dissertation, Harvard Business School.

Hrebiniak, L. G., & Joyce, W. J. (1985). Organizational adaptation: Strategic choice and environmental determinism. *Administrative Science Quarterly, 30,* 336-349.

Imai, K.-I., Nonaka, I., & Takeuchi, H. (1985). Managing the new product development process: How Japanese companies learn and unlearn. In K. Clark, R. Hayes, & C. Lorenz (Eds.), *The uneasy alliance* (pp. 337-374). Cambridge, MA: Harvard Business School Press.

Itami, H. (1983). *The case for unbalanced growth of the firm* (Research Paper Series No. 681). Stanford, CA: Stanford University, Graduate School of Business.

Kanter, R. M. (1982, July-August). Middle managers as innovators. *Harvard Business Review, 60,* 95-105.

Kimberly, J. R., & Miles, R. H. (Eds.). (1980). *The organizational life cycle.* San Francisco: Jossey-Bass.

Langton, J. (1984). The ecological theory of bureaucracy: The case of Josiah Wedgewood and the British pottery industry. *Administrative Science Quarterly, 29,* 330-354.

Levitt, B., & March, J. G. (1988) Organizational learning. In B. Staw & L. L. Cummings (Eds.), *Research in organizational behavior* (Vol. 10). Greenwich, CT: JAI.

Lewis, E. (1980). *Public entrepreneurship.* Bloomington: Indiana University Press.

Maidique, M. A., & Zirger, B. J. (1985). The new product learning cycle. *Research Policy, 14,* 299-313.

March, J. G. (1978). Bounded rationality, ambiguity, and the engineering of choice. *Bell Journal of Economics and Management Science, 9,* 435-457.

March, J. G. (1981a). Decisions in organizations and theories of choice. In A. H. Van de Ven & W. F. Joyce (Eds.), *Perspectives on organizational design and behavior.* New York: John Wiley.

March, J. G. (1981b). Footnotes to organizational change. *Administrative Science Quarterly, 26,* 563-577.

March, J. G. (1988, Spring). Wild ideas: The catechism of heresy. *Stanford Magazine.*

McKelvey, B. (1982). *Organizational systematics: Taxonomy, evolution, classification.* Berkeley: University of California Press.

McKelvey, B., & Aldrich, H. E. (1983). Populations, organizations and applied organizational science. *Administrative Science Quarterly, 28,* 101-128.

Miles, R. E., & Snow, C. C. (1978). *Organizational strategy, structure, and process.* New York: McGraw-Hill.

Miles, R. H., & Cameron, K. (1982). *Coffin nails and corporate strategies.* Englewood Cliffs, NJ: Prentice-Hall.

Miller, D., & Friesen, P. H. (with the collaboration of H. Mintzberg). (1984). *Organizations: A quantum view.* Englewood Cliffs, NJ: Prentice-Hall.

Mintzberg, H. (1978). Patterns in strategy formation. *Management Science, 24,* 934-948.

Mintzberg, H. (1979). *The structuring of organizations.* Englewood Cliffs, NJ: Prentice-Hall.

Mintzberg, H., & McHugh, A. (1985). Strategy formation in an adhocracy. *Administrative Science Quarterly, 30,* 160-197.

Mintzberg, H., & Waters, J. A. (1982). Tracking strategy in an entrepreneurial firm. *Academy of Management Journal, 25,* 465-499.

Nelson, R. R., & Winter, S. G. (1982). *An evolutionary theory of economic change.* Cambridge, MA: Harvard University Press.

Ouchi, W. (1980). Markets, bureaucracies, and clans. *Administrative Science Quarterly, 25,* 129-141.

Padgett, J. F. (1980). Managing garbage can hierarchies. *Administrative Science Quarterly, 25,* 583-604.

Penrose, E. T. (1968). *The theory of the growth of the firm.* Oxford: Basil Blackwell.

Pettigrew, A. (1979). On studying organization cultures. *Administrative Science Quarterly, 24,* 570-581.

Pfeffer, J. (1981). Management as symbolic action: The creation and maintenance of organizational paradigms. In B. Staw (Ed.), *Research in organizational behavior* (Vol. 3, pp. 1-52). Greenwich, CT: JAI.

Quinn, J. B. (1982). *Strategies for change.* Homewood, IL: Irwin.

Romanelli, E., & Tushman, M. L. (1986). Inertia, environments, and strategic choice: A quasi-experimental design for comparative-longitudinal research. *Management Science, 32*(5), 608-621.

Rosenberg, N., & Birdzell, L. E., Jr. (1986). *How the West grew rich.* New York: Basic Books.

Rumelt, R. P. (1974). *Strategy, structure, and economic performance.* Cambridge, MA: Harvard University, Graduate School of Business Administration.

Rumelt, R. P. (1987). Theory, strategy and entrepreneurship. In D. J. Teece (Ed.), *The competitive challenge* (pp. 137-158). Cambridge, MA: Ballinger.

Scott, W. R. (1981). *Organizations: Rational, natural, and open systems.* Englewood Cliffs, NJ: Prentice-Hall.

Selznick, P. (1957). *Leadership in administration.* New York: Harper & Row.

Shephard, H. A. (1967). Innovation-resisting and innovation-producing organizations. *Journal of Business, 40.*

Singh, J. V. (1986). Performance, slack, and risk-taking in organizational decision making. *Academy of Management Journal, 29*, 562-585.

Singh, J. V., House, R. J., & Tucker, D. J. (1986). Organizational change and organizational mortality. *Administrative Science Quarterly, 31*, 587-611.

Singh, J. V., Tucker, D. J., & House, R. J. (1986). Organizational legitimacy and the liability of newness. *Administrative Science Quarterly, 31*, 171-193.

Singh, J. V., Tucker, D. J., & Meinhard, A. (1988, August). *Are voluntary organizations structurally inert? Exploring an assumption in organizational ecology.* Paper presented at the annual meetings of the Academy of Management, Anaheim, CA.

Snow, C. C., & Hrebiniak, L. G. (1980). Strategy, distinctive competence, and organizational performance. *Administrative Science Quarterly, 25*, 317-336.

Staw, B., Sandelands, L. E., & Dutton, J. E. (1981). Thrust-rigidity effects in organizational behavior: A multilevel analysis. *Administrative Science Quarterly, 26*, 147-160.

Stevenson, H. E. (1976). Defining corporate strengths and weaknesses. *Sloan Management Review, 17*, 51-58.

Stinchcombe, A. L. (1965). Social structure and organizations. In J. G. March (Ed.), *Handbook of organizations* (pp. 142-193). Chicago: Rand McNally.

Teece, D. J. (1982). Towards an economic theory of the multi-product firm. *Journal of Economic Behavior and Organization, 3*, 39-63.

Tushman, M. L., & Romanelli, E. (1985). Organizational evolution: A metamorphosis model of convergence and reorientation. In B. M. Staw & L. L. Cummings (Eds.), *Research in organizational behavior* (Vol. 7, pp. 171-222). Greenwich, CT: JAI.

Van de Ven, A. H. (1986). Central problems in the management of innovation. *Management Science, 32*(4), 590-607.

Weick, K. E. (1976). Educational organizations of loosely coupled systems. *Administrative Science Quarterly, 21*, 1-19.

Weick, K. E. (1979). *The social psychology of organizing.* Reading, MA: Addison-Wesley.

Weick, K. E. (1987). Substitutes for corporate strategy. In D. J. Teece (Ed.), *The competitive challenge.* Cambridge, MA: Ballinger.

Williamson, O. E. (1970). *Corporate control and business behavior.* Englewood Cliffs, NJ: Prentice-Hall.

8

Founding Characteristics, Imprinting, and Organizational Change

DAVID J. TUCKER
JITENDRA V. SINGH
AGNES G. MEINHARD

The emergence of population ecology as an important paradigm in organization science has established the problem of how populations of organizational forms change over time as central in organizational theory. At a theoretical level, it is argued that population change occurs through differential founding and disbanding and through differential rates of change in organizational forms (Hannan & Freeman, 1989; Singh, Tucker, & Meinhard, in press). While empirical studies of differential founding and disbanding rates in populations of organizations have proliferated in recent years, there have been relatively few theoretical treatments and empirical studies of rates of change in organizational forms (but see Aldrich, 1979; Aldrich & Auster, 1986; Singh, Tucker, & Meinhard, 1988, in press).

We attempt in this chapter to explore empirically the effects of environmental and organizational founding characteristics on rates of change in organizational features. Using data from a population of voluntary social service organizations (VSSOs) located in metropolitan Toronto, Canada, we investigate whether rates of change in organizational features are influenced by differences in organizational and environmental conditions at founding after accounting for the influence of changes in environmental conditions over time.

Authors' Note: This research was supported by grant number 410-84-0632 from the Social Sciences and Humanities Research Council, Ottawa, Canada, and grant number 4555-55-7 from the National Welfare Grants Directorate, Ottawa, Canada.

The rationale for studying the relationship between founding conditions and rates of change in organizational features is, in part, suggested by the findings of our recent study of the effects of founding conditions on mortality rates of organizations (Tucker, Singh, & Meinhard, 1988). We found that differences at founding between organizations in selected organizational characteristics and environmental conditions significantly influenced differential mortality rates. Based on these findings, and on Stinchcombe's (1965) observation that an organization's founding conditions have an enduring effect on its structure and behavior, it seems reasonable to expect that organizations founded under different environmental conditions, and with different initial characteristics, would exhibit different rates of change.

The analysis reported in this chapter is exploratory. Our purpose is not to test hypotheses and confirm theoretical arguments but to appraise the empirical viability of understanding organizational change by studying the effects of conditions at founding on propensities to change. We see this study as a first step in disentangling the complexities of organizational change processes.

IMPRINTING IN ORGANIZATIONS

How an organization is structured and how it behaves over the period of its life span are believed to be influenced, in part, by the conditions and circumstances surrounding its formation. Stinchcombe (1965) was one of the first organizational theorists to emphasize this. In what is currently known as his "imprinting" hypothesis, he argues that organizations construct their social systems with the social resources available at the time of their founding and that they tend to retain the characteristics they acquired at founding over the course of their life spans. The processes accounting for this preservation of founding characteristics are threefold (Stinchcombe, 1965, pp. 167-169; see also, Aldrich, 1979, pp. 194-195; Scott, 1986, p. 158). First, the founding characteristics may be the most efficient for a given purpose. Accordingly, they persist because they give a competitive advantage over other arrangements. Second, founding characteristics may be preserved because organizations are insulated from environmental pressures by support from vested interests, traditionalizing forces, or a strongly legitimated ideological position. Third, the organization may not be confronted with competitive forces. Thus it is under no pressure to change in order to survive.

Although imprinting arguments are frequently invoked in the literature (e.g., Aldrich, 1979; Daft, 1983; Pennings, 1980: Tolbert & Zucker, 1983), to date, few empirical studies of imprinting have actually been done. Generally, the few studies that deal with related questions support Stinchcombe's view that an organization's founding environment and characteristics have an enduring effect on its structure and behavior. For example, in a study of 123 sheltered workshops, Kimberly (1975) showed that the dates and social conditions of their founding had a strong and continuing influence on the orientations they adopted in implementing their goals. In a later study of the development of a medical school, Kimberly (1979) concludes that the environment at founding, the personality of the founder, and the nature of initial decisions all have lasting effects on organizational structure and behavior. More recently, Boeker (1988), in a study of 62 semiconductor firms, found that the characteristics of the founding members and of the founding environmental context both have strong influences on the development of the organization's initial strategy.

We look for evidence of imprinting in our population of VSSOs by examining relationships between the founding characteristics of organizations and propensities to change. In particular, we examine the effects of institutional and ecological components of the environment and organizational characteristics, or rates of change in organizational features. An important reason for studying the effects of founding characteristics on rates of changes in VSSOs is that, to date, imprinting effects generally have been treated as permanent. This may not be the case for VSSOs because of their nature. We have argued elsewhere that a significant feature of VSSOs is that they have fairly indeterminate technologies (Singh, Tucker, & House '986; Tucker, 1981; Tucker, Singh, Meinhard, & House, 1988). Thus they are unable to demonstrate their effectiveness using conventional output, efficiency, or process criteria. Under these conditions, social criteria, such as the satisfaction and approval of external constituencies, are more likely to be used to judge effectiveness. This suggests that VSSOs are specifically vulnerable to the effects of external influences. Because of this ongoing openness of VSSOs to external influences, it may be that imprinting effects of founding conditions erode fairly quickly and that existing organizational features are best explained by contemporaneous environmental events. How imprinting effects work when changes in environmental conditions over time are taken into consideration is a central concern of this chapter.

Environmental Conditions at Founding

Currently, organizational environments are conceived of as having ecological and institutional components (Carroll & Huo, 1986; Hannan, 1986; Scott, 1983; Tucker, Singh, & Meinhard, 1990; Tucker, Singh, Meinhard, &

House, 1988). Ecological components of the environment are the availability and distribution of tangible resources (Aldrich, 1979; Scott, 1983). Institutional components are the rules and beliefs about the creation and structuring of organizations as well as the relational networks of other formal organizations (DiMaggio & Powell, 1983; Meyer & Rowan, 1977; Scott, 1983).

Institutional environments have been defined in terms of the decisions and activities of a few powerful institutional actors (Tolbert & Zucker, 1983). Based on this approach, we have argued that the state is perhaps the most significant actor in the institutional environments of VSSOs (Tucker, Singh, Meinhard, & House, 1988). Through changes in their policies and programs, different levels of government in Canada historically have created conditions that first enhanced, but later undermined, the legitimacy of creating VSSOs to help solve social problems. This raises the question of how being founded in a favorable institutional environment, as opposed to being founded in an unfavorable one, affects the propensity of an organization to change its features. One possible answer is that an important reason organizations tend to retain their founding features is that they may be insulated from environmental pressures by support from vested interests, traditionalizing forces, or a strongly legitimated ideological position (Aldrich, 1979; Stinchcombe, 1965). Consequently, they are not under pressure to change. In this regard, we have argued elsewhere that organizations founded in favorable institutional environments have higher levels of external legitimacy and institutional support than organizations founded in unfavorable environments precisely because they are able to gain the acceptance of vested interests (Tucker, Singh, & Meinhard, 1988; see also Aldrich, 1979; Astley, 1985). Thus organizations founded in favorable institutional environments will show a lower propensity to change. Obversely, organizations founded in unfavorable institutional environments will not be insulated from environmental pressures to change. Therefore, they will demonstrate a higher propensity to change. Overall, being founded in a favorable institutional environment will decrease rates of change, and being founded in an unfavorable institutional environment will increase rates of change.

Related to the ecological components of the environment, we examine the effects of density and resource concentration. Density, the number of organizations in the population, has been extensively shown to affect the founding and disbanding processes of organizations (Delacroix & Carroll, 1983; Hannan & Freeman, 1987; Singh et al., in press; Tucker, Singh, & Meinhard, 1988; Tucker, Singh, Meinhard, & House, 1988). While Carroll and Hannan (Chapter 5, this volume) have investigated the effects of density at founding on the mortality rates of organizations, to the best of our knowledge, whether density at founding had an imprinting effect on rates of change has not been studied. An argument concerning the effect of density at founding on rates of change is that since variation in density means variation in the intensity of competition effects in populations of organizations, with higher levels of density implying more intense competition (Hannan & Freeman, 1988; Tucker, Singh, Meinhard, & House, 1988), it follows that the higher the level of density at founding, the more intense the competition the organization is exposed to during its founding stage (see also Carroll & Hannan, Chapter 5, this volume). One important strategy organizations can use when confronted with intense competition due to niche crowding is to change their features so as to at least give the appearance of not duplicating other organizations or overlapping with them. In this way, the initial organizational niche is enlarged and the negative effects of competition are lessened (Delacroix, Swaminathan, & Solt, 1989, p. 247; Hawley, 1986, p. 56; Usher, 1989). It is plausible, therefore, that organizations founded in more dense environments, when compared with organizations founded in less dense environments, are more likely to be imprinted with a higher propensity to change. Thus they are more likely to show increased rates of change.

Similar to density, the imprinting effects of resource concentration at founding on rates of change have not been investigated. If there is a relationship, we expect that organizations that are founded in concentrated environments have lower rates of change. The argument we explore is similar to the effects of the founding institutional environment. As we use the term, a concentrated environment is one in which resources are distributed among a few resource allocators as opposed to being evenly distributed among a large number of resource allocators. Concentrated environments exert more control by heightening the dependence of organizations on resource allocators by presenting them with fewer alternatives (Pfeffer & Salancik, 1978, pp. 50-51). These concentrated environments make it more difficult to found new organizations but also insulate such organizations from selection pressures (Tucker, Singh, & Meinhard, 1988). Since insulation from external pressures decreases the probability that an organization will learn how to change (Aldrich, 1979; Stinchcombe, 1965), we think that organizations founded in highly concentrated environments will have lower rates of change.

Founding Organizational Characteristics

One of the important ways organizations differ from each other at founding concerns whether they are specialists or generalists (Hannan & Freeman, 1977; Tucker et al., 1990; Tucker, Singh, & Meinhard, 1988). A specialist

organization is one that operates in a single domain, whereas a gen
organization is one that operates in multiple domains. We think that w
an organization is founded as specialist or generalist will affect its propensity
to change. Our earlier research has shown that the founding and disbanding
processes for specialists, when compared to generalists, are more influenced
by environmental conditions due partially to the circumstances of their
founding — that is, the creation of specialist organizations is more opportu-
nistically motivated, and more easily achieved, than for generalist organizations (Tucker et al., 1990). Since vulnerability to environmental pressures is
an important condition for the occurrence of change (Aldrich, 1979;
Stinchcombe, 1965), we expect that organizations founded as specialists will
have higher rates of change and that organizations founded as generalists will
have lower rates of change.

In addition to organizational form, we also examine the effect of board
size at founding on organizational propensities to change. We found in earlier
research that having a larger board size at founding increased rates of change
(Singh et al., 1988, in press). Since boards of directors are one important way
VSSOs try to build links with other institutional actors (Singh, Tucker, &
House, 1986), one plausible way to interpret these findings is that larger
boards bring into organizations more diverse external influences, thereby
enhancing rates of change. In this study, we explore the validity of this
argument more fully by examining whether the effects of board size at
founding are maintained after controlling for other relevant variables.

METHOD

Population and Data Collection

The study population is composed of all VSSOs that came into existence
in metropolitan Toronto during the period 1970-1982, and numbers 389.
VSSOs are defined as "organizations governed by a board of directors and
that operate on a nonprofit basis and are concerned with changing, constrain-
ing and/or supporting human behavior" (Singh, Tucker, & House 1986,
p. 175). Data sources are mainly archival, including (a) files, documents, and
indexes maintained by the federal, provincial, and municipal levels of
government; (b) files, lists, and documents made available by local planning,
coordinating, and funding agencies (e.g., the United Way, the Community
Information Center); and (c) the annual reports of individual VSSOs. More
extensive information on the nature of the VSSO population, and on the data

sources and the data collection procedures, can be found in Singh, Tucker, and House (1986) and Singh, House, and Tucker (1986).

Measurement

Rates of organizational change. We gathered data on changes in name, sponsor, location, service area, goals, client groups, conditions of service provision, chief executive, and structure. The propensity of organizations to change is described by a stochastic function, the instantaneous transition rate, $r(t)$. Conceptually, this transition rate is similar to the instantaneous disbanding rate, $h(t)$, the hazard of disbanding studied in other research (Carroll & Delacroix, 1982; Freeman, Carroll, & Hannan, 1983; Singh, Tucker, & House, 1986), although substantive differences between disbanding and change introduce peculiarities into estimating rates of change. The instantaneous rate of change is given by:[1]

$$r(t) = \lim_{\Delta t \to 0} \frac{\Pr(\text{change } t, t + \Delta t)}{\Delta t}$$

Unlike the hazard of disbanding, this rate is not conditional upon the event not having occurred until time t. Intuitively, higher rates of change imply shorter average waiting times between changes, and vice versa.

Name change refers to an actual change in the identifying title of the organization. *Sponsor change* refers to a change in the organization that supported, promoted, or otherwise actively sponsored the focal organization. *Location change* measures a change in the physical location of the organization. *Service area change* refers to a change in the domain in which an organization offered services — legal, socio-rehabilitative, educational, and so on. *Goal change* measures whether the goals of the organization — such as advocacy, information and referral, raising and allocating funds — have changed. *Client group change* refers to whether an organization has changed the client group to whom it was offering services, such as families, the elderly, or children. *Change in conditions of service* measures whether there has been a change in the criteria or conditions to be satisfied by a client in order for services to be provided by the organization, for example, crime victim, physically handicapped, geographic location, or economically disadvantaged. *Chief executive change* measures whether there has been a succession in the executive head of the organization. Finally, *structural change* refers to a change in the structure of the organization, through the addition or deletion of subunits. All occurrences of these changes, and their timing, were noted. The change variables were coded 1 in the year the change occurred, and 0 otherwise.

Form. In our population, one of the key ways in which individual VSSOs differ from each other at founding is the number of domains in which they provide services. Some provide service in a single domain; others operate in multiple domains. Approximately 48% of the VSSOs occupied a single domain (e.g., health or leisure or education), 33% occupied two domains, and the remaining 19% were involved in three or more domains. In this study organizational form at founding was measured using two separate dummy variables for specialist (single domain) and generalist (three or more domains) organizations.

Board size. Board size is the number of persons serving on a VSSO's board of directors at the time of its founding.

Resource concentration. The measurement of resource concentration involved assuming the existence of a resource space capable of supporting a population of VSSOs (Brittain & Freeman, 1980, p. 293). This resource space was defined as being composed of a mix of 13 major resource allocators, including departments of the federal, provincial, and municipal governments as well as voluntary funding agencies. Resource concentration measured the extent to which a small number of these resource allocators controlled large amounts of resources, rather than resource control being evenly distributed. It was operationalized by calculating Gini coefficients given by:

$$G = \int_0^{100} \frac{[x - f(x)]\, dx}{\frac{1}{2}(100)^2}$$

where G = Gini coefficient of concentration, x = cumulative percentage of resource allocators, and $f(x)$ = cumulative percentage of resources allocated.

Institutional environment. As in earlier studies (Singh et al., in press; Singh, House, & Tucker, 1986; Tucker et al., 1990; Tucker, Singh, Meinhard, & House, 1988), we characterized the institutional environment in terms of the occurrence of two historical events, the Opportunities for Youth (OFY) period, from 1971 to 1975, and the Provincial Restraint (RES) period, lasting from 1976 to 1981. OFY corresponds to a period when involvement in the creation of new VSSOs was accepted as a preferred way of contending with social problems (Best, 1974; Houston, 1972; Loney, 1977; Wharf & Carter, 1972). RES corresponds to a period characterized by fiscal restraint (McKeough, 1975, 1976; Miller, 1980; Puckett & Tucker, 1976), with more emphasis on increasing the productivity of existing organizations than on legitimating the creation of new ones (Economic Council of Canada, 1976,

1977). OFY and RES are treated as dummy variables, coded 1 when present and 0 otherwise (for detailed description of OFY and RES, see Singh et al., in press; Tucker, Singh, Meinhard, & House, 1988).

Density. Density is the total number of VSSOs alive at any time. It is calculated by:

$$\text{density}_t = \text{density}_{t-1} + (\text{births}_{t-1} - \text{deaths}_{t-1})$$

ANALYSIS AND RESULTS

Descriptive Statistics

Table 8.1 presents descriptive data on frequencies for each type of organizational change in our population of VSSOs. These data show that some changes occurred frequently (e.g., changes in location, chief executive, and structure), whereas other changes (e.g., name, sponsor, and goals) occurred much less frequently. This suggests that some organizational features are more susceptible to change than others and that change in some features occurred frequently in this population. Of course, to explore whether the founding characteristics play a role in influencing rates of change in this population, it is necessary to study parametric models of rates of change.

Models

The descriptive statistics suggest the occurrence of multiple changes in organizations. In order to take this into account, we used multiple-spells models to estimate the impact of founding characteristics on rates of change, each spell being made up of a single year (Singh et al., in press; Singh, House, & Tucker, 1986; Singh, Tucker, & House, 1986). Based on approaches used in earlier research (Singh, House, & Tucker, 1986; Tucker, Singh, Meinhard, & House, 1988), we used multiple-spell Gompertz models, with the covariates being models in the β vector:

$$r(t) = \exp(\beta_o + \sum_i \beta_i X_i) \, \exp(\gamma_o t) \qquad [1]$$

where $\exp(\beta o)$ gives the portion of the change rate at founding that is attributable to the infancy of the organization, X_i refers to the founding characteristics, and the parameter γo gives the rate at which the change rate

TABLE 8.1: Frequencies of Organizational Change

Type of Change	Number of Organizations That Experience No Change	Number of Organizations That Experience Change
Name	339 (87.1)	50 (12.1)
Sponsor	344 (88.4)	45 (11.6)
Location	188 (48.3)	201 (51.7)
Service area	346 (88.9)	43 (11.1)
Goals	325 (82.5)	64 (17.5)
Client groups	381 (97.9)	8 (2.1)
Conditions of service	374 (96.1)	15 (3.9)
Chief executive	199 (51.2)	190 (48.8)
Structure	128 (47.4)	142 (52.6)

SOURCE: Singh et al. (1988).
NOTE: $N = 389$ except for structural change. Because structural change data were collected during interviews, and some organizations were already disbanded, data could be gathered on only 270 organizations.

approaches the null asymptotic change rate. We chose to model variables in the β vector because, in using multiple-spells models with yearly spells, it seems equally meaningful to insert covariates into either the β or γ vectors, as their substantive interpretations are not very different (Singh, House, & Tucker, 1986, p. 603).

The model described in equation 1 does not take into account the effects of changes in environmental conditions over time on rates of change, which are probably significant. Thus it seems plausible that initial analyses may show differential rates of change related to founding conditions, but controlling for changing environmental conditions may nullify such findings. Earlier we had argued that this may be particularly true for VSSOs, since, for a variety of reasons, they can be expected to remain specifically vulnerable to external influences. In addition, available longitudinal research indicates that rates of change are affected by changing environmental conditions (Meyer & Brown, 1977; Singh et al., in press). We incorporated several control variables into the analysis—institutional environmental conditions, density,

TABLE 8.2: Maximum Likelihood Estimates: Effects of Founding Conditions on Rates of Change, Gompertz Models (multiple spells)

Change Type	$\beta0$	Specialist $\beta1$	Generalist $\beta2$	B.Size $\beta3$	OFY $\beta4$	RES $\beta5$	Dens. $\beta6$	Cono. $\beta7$	OFYtv $\beta8$	REStv $\beta9$	DENs.tv $\beta10$	Dens.tv^2 $\beta11$	Cono.tv $\beta12$	γ^0	x^2	df	p-level
Name	-18.85** (9.787)	-0.147 (0.315)	-0.413 (0.428)	0.052** (0.023)	0.687** (0.438)	1.214** (0.728)	1.727*** (0.601)	0.335 (0.439)	-0.161 (0.904)	1.179*** (0.542)	0.073** (.040)	-0.00009*** (0.00004)	-0.060* (0.043)	0.574** (0.151)	36.98	13	0.001
Sponsor	-28.12** (3.765)	0.315 (0.360)	0.221 (0.444)	-0.011 (0.029)	0.574 (0.496)	2.003*** (0.686)	0.533 (0.539)	0.046 (0.465)	-0.496 (0.982)	0.748 (0.674)	0.084** (0.051)	-0.0001** (0.00005)	0.114 (0.115)	0.140 (0.173)	33.97	13	0.001
Location	10.48** (4.208)	-0.039 (0.142)	0.274** (0.161)	0.002 (0.012)	-0.316** (0.149)	0.086 (0.247)	1.480*** (0.254)	-0.309** (0.179)	-0.047 (0.361)	1.248*** (0.230)	0.040*** (0.017)	-0.00006*** (0.00002)	-0.011 (0.026)	0.407*** (0.058)	91.17	13	0.000
Goals	-16.32 (13.72)	0.713*** (0.368)	1.103*** (0.389)	0.014 (0.023)	0.593** (0.358)	0.512 (0.576)	1.269** (0.547)	0.185 (0.414)	3.450*** (1.385)	1.495*** (0.653)	0.011 (0.049)	-0.000006 (0.000058)	0.010 (0.115)	0.406*** (0.138)	45.66	13	0.000
Chief executive	-16.58*** (4.133)	0.169* (0.122)	-0.238* (0.166)	0.017** (0.009)	0.132 (0.143)	0.815*** (0.235)	1.386*** (0.217)	-0.247* (0.161)	0.154 (0.392)	1.119*** (0.197)	0.061*** (0.016)	-0.00007*** (0.00002)	-0.023 (0.025)	0.530*** (0.053)	137.63	13	0.000
Structure	-17.88*** (4.834)	0.224* (0.156)	0.410** (0.174)	0.010 (0.012)	1.138*** (0.199)	0.346* (0.244)	0.031*** (0.003)	0.023 (0.027)	2.978*** (0.655)	2.576*** (0.334)	0.061*** (0.019)	-0.00006*** (0.00002)	-0.374*** (0.070)	1.231*** (0.107)	177.67	13	0.000
Client groups	43.55 (57.17)	0.517 (1.179)	0.945 (1.260)	-0.006 (0.086)	3.983 (3.479)	1.229 (5.269)	-0.156 (3.546)	0.895 (3.291)	-2.097 (4.129)	2.096 (2.550)	-0.221 (0.197)	0.0002 (0.0002)	0.116 (0.339)	0.385 (0.551)	19.82	13	0.100
Conditions of service	2.695* (1.785)	0.237 (0.616)	-0.277 (0.867)	-0.003 (0.053)	-0.037 (0.658)	-1.503 (1.344)	-0.470 (1.546)	1.067 (1.027)	3.927** (2.085)	1.927** (1.070)	-0.177** (0.085)	0.0002** (0.0008)	0.195 (0.156)	0.016 (0.295)	13.81	13	0.387
Service area	-0.867 (1.792)	0.274 (0.474)	-0.438 (0.693)	0.027 (0.035)	0.059 (0.537)	0.177 (0.822)	1.015 (0.849)	-0.113 (0.654)	-0.097 (1.381)	0.746 (0.813)	-0.031 (0.063)	0.00002 (0.0006)	0.068 (0.152)	0.288* (0.208)	9.78	13	0.712

*p < .10; **p < .05; ***p < .01.

and resource concentration — in order to rule out confounding due to environmental change.

In order to account for the effects of founding characteristics and environmental changes over time simultaneously, we used a more general form of the model in equation 1 and controlled for OFY, RES, density, and resource concentration as time-varying covariates in a model of the form:

$$r(t) = \exp\{\beta_o + \sum_i \beta_i X_i + \sum_j \beta_j X_j(\tau)\} \; \exp(\gamma_o t) \qquad [2]$$

where the X_js are the time-varying control variables. Table 8.2 presents the parameter estimates and standard errors for the various rates of change.

The results in Table 8.2 show that while the Gompertz models of the rates of change for service area, client groups, and conditions of service were not significant compared to constant rate models ($p > .05$), the remaining six models of rates of change for name, sponsor, location, goals, chief executive, and structure were all highly significant. An examination of the parameter estimates for these six models showed that of all the founding conditions the patterns for OFY, RES, and density are the strongest. The effects of OFY on name change, goal change, and structure change are positive and significant. But for location change, the effect of OFY is negative and significant. Generally, these findings do not support our argument that organizations founded in favorable institutional environments have lower rates of change, with the exception of location change. The effects of RES on rates of name change, sponsor change, chief executive change, and structure change are all positive and significant. These results are consistent with our expectation that unfavorable conditions in the institutional environment at founding lead to higher rates of change.

Our argument for density proposed that because of competition effects, high density at founding would be associated with higher rates of change. The results in Table 8.2 provide strong support for this argument. They show that the higher the density at founding, the higher the rates of change for name, location, goals, chief executive, and structure.

The overall pattern of findings for resource concentration, board size, and form, while not as strong as for OFY, RES, and density, provide partial support for our arguments. The parameter estimates for resource concentration at founding are significant for rates of location and chief executive change. In both cases, the signs are negative, which is consistent with our arguments. For board size, the findings show that having a larger board at founding is associated with higher rates of name and chief executive change, which is also consistent with expectations.[2] Finally, the results also show that being founded as a specialist is associated with higher rates of change for goals, chief executive, and structure, though for the last two types of change, the effects are only marginally significant ($p < .10$). Being founded as a generalist had a positive effect on rates of change in location, goals, and structure and a negative effect on rate of chief executive change. These results provide some support for the argument that organizations founded as specialists have higher rates of change because of greater vulnerability to environmental pressures. However, the argument that organizations founded as generalists have lower rates of change is generally not supported, with the exception of rate of chief executive change.

Although not of central theoretical concern here, it is interesting that some of the control variable also affected rates of change. Specifically, OFY had positive effects on rates of change in goals and structure and RES had positive effects on rates of change in name, location, goals, chief executive, and structure. This suggests that while both favorable and unfavorable institutional environmental changes increase rates of change in organizational features, the effects of unfavorable institutional changes are more comprehensive. This is in line with our findings reported in earlier research that changes in the institutional environment positively affect rates of change in organizations (Singh et al., in press). This generally appears to support the argument that organizations attempt to align their structures with the institutional environment (Meyer & Rowan, 1977).

The effects of changes in density over time are also interesting. Based on earlier arguments and results (Hannan & Freeman, 1988; Singh et al., in press; Tucker, Singh, Meinhard, & House, 1988), we modeled curvilinear effects of time-varying density on rates of change. The findings clearly indicate curvilinear effects of density on rates of change for name, sponsor, location, chief executive, and structure, with an initially increasing and then decreased effect. This suggests that increasing density increases rates of organizational change only up to a certain point. After that, increasing density has the effect of lowering rates of organizational change. While these findings are similar to our earlier findings on the effects of change in density over time on the death rates of VSSOs (Tucker, Singh, Meinhard, & House, 1988), they are not in line with arguments that the effects of low levels of density are positive because of mutualism, but the effects of high density levels are negative because of competition (Barnett & Carroll, 1987; Hannan & Freeman, 1988). Neither are they in line with the view that, because the effects of increasing density are strictly competitive (Barnett & Amburgey, Chapter 4, this volume), it is reasonable to expect, based on conventional thought, that under conditions of increasing density, organizations will be more adaptive in their behavior. One plausible interpretation is that organizational change, as a means of dealing with increasing competition, is a viable option only up to a certain point. Under conditions of intense competition, other more mutualistic forms of behavior, such as cooperation, are more useful. The question of how change in density over time affects organizational behavior in general is one that requires much additional research.

DISCUSSION

This chapter has presented results from an investigation of organizational imprinting in a population of voluntary social service organizations. The central theoretical thrust was to study the effects of the founding conditions on organizational change.

The results show relatively strong patterns for the effects of founding conditions on rates of change. Being founded in favorable or unfavorable institutional environments, and under conditions of high density, generally increases rates of change. Being founded in concentrated environments decreases rates of location and chief executive change. Organizations founded as specialists had increased rates of change in goals, chief executive, and structure, though the evidence for the last two changes is only marginal. The results for being founded as a generalist are mixed, with rates of change in location, goals, and structure being increased and rate of chief executive change being decreased. Finally, organizations founded with larger boards have increased rates of name and chief executive change.

Estimates of the effects of specific environmental and organizational characteristics show partial support for our arguments. On the one hand, the analyses strongly support our arguments concerning the effects of unfavorable institutional environments and dense environments on organizational rates of change. Though not as strong, the findings for the effects of resource concentration and board size are also in accord with our arguments. On the other hand, our arguments concerning the effects on rates of change of favorable institutional environments and organizational form are not supported by the analysis.

For organizations founded in favorable institutional environments, the findings generally show increased rates of change. This is opposite to our expectations. Since being founded in an unfavorable institutional environment also increased rates of change, this finding is puzzling. One possible explanation can be derived by recalling that organizational change can be expected to occur in most organizations due to the impact of environmental turbulence and change (Singh et al., in press). Consequently, the real question is not whether organizational change will occur, but whether the types of change made will differ depending upon the nature of the institutional environment at founding. Examination of the findings in Table 8.2 does show differences in the types of changes made. Generally speaking, being founded in a favorable institutional environment results in more core changes (e.g., changes in goals and structure), whereas being founded in an unfavorable institutional environment results in more peripheral changes (e.g., changes in sponsor and chief executive. For elaboration, see Hannan & Freeman, 1984; Singh, House, & Tucker, 1986, particularly pp. 60-61). A reason for this may be that, because it is easier to found organizations in favorable institutional environments (Tucker, Singh, Meinhard, & House, 1988), they come into existence more quickly, in a relatively unplanned or "premature" state. Subsequently, they tend to have to make more fundamental changes in order to survive. Alternatively, the founding processes for organizations created under unfavorable institutional conditions are more deliberate because the environment is more hostile. Therefore, the changes such organizations have to make in order to survive tend to be more peripheral. This points to the need for research dealing not only with the nature and source of organizational change but also, simultaneously, with its timing and subsequent effects on the life chances of organizations.

The findings for organizational form are that being founded as a generalist usually has a positive effect on rates of change. The effects on rates of change of being founded as a specialist organization are not strong enough to permit a meaningful systematic claim. These findings are not in accord with our arguments, which proposed that being founded as a specialist would increase rates of change and being founded as a generalist would decrease them. A possible interpretation is that generalist organizations, because they are more diverse and interact more comprehensively with the environment, are more likely to be under pressure to change.[3] Obviously, additional research is required to clarify this issue.

The findings of this research are subject to certain limitations. As noted earlier, voluntary social service organizations are a fairly unique form, thus the results reported here are not necessarily generalizable to other populations. Also, the time period covered, 13 years, is relatively short. This made it impossible to disentangle what may be short-term imprinting effects of founding conditions from more long-term effects. These limitations point to the need for similar studies in diverse populations, covering longer periods of time.

Since the issue of imprinting and organizational change has not been investigated in this manner by other researchers, it is not possible to compare our findings with those of other studies. Nonetheless, we think that the general finding of this study that organizations are imprinted by founding conditions with propensities to change has two significant implications. First, this study showed stronger effects on rates of change for environmental conditions at founding than for founding organizational characteristics. This aligns with Stinchcombe's (1965) general expectation that organizations are imprinted with the social conditions extant at the time of their founding and supports earlier findings by Kimberly (1975, 1979) and by Meyer and Brown (1977). Similar to what has been discovered for organizational disbandings, it appears from the findings of this research that progress in constructing theories aimed at generating comprehensive explanations of organizational change requires contending simultaneously with the effects of events that occurred earlier in the organization's life, as well as with changes in current environmental threats and opportunities.

Second, the findings of this research imply a refinement of Hannan and Freeman's (1984) argument that inertia—that is, the tendency of organizations to resist change—occurs as a consequence of environmental selection pressures. According to Hannan and Freeman, selection processes in modern societies favor organizations with high reliability and high accountability. A fundamental requirement for reliability and accountability is that organizational structures be highly reproducible, which is achieved through the process of institutionalization. While institutionalization economizes on the costs of collective action by giving the organization a taken-for-granted character, it also makes it resistant to change. Therefore, environmental selection processes favor organizations with higher inertia. We found in this research that whether or not organizational change occurs is influenced, in part, by founding conditions. This suggests that organizational imprinting is another source of inertia in populations of organizations, and that incorporating it into future studies will help extend understanding of conditions under which inertia occurs.

NOTES

1. Our discussion and description of the measurement of rates of organizational change is based on an earlier paper by Singh et al. (1988). Descriptions of the measurement of the variables of form, board size, resource concentration, and institutional environment are also based on earlier papers (see Singh, House, & Tucker, 1986; Singh, Tucker, & House, 1986; Tucker et al., 1990; Tucker, Singh, Meinhard, & House, 1988).

2. These findings are not as strong as those reported in earlier research, where we found that board size at founding had a significant, positive effect on rates of change for name, sponsor, location, service area, goals, conditions of service, chief executive, and structure (Singh et al., in press). Significantly, the models of rates of change derived in this earlier study were not as fully specified as the models derived in this study, which suggests revisions to our earlier conclusions.

3. The particular findings for generalists are that rates of change are positive for location, goals, and structure, but are negative for chief executive. This finding for chief executive change is interesting in light of arguments that change in chief executive is one of the more important ways organizations adapt to changing environments (Pfeffer & Salancik, 1978). A possible interpretation is that since we are dealing here with the overall form of the organization and, overall, generalists are more adaptive than specialists, the significance of chief executive change as an adaptive change varies in importance according to organizational form, meaning that, all other things being equal, the higher the level of generalism, the lower the level of executive change. Our findings for specialists and generalists, though not strong, are consistent with this argument.

REFERENCES

Aldrich, H. E. (1979). *Organizations and environments.* Englewood Cliffs, NJ: Prentice-Hall.

Aldrich, H., & Auster, E. (1986). Even dwarfs started small: Liabilities of size and age and their strategic implications. In B. Staw & L. L. Cummings (Eds.), *Research in organizational behavior* (Vol. 8, pp. 165-198). Greenwich, CT: JAI.

Astley, W. G. (1985). The two ecologies: Population and community perspectives on organizational evolution. *Administrative Science Quarterly, 30,* 224-241.

Barnett, W. P., & Carroll, G. R. (1987). Competition and mutualism among early telephone companies. *Administrative Science Quarterly, 32,* 400-421.

Best, R. S. (1974). Youth policy. In G. B. Doern & V. S. Wilson (Eds.), *Issues in Canadian public policy* (pp. 137-165). Toronto: Macmillan.

Boeker, W. (1988). Organizational origins: Entrepreneurial and environmental imprinting at the time of founding. In G. R. Carroll (Ed.), *Ecological models of organizations* (pp. 33-51). Cambridge, MA: Ballinger.

Brittain, J. W., & Freeman, J. (1980). Organizational proliferation and density-dependent selection: Organizational evolution in the semiconductor industry. In J. R. Kimberly & R. H. Miles (Eds.), *The organizational life cycle* (pp. 291-338). San Francisco: Jossey-Bass.

Carroll, G. R., & Delacroix, J. (1982). Organizational mortality in the newspaper industries of Argentina and Ireland: An ecological approach. *Administrative Science Quarterly, 27,* 169-198.

Carroll, G. R., & Huo, Y. P. (1986). Organizational task and institutional environments in evolutionary perspective: Findings from the local newspaper industry. *American Journal of Sociology, 91,* 838-873.

Daft, R. L. (1983). *Organization theory and design.* New York: West.

Delacroix, J., & Carroll, G. R. (1983). Organizational foundings: An ecological study of the newspaper industries of Argentina and Ireland. *Administrative Science Quarterly, 28,* 274-291.

Delacroix, J., Swaminathan, A., & Solt, M. (1989). Density dependence versus population dynamics: An ecological study of failings in the California wine industry. *American Sociological Review, 54*, 245-262.

DiMaggio, P. J., & Powell, W. W. (1983). The iron cage revisited: Institutional isomorphism and collective rationality in organizational fields. *American Sociological Review, 48*, 147-160.

Economic Council of Canada. (1976). *People and jobs: A study of the Canadian labour market.* Ottawa: Information Canada.

Economic Council of Canada. (1977). *Into the 80s.* Ottawa: Information Canada.

Freeman, J. H., Carroll, G. R., & Hannan, M. T. (1983). The liability of newness: Age dependence in organizational death rates. *American Sociological Review, 48*, 692-710.

Hannan, M. T. (1986). *A model of competitive and institutional processes in organizational ecology* (Technical Report 86-13). Ithaca, NY: Cornell University, Department of Sociology.

Hannan, M. T., & Freeman, J. (1977). The population ecology of organizations. *American Journal of Sociology, 82*, 929-964.

Hannan, M. T., & Freeman, J. (1984). Structural inertia and organizational change. *American Sociological Review, 49*, 149-164.

Hannan, M. T., & Freeman, J. (1987). The ecology of organizational founding rates: The dynamics of foundings of American labor unions, 1836-1975. *American Journal of Sociology, 92*, 910-943.

Hannan, M. T., & Freeman, J. (1988). Density dependence in the growth of organizational populations. In G. R. Carroll (Ed.), *Ecological models of organizations* (pp. 7-31). Cambridge, MA: Ballinger.

Hannan, M. T., & Freeman, J. (1989). *Organizational ecology.* Cambridge, MA: Harvard University Press.

Hawley, A. H. (1986). *Human ecology: A theoretical essay.* Chicago: University of Chicago Press.

Houston, L. F. (1972). The flowers of power: A critique of OFY and LIP programmes. *Our Generation, 7*, 52-61.

Kimberly, J. R. (1975). Environmental constraints and administrative structure: A comparative analysis of rehabilitation organizations. *Administrative Science Quarterly, 20*, 1-9.

Kimberly, J. R. (1979). Issues in the creation of organizations: Initiation, innovation, and institutionalization. *Academy of Management Journal, 22*, 437-457.

Loney, M. (1977). The political economy of citizen participation. In L. Panitch (Ed.), *The Canadian state: Political economy and political power* (pp. 346-372). Toronto: University of Toronto Press.

McKeough, W. D. (1975). *Ontario budget 1975.* Toronto: Ministry of Treasury, Economics and Intergovernmental Affairs.

McKeough, W. D. (1976). *Ontario budget 1976.* Toronto: Ministry of Treasury, Economics and Intergovernmental Affairs.

Meyer, J. W., & Rowan, B. (1977). Institutionalized organizations: Formal structures as myth and reality. *American Journal of Sociology, 83*, 340-363.

Meyer, M. W., & Brown, M. C. (1977). The process of bureaucratization. *American Journal of Sociology, 83*, 364-385.

Miller, F. S. (1980). *Ontario budget 1980.* Toronto: Ministry of Treasury and Economics.

Pennings, J. M. (1980). Environmental influences on the creation process. In J. R. Kimberly & R. H. Miles (Eds.), *The organizational life cycle* (pp. 135-160). San Francisco: Jossey-Bass.

Pfeffer, J., & Salancik, G. R. (1978). *The external control of organizations.* New York: Harper & Row.

Puckett, T., & Tucker, D. J. (1976). Hard times for Ontario's social services. *Canadian Welfare, 52*, 8-11.

Scott, W. R. (1983). The organization of environments: Network, cultural, and historical elements. In J. W. Meyer & W. R. Scott (Eds.), *Organizational environments* (pp. 155-175). Beverly Hills, CA: Sage.

Scott, W. R. (1986). *Organizations: Rational, natural, and open systems* (2nd ed.). Englewood Cliffs, NJ: Prentice-Hall.

Singh, J. V., House, R. J., & Tucker, D. J. (1986). Organizational change and organizational mortality. *Administrative Science Quarterly, 31*, 587-611.

Singh, J. V., Tucker, D. J., & House, R. J. (1986). Organizational legitimacy and the liability of newness. *Administrative Science Quarterly, 31*, 171-193.

Singh, J. V., Tucker, D. J., & Meinhard A. (1988, August). *Are voluntary organizations structurally inert? Exploring an assumption in organizational ecology.* Paper presented at the annual meetings of the Academy of Management, Anaheim, CA.

Singh, J. V., Tucker, D. J., & Meinhard, A. G. (in press). Institutional change and ecological dynamics. In W. W. Powell & P. J. DiMaggio (Eds.), *The new institutionalism in organizational analysis.* Chicago: University of Chicago Press.

Stinchcombe, A. L. (1965). Social structure and organizations. In J. G. March (Ed.), *Handbook of organizations* (pp. 142-193). Chicago: Rand McNally.

Tolbert, P., & Zucker, L. G. (1983). Institutional sources of change in the formal structures of organizations: The diffusion of civil service reform. *Administrative Science Quarterly, 28*, 22-39.

Tucker, D. J. (1981). Voluntary auspices and the behavior of social service organizations. *Social Service Review, 55*, 605-627.

Tucker, D. J., Singh, J. V., & Meinhard, A. G. (1988). *Founding conditions, environmental selection and organizational mortality.* Unpublished manuscript, McMaster University, School of Social Work.

Tucker, D. J., Singh, J. V., & Meinhard, A. (1990). Organizational form, population dynamics, and institutional change: A study of founding patterns of voluntary organizations. *Academy of Management Journal, 33*, 151-178.

Tucker, D. J., Singh, J. V., Meinhard, A. G., & House, R. J. (1988). Ecological and institutional sources of change in organizational populations. In G. Carroll (Ed.), *Ecological models of organizations* (pp. 127-151). Cambridge, MA: Ballinger.

Tuma, N. (1980). *Invoking RATE.* Menlo Park, CA: SRI International.

Usher, J. M. (1989). *Exploring the role of density-dependent organizational change in population-level change.* Unpublished manuscript, University of Alberta, Faculty of Business.

Wharf, B., & Carter, N. (1972). *Planning for social services: Canadian experiences.* Ottawa: Canadian Council on Social Development.

9

Organizational Adaptation, Environmental Selection, and Random Walks

DANIEL A. LEVINTHAL

An important debate in the organizational literature has addressed the relative importance of organizational adaptation and environmental selection in determining the range of organizational structures and behaviors that we observe (Child, 1972; Hannan & Freeman, 1977, 1984; Romanelli & Tushman, 1986; Singh, House, & Tucker, 1986). Contingency theory, which for many years had been the dominant paradigm in explaining the variation of organizational structures across environments, emphasizes the role of management in effecting organizational change (Lawrence & Lorsch, 1967; Thompson, 1967). More recent discussions of adaptation processes offer a less intentionally rational vision of managerial behavior (Levitt & March, 1988; March, 1981). Nevertheless, both models of adaptive learning and contingency theory contrast with an ecological perspective that postulates that organizations themselves are largely inert and that change occurs at the population level through selection processes (Hannan & Freeman, 1977). For the most part, this contrast between adaptation and selection has been at a theoretical level (Astley & Van de Ven, 1983). Since the effects of both adaptation and selection processes on the observed characteristics of a population of organizations are quite complex, in order to develop further insight into the role of these processes a simple analytical model is developed that allows us to derive the empirical implications of adaptation and selection processes for the pattern of survival for a population of organizations.

Author's Note: I thank Glenn Carroll, Mark Fichman, Jim March, Steve Mezias, Jerry Ross, Jitendra Singh, and Brian Uzzi for comments on a prior draft of this chapter.

In developing such a model, it is important that the underlying assumptions be sound and that the model generate results consistent with the existing set of empirical results regarding the survival patterns over time of organizations. One of the robust findings regarding the pattern of organizational survival is that the rate of organizational dissolution declines with an organization's age (Carroll, 1983; Carroll & Delacroix, 1982; Freeman, Carroll, & Hannan, 1983). While there is some evidence that organizations may experience a brief "honeymoon period" in which the initial probability of dissolution is low (Aldrich & Staber, 1983; Carroll & Huo, 1985; Fichman & Levinthal, 1988; King & Wicker, 1988; Singh, Tucker, & House, 1986), it is clear that there is a tendency for the death rate to decline over time and that it typically asymptotes to a low level. This negative duration dependence is referred to in the literature as the "liability of newness" (Stinchcombe, 1965).

In addition to developing a model that generates results that are consistent with what we think we know about survival patterns of organizations, it would be desirable for such an analysis to suggest new hypotheses that will advance the current literature. In particular, much of the discussion of the importance of adaptation versus selection processes has been polemical in nature. An important exception to this is the work of Singh, House, and Tucker (1986), who have examined the effects of organizational changes on the likelihood of organizational survival for a population of voluntary social service organizations. They directly measured various organizational changes, such as change in organizational goals or chief executive, and statistically estimated the impact of these changes on organizational death rates. Such an analysis requires more detailed information than is usually available from archival sources. This poses a serious problem for researchers using an ecological perspective, since they often must track populations of organizations over considerable periods of time. If, however, adaptation and selection processes resulted in qualitatively different patterns of survival of organizations over time, then the two theories could be tested in the absence of such direct measures. In the context of the analytic model developed here, such a test is derived.

A canonical learning model is developed in order to represent adaptation processes. This, in turn, is embedded in an environment that selects out poorly performing organizations. In particular, the learning model uses the T-maze decision problem under stochastic reward that has formed the basis for much of the research on learning theory (Bower & Hilgard, 1981). Pure selection processes are modeled by assuming that some attribute of the organization is stable over time and differential selection rates occur as a result of variation in this attribute in the population of organizations. In the context of the simple model developed here, the attribute over which organizations vary is the decision rule. Organizations are considered to "die" when their stock of capital drops below some threshold level. A cohort of such organizations is analyzed in which particular organizations may have different initial endowments of wealth and different decision rules, and vary in their adaptation rates. In particular, the focus of the analysis is on a comparison of the failure rate of organizations that do not adapt to their environments with the failure rate for organizations that do adapt to their environments.

MODEL STRUCTURE

Lave and March (1975) characterize adaptive rationality as learning in a regular manner from trial and error: "An action is taken; the world responds to the action; and the individual infers something about the world and then adapts his behavior so as to secure desirable responses" (p. 248). The standard learning paradigm is the T-maze problem. Imagine a mouse placed in a maze in the shape of a T. If the mouse turns left at the top of the T and enters a trap door, it receives a reward, which we shall label W_L. Alternatively, if it turns right and enters the trap door on that side, it receives W_R. Presumably, the mouse will learn to turn in the direction of the more attractive reward (for instance, cheese rather than nothing). In particular, if the mouse turned left and received the desirable reward, then the probability of its turning left next time is assumed to be characterized as follows:

$$P_L(t) = (1 - \alpha)^* P_L(t - 1) + \alpha^* 1$$

where $P_L(t - 1)$ is the prior probability of turning left and α, where $0 \le \alpha \le 1$, represents the learning rate. For instance, if $\alpha = 0$, then the mouse's behavior remains constant despite the positive outcome (i.e., $P_L(t) = P_L(t - 1)$). Alternatively, if $\alpha = 1$, then, with certainty, the mouse will turn left next time given its success during the previous time period. In contrast, if the mouse turned left and did not receive the desirable reward, the probability of its turning left the next time is characterized by the following equation:[1]

$$P_L(t) = (1 - \alpha)^* P_L(t - 1)$$

An analogous set of learning rules are assumed to hold with respect to feedback from the environment subsequent to a decision to turn right. Clearly, this is a very stylized representation of a learning process. However, over a wide variety of experimental settings, this model has been shown to represent well not only the behavior of mice, but the behavior of well-educated human decision makers (Bower & Hilgard, 1981; Kintsch, 1970). Furthermore, this structure has also formed the basis for both theoretical and empirical models of organizational behavior (Cyert & March, 1963; Levinthal & March, 1981).

Most learning situations of interest involve a great deal of uncertainty. Not only are outcomes a function of one's decision and the nature of the environment, often they are also a function of purely chance events. To reflect this, a common enrichment of the above model is to make the reward from the environment stochastic. Let P_E represent the probability that the desirable reward is present on the left side of the T-maze and $1 - P_E$ that it is present on the right side. Given this structure, one can show that over time a decision maker who obeyed the above learning rules would turn left with probability P_E. This result is known in the learning theory literature as *probability matching* and, indeed, the behavior of both mice and human subjects has been shown to have this property (Bower & Hilgard, 1981, pp. 223-224). This tendency toward probability matching does not correspond to payoff-maximizing behavior, which would consist of choosing each time the direction that yields the higher expected outcome. Since P_E is assumed to be constant over time, payoff-maximizing behavior would result in the same decision each time.

This two-state representation of the environment has been used not only by learning theorists, but also by researchers using ecological models of selection to illustrate the notion of grain and the desirability of specialist and generalist strategies:

> Consider an environment which can take on only two states and in every period falls in state one with probability p and in state two with probability $q = (1 - p)$. Assume further that variations in environmental states are Bernoulli trials (independent from period to period). For this situation Levins (1962, 1968) has shown that optimal niche width depends on p and the "distance" between the two states of the environment. (Hannan & Freeman, 1977, p. 950)

Since each organization faces two environments, its fitness depends on fitness in this pair of environments. Hannan and Freeman summarize the ability of the organization to succeed in the two environments by plotting the payoffs in state 1 and state 2 on a graph, the axes of which are the payoffs (i.e., fitness) in state 1 and state 2. In the decision context developed here, the plot would consist of a straight line with a slope of -1. By varying its probability of turning left, the organization can achieve any point on this line. Hannan and Freeman (1977) refer to this set of points as a "fitness set." They are interested in which of these points will be favored by natural selection. To address this, they introduce the additional concept of grain. An environment is viewed as "fine-grained when the typical durations in states are short relative to the lifetime of organizations" (p. 952). Otherwise, the environment is viewed as coarse-grained. Coarse-grained changes would correspond to changes such as a change in the regulatory environment. Most products and services would be viewed as facing a fine-grained environment. If the environment is fine-grained, organizations experience a large number of trials with different states of the environment, and their fit with the environment can be represented by their average performance. Thus the fit of a given strategy in a fine-grained environment is simply the probability of state 1, P_E, times the payoff in that state for a given strategy plus the probability of state 2, $1 - P_E$, times the payoff in that state for the same strategy. In our context, we can express this as follows:

$$\text{fit} = P_E * P_L * W_1 + (1 - P_E) * (1 - P_L) * W_2$$

In this structure, as long as $P_E * W_1 \neq (1 - P_E) * W_2$, specialism is the preferred strategy. In particular, if $W_1 = W_2$, then $P_E > 1/2$ implies that the optimal strategy is $P_L = 1$ and $P_E < 1/2$ implies that the optimal strategy is $P_L = 0$. When $P_E = .5$, all values of P_L yield the same payoff and, hence, fitness.

Since specialism is the optimal strategy, adaptive behavior, which has been shown to lead to probability matching, does not maximize fitness. As Hannan and Freeman (1984) suggest, inertia — that is, a lack of adaptation — can be survival enhancing. In a world where specialism is desirable, adaptive behavior has the liability that it cannot sustain such extreme policies. Suppose that the organization "learns" that a high P_L is desirable. As long as $P_E < 1$, there is some probability that the organization will incur an unfavorable outcome given the decision to go left. When this occurs, the organization will then adapt its policy so as to decrease the probability of going left. The ideal learning process, assuming that the payoff structure is stable, would have the rate of adaptation decline with time. Early on in the learning process, the organization may be far from the appropriate strategy and a high rate of adaptation facilitates, on average, a survival-enhancing change in its policies. Later on, when the organization's policy is, on average, closer to the optimum, a lower rate of adaptation enables the organization to replicate this policy over subsequent periods. This pattern can be viewed as an increasing institutionalization of an organization's policies and suggests that if specialism is optimal, the survival rates of older organizations that are inert should be higher than those of organizations that adapt. However, this proposition is silent on whether the *cumulative* survival rate of inert organizations is higher than that of organizations that adapt to experience. Adaptive organizations may have a superior survival rate in early periods. Whether or not this holds would depend on the fitness of the policies of newly founded inert organizations.

Another common feature of adaptive learning models is that the tendency for the organization to change its current policy reflects how the organization's current performance corresponds to its aspirations (Cyert & March, 1963). Prior researchers have noted the tendency of organizations to engage in "problemistic search" (Cyert & March, 1963; Lindblom, 1959; March & Simon, 1958; Steinbruner, 1974). The organization is assumed to have a performance target, or goal, against which it compares actual performance. If the target exceeds performance, an organization searches for solutions to the problem, emphasizing immediate refinements to the current policy. Thus one may want to assume that adaptive behavior occurs only when actual performance falls short of the organization's aspiration level. Furthermore, the organization's aspiration level itself may adapt over time in response to actual performance. For simplicity, in the current analysis, such complications are ignored and the adaptive organizations are assumed to respond to all feedback, both favorable and negative, from the environment.

This discussion of organizational survival presupposes a criterion or process by which organizations fail to persist. Going back to the metaphor of a mouse choosing directions in a T-maze, we may view death as occurring when the mouse has failed to obtain food and water over some interval of time. Corporations, excluding the case of merger or acquisition, cease to exist when they are unable to meet their financial obligations to creditors. In the stylized model developed here, an organization is defined as failing if its wealth falls to zero. In keeping with this definition, successful and unsuccessful outcomes are characterized in terms of monetary units. For simplicity, we define the favorable outcome as a positive increment in wealth by one unit and an unfavorable outcome as a decrease in wealth by one unit. Thus the model assumes that the survival of the organization is tied to its performance. While this assumption is likely to be valid in many environments, Meyer and Zucker's (1989) work on permanently failing organizations indicates that this linkage between performance and survival is not universal.

In addition to realizing these changes to its wealth over time, the organization may start its life with an initial stock of capital. Companies, whether the product of an individual entrepreneur or a well-financed, venture-capital-backed enterprise, typically start with some initial commitment of financial resources (Fichman & Levinthal, 1988). Analogously, voluntary social service organizations (VSSOs) have been shown to start their lives with some initial stock of legitimacy, as evidenced by the presence of external institutional support (Singh, Tucker, & House, 1986).

ANALYSIS

The interest here is in the survival rates of populations of organizations that differ in their degree of inertia. A population of organizations that adapt their policies in response to feedback from the environment (i.e., $\alpha > 0$) is contrasted with a population of organizations that are inert (i.e., $\alpha = 0$). Figure 9.1 displays the hazard rate over time for a population of adaptive organizations in which $\alpha = .25$.[2] The data are generated by simulating the experience of a population of 10,000 organizations and calculating the hazard rate (the ratio of the number of deaths divided by the number of organizations that had survived until the prior period). In addition to specifying the learning rate, it is necessary to characterize the initial wealth endowment of the organizations. Half of the organizations are assumed to have an endowment of one unit and the other half an endowment of two units.[3] The initial value of P_L (i.e., the decision rule) is set at .5. That is, initially, the organization is equally likely to choose to go left or right. Finally, the value of the environment parameter, P_E, is set at .1.[4] We observe the classic pattern of negative duration dependence found in nearly all empirical estimates of organizational mortality (Carroll, 1983; Carroll & Delacroix, 1982; Freeman et al., 1983). It appears that as time goes on, organizations adapt their decision rules to be a more appropriate fit to the environment.

An adaptive model meets the minimal empirical test of being consistent with the observed pattern of duration dependence; however, it remains to be seen whether it provides a better explanation than a model based on selection. In order to model a selection process, the learning rates are set at 0 (i.e., $\alpha = 0$) and a distribution of decision rules is postulated for the population of organizations. There are assumed to be two types of organizations that are represented in equal numbers: one with a probability of going left of .1 and the other a probability of going left of .9. For each type of organization, half have an initial endowment of one unit and half an endowment of two units. Figure 9.2 indicates the hazard rate over time for such a population. We again observe the familiar pattern of negative duration dependence. But in this case, the forces generating this pattern of negative duration dependence appear to

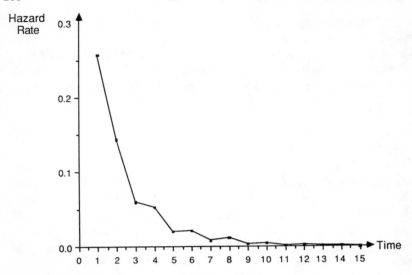

Figure 9.1. Hazard rate under adaptation. $N = 10,000$; $\alpha = .25$; $P_L = .5$.

be quite different. An organization with a decision rule that is a poor fit with the environment — that is, a probability value that is far from 0 given that $P_E < .5$ — would tend to be selected out in early periods. As a result, those organizations that have survived for several periods are more likely to be organizations with decision rules that are a good fit with the environment and, as a result, the hazard rate would tend to be lower in these later periods. However, the results are rather discouraging with respect to the agenda of generating differentiating empirical implications from adaptation and selection processes. While the two processes do generate different quantitative predictions, the differences in the actual magnitudes are not robust and are sensitive to the distribution of decision rules postulated for the population of inert organizations.

One response to the similarity in predictions of the two conceptually distinct processes would be to label this an unfortunate (at least from the researcher's perspective) case of equifinality. An alternative response is to ask whether in fact there is some third factor that is generating this pattern of negative duration dependence. As a suggestive test as to whether there is any basis for such an explanation, consider the results for a population of organizations that are inert and homogeneous. That is, neither adaptive learning nor selection is occurring. Figure 9.3 presents the results of such a run where the decision for all organizations is set at $P_L = .5$. Organizations

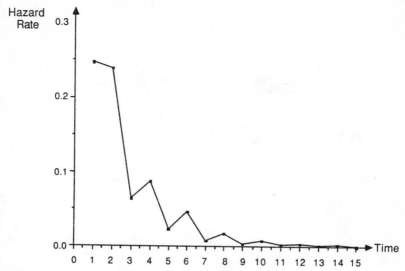

Figure 9.2. Hazard rate under selection. $N = 10,000$; $\alpha = 0$; $P_L = .1$ and $.9$.

are identical and the choices they make each period are purely random. Despite the total lack of intelligence, whether acquired by the organization through adaptation or obtained at the population level through selection, we can observe the familiar pattern of negative duration dependence. Neither adaptation nor selection processes are necessary to generate the qualitative pattern of organizational mortality that has formed one important baseline model for ecological analysis (Carroll, 1984, p. 85). The need for a third, perhaps more fundamental explanation, appears compelling.

In fact, the explanation is quite simple. Consider an organization with an initial capital stock of one unit. If the organization is unlucky, its capital stock will be reduced by one unit and it will not survive. Alternatively, if the organization is lucky in the initial period, not only does it not die, but its capital stock is actually increased by one unit. This, in turn, implies that this organization faces a low probability of dying in the next few periods. More generally, conditional on survival, the estimate of the capital stock increases. This result would hold for any model in which an organization's probability of survival is related to its performance. A high capital stock, in turn, buffers the organization from death, regardless of the wisdom of its decision rule. The apparent selection or adaptation process indicated in Figure 9.3 reflects the outcome of a series of random "successes" and "failures" and, most important, how survival up to a given duration is informative about the likely

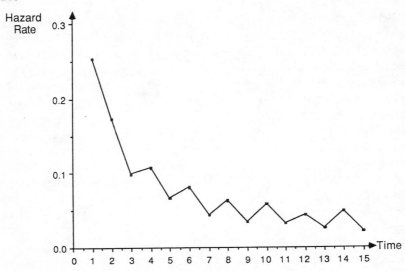

Figure 9.3. Hazard rate under random model. $N = 10,000$; $\alpha = 0$; $P_L = .5$.

relationship between the number of prior successful and unsuccessful outcomes. This relationship, in turn, has important implications for the probability of survival. Both adaptation and selection processes can influence the characteristics of the population and, as a result, organizations' life chances, but these effects pale in comparison to the purely stochastic influences of changes in wealth as an explanation of the pattern of organizational survival. Unaided intuition might suggest that if organizations did not adapt and there were no variation in the population, the hazard rate would be constant over time. This is far from the case.

The characterization presented here of largely random changes in wealth driving the pattern of survival rates is quite close to one of the summary conclusions drawn by Carroll (1983) in his extensive review of empirical work on patterns of organizational mortality:

> Several studies also point out that firms dying at young ages frequently have never experienced success. Typically, these firms did not experience a change in fortune from good times to bad times; they simply held out through bad times as long as possible. (p. 304)

Similarly, in the simulation results, early failures result in death, whereas early success results in an increase in the capital stock that, in turn, buffers the organization in future periods.

Before dismissing these results as an artifact of a highly stylized model, one should consider the survival probability of organizations with varying degrees of wealth. Take the example of universities, where there literally exist endowments. Suppose that Harvard University engaged in a radical restructuring, such as instituting a policy of no formal courses and adopting a tutorial system, or admitting half of the students at random. What would be the survival implications of such a change? We would suggest that these changes would not have any immediate survival implications, that Harvard would have to engage in inappropriate behavior for decades in order to find its survival in question. Contrast this scenario with a small, private college with a modest endowment. The wisdom of the decisions made by its administrators will have far greater survival implications than will the decisions made by Harvard's administrators. For one university survival is a meaningful question, for the other it is not.

The notion that some organizations may be buffered from selection pressures has been noted previously in the organizational theory literature. Aldrich (1979) suggests that "organizational forms may be insulated against environmental pressures because of government protection or regulation, support from powerful elites, or shared beliefs and values that selectively screen out potentially disruptive external events" (p. 196). Indeed, Aldrich cites the particular example of "private universities with substantial endowments [that] have been able to resist pressures to modify their traditional practices regarding student-teacher ratios, course offerings, and use of the summer session's slack time more easily than publicly supported universities" (p. 196). Size per se has been argued to buffer organizations from selection pressures. Pfeffer and Salancik (1978) state that "growth enhances the organization's survival value, then, by providing a cushion, or slack, against organizational failure" (p. 139). The notion that some organizations may be buffered from selection pressures is a principal focus of Miner, Amburgey, and Stearns (1987), who define an organizational buffer "as an intervening factor that shields an organization from external threats such that the organization gains a lower intensity of selection than would otherwise have occurred" (p. 2). They identify two basic classes of buffering mechanisms: those that are resource based and those that are institutional. In the former case, the basis of protection is access to factors of production or technology, while in the latter case it is based on factors "such as legitimacy and professional norms, or more formal structural arrangements such as regulation or licensing requirements" (pp. 2-3). The analysis developed here suggests that buffering may also result from the chance occurrence of prior successes.

The ability of a random walk on wealth levels to represent the observed pattern of duration dependence is analogous to the results regarding the ability of stochastic growth models to explain the observed distribution of firm sizes (Ijiri & Simon, 1977). From an initial condition of symmetry, high levels of concentration may emerge as a result of random growth rates.[5] Scherer (1980) summarizes this line of research as follows:

> Why do concentrated firm size distributions arise from initial conditions that seemingly give each firm an equal chance? The answer, in a word, is luck. Some firms will inevitably enjoy a run of luck, experiencing several years of rapid growth in close succession. Once the most fortunate firms climb well ahead of the pack, it is difficult for laggards to rally and rectify the imbalance for, by definition, each firm — large or small — has an equal chance of growing by a given percentage amount. (p. 146)

As Scherer suggests, there are several "aspects of business enterprises in which luck plays a significant role — e.g., in the hiring of key executives, in research and new product development decisions, in legal disputes involving critical patents, in the choice of advertising campaign theme, or in a thousand and one other decisions among attractive but uncertain alternative courses of action" (p. 147).

The fact that a random walk over wealth levels can replicate the pattern of organizational mortality that we observe does not negate the possibility that processes of adaptation or selection are at work. The results do, however, imply that a pattern of negative duration dependence is not *prima facie* evidence for the importance of selection processes. Furthermore, the results suggest that management practitioners should be cautious in drawing strong lessons from the observed behavior of apparently successful organizations (Peters & Waterman, 1982). This is essentially the conclusion that March and March (1977) reach in their study of job matches, in which they find that the pattern of mobility of school superintendents across jobs is consistent with a simple Markov model in which individuals and jobs are homogeneous and changes in jobs are random:

> The normative lesson is much narrower. It is that the same behaviors, abilities, and values that produce successful careers at the top will, on the average, produce unsuccessful ones also; that little can be learned about how to administer schools by studying a successful high-level administrator that could not be learned by studying unsuccessful ones; and that the stories we tell each other about success and failure in top management, like the stories we tell about success and failure in gambling, are in large part fictions intended to reassure us about justice and encourage the young. (p. 408)

ADAPTATION VERSUS SELECTION

The prior analysis provides important insight as to how simple properties of a series of random successes and failures can generate a pattern of negative duration dependence. Yet, up to this point, the analysis has failed to provide a basis for empirically distinguishing between adaptation and selection processes. The preceding discussion of the importance of the organization's capital stock does, however, provide some suggestion as to how one might construct such a test. In prior research, all organizations that are currently active are considered to be at risk of failure. Organizations with a large capital stock are, however, as a practical matter, not at risk of failure in the current time period. Therefore, the notion of a refined risk set is introduced. An organization is defined to be in the refined risk set if its financial situation is such that it faces a real threat of failure in the current time period. This notion of a refined risk set is closely related to Miner et al.'s (1987) concept of partial selection. In their view, organizations that are buffered from the environment are subject to less intense selection pressures. Within the context of the stylized model developed here, categorizing organizations using this definition of a refined risk set is straightforward. An organization is at risk if its current capital stock is equal to one. In a more realistic setting, such a categorization becomes more difficult, but is probably still feasible. For instance, business firms could be identified by a traditional measure of financial health, such as the ratio of current liabilities to current assets. For private universities, one might use the size of the endowment, either as an absolute measure or expressed as a ratio, such as the endowment per student or endowment per employee.

This notion of a refined risk set having been introduced, it remains to be seen how it can be exploited to distinguish the effects of adaptation and selection processes. Let us consider the hazard rate with respect to the refined risk set. If all organizations are alike and their choices in each time period are purely random, then the hazard rate with respect to the refined risk set should be constant over time. In stark contrast to this, we have seen how at the *population* level such a process generates a declining hazard rate over time. Alternatively, consider the setting in which individual organizations are inert, but the population is subject to selection forces. In early time periods, having a low capital stock is more a reflection of the organization's initial endowment and the organization's luck with respect to the stochastic realizations of successful and unsuccessful outcomes. In later time periods, however, a low capital stock is likely to be more a statement about the organization itself. Older organizations that are selected out are quite likely to have a poor fit with their environments, while organizations that are selected out in earlier periods are likely just to have been unlucky. This suggests that under a selection process, the hazard rate for the refined risk set should increase over time. Finally, consider the hazard rate over time for a population of adaptive organizations. While the learning process is not perfect due to the noise in the feedback from the environment (i.e., good decisions are not always rewarded with good outcomes), there will be a general tendency for organizations to improve their fit with the environment over time. Those organizations that find themselves in the refined risk class are likely to be unlucky, both in the sense of incurring negative outcomes from the environment and in the sense of receiving misleading signals from their performance. Nevertheless, even for these unfortunate learners, there should be a general tendency to improve their decision rules over time. This suggests, in turn, that there should be a tendency for the hazard rate with respect to the refined risk class to decline with time under an adaptation process.

Figure 9.4 indicates the average propensity to choose "left" (i.e., the decision rule) for those organizations that are in the refined risk set for (a) a population of homogeneous, inert organizations; (b) a heterogeneous population of inert organizations; and (c) a population of adaptive organizations.[6] We observe qualitatively distinct patterns in the decision rule over time for the three populations. The decision for the population of homogeneous, inert organizations is constant over time. In contrast, the propensity to choose "left," the inferior choice, for a population of inert organizations subject to selection pressures tends to be relatively high. Finally, the propensity to choose "left" for adaptive organizations declines with time.[7] Of course, these predictions are made with respect to pure forms of the alternative processes in that adaptation and selection are modeled such that one occurs exclusive of the other. If, as is perhaps more realistic, both adaptation and selection processes are present, predicting the pattern of duration dependence for the refined risk set becomes considerably more complex. However, the results derived here would hold in populations in which a process of either adaptation or selection was the dominant mechanism by which the population of organizations changed.

This pattern of time dependence in the decision rule is reflected as well in the change in the hazard rate with respect to the refined risk set. Table 9.1 indicates the hazard rate with respect to the refined risk set over time. One difficulty in interpreting these results is that the number of organizations that are in the refined risk category declines sharply over time. Therefore, the empirical hazard rates for later periods are based on a smaller sample size. In order to estimate the statistical significance of the results explicitly, the

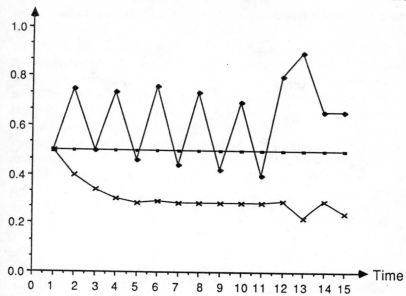

Figure 9.4. Average propensity for organizations in refined risk set. x: $\alpha = .25$; $P_L = .5$. Diamonds: $\alpha = 0$; $P_L = .1$ and $.9$. Boxes: $\alpha = 0$; $P_L = .5$.

hazard rates are compared with the expected hazard rate for Period 1. The expected hazard rate equals the probability of an unfavorable outcome for those organizations in the refined risk set. Given a decision rule of P_L, the probability of an unfavorable outcome is: $P_E(1 - P_L) + (1 - P_E)P_L$. With an equal number of organizations with $P_L = .1$ and $P_L = .9$, the average probability of failure is $.5$ under the selection process. The expected probability of failure in the first period is also $.5$ for the population of adaptive organizations, since the initial value of P_L is set at $.5$. The question is whether the hazard rate for subsequent periods is greater or less than this value.

The empirical hazard rate for the refined risk set is merely the ratio of those organizations that fail over the total number of organizations that are in the refined risk set. Let N represent the number of organizations that are in the refined risk set and K the number of those that fail. The statistical test consists of examining the likelihood that K organizations out of N would fail if the probability of failure were the Period 1 expected hazard rate. For large values of N, we can use a χ^2 test with one degree of freedom to test this relationship (DeGroot, 1975). For the population of adapting organizations, the hazard rates for Periods 2 through 8 are, at $p < .005$ level or lower, significantly

TABLE 9.1: Hazard Rate for Organizations in the Refined Risk Group

Time	Adaptive Number Failed/ Refined Risk Set	Ratio	Selection Number Failed/ Refined Risk Set	Ratio
1	2,576/5,000	.53	2,466/5,000	.49
2	1,063/2,570	.41***	1,792/2,557	.70***
3	376/1,041	.36***	267/719	.51
4	312/916	.34***	466/703	.66***
5	113/357	.32***	110/239	.46
6	117/381	.31***	217/294	.74***
7	46/147	.31***	39/80	.49
8	66/185	.36***	82/111	.74***
9	22/64	.34*	14/30	.47
10	23/78	.29***	35/51	.69**
11	8/25	.32	9/16	.56
12	14/42	.33*	13/16	.81***[a]
13	4/16	.25*[a]	3/3	1.00**[a]
14	8/27	.30*[a]	9/10	.90***[a]
15	2/18	.11***[a]	0/0	na

NOTE: The significance levels reflect the probability that the true value is .5.
a. Due to the small sample size, the significance test is based on the binomial distribution, not the X^2.
*$p < .05$; **$p < .01$; ***$p < .005$.

lower than the expected Period 1 hazard rate. With the exception of the Period 11 hazard rate, the remaining values are significantly lower than .5 at the $p < .05$ level or lower. Thus the statistical results generally confirm the prior intuition that an adaptation process generates a hazard rate with respect to the refined risk set that decreases with time.

The results are robust with respect to changes in the learning rate. At low rates of learning, the hazard rate with respect to the refined risk class is significantly lower than .5 for later time periods, but not necessarily for early time periods. For instance, when $\alpha = .05$, the hazard rates for Periods 2, 5, 7, and 9 are not significantly different from .5, while, for the remaining time periods, the hazard rate is significantly lower than .5 at the $p < .01$ level. In contrast, for high rates of learning the hazard rate in early time periods is significantly lower than .5, while for later time periods it tends not to be significantly different. For instance, when $\alpha = .5$, the hazard rates for Periods 2 through 8 are, at the $p < .01$ level, significantly lower than .5. The hazard rates for Periods 9, 11, and 13 through 15, in contrast, are not significantly different from .5. Rapid learning facilitates performance early on in the organization's life. It has, however, the liability mentioned earlier, that organizations subsequently will also rapidly unlearn in response to false signals from the environment. Organizations with slow rates of learning do not appear very adaptive in early periods of their lives, but they are more capable of retaining the intelligence acquired through adaptation.

For the selection results, all of the even-numbered time periods are, at the $p < .01$ level or lower, significantly higher than the expected Period 1 hazard rate. In contrast, only one of the odd-numbered time period rates is significantly different from the expected Period 1 hazard rate. Thus, while there is some strong evidence in support of the argument that the hazard rate with respect to the refined risk set increases over time under a selection process, this result does not appear to be robust. Indeed, this mixed result points to an important qualification with respect to the results regarding selection processes. It is always true that the proportion of the misfit organizations that are in the refined risk set increases over time. It is this phenomenon that results in the hazard rate increasing over time. If, however, misfit organizations are nearly all selected out in the initial time periods, then the proportion of organizations in the refined risk set that are misfit may actually be smaller in later periods than in early periods.

With this in mind, let us now reconsider the results in Table 9.1 for a selection process. Due to the discreteness of the payoff structure, only those organizations with an initial endowment of one unit will fail in odd-numbered time periods, whereas only those organizations with an initial endowment of two units would fail in even-numbered time periods. Therefore, the results indicate that if the initial endowment of all organizations is one unit, then the hazard rate for the refined risk set is not statistically different across time periods. In contrast, if the endowment of organizations was uniformly distributed from Period 1 to Period 3, then the results under the selection process would be statistically significant for all time periods.[8] Thus, with some minimal level of initial endowment in the population of organizations, the prediction regarding selection processes holds.

These results also appear to be robust to changes in the distribution of the decision rule across organizations. Reducing the variation in the distribution of decision rules across organizations, not surprisingly, diminishes somewhat the strength of the results regarding selection processes. With half of the organizations having a decision rule of .3 (i.e., P_L = .3) and half a decision rule of .7, three of the hazard rates with respect to the refined risk set are significantly greater than .5 ($p <$ .025) and none of the other estimated hazard rates is significantly different from .5. If, however, one increases the initial endowment level such that half the organizations have an endowment of two units and half an endowment of three units, one obtains strong results regarding the hazard rate for the refined risk set even with the reduced variation in organizational types. With these endowment levels and half the organizations having a propensity of .3 and half one of .7, the hazard rates in Periods 2 through 7 are, at the $p <$ .005 level, significantly greater than .5. Of the remaining eight time periods, three have a hazard rate significantly greater than .5 at the $p <$ .01 level and the others are not significantly different from .5.

While exploring the notion of the hazard rate with respect to a refined risk set provides an agenda for future empirical work, it is also worth considering whether any existing empirical analyses can be interpreted in this light. One such opportunity is present in the work of Singh, Tucker, and House (1986). They are concerned with the ability of VSSOs to acquire legitimacy and, in turn, other resources from their environment. One measure that Singh et al. examine is the acquisition, and possible loss, of a community directory listing. The community directory listing is an important reference source for acceptable services and is consulted by clients and referral services. Of the 389 organizations that they studied, 146 acquired community directory listings. Of these, 15 were eventually dropped from the community directory. While there was a general pattern of the hazard rate declining over time for the population as a whole, the hazard rates for those organizations that lost their community directory listings increased as a function of time. If we interpret the loss of a community directory listing as placing an organization in the refined risk set, then the results suggest a process in which the VSSOs are largely inert, but vary in their fitness to the environment.

DISCUSSION

The analysis raises two basic research questions. One is the empirical question concerning what the nature of time dependence is for the hazard rate with respect to the refined risk set. The other relates to the model itself and the possible enrichments to the model structure. In particular, this is not a true ecological model in the sense that both the behavior and survival chances of organizations are not interdependent. From an adaptation perspective, this rules out the possibility of imitation (Levitt & March, 1988). In terms of selection theory, issues of density-dependent selection processes are not addressed (Brittain & Freeman, 1980). Ignoring such issues is, however, consistent with Freeman and Hannan's (1983) initial empirical application of the population ecology approach to the restaurant industry:

> Because restaurants in a city compete for customers and staff, survival of restaurants attempting to occupy the same niche is probably not completely independent.... [However,] knowing the timing of the death of one establishment probably does not help much in predicting the dates of events for others. We assume as a first approximation that competition is diffuse, that all establishments compete for common resources but do not face strong head-on competition. (p. 1138)

In the language of economic theory, this reflects a setting of perfect competition in which the environment (i.e., market price) is independent of the behavior (i.e., output choice) of any one firm. Thus one important direction of further research would be to develop a model of a truly ecological process in which the survival probabilities of individual organizations depended on the population of organizations through density-dependent selection pressures and the opportunity for imitative behavior and processes of institutionalization is present. One could also consider the internal ecology of organizations and model a process in which individual subunits of the organization change in an adaptive manner and some core feature of the organization is stable over time and is subject to selection pressures.

The present structure does, however, provide considerable insight into the nature of selection processes. If prior success buffers an organization from selection pressures, then negative duration dependence can be expected to be observed regardless of whether or not organizations adapt to the environment or if organizations' behavior is purely random. Therefore, the existence of negative duration dependence may mean that there is a liability of newness (Stinchcombe, 1965), but the explanation may be quite different from conventional ones. A purely random process of organizational behavior, in conjunction with environmental selection, can replicate the basic stylized facts by which theoretical analyses have tended to be judged. The notion of a refined risk set is introduced as a way out of this basic indeterminacy. Indeed, we find support for the hypothesis that duration effects with respect to the refined risk class are qualitatively different under selection and adaptation processes.

One of the principal criticisms of the application of ecological theory to the study of organizations is whether biological organisms are an appropriate analogue to organizations. A particular focus of this concern is that organizations, unlike biological species, are able to change their form (Perrow, 1986). The analysis developed here points to a different distinction between biological and organizational selection processes. Human organizations are able to accumulate slack resources. In the context of corporations, this slack often takes the form of financial assets — that is, capital. Biological organisms are far less able to live off of their "fat." The reduction in selection pressures associated with the accumulation of slack resources is importantly different from what results from a benign, or resource-rich, environment. In the latter case, all organizations of a particular form benefit from the benign nature of the environment. In contrast, the accumulation of slack resources is a function not only of the nature of the environment, but of the past history of the organization. It is this history-dependent nature of selection pressures that allows for chance events, such as random changes in wealth levels, to have profound implications for the pattern of organizational mortality.

NOTES

1. For simplicity, the learning rate with respect to negative reinforcement has been defined to be the same as the learning rate with respect to positive reinforcement.

2. The results are quite robust to the particular value of the learning rates.

3. The motivation for postulating a distribution of endowments is due to the lumpiness of the payoff structure. For instance, consider organizations that have an initial endowment of one unit. Those organizations that are unsuccessful in the first period fail. The survivors, those organizations that received a favorable outcome in the first period, have a zero probability of death in the second period. Such discontinuities in the hazard rate are avoided by having two different levels of initial endowments. More substantively, prior researchers have shown that the size of organizations at founding varies considerably (Birch, 1979; Freeman et al., 1983), which lends more realism to this assumption.

4. A relatively extreme value of P_E — that is, close to 0 or 1 — makes both adaptation and selection processes more significant. Indeed, as was noted earlier, if $P_E = .5$, then the performance of organizations is independent of their behavior.

5. Much of this research adopts the assumption of Gibrat's law of proportionate growth, which states that the distribution of growth rates for each firm is the same and, in particular, is independent of both firm size and the firm's past history of growth. A stochastic process adhering to Gibrat's law generates a distribution of firm size that is lognormal. Recent work by Hannan, Ranger-Moore, and Holl (1988) further develops this line of research by introducing ecological considerations such as the carrying capacity of a niche, entries and exists, and localized competition.

6. For the populations of homogeneous, inert organizations and adaptive organizations, the initial decision rule is $P_L = .5$. For the heterogeneous population, half have a decision rule of $P_L = .1$ and half a decision rule of $P_L = .9$.

7. Under adaptation, the average propensity for the population of surviving organizations as a whole corresponds to the prediction of probability matching and reaches the value of P_E. The propensity for those organizations in the refined risk set approaches this rate, but, not surprisingly due to the fact that this set is composed of those organizations that have performed poorly, the average propensity is somewhat about the population level.

8. For Periods 2 through 11 the result is significant at the $p < .005$ level and for three of the four remaining periods at $p < .01$ level. Only in Period 14 are the results relatively weak, with a significance level of $p < .10$.

REFERENCES

Aldrich, H. E. (1979). *Organizations and environments.* Englewood Cliffs, NJ: Prentice-Hall.

Aldrich, J. E., & Staber, U. (1983). *The organizations of business interest associations* (Tech. Rep.). University of North Carolina, Chapel Hill.

Astley, W. G., & Van de Ven, A. H. (1983). Central perspectives and debates in organization theory. *Administrative Science Quarterly, 28,* 245-273.

Birch, D. (1979). *The job generation process.* Cambridge: MIT, Center for the Study of Neighborhood and Regional Change.

Bower, G. H., & Hilgard, E. R. (1981). *Theories of learning.* Englewood Cliffs, NJ: Prentice-Hall.

Brittain, J. W., & Freeman, J. (1980). Organizational proliferation and density-dependent selection: Organizational evolution in the semiconductor industry. In J. R. Kimberly & R. H. Miles (Eds.), *The organizational life cycle* (pp. 291-338). San Francisco: Jossey-Bass.

Carroll, G. R. (1983). A stochastic model of organizational mortality: Review and reanalysis. *Social Science Research, 12,* 303-329.

Carroll, G. R. (1984). Dynamics of publisher succession in newspaper organizations. *Administrative Science Quarterly, 29,* 93-113.

Carroll, G. R., & Delacroix, J. (1982). Organizational mortality in the newspaper industries of Argentina and Ireland: An ecological approach. *Administrative Science Quarterly, 27,* 169-198.

Carroll, G. R., & Huo, Y. P. (1985). *Losing by winning: The paradox of electoral success by organized labor parties in the Knights of Labor era* (Tech. Rep.). Berkeley: University of California.

Child, J. (1972). Organization structure, environment, and performance: The role of strategic choice. *Sociology, 6,* 1-22.

Cyert, R., & March, J. (1963). *Behavioral theory of the firm.* Englewood Cliffs, NJ: Prentice-Hall.

DeGroot, M. H. (1975). *Probability and statistics.* Reading, MA: Addison-Wesley.

Fichman, M., & Levinthal, D. A. (1988). *Honeymoons and the liability of adolescence: A new perspective on duration dependence in social and organizational relationships.* Paper presented at the annual meetings of the Academy of Management, Anaheim, CA.

Freeman, J., Carroll, G. R., & Hannan, M. T. (1983). The liability of newness: Age dependence in organizational death rates. *American Sociological Review, 48,* 692-710.

Freeman, J., & Hannan, M. T. (1983). Niche width and the dynamics of organizational popula-tions. *American Journal of Sociology, 88,* 1116-1145.

Hannan, M. T., & Freeman, J. (1977). The population ecology of organizations. *American Journal of Sociology, 82,* 929-964.

Hannan, M. T., & Freeman, J. (1984). Structural inertia and organizational change. *American Sociological Review, 49,* 149-164.

Hannan, M. T., Ranger-Moore, J., & Holl, J. B. (1988, December). *Competition and the evolution of organizational size distributions* (Tech. Rep.). Ithaca, NY: Cornell University.

Ijiri, Y., & Simon, H. A. (1977). *Skew distributions and the sizes of business firms.* Amsterdam: North-Holland.

King, J. C., & Wicker, A. W. (1988). The population demography of organizations: An applica-tion to retail and service establishments. In F. Hoy (Ed.), *Academy of management best paper proceedings.* New York: Academy of Management.

Kintsch, W. (1970). *Learning, memory, and conceptual processes.* New York: John Wiley.

Lave, C. A., & March, J. G. (1975). *An introduction to models in the social sciences.* New York: Harper & Row.

Lawrence, P. R., & Lorsch, J. W. (1967). *Organization and environment: Managing differenti-ation and integration.* Cambridge, MA: Harvard University, Graduate School of Business Administration.

Levins, R. (1962, November-December). Theory of fitness in a heterogeneous environment I: The fitness set and adaptive function. *American Naturalist, 96,* 361-378.

Levins, R. (1968). *Evolution in changing environments.* Princeton, NJ: Princeton University Press.

Levinthal, D., & March, J. (1981). A model of adaptive organizational search. *Journal of Economic Behavior and Organization, 2,* 307-333.

Levitt, B., & March, J. G. (1988) Organizational learning. In B. Staw & L. L. Cummings (Eds.), *Research in organizational behavior* (Vol. 10). Greenwich, CT: JAI.

Lindblom, C. E. (1959). The science of muddling through. *Public Administration Review, 19,* 79-88.

March, J., & Simon, H. (1958). *Organizations.* New York: John Wiley.

March, J. C., & March, J. G. (1977). Almost random careers: The Wisconsin school superinten-dency. *Administrative Science Quarterly, 22,* 377-409.

March, J. G. (1981). Footnotes to organizational change. *Administrative Science Quarterly, 26,* 563-577.

Meyer, M. W., & Zucker, L. G. (1989). *Permanently failing organizations.* Newbury Park, CA: Sage.

Miner, A. S., Amburgey, T., & Stearns, T. (1987, December). *Partial selection in organizational populations* (Tech. Rep.). Madison: University of Wisconsin, School of Business.

Perrow, C. (1986). *Complex organizations.* New York: Random House.

Peters, T., & Waterman, R. (1982). *In search of excellence.* New York: Harper & Row.

Pfeffer, J., & Salancik, G. R. (1978). *The external control of organizations.* New York: Harper & Row.

Romanelli, E., & Tushman, M. L. (1986). Inertia, environments, and strategic choice: A quasi-experimental design for comparative-longitudinal research. *Management Science, 32*(5), 608-621.

Scherer, F. M. (1980). *Industrial market structure and economic performance.* Chicago: Rand McNally.

Singh, J. V., House, R. J., & Tucker, D. J. (1986). Organizational change and organizational mortality. *Administrative Science Quarterly, 31*, 587-611.

Singh, J. V., Tucker, D. J., & House, R. J. (1986). Organizational legitimacy and the liability of newness. *Administrative Science Quarterly, 31*, 171-193.

Steinbruner, J. D. (1974). *The cybernetic theory of decision.* Princeton, NJ: Princeton University Press.

Stinchcombe, A. L. (1965). Social structure and organizations. In J. G. March (Ed.), *Handbook of organizations* (pp. 142-193). Chicago: Rand McNally.

Thompson, J. D. (1967). *Organizations in action.* New York: McGraw-Hill.

10

Evolution in Communities of
Voluntary Organizations

J. MILLER McPHERSON

Implicit in the bioevolutionary literature are two analytically separable approaches to the study of evolution. The first, and by far the best known, is the approach often attributed to Fisher and Haldane (see Bowler, 1984), which takes as its fundamental datum the physical structure of each species and relates this structure to the process of speciation. Traits such as beak size or brain mass are shown to have developed over the course of time as a result of the selection process. The statistical distribution of these traits in the populations in the classical Fisher-Haldane view are understood to reflect Mendelian processes of inheritance. Changes in these distributions are created by selection, migration, or mutation. The focus is on the physical character of the organisms themselves, as expressions of their genetic makeup.

An alternative approach centers on the niche occupied by the population. Perhaps the purest expression of this perspective is in Sewall Wright's (1931) landmark paper "Evolution in Mendelian Populations," which served as the rallying point for opponents of the Fisher-Haldane view. In a subsequent paper, Wright (1932) developed the notion of the *adaptive landscape*, which argues that species adjust their niche to a local, rather than a global, maximum. The key part of Wright's argument, for our purposes, is that small

Author's Note: Work on this chapter was supported by National Science Foundation grants SES-8120666, SES-8319899, and SES-8821365, J. Miller McPherson, principal investigator. Part of the analysis was conducted under a grant from the Cornell National Supercomputer Facility, a resource of the Cornell Theory Center. Additional support was provided by the Cornell Institute for Social and Economic Research. All interpretations and analysis are the responsibility of the author.

subpopulations of species that are geographically localized can adapt to local conditions at a much higher rate than the main populations, and are able to move to new maxima in the adaptive landscape much more readily.

Wright thus subtly shifted attention from physical traits as expressions of genetic makeup to ecological niches as expressions of genetic makeup. The necessity for this shift derived from the fact that the Fisher-Haldane approach did not, in Wright's view, satisfactorily explain how adaptation can occur. Wright's argument is that large populations will tend to have evolutionarily stable distributions of traits; smaller populations that allow random fluctuations of these traits will be able to shift their niches more readily.

This division in bioecology has an analogue in the organizational literature. The evolution of organizations has been presented mainly as the evolution of organizational culture (see McKelvey, 1982; McKelvey & Aldrich, 1983), in the sense that behavioral and normative regularities in the organization are regarded as the unit of selection. This view is parallel to the idea that the relevant evolutionary focus is on physical traits.

The model of organizational evolution presented in this chapter is more akin to Wright's approach to evolution than to Fisher and Haldane's, in two ways. First, it examines small localized populations of elements under selection: the members of an organization as they are recruited and lost to attrition. Second, the groups are considered to be populations situated in something very much like an adaptive landscape. I will argue that prior explicit approaches to organizational evolution, such as the McKelvey-Aldrich approach, are trying to explain phenomena that we are not yet theoretically equipped to address. I argue that we need to model changes in the niche of the organization, rather than in its cultural or organizational form. The relevant unit of selection for this approach is the human individual, rather than some less well-defined behavioral or normative unit. The concreteness of these units, and the massive amount of prior knowledge about the distribution of characteristics across them (i.e., human demography, survey research), confers significant advantages on such a theory, in comparison to work that depends on tracing organizational characteristics back into history.

There was a great deal of effort invested in applying evolutionary ideas to social and cultural systems even at the time of the basic advances in evolutionary biology. Some of the reasons for the failure of the early social evolutionists like Spencer are still facing us as major problems. I will sketch a few of these problems and propose a solution to a subset of them, in the form of a model of evolutionary change in systems of voluntary organizations.

The glaring fact facing Darwin was the great diversity of forms; the second obvious fact was that these forms perpetuated themselves from one generation to the next. Finches reliably produced finches, while tortoises did likewise. Although the reproduction of characteristics was not exact from one generation to the next, the observable fact that one species could not inter-breed with others gave a valid foundation for thinking about the process.[1]

Social evolutionists are in a more difficult position. First, the units that make up the populations of interest are not clear. Should we take as our population member the individual, the behavior, the group, the state, the cultural trait, or the ethnic category? Second, the generations are not clear: When does one unit leave off and another begin? Third, the forms we observe show no obvious stability like that of biological traits. The bioevolutionists had the advantage of seeing structural features, such as number of legs, reproduced from generation to generation.

Despite heroic efforts, the state of the art in the study of cultural evolution (e.g., Boyd & Richerson, 1985; Cavalli-Sforza & Feldman, 1981) is not yet sufficient to allow us to model organizational evolution on the cultural level. While there are some fine examples of attempts to trace the evolutionary process for organizations (McKelvey, 1982), I think that we still do not have the theoretical apparatus in place to allow organizational phylogenetic anal-ysis. We need to remember that the phylogenetic tree of the most studied species *Homo sapiens* was subject to continual revision as long as the fossil record was the primary source of evidence (e.g., Lewin, 1988). Only when biochemical analysis allowed independent dating of fossil territory and the decoding of DNA allowed comparison of genetic similarities among existing species did various authorities begin to reach consensus on even the rough shape of human evolution.

A major difficulty in modeling cultural evolution is that we still have not solved the unit problem. While it is obvious that the concept of the "comp" represents a great stride over past notions, the exact nature of the unit is still somewhat unclear. The comp can be thought of as the elementary unit that combines to produce the structure of an organizational form. However, whatever unit one chooses to focus on, it can be reduced to a lower form or aggregated to a higher form. For instance, does the comp brought to the organization by the secretary consist of typing skills, spelling, motor skills, or, in the other direction, competence in the language, ability to take direc-tion, or what? There is a hierarchy of comps that nest together in a probably endless recursion. The problem lies in choosing the appropriate level. At higher levels (e.g., language) the comp is probably shared by all members of the organization. At lower levels, it is probably unique. Until we have a clearer understanding of general cultural transmission, we will have prob-lems in attacking organizational evolution at this cultural level. The same arguments can be made for the organizational routine level of explanation (Nelson & Winter, 1982; Winter, Chapter 12, this volume).

Given this problem, we will not be able to trace the phylogenetic trees of different organizational forms unambiguously in the fashion of modern evolutionary biology.[2] Since an organization on this level of analysis is an assemblage of these units, I think that our inability to specify clearly the unit character seriously hinders the development of models that specify how these units work together over evolutionary time scales.

The evolutionary theory of this chapter sidesteps the problem by focusing attention on units well known to be essential components of human organizations: human individuals. The core imagery of the model uses ideas akin to Wright's adaptive landscape, although the theory was developed independently of Wright's ideas. The goal of this theory is to explain the dynamic behavior of groups[3] and organizations in a multidimensional niche space. The theory contains an explanation of (a) why groups are localized in this property space, (b) how much of this space they occupy, (c) under what conditions the group is likely to change its location in this property space, (d) under what conditions the group will grow or decline in numbers, and (e) when a new group is likely to form or an old one to die.

NICHES AND BLAU SPACE

The first premise of my evolutionary theory of voluntary organization is that groups form through the combination of individuals mediated by social networks. New groups can form where individuals are linked to one another by bonds of friendship, kinship, acquaintanceship, or some other network relation. Existing groups obtain new members through network contacts between members and nonmembers. Group growth and decline are determined by the balance between recruitment of new members and the loss of old ones. Thus the process of member recruitment and loss determines the character of the group, its size, and most other important characteristics. In order to dissect the processes of recruitment and loss, we need to develop first a way of thinking about the problem that incorporates useful information about the units that make up the groups in this scheme: the individuals.

The image of the individual I use is the person as a point in multidimensional space, which could be called Blau space (e.g., Blau, 1977).[4] In Blau's view, the most important features of the social system are captured by the dimensions of social structure that make a difference in the relations people have with one another. These characteristics are the basic sociodemographic variables — age, sex, race, education, and so forth.[5] In Blau space, each individual is a point representing concrete values of the Blau dimensions. The dimensions of age, education, and so forth define a region in which each person's relationship to everyone else in the system is measurable in Euclidean distance.

The simple fact of social life that Blau has highlighted is that the probability that two individuals will be connected to one another behaviorally (and thus culturally, materially, organizationally) is a monotonic declining function of the distance between the two points representing the individuals in Blau space. This fact is the basic empirical generalization in the social network literature (Marsden, 1987, in press; Marsden & Campbell, in press); it is called the homophily principle (see McPherson & Smith-Lovin, 1986). This principle tells us that connections between ideas in Blau space decrease with distance.

Organizations exist in this Blau space as well. They are localized in this space by the fact that organizations recruit and maintain their members through the social networks that tie individuals together (McPherson & Smith-Lovin, 1987). Since all known social networks are homophilous, the organization will come to be composed of similar people; it will be limited in the extent to which it can span Blau space. The organizations are restricted in their range in Blau space by the recruitment process; this range can be thought of as the niche that an organization occupies. The classical definition of a niche is the combination of resources that sustains a population; the niche of the organization in Blau space is the combination of human resource characteristics that sustains the organization.

Notice that focusing on niches defined in terms of individuals, which are bounded, rather than on cultural characteristics solves the unit problem and allows us to sidestep the issue of the phylogenetic tree, with all its inherent problems. We can look at the unfolding of dynamics in the niche space over whatever period of time we wish, without locking ourselves into possibly untenable hypotheses about historical events in the formation of new organizational traits. As will be seen, the evolutionary view that I am developing is history free; the information needed to predict the (short-term) future state of the system is contained in the present structure of the system.

WHY DO ORGANIZATIONAL NICHES FORM?

Since organizations recruit primarily through social network contacts between members and nonmembers, the potential pool of members for an organization at any given time will be the individuals connected to the current members. Since networks are homophilous, these potential members will be similar to the current members. Thus the organization develops a distinctive character defined by the current members of the group.

The inherent conservatism in recruitment processes thus created is magnified by the likelihood that recruitment to a given group is enhanced by multiple contacts. That is, it is very likely that recruitment to a group becomes more probable when a given potential member knows more current members. If this is true, groups will be even more localized in niche space than would be expected on the basis of the homophily principle alone.

Notice that the recruitment process is a form of natural selection. Memberships are born and die according to rules of selection and retention. Groups that are maintaining their niches selectively recruit members from that niche. At the organizational level, the distribution of the individual traits bears some analogy to the distribution of genes in a biotic population. Organizations maintaining their niche will recruit new members like themselves. Normal processes of recruitment and attrition will result in stable niches through stable selection processes. When the population of members (the group) expands or contracts its niche space, it does so by recruiting or losing members at the edges of the niche. New members who are significantly different from the old are like mutations whose viability is being tested. If the new mutation survives, the group adapts in the direction of the new member, who will be recruiting more members of like character. If the new mutation dies (leaves the group), the group maintains its old niche. Thus selection of members is adaptation at the level of the group.

There is an interesting duality between the distribution of individual characteristics inside the group and the group's location in niche space.[6] When a group occupies a large range of a dimension in Blau space, it is a *generalist* in that dimension. It is using a relatively large segment of the resources in the community. Internally, the group is heterogeneous on the variable in question. The internal and external consequences of generalism are different.

Internally, when an organization is heterogeneous, it will have to cope with increased coordination problems inherent in managing regular contacts between people of different backgrounds. Since people from diverse origins are less likely to share any given social characteristic, communication between such persons is more problematic. People from different social classes will bring to the organization different assumptions about the world, different styles of interaction, different interests, and, perhaps most important, different connections to the outside world. The greater the level of internal heterogeneity, then, the greater the difficulty of reconciling the diversity of membership characteristics.[7] We would expect, then, that groups that are extremely diverse will be selected against in the long run.

From the point of view of the larger system, generalism makes the group compete with a larger number of other groups for its members. When an organization occupies a larger region of the total social space, it overlaps with a greater number of other groups in that space. The advantage of the generalist group is that it can capitalize on opportunities in a wide area of the system. The disadvantage of the generalist is that it cannot compete intensively anywhere. The local density of the network contacts for specialist groups will be higher in its niche than the local density of the contacts for generalists. Since recruitment to the group is likely to be an increasing function of the number of local contacts, the generalist will be at a competitive disadvantage with the specialist in the specialist's niche.

Thus organizational niches form because organizations recruit through homophilous social networks, and because there are good internal reasons to maintain group homogeneity.

HOW MIGHT ORGANIZATIONAL NICHES CHANGE?

A group may change its niche by systematic selection in the niche space, as suggested above. A change in the distribution of characteristics in the organization can result in specialization, generalization, maintenance, or drift in the niche. When the organization recruits systematically in one direction, the niche expands in that direction. If it systematically loses members in the other direction, the niche shifts, while the niche width stays the same. Groups that recruit only from the center of the niche will specialize, while those that recruit at the edges will generalize.

All these outcomes are relatively obvious once the connection between membership dynamics and niche movement is made. Before we have a complete understanding of the adaptation processes, however, we must posit a mechanism that would generate these systematic forces in membership selection and retention.

The key to such a mechanism lies in the concept of the carrying capacity. The carrying capacity for a biotic system is the maximum biotic load that the system can sustain. The carrying capacity for a population is the total number of individuals of that population that can be sustained in the system. In ecological theory, the numbers in the population will expand until the limit set by the carrying capacity, *or the limit induced by interference and competition from other populations,* is reached.

We must ask at this point what limits to the growth of a voluntary organization (and perhaps, by extension, other kinds of organization) there are. First, there is the number of persons in the community. No organization localized in the community can exceed this number. Second, there is the subset of that number that fits the criteria for membership; that is, the number that falls into the niche of the organization. This number is an absolute upper limit to the size of a group *in the absence of interference or competition from other groups.* However, we know that there are all sorts of competitors for the time and resources of people. Work demands, family activities, and other voluntary groups consume major portions of the time budgets of individuals. Thus any given region of social space will be crowded with large numbers of competitors for the attention of the individuals in that space. Thus we do not expect a given group to be able to exhaust all the resources in its niche by attracting all potential members; the competition of other groups reduces the carrying capacity for a given group far below the gross number of people in the niche.

Since there are many sources of competition for potential members, we must infer the carrying capacity for an organization indirectly. One approach to this is to map the actual distribution of groups in Blau (or niche) space and compare it with the distribution of individuals in that space. Figure 10.1 maps the distribution of individuals and memberships along the dimension of years of education for the city of Lincoln, Nebraska, in 1983.[8] The solid line is the relative frequency of individuals, and the dotted line represents memberships. Note that the area under both curves adds up to unity, since the data are expressed in relative frequency.

The thing that stands out in this view of the data is the relative disparity in the two curves above 12 years of education and below 17 years. For the period 13 to 15 years, the membership curve is substantially below the individual curve, while at 15 to 16 years, it is substantially above. One way of looking at this fact is that the people with some college are underexploited by the organizations relative to the average person, while the college graduates are overexploited. The college graduates are members of more organizations per capita than is typical of people with more or less education, while the people with some college are members of fewer.

Figure 10.2 emphasizes this fact, in the form of what I call the *resource exploitation curve.* It is simply the difference between the two curves of Figure 10.1. Where the membership curve is above the individual curve in

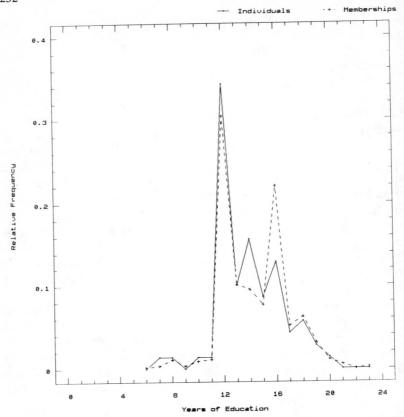

Figure 10.1. Relative frequency of individuals and memberships by years of education, Lincoln, Nebraska, 1983. Solid line indicates individuals; dashed line indicates memberships.

Figure 10.1, the resource exploitation curve is positive. Where the individual curve is above the membership curve, the resource exploitation curve is negative. The strong peak in the resource exploitation curve at 16 years of age is the large disparity of the previous paragraph. The curve is relatively flat where there is a good match between the individual and membership functions of Figure 10.1. The vertical dimension maps the exploitation of individual resources by the organizations in the system. Where the curve is high, resources are being overexploited; where the curve is low, there is underexploitation.[9]

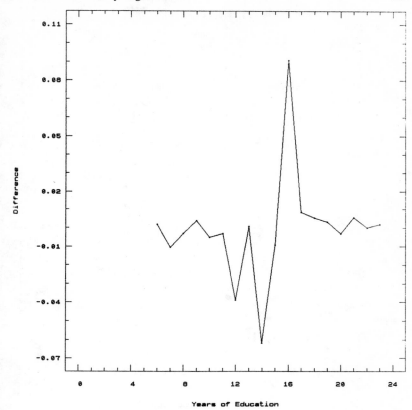

Figure 10.2. Resource exploitation curve for Lincoln in education dimension.

The model predicts that organizations in different locations on this resource exploitation curve will have different selective pressures on their members. Groups in regions of high exploitation will either move away from their location by selective attrition of members and a selective inability to recruit new members or decline in size. Groups in regions of low exploitation will find it easier to recruit new members and to retain their current ones, and will thus tend to stay located in that region and grow in size. Groups perched on the edge of a region of unexploited resources will tend to be drawn into that region by the differential ability to recruit and retain members in that direction. The organization will grow into low-exploitation regions and away from high-exploitation regions. Groups in regions of average exploitation,

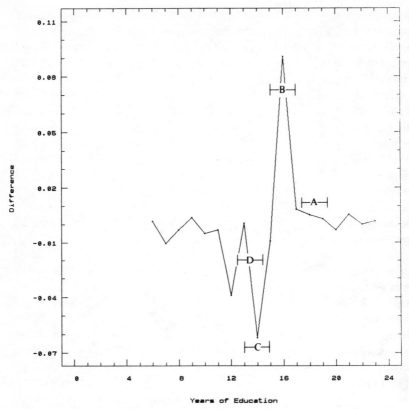

Figure 10.3. Resource exploitation curve for Lincoln, with organizations.

with no substantial slope in the resource exploitation curve in their vicinity, will tend to remain stable in their location and in their size.

The logic of the model suggests that only groups poised on the edge of an opportunity will be able to take advantage of it. Only an organization in the vicinity of a valley in the exploitation curve will be able to adapt itself into it, since groups can grow only through the homophilous network connections of their members.

Figure 10.3 presents four observed groups from the Ten Towns data,[10] mapped onto the resource exploitation curve. The location of the letter labeling the group is the mean of education for the group, and the arms projecting indicate a one-standard-deviation window around the mean of the group. Group A, the Near South Neighborhood Association, is mostly college graduates and professional people. Since it is in a relatively level region of the resource exploitation curve, the model predicts that, over time, it should remain stable in size and composition. Such organizations are at equilibrium with their competitors.

Group B, the Knights of Columbus, is located near the peak of the exploitation curve, at about 15.5 years of education. According to the model, this group will (a) gain more members with less education and (b) lose more members at the peak exploitation value of 16 years. As a result, the group should shift its niche to the left on the education dimension, and should continue to lose members until either the resource exploitation curve has leveled out or the group has moved its niche to a less exploited region. In fact, inspection of the scattergram for this group that relates the education of the member to the member's tenure in the group suggests that newer members tend to have come from the less exploited region.

On the other hand, organizations like Group B will be unstable. It is in a region where the slope of the exploitation curve is steep and significantly away from zero. Since there are relatively fewer unaffiliated college graduates in the system, they are less likely to be available to join the group and more likely to have other competing demands on their time and energy. When Group B moves toward the underexploited region by shifting downward in mean education, it will generate more memberships among those with some college, which will begin to reduce the differential between the college graduates and the areas on either side of the region. When enough groups have invaded the area around 14 years of education, the system will be back in equilibrium, and the resource exploitation curve will flatten out.[11]

Group C, a Dungeons and Dragons club,[12] is located directly in the least exploited region of the space. This group should have no trouble recruiting new members and retaining the old ones; it should grow in size and retain its current niche.

The model also shows why some groups become specialists and others generalists. Specialists are created by valleys in the resource exploitation function, while generalists have grown into opportunities at their edges. Group D, the Lincoln Rose Society, has mean education of 13.1 years and is poised on the edge of the substantial dip in resource exploitation bottoming out at 14 years. Since this group is already in a region of underexploitation (already on a part of the curve below the zero value), it will be expected to have no trouble growing by recruiting new members and retaining the old ones. However, the model suggests that new members at 14 years of education will be much more easily obtained than even the readily available ones in the current niche. This group should grow into the resource-rich region at 14 through recruitment, and stay in the already rich current niche.

The model specifies the conditions under which an organization will grow or decline.[13] When a group is trapped in a region of the exploitation function significantly above the mean, the group will have an imbalance of loss and gain of members; it will decline in size.[14] If the height of the exploitation curve is great enough, and the group cannot adapt into a more congenial region, the competitive pressure could be great enough to make it disappear entirely.[15] The horizontal location of a group (and the proximity to upward or downward slopes) gives us information about the likely future composition of the group.

Finally, the model gives us an idea about the formation of new groups by fission. When a group generalizes in one or more dimensions beyond the level sustainable, the group will be more likely to split into two separate systems, each with a more or less distinctive niche.

In sum, the resource exploitation curve controls the movement of organizations through the niche space. Groups will tend to move toward regions of opportunity and away from regions of overexploitation. They will grow when they are in a region of opportunity and decline when in a resource-poor area. They will generalize when growth is possible in an adjacent region without loss of current members, and they will specialize when squeezed by steep walls of a valley in the exploitation curve.

CHALLENGES TO THE MODEL:
EMPIRICAL AND THEORETICAL

The crucial empirical question for testing the model is that of order versus chaos. If the system of organizations is too stable, on the one hand, there will not be enough mismatch between resource exploitation and resources to detect the effects produced under the model. In essence, a too-stable system would behave as though there were no effects of competition, since the equilibrium condition would freeze the system, producing stasis. The available evidence on the dynamics of these systems suggests that we can safely discount this possibility.

It is useful to consider explicitly some potential sources of turbulence in the system, since the model assumes such turbulence. First, there are demographic sources. Processes of individual death, birth, aging, migration, sickness, and so on will produce constantly shifting patterns of affiliation, which will produce local opportunities in the niche space. These changes will affect patterns of joining and leaving organizations that will in turn alter the exploitation rate.

For instance, new immigrants to a community will join groups in the system at a much higher rate until they approximate the level of affiliation characteristic of people in their social position. Out-migrants will shift both the individual and membership functions. People going through life-cycle stages such as parenthood or job changes will shift their affiliation patterns. All of these forces will produce immediate and lagged effects on the system.

Second, there are external shocks to the system that can produce demographic shifts. A new factory moves to town, introducing changes in the life circumstances of many residents, and increasing the in-migration rate. Or an old factory closes. A new road is opened up, increasing the effective population size of the system.

Third, there are exogenous shocks not necessarily operating through demographic processes. The economy bottoms, increasing the economic resources of the residents. Overtime work at the factory skyrockets, decreasing leisure time. Or the economy busts, forcing people to take on two jobs, or possibly throwing marginal workers out of the labor force entirely. A new recreational center becomes available, making it much easier to form new sports. The federal government withdraws its support for extension clubs, forcing most of them to fold or to change their system of operation.

Finally, there are stochastic fluctuations in almost all large-scale multivariate systems. Even simple predator-prey systems show regular fluctuations over time. Most natural systems have both irregular and regular cyclic dynamic components.

Some other suggestive data exist on the issue. McPherson and Lockwood (1980) found in a panel analysis of individual affiliation that the rate of joining was strongly related to the life cycle (see also Knoke & Thomson, 1977). McPherson (1981) found that a simple stochastic process model described the flow of individuals into and out of organizations, but that age had an exogenous impact on the process. Thus there is almost certainly turbulence in the system created by demographic process.

The other side of the coin is chaos. If the system is too turbulent, then movement in the niches will be Brownian over time periods longer than a few membership cycles; most groups appear to operate in yearly membership cycles. Those who are very informal (and small) tend to have shorter periods. A few, such as those related to churches and other larger structures, may have longer periods. This possibility is essentially an empirical question. The best visible evidence suggests that the modal membership is longer than five years (McPherson, 1981, p. 719).

Data from McPherson (1983a) suggest that the rates of gain and loss of members in different types of groups are in rough equilibrium at the aggregate level in Omaha, one of the communities in the present study. Since the 1983 data are at a higher level of aggregation than would be ideal to test the model, conclusions about these dynamics must be tentative. However, the evidence suggests that the flow of members through organizations tends toward equilibrium at the level of organizational types. This result is consistent with the underlying premise of the model that there is a balance between exploitation and potential in the long run.

Thus there is reasonable evidence to suggest that there is a balance between order and chaos in the system of organizations. It is hoped that this balance allows enough change to produce the effects posited by the model, but not so much change as to swamp the system in variation. I turn now to some hypotheses from the model.

HYPOTHESES

(1)   Growth will be directly related to resource underexploitation.

Organizations located in underexploited regions of a resource space will have less competitive pressure, will be able to recruit new members at a high rate and to retain the old members longer. This hypothesis is a form of the general density-dependence argument from bioecology (Hannan & Freeman, 1988; Ricklefs, 1979). The other side of this hypothesis is that declines will occur in regions of overexploitation. The extreme form of the hypothesis predicts organizational deaths and births for extreme values of deviation from the expected resource curve.

(2)   The direction of niche movement will be a function of the local shape of the exploitation curve.

Organizations in the region of a dip in the exploitation curve will tend to drift in the direction of the dip because they will be more successful at gaining new members from that region and at retaining such members already present. Organization will drift away from bumps in the curve for similar reasons.

A related hypothesis at the community level is that the overall amount of niche movement for all organizations will be a direct function of variance in the resource exploitation curve. Organizations located in more turbulent systems will be jostled by their neighbors more than those in quieter systems. The jaggedness of the curve should predict which regions of the resource space are most active.

At the individual level, persons in regions of underexploitation should be recruited at a higher rate. The individuals who are already members of groups will be retained at a higher rate if they are located in underexploited regions and at a lower rate if the opposite is true.

(3) The rate of niche movement will be inversely related to the amount of homophily in the network.

The more homophily in the social network connecting individuals, the narrower the range (in the resource space) of associates that will be immediately accessible to the organization through its members. Homophily determines the field of potential members for the group; the narrower the range of associates in, say, the education dimension, the more slowly the organization is able to move through that dimension, since each new member added will tend to be close to the current members in social space. If the typical person has friends who are within one year of his or her education, then the organization is constrained to move more slowly through the resource space than if the typical person in the system knows people at ten years remove. This proposition is an organizational form of the weak tie hypothesis of Granovetter (1973).

(4) The rate of niche movement will be related to the density of the social network.

The greater the number of contacts in the network, the greater the possibility for recruitment through those contacts. The local topology of the network may play a significant role in the shape of the niche. If there are local peaks and valleys in the density of the network, the organization will find it difficult to span these barriers. Some indirect evidence on this proposition has been gathered by Liedka (1988), who analyzed patterns of niche location and social network topology in the General Social Survey data from 1984 through 1986. His results suggest that there may be a substantial relationship between the local density of social networks and the presence of organizations in that locale.

(5) The rate of niche movement will be a positive function of the rate of turnover in the organization.

The greater the loss and/or gain of members, the greater the chances that the group will be mobile in the resource space. Note that this turnover rate will be a function of the amount of resource exploitation in the region of the organization. If the group is in a region of high exploitation, the rate of loss will be high, and the group mean may move by virtue of systematic loss, or random fluctuation. If there is low exploitation locally, then the organization will be gaining new members at a higher rate, and has the potential to change its location through selective recruitment.

(6) The rate of niche movement will be inversely related to the size of the group.

The larger the group, the less influence any given member's presence (or absence of any given old member) has on the overall position of the group in the niche space. The mean of the group on any given resource dimension will be less responsive to given numbers of gain or loss in membership. This hypothesis will not be supported if groups actually have characteristic rates of gain and loss independent of organizational size. If groups gain and lose, say, 10% of their members in a given year on the average, regardless of size, then the rate of niche movement can be the same for small and large groups. In the absence of some mechanisms promoting stability for larger groups (e.g., institutionalization), large groups could move in response to opportunities as quickly as small ones.

(7) The rate of niche movement will be directly related to generalism.

Groups spanning larger regions of the resource space will have more members who have extreme values of the resource than will specialists. These extreme values will have a larger effect on the mean location of the organization in the niche space should they drop their membership or recruit more members like them. Of course, there is the possibility that there is a strong relationship between size and generalism, as suggested by Carroll (1985). If so, Hypotheses 6 and 7 will be linked empirically.

(8) Generalism will be inversely related to homophily in the social network.

The greater the homophily in the social network, the more localized are social associations in the network. Groups will tend to exploit intensively a local region in the network, since most ties will be local rather than spanning.

One consequence of the relationship between generalism and homophily is that when generalist organizations do exist in homophilous systems, they will tend to generate more bridging ties than in less homophilous systems. Their integrative function (Babchuk & Edwards, 1969) will be heightened.

DISCUSSION

The theory outlined above is aggressive. It purports to explain why groups form, what kinds of people are in them, what will happen to them in the short-term future, and why they die. Clearly, the predictions are formulated for the evolutionary short term, but one could readily argue that all changes occur in the short term, and the long term is simply accumulation (see Dawkins, 1986).

The essence of the model is the commonsense idea that groups will recruit new members like the old ones. The power of the model comes from specifying exactly what kind of similarity is important, and what potential for recruitment is out there. The model has the potential to tie together theories of social networks and organizations in such a way as to afford us a detailed understanding of the operation of communities of organizations over time. The model contains within it the potential for the extension of population ecology to encompass community ecology — the interactions of populations of organizations over time.

The model solves the problem posed early in the chapter, that is, the issue of the appropriate unit of selection in organizational evolution. At least for voluntary organizations, the correct unit is the individual member. Thinking of the process this way leads to the realization that the organization's niche is the key property of the organization to study. Focusing on the behavior of the niche over time allows us to develop a systematic model that generates testable predictions.

It remains to be seen, of course, to what extent there is empirical support for the model, and to what extent one can generalize to other types of organizations. One can think of a number of advantages of a model of this sort applied to other types of organizations, such as firms or general nonprofits such as universities. The clear way in which the composition of the group is linked to the dynamics of growth and decline by the model may pave the way for a new theoretical synthesis of the literature on career paths and organizational analysis. The model has the potential for connections to literatures as diverse as social movements, the professions, leisure, and religion. These connections will be the subject of future effort.

NOTES

1. This rule is, of course, not ironclad. Wright (1948) discusses a number of interesting exceptions, including rings of species in which close pairs of species may interbreed and distant pairs may not, with gradients of speciation based on geographical distance.

2. Not the least of the problems in tracing phylogenetic trees for organizations is the fact that the phylogenetic trees in bioevolution are divergent. That is, branches, once formed, remain distinct. This fact means that the bioevolutionary trees have a much simpler structure than trees that allow branches to reconverge, as would almost certainly occur for organizational forms.

3. From the point of view of the theory, groups and organizations are the same sort of phenomena, although possibly differing in terms of formalization, institutionalization, persistence, activity, and so forth. I use the terms more or less interchangeably. Researchers who identify strictly with the complex organization literature may feel less comfortable with an approach that treats bridge clubs and major corporations as aspects of the same phenomenon.

4. There is some similarity between this conception and that of Lumsden and Singh (Chapter 6, this volume). The main difference is that the Blau dimensions are well known to have the property of homophily, which is central to the model. The Lumsden and Singh opportunity space has no clearly defined link to past research.

5. Actually, as I point out in another paper, the dimensions that can be incorporated into the model are virtually unlimited, including time, space, and other social characteristics (McPherson, 1983b).

6. The internal distribution of members with respect to the Blau dimensions is the demography of the organization (Stewman, 1988).

7. Diversity itself can be a resource for certain types of groups. For instance, research on group decision making suggests that the presence of outliers can create conditions for more imaginative solutions to group problems. In another sense, diversity can connect the group to a wider range of information from the total network; distant contacts in the network are more likely to have nonredundant information. For those organizations that need to have system-spanning information, diversity may be an advantage.

8. The data come from the Ten Towns project (McPherson, 1982), and are described in more detail in McPherson and Smith-Lovin (1986, 1987).

9. The two figures summarize a great deal about the system. For instance, a positive correlation between the variable and the affiliation rate would produce an upward trend in Figure 10.2. Such correlations have been reported and discussed by research in the major journals for several decades. Should we want to apply the model to a system with such a correlation, we could simply detrend the curve. In other words, the model can easily be articulated to deal with the fact that some resource dimensions, such as age and education, are correlated with affiliation. Thus we can take into account the fact that one end of a continuum has greater utility to groups (e.g., income) than the other, as reflected in a higher general exploitation rate at one end than the other. Or, we could residualize the curve by another variable to remove its influence. The method is flexible in its ability to incorporate a priori information.

10. I use actual groups from the study to give the reader some flavor of the substantive context. These allow us to see that the model is multidimensional rather than unidimensional. The groups are actually operating in a K-dimensional space, with peaks and valleys in a generalized topography not unlike Wright's adaptive landscape. The picture in the text is essentially the marginals of that space in one dimension.

11. The system does not actually have to reach equilibrium. The model gives predictions about the forces acting on the organizations in the relatively short run. The general turbulence

in the system (represented by waves in the membership function) created by variations in exogenous variables, organizational births and deaths, and general movement in the system (see the discussion in a later section) should continually produce opportunities for organizations to exploit. The model depends on transients in the system, with a trend toward equilibrium created by competition.

12. This group suggests some interesting ways in which our ecological model interacts with institutional theories of organization (see Scott, 1988). The Dungeons and Dragons organizing theme is probably an ephemeral form, generated by mimetic processes (DiMaggio & Powell, 1983). However, the great potential for exploitation in this region is probably the reason for the presence of the group here in the first place. Trendy groups can take root here, where the potential for group formation and growth is high. An interesting theme to play out in these data would be whether such groups actually do grow, as predicted by the model, or whether they disappear when the popularity of their activities begins to decline generally. A strong (and probably unlikely) result supporting our model would be organizational transformation rather than death. That is, our belief in the model would increase if the group shifted to some newer and trendier game rather than disbanding. In a sense, these institutional forces are the residuals of the model.

13. A region of high opportunity can be capitalized upon in three ways, ordered in the priority I expect: (a) Groups in the region can grow in size, (b) neighbors can move into the territory, and (c) new groups can form. The probability of the third way should be an increasing function of opportunity, under the model. Note that this view of the origin of social groups is a novel complement to the emerging network-based understanding of the process of organizational birth (see Granovetter, 1978). Of course, institutional forces can alter the relative probability of these three ways. For instance, since the size of sports teams is often fixed, one would expect the formation of new ones in response to opportunity, while the size of some other types of groups, such as stamp collectors, can expand virtually without limit. The relationship between the size and number of groups is a major theme running through much of my work on these groups (McPherson, 1981, 1982, 1983b; McPherson & Smith-Lovin, 1982, 1986).

14. McPherson (1981) shows that the mean affiliation rate for the system is the ratio of the rate of joining to the rate of leaving organizations, under plausible assumptions about the system. The model of this proposal can be interpreted as a further specification of the relation between the mean affiliation rate and the actual process of membership birth and death. When the mean affiliation rate locally exceeds the level sustainable by the system, the increased rate of attrition will act to bring the mean back down toward the average level for the system.

15. Predictions about growth and decline in size will depend upon the multivariate distribution of resources. What we see in the exploitation curves is actually the marginal distribution of a hyperspace in which all relevant dimensions generate a geography of resource exploitation. Groups will grow and decline in response to this total picture of the resources available.

REFERENCES

Babchuk, N., & Edwards, J. N. (1969). Voluntary associations and the integration hypothesis. *Sociological Inquiry, 35*, 149-162.

Banaszak-Holl, J. (1988). *The community ecology of voluntary associations: Evidence from the General Social Survey.* Unpublished manuscript, Cornell University.

Bidwell, C. E., & Kasarda, J. D. (1985). *The organization and its ecosystem.* Greenwich, CT: JAI.

Blau, P. M. (1977). *Inequality and homogeneity.* New York: Free Press.

Bowler, P. J. (1984). *Evolution: The history of an idea.* Berkeley: University of California Press.

Boyd, R., & Richerson, P. J. (1985). *Culture and the evolutionary process.* Chicago: University of Chicago Press.

Burt, R. S. (1985). General Social Survey network items. *Connections, 8,* 119-123.

Carroll, G. R. (1985). Concentration and specialization: Dynamics of niche width in populations or organizations. *American Journal of Sociology, 90,* 1262-1283.

Carroll, G. R. (Ed.). (1988). *Ecological models of organizations.* Cambridge, MA: Ballinger.

Cavalli-Sforza, L. L., & Feldman, M. W. (1981). *Cultural transmission and evolution.* Princeton, NJ: Princeton University Press.

Dawkins, R. (1986). *The blind watchmaker.* New York: W. W. Norton.

DiMaggio, P. J., & Powell, W. W. (1983). The iron cage revisited: Institutional isomorphism and collective rationality in organizational fields. *American Sociological Review, 48,* 147-160.

Feld, S. L. (1981). The focused organization of social ties. *American Journal of Sociology, 86,* 1015-1035.

Freeman, J. H., & Hannan, M. T. (1983). Niche width and the dynamics of organizational populations. *American Journal of Sociology, 88,* 1116-1145.

Granovetter, M. S. (1973). The strength of weak ties. *American Journal of Sociology, 78,* 1360-1380.

Granovetter, M. S. (1978). Threshold models of collective behavior. *American Journal of Sociology, 83,* 1420-1443.

Granovetter, M. S. (1985). Economic action and social structure: The problem of embeddedness. *American Journal of Sociology, 91,* 481-510.

Hannan, M. T., & Freeman, J. (1977). The population ecology of organizations. *American Journal of Sociology, 82,* 929-964.

Hannan, M. T., & Freeman, J. (1988). Density dependence in the growth of organizational populations. In G. R. Carroll (Ed.), *Ecological models of organizations* (pp. 7-32). Cambridge, MA: Ballinger.

Knoke, D., & Thomson, R. (1977). Voluntary association membership trends and the family life cycle. *Social Forces, 56,* 48-65.

Laumann, E. O. (1973). *Bonds of pluralism: The form and substance of urban social networks.* New York: Academic Press.

Levins, R. (1968). *Evolution in changing environments.* Princeton, NJ. Princeton University Press.

Lewin, R. (1988). *Bones of contention: Controversies in the search for human origins.* New York: Touchstone.

Liedka, R. (1988). *Who do you know in the group: Organizations and networks.* Unpublished manuscript, Cornell University.

Marsden, P. V. (1987). Core discussion networks of Americans. *American Sociological Review, 52,* 122-131.

Marsden, P. V. (in press). Homogeneity in confiding relations. *Social Networks.*

Marsden, P. V., & Campbell, K. E. (in press). Recruitment and selection processes: The organizational side of job searches. In R. L. Breiger (Ed.), *Social mobility and social structure.* New York: Cambridge University Press.

McKelvey, B. (1982). *Organizational systematics: Taxonomy, evolution, classification.* Berkeley: University of California Press.

McKelvey, B., & Aldrich, H. E. (1983). Populations, organizations and applied organizational science. *Administrative Science Quarterly, 28,* 101-128.

McPherson, J. M. (1977). Correlates of social participation: A comparison of the ethnic community and compensatory theories. *Sociological Quarterly, 18*, 197-208.

McPherson, J. M. (1981). A dynamic model of voluntary affiliation. *Social Forces, 59*, 705-728.

McPherson, J. M. (1982). Hypernetwork sampling: Duality and differentiation among voluntary associations. *Social Networks, 3*, 225-249.

McPherson, J. M. (1983a). An ecology of affiliation. *American Sociological Review, 48*, 519-532.

McPherson, J. M. (1983b). The size of voluntary organizations. *Social Forces, 61*, 1044-1064.

McPherson, J. M. (1988a). *Evidence for ecological competition in voluntary organizations.* Unpublished manuscript.

McPherson, J. M. (1988b). A theory of voluntary organization. In C. Milofsky (Ed.), *Community organizations* (pp. 42-76). New York: Oxford University Press.

McPherson, J. M., & Lockwood, W. G. (1980). The longitudinal study of voluntary association memberships. *Journal of Voluntary Action Research, 9*, 74-84.

McPherson, J. M., & Smith-Lovin, L. (1982). Women and weak ties: Differences by sex in the size of voluntary associations. *American Journal of Sociology, 87*, 883-904.

McPherson, J. M., & Smith-Lovin, L. (1986). Sex segregation in voluntary associations. *American Sociological Review, 51*, 61-79.

McPherson, J. M., & Smith-Lovin, L. (1987). Homophily in voluntary organizations: Status distance and the composition of face to face groups. *American Sociological Review, 52*, 370-379.

McPherson, J. M., & Smith-Lovin, L. (1988). A comparative ecology of five nations: Testing a model of competition among voluntary organizations. In G. R. Carroll (Ed.). *Ecological models of organizations* (pp. 85-110). Cambridge, MA: Ballinger.

Nelson, R. R., & Winter, S. G. (1982). *An evolutionary theory of economic change.* Cambridge, MA: Harvard University Press.

Ranger-Moore, J. (1988). *Movement of voluntary association types through a multidimensional resource space.* Unpublished manuscript, Cornell University.

Ricklefs, R. E. (1979). *Ecology.* New York: Chiron.

Scott, W. R. (1988). The adolescence of institutional theory. *Administrative Science Quarterly, 32*, 493-511.

Snow, D. A., Zurcher, L. A., Jr., & Eckland-Olson, S. (1980). Social networks and social movements: A microstructural approach to differential recruitment. *American Sociological Review, 45*, 787-801.

Stewman, S. (1988). Organizational demography. In W. R. Scott & J. Blake (Eds.), *Annual review of sociology* (Vol. 14, pp. 173-202). Palo Alto, CA: Annual Reviews.

Tuma, N. B., & Hannan, M. T. (1984). *Social dynamics: Models and methods.* New York: Academic Press.

Wright, S. (1931). Evolution in Mendelian populations. *Genetics, 16*, 97-159.

Wright, S. (1932). The roles of mutation, inbreeding, crossbreeding, and selection in evolution. *Proceedings of the Sixth International Congress of Genetics, 1*, 356-366.

Wright, S. (1948). Organic evolution. *Encyclopedia Britannica* (Vol. 8, pp. 915-929). Chicago: Encyclopedia Britannica.

Young, D. R., & Finch, S. J. (1977). *Foster care and non-profit agencies.* Lexington, MA: D. C. Heath.

Zald, M. N. (1970). *Organizational change.* Chicago: University of Chicago Press.

Zald, M. N., & Denton, P. (1963). From evangelism to general service: The transformation of the YMCA. *Administrative Science Quarterly, 8*, 214-234.

11

Competition and the Evolution of Organizational Size Distributions

MICHAEL T. HANNAN
JAMES RANGER-MOORE
JANE BANASZAK-HOLL

This chapter reports early steps in research that seeks to clarify how ecological dynamics interact with organizational growth in shaping the evolution of organizational populations. It considers the evolution of size distributions over the histories of populations using both simulated and real historical populations.

The full dynamics of populations of organizations involve vital rates (of founding and mortality) as well as growth and decline of individual organizations. However, in the interest of analyzing data on diverse populations over long periods, recent research in organizational ecology has emphasized vital rates (see, for example, the chapters by Aldrich et al., Barnett & Amburgey, Carroll & Hannan, and Freeman in this volume). This emphasis may have slighted issues of growth and contraction at the organizational level (see Winter, Chapter 12, this volume). The research described here seeks to redress the balance by building models of organizational ecologies in which individual organizations grow and contract. It explores the implications of adding *growth at the organizational level* to models of organizational ecol-

Authors' Note: This research was supported by National Science Foundation grant SES-8809006. Computations were performed on the Cornell National Supercomputer Facility, which is supported by the National Science Foundation, New York State, and IBM. We appreciate the comments of Glenn Carroll and Jitendra Singh on an earlier draft of this chapter.

ogy. Current prospects for complete analytic characterizations of the dynamics of organizational populations are poor because the processes involved are complicated. In particular, they involve linkages between microdynamics and macrodynamics. Although we have begun to understand various aspects of dynamics at each level, we do not yet know how to integrate them analytically. Therefore, we use a combination of empirical analysis and microsimulation.

We concentrate on size distributions for two reasons. First, size distributions tell a great deal about the structure of power and dominance in the world of organizations. Understanding the evolution of size distributions has potential value for linking change in organizational populations with change in macrostructures (Hannan, 1988).

The second motivation is practical. It is costly and difficult to obtain data suitable for estimating models of growth for complete populations over long historic periods, as is appropriate for ecological studies. Yet available data sometimes provide snapshots of a series of size distributions in the evolution of populations even when panel data on the sizes of individual organizations are not available. We think that we can learn about both the ecology of organizations and growth at the organizational level by studying the dynamics of size distributions. By learning the consequences of the features of growth processes for the evolution of size distributions in cases for which rich data are available, we seek to uncover patterns that can be used to infer dynamics when size distributions are available but microdata are not.

CLASSICAL MODELS OF SIZE DISTRIBUTIONS

Modern research on organizational size distributions began with Gibrat's (1931) claim that the sizes of firms, like those of other "naturally occurring" economic units, follow a lognormal distribution. The main idea is Kapteyn's (1903) "law of proportionate effect," which holds that growth is proportional to size and the factor of proportionality is random.[1] Let S_{it} denote the size of an organization in period t. Assume that the size of each organization in each period is a multiple of its size in the previous period:

$$S_{it} = S_{i,t-1}(1 + u_{it})$$ [1]

where u_{it} is a random growth rate. According to equation 1, S_{it} depends on initial size, S_{i0}, and the history of random growth rates:

$$S_{it} = S_{i0}(1 + u_{it}) \ldots (1 + u_{i0}) \qquad [2]$$

If periods are short enough that growth rates are small (or if time is regarded as a continuous parameter), then equation 2 can be well approximated by:

$$\log S_{it} = \log S_{i0} + u_{it} + \ldots + u_{i0} \qquad [3]$$

Gibrat's model for the growth of firms assumes that the random growth rate, u_{it}, is (a) independent from period to period and among firms in each period, (b) independent of current size (Gibrat's law), and (c) reflects the operation of many forces, each with small effect, which means that it can be approximated by a normal distribution. That is, Gibrat assumes that u_{it} are independent, identically distributed, normal random variables with mean μ and variance σ^2. Then $\log S_{it}$ has the form:

$$\log S_{it} = \log S_0 + \in_{it} \qquad [4a]$$

where

$$\in_{it} \sim N(\mu t, \sigma^2 t) \qquad [4b]$$

In other words, the size distribution has a *lognormal* distribution, the mean and variance of which grow linearly over time.

As Steindl (1967) points out, analysts were attracted to size distributions because of their temporal stability. The source of the stability was the major analytic puzzle. However, Gibrat's model is not stable. Rather, it is explosive in the sense that both the mean and variance of log-size grow without bound as time passes. So subsequent research sought ways to stabilize distributions within the general framework developed by Gibrat.

The key innovation, due to Simon and his collaborators in a classic series of papers (Ijiri & Simon, 1964, 1974, 1977; Simon, 1955; Simon & Bonini, 1959), introduced an entry process into the smallest size category to stabilize the process.[2] Simon (1955) initially proposed two models; only one has been used in subsequent research on organizations. He developed the models to explain distributions of word frequencies in texts. Both models assume that growth is random across a set of ordered size categories with rates following Gibrat's law and that entries occur at a constant rate and only in the smallest size category. The first model considers an expanding text in which new words enter and existing words remain. The second considers a text of fixed length in which words enter and vanish. The first model is the one that Simon and his collaborators applied to distributions of firm sizes. The second model, which was developed much more fully by Steindl (1965), is closer to the one used here.

The first model (of an expanding text) implies that the upper tail of the distribution converges to a Pareto distribution.[3] This distribution implies the famous *rank-size rule*: a linear relationship between log-rank and log-size (in the upper tail). Applications of Simon's first model to size distributions of organizations relied on plots of log-rank against log-size to check the fit of the model to data. Simon and Bonini (1958) have shown that the model provides a reasonably good fit to data on giant industrial firms in the United States.

In subsequent research, Simon and his collaborators noted that plots of log-rank against log-size tend to bend (are convex from below). Ijiri and Simon (1974) conclude that a combination of autocorrelation in growth rates and mergers accounts for the upward bow in plots of log-rank against log-size. In this and related simulations, these researchers have demonstrated that adding various complications does not have much impact on the qualitative implications of Simon's first model. However, in each simulation, firms were allowed to grow but not to contract, and the possibility of mortality was excluded in most simulations. So the model as implemented in organizational research was a highly restricted one.

The research reported here builds on the tradition begun by Simon. However, we propose a major shift in emphasis — from statics to dynamics and from attention to the upper tail to study of complete size distributions. In the sections that follow, we attempt to show that fresh issues arise when one considers how empirical size distributions evolve over time rather than simply attending to equilibrium implications of processes. We also suggest that some of the most interesting features of organization size distributions concern the middle range rather than the upper tail. We argue in favor of considering complete distributions.

TOWARD ECOLOGICAL MODELS OF SIZE DISTRIBUTIONS

This section describes our strategy of building ecological models to explain the evolution of size distributions over time. We begin by reviewing the results of simulations that relax the restrictive assumptions used in the prior simulation studies.

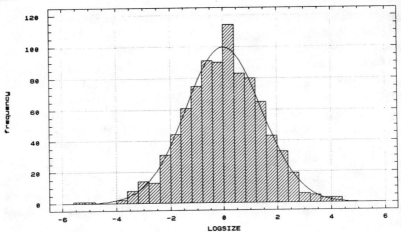

Figure 11.1. Baseline simulation (equation 4).

Before considering these complications, we discuss our baseline simulation. We start with the Gibrat's model, the growth process in equation 4. The first stage of research confirmed that our baseline program yields size distributions that converge rapidly to a lognormal distribution beginning with either a uniform distribution of initial sizes or a lognormal distribution of initial sizes. (In the latter case, the initial distribution contains many very small organizations and a few larger ones.) Since the latter assumption appears to be more realistic and is consistent with our approach to handling entries, we use it in subsequent steps. In the baseline program the initial distribution is chosen by taking the antilog of a random deviate chosen from a normal distribution with mean zero and variance of 0.00329. Therefore the initial population is lognormal with expected value equal to 1.002.[4] On the average, 16% of the organizations in the initial population exceed the mean size by 25% or more. Figure 11.1 provides a frequency distribution of log-size for one example of such a process after 500 periods for comparison with results from other models. In this and the figures that follow, the continuous line depicts the density of a lognormal distribution implied by the sample mean and variance of size. Clearly, the simulated distribution agrees closely with the lognormal.

Introducing a Carrying Capacity

Next we introduce a form of ecological control that causes the sizes of organizations to contract as well as grow. Our growth model uses the notion of a *carrying capacity* for a population in an environment, following the lead of Lotka (1925) and Volterra (1927/1978). The carrying capacity indicates the upper limit on the growth of the population given a set of social, political, and economic conditions.

Let S_t indicate the *mass* (the aggregate size of all organizations) of the population:

$$S_t = \sum_{i=1}^{N_t} S_{it}$$

where N_t is the number of organizations in the population at time t. Further, let the carrying capacity for the population in period t be indicated by S_t^*. In general, a carrying capacity reflects changeable socioeconomic conditions and consequently changes over time. In the simulations reported here, we specify that the carrying capacity is constant in order to make it possible to distinguish patterns that arise from internal dynamics alone from those that reflect interactions of such dynamics with changing external circumstances. We do not yet know whether the simplification to constant carrying capacities affects the qualitative dynamics of these systems. We plan to experiment with time-varying carrying capacities in subsequent research.

The aggregate size of the population tends to expand or contract depending on whether it is below or above the carrying capacity. In particular, we assume that the growth of each organization is governed by the process:

$$S_{it} = S_{i,t-1} \left[\frac{S_{t-1}^*}{S_{t-1}} \right] e^{\epsilon_{it}} \qquad [5]$$

where $\in_{it}$ is a normal random variable with mean zero.[5] According to this model, the ratio of an organization's size in adjacent periods depends on the population's distance from the carrying capacity and the random growth multiplier. Aside from the term in brackets, this is the lognormal model of population growth discussed above. In other words, this model asserts that population growth is lognormal with expected growth of essentially zero[6] when the population is at the carrying capacity.

From a formal perspective, the model in equation 5 is much more complicated than the lognormal since the growth of each organization depends on the sizes of all others. This is the classical form of ecological control that has been called *diffuse competition* (Tuma & Hannan, 1984, chaps. 11-14). Under diffuse competition, all members of the population compete for the same set of resources. Growth of any one organization impedes the growth of others. But, unlike Simon's first model, members of the population do not necessar-

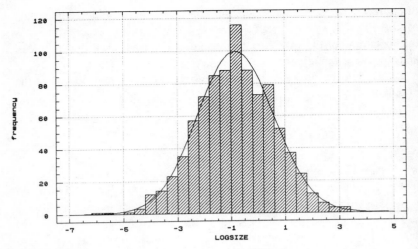

Figure 11.2. Baseline with carrying capacity (equation 5).

ily retain resources indefinitely — organizations decline as well as grow. Because the carrying capacity limits growth in the mass of the population, the emergence of one or more very large organizations depresses the growth rates of other organizations. So the carrying capacity causes mean size to decline gradually over time as maximum size trends upward, whereas mean size is stationary under the conditions we use in generating the lognormal (Hannan & Ranger-Moore, 1990; Ranger-Moore, 1989). Figure 11.2 displays a typical empirical distribution after 500 periods.

Entries and Exits

The next step adds entries and exits. Recall that Simon's model allows entries into only the smallest size class. Since we treat size as continuous, there is no natural way to choose a size at which entries occur. Moreover, choosing any particular value of size as the entry point introduces a spike into the distribution at that point. Because data on foundings reveal considerable variability in initial size, we allow such variability in the simulation. So the entry process contains two parts. The first is a Poisson process that generates entries at a constant rate, as in Simon's models.[7] The second part of the entry process assigns a random size to each entrant. Our simulation program chooses an initial size from a lognormal distribution with mean and variance equal to those of the initial cohort. Addition of this process to the baseline process in equation 4 tends to produce distributions that are approximately lognormal but skewed toward smaller sizes, as expected.

We specify a mortality process that reflects liabilities of newness and liabilities of smallness. Based on results by Hannan (1989) and Hannan and Freeman (1989, chap. 10), we use a discrete-time version of the Weibull model in expressing the effects of aging. And following Freeman, Carroll, and Hannan (1983), we assume that size decreases mortality at a decreasing rate. Combining these two assumptions gives the following model for the probability of mortality as a function of age, t, and size, S:

$$\Pr\{\text{mortality between } t \text{ and } t + 1\} = \alpha t_i^{\alpha-1} S_{it}^{-\beta} \qquad [6]$$

with $0 < \alpha < 1$ and $0 < \beta < 1$.

As expected, such a mortality process (with parameters based on estimates from empirical populations) tends to produce a negative skew in the distribution of log-size, by eliminating many of the smallest organizations. At later times, when the liability of newness wears off for some small organizations, the skew shifts back toward the left. However, the size of the largest firm tends to rise only slightly in this variation and many organizations remain close in size to the largest.

Combining entries, mortality, and a carrying capacity produces a mixture distribution. The region to the left contains a subdistribution of new and recent entrants whose size distribution is essentially lognormal. To the right are a small number of older, larger organizations. As long as the flow of entrants continues unabated, the two subdistributions persist. The combined distribution is far from lognormal. Standard nonparametric tests of distributions, such as chi-square tests and Kolmogorov-Smirnov tests, indicate that the departure is significant beyond sampling fluctuations with the setup we use.

Relaxing Gibrat's Law

We noted above that the classic models build on what has come to be known as "Gibrat's law," which holds that growth rates are statistically independent of size. Empirical studies of growth of firms have found mixed support, at best, for Gibrat's law. Hart and Prais (1956) studied firms quoted on the London Stock Exchange and concluded that Gibrat's Law was not violated. But Mansfield's (1962) study of steel, petroleum, rubber tire, and automobile industries in the United States found that growth rates and the variance of growth rates decline with size, violating Gibrat's law. Since those

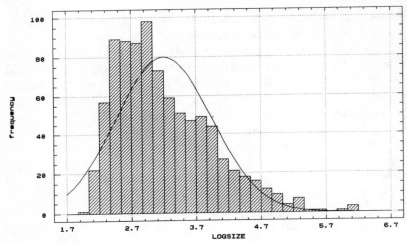

Figure 11.3. Baseline with growth rate declining with size.

two initial studies, a debate has persisted. Some research has supported Gibrat's Law (Archer & McGuire, 1965); some has indicated that growth rates are size independent but the variance diminishes with size (Hart, 1962; Hymer & Pashigian, 1962); some finds that Gibrat's law holds well for large organizations but not for small ones (Aaronovitch & Sawyer, 1975; Engwall, 1968; Hall, 1987); and some finds that Gibrat's law fails, as growth rates diminish with increasing size[8] (Chesher, 1979; Evans, 1987a, 1987b; Hall, 1987; Kumar, 1985).

Early studies suffered from focusing on selectively biased population samples (for example, only large organizations, or only firms quoted on the stock exchange) and did not control for censoring, heteroscedasticity, and variable hazard rates due to size (Collins, 1973). Recent econometric studies that have addressed these complications point to departures from Gibrat's law (Evans, 1987a, 1987b; Hall, 1987; Kumar, 1985).

Given these findings, we explore the implications for size distributions of a process in which the growth rate (but not its variance) declines with size. We used a model in which equation 5 is multiplied by a monotonically declining function of size:

$$S_{it} = S_{i,t-1} \left[\frac{S^*_{t-1}}{S_{t-1}}\right] e^{\varepsilon_{it}} \left[1 + e^{-\theta S_{i,t-1}}\right], \quad \theta > 0 \qquad [7]$$

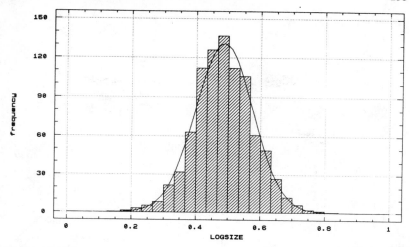

Figure 11.4. Baseline with carrying capacity, growth rate declining with size (equation 7).

The multiplier, the right-most term in equation 7, ranges between 1, as size approaches infinity, and 2, as size approaches zero. So this multiplier makes the rate of growth and decline of tiny organizations roughly twice as large as those of huge organizations. The parameter θ governs the speed with which the volatility due to small size wears off with growth. This specification implies that Gibrat's law holds asymptotically.

Figure 11.3 shows the result of making this modification to the growth rate in the "pure" lognormal process in equation 4, in which there are no entries and exits. Because growth rates on average are slightly greater than unity (as explained in note 4), this modification has a major impact on the distribution. Figure 11.3 shows a typical result, with $\theta = 0.5$. Note that the distribution of organizations by log-size is truncated on the left and that the modal size is much larger than in Figure 11.1 for the pure lognormal. It is clear that the fit to a lognormal is quite poor. Results of standard nonparametric tests indicate that the resulting distributions differ significantly from the lognormal.

Figure 11.4 provides plots parallel to those just discussed but for the process with a carrying capacity, entry, and mortality as discussed in previous sections. This time the qualitative implications of the failure of Gibrat's law are very different. The resulting distribution after 432 periods appears to be lognormal. Nonparametric tests indicate that this distribution is indistinguishable from a lognormal. Yet the range of variation in size is very small and the size of the largest organization is smaller than the average size of organizations in the population at the initiation of the process. In other words, the failure of Gibrat's law in this context results in extreme concentration of the distribution, with a great many similarly sized organizations.

Despite the differences in outcomes for the unbounded process and the one with a carrying capacity regarding the left tail of the size distribution, both have a tendency to produce a densely occupied region in the center of the distribution. This result provides an entering point of comparison with an ecological model to be discussed next.

Size-Localized Competition

Hannan and Freeman (1977) have suggested that organizations of very different sizes typically employ different strategies and structures and therefore rely on different mixes of resources. If this is so, then organizations compete most intensely with organizations of similar size. In particular, "competition between pairs of organizations in an activity will be a decreasing function of the distance separating them on the size gradient" (p. 945). They also suggest that the competitive balance among organizations of different sizes changes as the size distribution evolves:

> When large-sized organizations emerge they pose a competitive threat to medium-sized organizations but hardly any threat to small organizations. In fact, the rise of large organizations may increase the survival chances of small ones in a manner not anticipated in the classical model. When the large organizations enter, those in the middle of the size distribution are trapped. Whatever strategy they adopt to fight off the challenge of the larger form makes them more vulnerable in competition with small organizations, and vice versa. That is, at least in a stable environment the two ends of the size distribution can outcompete the middle. (p. 946)

This conjecture implies a pattern opposite the one produced by adding size-related growth rates to the baseline models. It holds that the center of the distribution will be sparse — not dense — relative to the lognormal.

Hannan and Ranger-Moore (in press) contrast simulation results of two different versions of the Hannan-Freeman argument. Both assume that the relationship is very strong in tightly packed regions of the size axis and that growth rates are relatively insensitive to variations in distance in the upper range. They use the following specification:

$$S_{it} = S_{i,t-1} \left[\frac{S_{t-1}^*}{S_{t-1}} \right] D_{i,t-1}^\gamma \, e^{\varepsilon_{it}} \qquad [8]$$

with $0 < \gamma < 1$. Here D is a measure of distance along the size axis.

The first scenario assumes that the intensity of competition facing each organization depends on the exact position of every other organization in the population. Hannan and Ranger-Moore use the Euclidean distance of each organization from all others in terms of size:

$$D_{it} = \sqrt{\sum_{j=1}^{N_t} (S_{it} - S_{jt})^2} \qquad [9]$$

In the second scenario, competition is restricted to "windows" of the size axis. Organizations are assumed to compete only with organizations within some range of their own size, the window. That is, the measure of distance is

$$D_{it} = \sqrt{\sum_{\substack{S_{jt}: \\ |S_{jt} - S_{it}| \leq \kappa}} (S_{jt} - S_{it})^2} \qquad [10]$$

where κ is the width of the window. Using the functional form in equation 10 with windows localizes the competition process by disregarding the presence of organizations outside a window.

The first scenario does not produce gaps in the distribution. Rather, it generates extreme monopolies. Once an organization has moved away from the pack, it receives a big relative increase in growth and the process is self-accelerating. The second scenario does tend to produce the predicted qualitative pattern of gaps in the center of the distribution. Figure 11.5 illustrates the consequences of the competitive process with discrete windows, entries, and mortality. In the simulation whose result is reported in Figure 11.5, the window was made an increasing function of size: $\kappa = \pm(10 + S_i/2)$. That is, this version assumes that large organizations compete over a broader band than small ones do.[9] The effect of distance on growth rates, γ in equation 8, was set to 0.10, which means that growth rates grow with distance from competitors at a sharply decreasing rate. Put differently, it means that growth rates fall sharply when localized competition becomes intense. Figure 11.5 shows that such localized competition does tend to depress the center of the distribution, as the Hannan-Freeman conjecture suggests would be the case. Notice the large gap in the right center of the

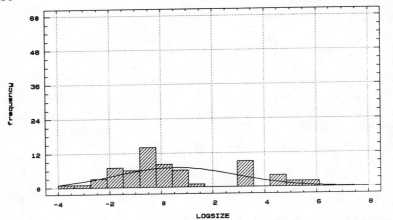

Figure 11.5. Size-localized competition, with entries, mortality, and carrying capacity.

distribution. Indeed, the departure from lognormality is significant at the .01 level ($\chi^2 = 25.0$ with 7 degrees of freedom).

Finally, we combined localized competition (with windows) with growth rates that decline with size, as discussed in the previous section. We imagined that the increased growth of small organizations would continually erode gaps in the distribution. This turns out not to be the case. Figure 11.6 reports a typical result. First, note that this variation produces many more organizations in the population and a reduction in the range of size. Yet, forcing growth rates does not eliminate the gap (a chi-square test against the lognormal yields $\chi^2 = 367.4$ with 17 degrees of freedom). Indeed, this scenario, which develops very rapidly from the initial lognormal distribution, appears to lead to isolated subpopulations. When we run the simulation for longer periods (as many as 2,500), the scenario in which growth rates decline with size tends to produce a deeper gap than does an otherwise similar process with growth rates independent of size.

SIZE DISTRIBUTIONS OF
BANKS AND INSURANCE COMPANIES

Now we consider two empirical trajectories of size distributions in order to see whether the processes depart from a lognormal and, if they do, whether they tend to clump in the center (as would be the case if growth rates decline with size and there is no size-localized competition) or whether gaps develop

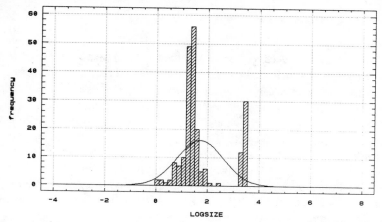

Figure 11.6. Localized competition with growth rates declining with size.

in the center of the distribution (as implied by the model of size-localized competition).

In designing empirical studies, the major strategy issue is whether to focus broadly or narrowly. The Simon tradition took a broad perspective, usually focusing on the "Fortune 500," the largest 500 industrial firms in the U.S. economy. This choice, presumably dictated by availability of data and interest in the dominant economic actors in the economy, yields a very diverse set of organizations. Some, like major oil companies, focus on one or a few industries and are strongly affected by events in those industries. Others, especially conglomerates, use a broadly generalized strategy and seek to compete in many markets. Although these giant firms all presumably compete in capital markets and in some labor markets, they do not all compete in product markets. Combining such diverse corporate actors in one size distribution combines two kinds of random variability: variation due to strategy choices and luck with an industrial market and random variations in the fortunes of industries.

We decided to take the other tack, to focus narrowly. Our goal was to collect information on firms that stand in direct competition in various kinds of markets and to eliminate the noise due to secular changes in the fortunes of industries. Indeed, we chose to study populations of firms in narrowly defined industries that also have a geographical concentration. Because we are interested in explaining the evolution of size distributions over time, we chose industries for which nearly complete enumerations are available by year over long periods. We have begun with banks operating in New York City and life insurance companies operating in New York State.

New York City Banks, 1830-1980

Information on the resources of New York City commercial banks prior to 1920 was found in two government sources: the *Annual Report of the Superintendent of Banks of the State of New York* and the *Annual Report of the Comptroller of the Currency of the United States*. Data were collected for every tenth year, beginning with 1830. Unavailability of certain data meant that the year 1911 was used instead of 1910 and that 1940 was not included in any of the preliminary results. The comptroller of the currency collected information on federally chartered banks after the establishment of a federal banking system in 1864. The New York State Banking Department, formed in 1951, collected information on the state-chartered and independent banks.[10] Information on independent banks is less reliable than the information on federally chartered and state-chartered banks.

After 1920, information on the resources of New York City banks was found in the *Rand McNally International Bankers' Directory* (final editions for each year were used). This directory includes voluntary financial information from all commercial and savings banks and trust companies within the United States. The directory receives lists of all financial institutions from federal regulatory agencies and then contacts the institutions for financial information. A discrepancy exists between earlier data, which include commercial banks, and data for years after 1920, which include commercial, savings, and trust companies; however, this problem will be addressed with data currently being collected.

Figures 11.7-11.11 report empirical distributions of the log of assets (measured in thousands of [nominal] dollars) for slices taken at 30-year intervals from 1860 to 1980 (we do not report 1830 because only 15 banks were operating in that year). Perhaps the most notable feature of these distributions is their *temporal instability*. It is certainly not the case that this population converged to some stable distribution early in its history and persisted. The initial distribution, 1860 (Figure 11.7), is close to a lognormal. According to a chi-square test, the null hypothesis of lognormality cannot be rejected at the .05 level. Over the subsequent 30 years, the distribution spreads out, as a lognormal process would (Figure 11.8). This distribution also does not differ significantly from a lognormal. By 1920 (Figure 11.9), the mean of log-size has increased considerably and the distribution has continued to spread out. There are no obvious gaps in the distribution, but now both tails appear to be thin relative to a lognormal. Yet a chi-square test does not lead to rejection of the null hypothesis of lognormality. The 1950 distribution (Figure 11.10) looks quite different. Despite a spike in the center of the distribution and a modest gap in the left-center again, this distribution

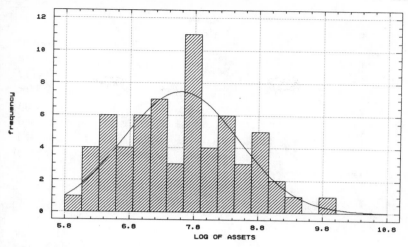

Figure 11.7. New York City banks, 1860.

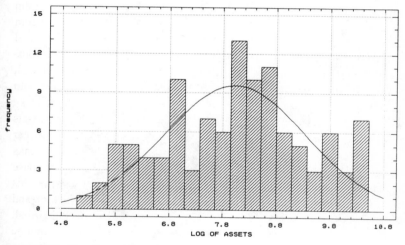

Figure 11.8. New York City banks, 1890.

too does not depart significantly from a lognormal. Finally, the 1980 distribution (Figure 11.11) seems to have the shape implied by the Hannan-Freeman conjecture. There is a noticeable gap in the left-center of the distribution and another smaller gap to the right-center. The departure from the implications of a lognormal is significant at the 0.05 level ($\chi^2 = 23.2$ with 10 degrees of freedom).

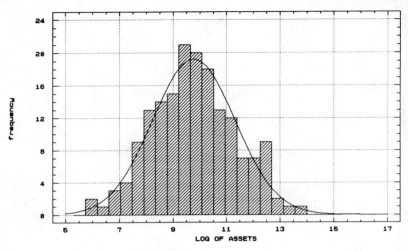

Figure 11.9. New York City banks, 1920.

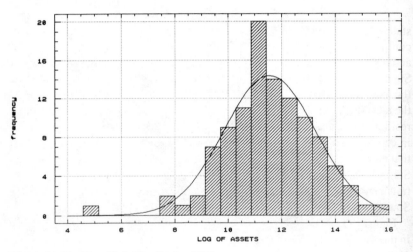

Figure 11.10. New York City banks, 1950.

Life Insurance Companies
Operating in New York State, 1860-1960

Data for the life insurance industry are being collected from the *New York Insurance Reports*, published by the commissioner of insurance of the State of New York starting in the year 1860. The volumes compile the annual

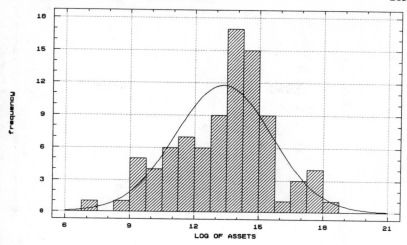

Figure 11.11. New York City banks, 1980.

statements that New York State regulations require of all life insurance companies doing business in the state. From these summaries of annual activities, the population can be defined in two ways: business in New York State only and total business. The first definition will be useful in analyzing the population as a size distribution. The second definition takes into account the fact that companies with diverse geographic holdings are likely to be more resilient to localized environmental change. It will therefore be more useful in ecological studies of vital rates, such as mortality. It is important to note that national business was recorded for all years, while business in New York State alone was not recorded until the late 1880s. In this chapter we concentrate on the distribution of total assets of all such firms operating in New York State.

Figures 11.12-11.15 report empirical distributions of log assets (measured in thousands of [nominal] dollars) for this population in the years 1870, 1900, 1930, and 1960. Again the overall impression is one of great temporal instability. Whatever dynamics have shaped this distribution have not been stable. The initial distribution (Figure 11.12) differs significantly from lognormality. The peak is too far to the left and the regions to the right-center are too sparsely occupied. Thirty years later (Figure 11.13) the distribution has shifted toward lognormality. Indeed, this distribution does not differ significantly from a lognormal. In 1930 (Figure 11.14) the distribution has developed sparse regions to the left-center, but still does not differ signifi-

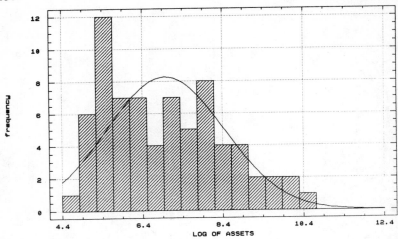

Figure 11.12. New York life insurance companies, 1870.

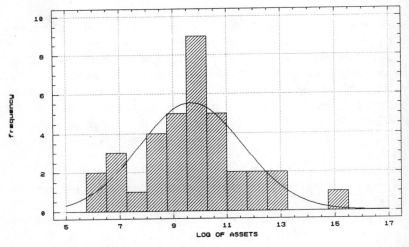

Figure 11.13. New York life insurance companies, 1900.

cantly from lognormality. Yet by 1960 (Figure 11.15) this trend has been accentuated. The center of the distribution is significantly depressed relative to a lognormal. A chi-square test against the lognormal yields $\chi^2 = 13.7$ with 6 degrees of freedom. So once again, the evolution of the size distribution appears to have operated in a manner that corresponds at least roughly with the implications of size-localized competition processes.

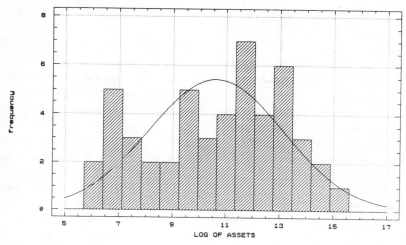

Figure 11.14. New York life insurance companies, 1930.

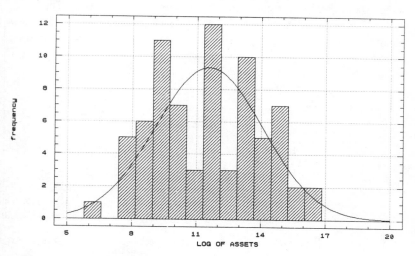

Figure 11.15. New York life insurance companies, 1960.

DISCUSSION

We are struck by the fact that these empirical size distributions change markedly over time. We suspect that these changes reflect both internal dynamics of populations and the effects of changes in external environments. Given that the empirical distributions cannot be characterized by a single simple stochastic process (such as the lognormal — or, presumably, the Yule or Pareto distribution), there is ample opportunity to model the evolution of organizational size distributions in substantive, theoretical frameworks.

We think that the initial results are encouraging as regards the Hannan-Freeman conjecture that competition tends to be localized on the size axis. Size distributions of both empirical populations evolve toward a pattern that is consistent with the argument, beginning with essentially lognormal distributions. However, our simulation structure creates gaps to the right-center of the distribution and both empirical populations develop gaps (or dips) to the left-center of the distribution. We do not yet understand the source or the implications of this difference. The next item on our agenda of simulations is to vary the scenario of localized competition in order to learn whether and how we can shift the gaps in the distribution.

The next major step in the empirical research is to relate the life history data on individual firms to the evolution of the size distribution. Two issues hold major interest. The first concerns patterns of mortality. Does location in the size distribution affect mortality rates net of age and size? That is, do firms that find themselves in densely occupied regions of the size distribution experience heightened mortality? Second, does a similar process hold for growth in size? That is, are growth rates of firms depressed in regions of intense size-localized competition?

NOTES

1. Useful surveys of the genesis of this model can be found in Aitchison and Brown (1957) and Steindl (1965).

2. Another approach, sketched by Kalecki (1945) and developed at length by Steindl (1965), introduces a negative relationship between the growth rate and size of a particular form to ensure that the variance of the distribution remains stable. Since recent economic research finds such a relationship we consider this possibility below. However, we also propose a different way of stabilizing the size distribution.

3. The second model implies that the upper tail of the distribution converges to Fisher's log-series distribution.

4. The mean of $\exp(\in)$ where $\in$ is a normally distributed random variable with a mean of zero and a standard deviation of σ is $\exp(\sigma^2/2)$; its variance is $\exp(\sigma)[\exp(\sigma) - 1]$ (Johnson & Kotz, 1970, p. 115).

5. In the versions of the simulation discussed here, we also assume that $\in_{it}$ is uncorrelated over time and over organizations in the population.

6. In fact, the expected growth is not zero in this model but depends on the variance of the random growth rate, as we note below. However, for substantively plausible levels of variability in growth rates, the expected rate is essentially zero.

7. The rate of the founding process, which equals the expected number of foundings per period, sets a time scale for the process. We use this as the main time scale and set parameters of the mortality rate appropriately.

8. Singh and Whittington (1975) find that growth rates *rise* (weakly but significantly) with size.

9. This specification also leads to one-sided competition, since a small organization may be in the window of a large one but not vice versa. We are also experimenting with windows of fixed width and with width that varies with the logarithm of size.

10. Information on banks within New York State prior to 1850 can be found in the New York State Assembly records. However, the information provided by the banks was not supervised by any regulatory agency, such as the later Department of Banking. The accuracy of the figures from this earlier period is questionable. However, we will be able to confirm whether the banks reported or not by using data currently being collected on the foundings and disbandings of the banks.

REFERENCES

Aaronovitch, S., & Sawyer, M. C. (1975). Mergers, growth and concentration. *Oxford Economic Papers, 27,* 136-155.

Aitchison, J., & Brown, J. A. C. (1957). *The lognormal distribution.* Cambridge: Cambridge University Press.

Archer, S. H., & McGuire, J. (1965). Organization size and probabilities of growth. *Western Economic Journal, 3,* 233-246.

Chester, A. (1979). Testing the law of proportionate effect. *Journal of Industrial Economics, 27,* 403-411.

Collins, L. (1973). Industrial size and stochastic processes. *Progress in Geography, 5,* 121-165.

Engw " l. (1968). Size distribution of organizations: A stochastic model. *Swedish Journal of Economics, 70,* 138-157.

Evans, D. S. (1987a). The relationship between organization growth, size, and age: Estimates for 100 manufacturing industries. *Journal of Industrial Economics, 35,* 567-581.

Evans, D. S. (1987b). Tests of alternative theories of firm growth. *Journal of Political Economy, 95,* 657-674.

Freeman, J., Carroll, G. R., & Hannan, M. T. (1983). The liability of newness: Age dependence in organizational death rates. *American Sociological Review, 48,* 692-710.

Gibrat, R. (1931). *Les inégalités économiques.* Paris: Sirey.

Hall, B. (1987). The relationship between firm size and firm growth in the U.S. manufacturing sector. *Journal of Industrial Economics, 35,* 583-606.

Hannan, M. T. (1988). Organizational population dynamics and social change. *European Sociological Review, 4,* 1-15.

Hannan, M. T. (1989). Age dependence in the mortality of national labor unions: Comparisons of parametric models. *Journal of Mathematical Sociology, 15,* 1-30.

Hannan, M. T., & Freeman, J. (1977). The population ecology of organizations. *American Journal of Sociology, 82,* 929-964.

Hannan, M. T., & Freeman, J. (1989). *Organizational ecology.* Cambridge, MA: Harvard University Press.

Hannan, M. T., & Ranger-Moore, J. (1990). The ecology of organizational size distributions: A microsimulation approach. *Journal of Mathematical Sociology, 15,* 65-89.

Hart, P. E. (1962). The size of growth of organizations. *Econometrica, 29,* 29-39.

Hart, P. E., & Prais, S. J. (1956). The analysis of business concentration. *Journal of the Royal Statistical Society* (Part II), *119,* 150-191.

Hymer, S., & Pashigian, P. (1962). Firm size and rate of growth. *Journal of Political Economy, 70,* 556-569.

Ijiri, Y., & Simon, H. A. (1964). Business firm growth and size. *American Economic Review, 54,* 77-89.

Ijiri, Y., & Simon, H. A. (1971). Effects of mergers and acquisitions on business organization concentration. *Journal of Political Economy, 79,* 314-322.

Ijiri, Y., & Simon, H. A. (1974). Interpretations of departures from the Pareto curve firm-size distributions. *Journal of Political Economy, 82,* 315-331.

Ijiri, Y., & Simon, H. A. (1977). *Skew distributions and the sizes of business firms.* New York: North Holland.

Johnson, N. L., & Kotz, S. (1970). *Distributions in statistics: Continuous univariate distributions* (Vol. 2). Boston: Houghton Mifflin.

Kalecki, M. (1945). On the Gibrat distribution. *Econometrica, 13,* 161.

Kapteyn, J. C. (1903). *Skew frequency curves in biology and statistics.* Astronomical Laboratory, Gronigen: Noordhoff.

Kumar, M. S. (1985). Growth, acquisition activity and organization size: Evidence from the United Kingdom. *Journal of Industrial Economics, 33,* 327-338.

Lotka, A. J. (1925). *Elements of physical biology.* Baltimore: Williams & Wilkins.

Mansfield, E. (1962). Entry, Gibrat's law, innovation, and the growth of organizations. *American Economic Review, 52,* 1023-1051.

Prais, S. J. (1976). *The evolution of giant firms in Britain.* Cambridge: Cambridge University Press.

Ranger-Moore, J. (1989). *Ecological dynamics of organizational size distributions.* Unpublished master's thesis, Cornell University.

Simon, H. A. (1955). On a class of skew distribution functions. *Biometrika, 52,* 425-440.

Simon, H. A., & Bonini, C. P. (1958). The size distributions of business firms. *American Economic Review, 48,* 607-617.

Singh, A., & Whittington, G. (1975). The size and growth of organizations. *Review of Economic Studies, 42,* 15-26.

Steindl, J. (1965). *Random processes and the growth of firms: A study of the Pareto law.* New York: Hafner.

Steindl, J. (1967). Size distributions in economics. In D. Sills (Ed.), *The International Encyclopedia of the Social Sciences.* New York: Macmillan.

Tuma, N. B., & Hannan, M. T. (1984). *Social dynamics: Models and methods.* New York: Academic Press.

Volterra, V. (1978). Variations and fluctuations in the number of coexisting species. In F. M. Scudo & J. R. Ziegler (Eds.), *The golden age of theoretical ecology: 1923-1940.* New York: Springer-Verlag. (Original work published 1927)

12

Survival, Selection, and Inheritance in Evolutionary Theories of Organization

SIDNEY G. WINTER

The extension of evolutionary modes of analysis into realms remote from biology is an intellectual activity with a long history and a great deal of current vitality. Although there remain some skeptics who continue to characterize the whole enterprise as a concoction of dubious biological analogies, anyone who approaches the contributions of the past decade with an open mind is likely to be impressed with the broad promise of the evolutionary approach.

Diversity and controversy are prominent features of contemporary discussions, as they are of the historical record. Even among committed evolutionists, there is much more agreement on the general outlines and value of an evolutionary approach than there is on the specific mechanisms involved. In particular, investigators in the broad area of cultural evolution have introduced a wide variety of terms to denote what is transmitted through time ("inherited") in cultural evolution. Dawkins (1976) writes of "memes," a concept that covers, for example, "tunes, ideas, catchphrases, clothes fashions, ways of making pots or building arches," which spread "via a process which in the broad sense, can be called imitation" (p. 206). Lumsden and Wilson (1981) note a number of synonymous or near synonymous terms in

Author's Note: I am indebted to the participants in the Wharton Conference on Organizational Evolution for stimulating and helpful discussions, and to Richard Nelson for helpful comments. I owe a special debt to Jitendra Singh for his careful review and thoughtful critique of an earlier draft of this chapter. Whatever errors and shortcomings remain are my own responsibility.

the literature (p. 7), and take some pains to argue the merits of their own preferred term, "culturgen" (pp. 26-30). As in the case of Dawkins's "meme," their concept is broad in scope and the comparably broad concepts of teaching, learning, and imitation are employed in the discussion of the transmission of traits.[1]

It is not easy to say how many distinct concepts are represented by these various terms. The conceptual distinctions are fuzzy, largely because little attention has been paid to the mechanism by which whatever-it-is-called is transmitted, to the precision of this replication mechanism, and to the taxonomic or measurement problems involved in determining whether the same or different traits are represented in two observed instances.[2]

Evolutionary theories of organization constitute a subfield of the broader inquiry into cultural evolution. Investigators in this subfield are interested in the evolution of the particular aspects of human culture involving the appearance and disappearance of organizations and ways of organizing. They do not fully share the concern of most cultural evolutionists with the links between cultural phenomena and biological evolution. The question of what is "inherited" and how the inheritance mechanism works is, however, just as central and just as far from definitive resolution as it is in cultural evolution generally.

In this chapter, I review and extend the approach to the inheritance question that Richard Nelson and I have taken in our effort to advance the evolutionary approach to economic organization. Compared with other contributors to the cultural and organizational evolution literatures, we have devoted disproportionate attention to spelling out a detailed theoretical picture of the mechanisms of inheritance, selection, and survival. We like to think of ourselves as extremists in this regard, arguing that the adequacy of the theoretical treatment of these mechanisms is a key indicator of the degree to which the "biological analogies" (Penrose, 1952) level of argument has been surpassed in developing an evolutionary approach to particular phenomena. Our concepts have been shaped to address a range of phenomena specific to organizational evolution. The "organizational ecology" approach to organizations (represented by many of the chapters in this volume) addresses empirical issues that are closely related to those of interest in evolutionary economics. A subsidiary purpose of this chapter is to assess some of the interpretations offered by this approach from the viewpoint of evolutionary economics. In particular, the focus of the comparative discussion is on the branch of organizational ecology that has focused on organizational birthrates and death rates — the "population ecology" school founded by Hannan and Freeman (1977) and represented in this volume by the chapters of Aldrich et al., Barnett and Amburgey, Carroll and Hannan, Freeman, and Hannan et al.

The next section reviews the basic concerns of evolutionary economics, and in the section that follows I make the case for "routines" as a fundamental unit of analysis in the evolutionary approach to organizations — a case premised on the concerns set forth in the next section. I then present a discussion of the concepts of survival, selection, and inheritance employed in economic evolutionary theory, relating them to organizational routines and to the role of large organizations. The final section relates the earlier parts of the chapter to some of the work done in the organizational ecology tradition, points out similarities and differences, and identifies specific issues that call for further research.

CONCERNS OF ECONOMIC EVOLUTIONARY THEORY

Thorstein Veblen was an early advocate of an evolutionary approach to economic theory. In his 1898 essay "Why Is Economics Not an Evolutionary Science?" he associates the evolutionary approach with the analysis of cumulative change and specifically characterizes the subject matter of evolutionary economics as follows:

> For the purpose of economic science the process of cumulative change that is to be accounted for is the sequence of *change in the methods of doing things* — the methods of dealing with the material means of life. (Veblen, 1898/1961)

Apart from the fact that an overly literal reading of the word *material* might lead to an interpretation inappropriate to economies increasingly dominated by the service sector, this characterization serves as well today as it did when Veblen wrote it.

"Methods of doing things" had changed a great deal in the two centuries before Veblen wrote, and they have changed even more in the period of almost a century since then. The aspirations that motivate the development of the evolutionary theory of economic change are to contribute to the understanding of this continuing process of change and to the development of constructive policies for guiding and controlling it. These aspirations have implications for the content and structure of the required theory.

First among the focal concerns of economic evolutionary theory is understanding the nature and sources of *productive competence*. It is clear enough that, in a metaphorical sense at least, organizations "know" how to do things. The application of science and technology to the production of goods and services is a distinctive and impressive feature of modern societies; for the most part this feature reflects the accomplishments of organizations — and often of large organizations. But what does it mean for an organization to "know" something, and how does organizational knowledge relate to individual knowledge? Is most of the knowledge that underlies the productive competence of an organization written down somewhere? If so, where? How, in fact, does the "knowledge" of an organization relate to its productive competence, that is, to its actual ability to produce valued goods and services? What sorts of events in the life of an organization might degrade or erase its memory?

To understand "methods of doing things" at a level relevant to economics is to understand "methods" not in a scientific or engineering sense, but as organizational performances. It is not the content of the recipe book that is principally of concern when one eats a meal in a restaurant, and it is not the level of engineering understanding that is of concern when one turns on a television set or picks up a telephone to make a call. What is of concern to the customer — and hence should be of intellectual interest to economists — is the ability of organizations actually to deliver what is wanted.

The second, closely related, concern of economic evolutionary theory is innovation. It is the pace and character of change in productive competencies that constitute the most striking phenomena to be accounted for. Just as productive competence cannot be understood in terms of culinary or engineering "recipes" alone, changes in productive competence cannot be understood simply in terms of inventions. As Schumpeter (1911/1934) emphasizes, the actual introduction into economic practice of new ways of doing things typically requires that many obstacles be overcome, obstacles that do not in a similar way impede the mere *conception* of new ways of doing things. Obstacles to change are, however, simply sources of continuity viewed from the other side. Whatever we may choose to mean by "inheritance" in evolutionary theories of organizations, it presumably will play the role of a major source of continuity in organizational performances. Accordingly, the attempt to understand inheritance leads into much the same territory as the attempt to understand innovation, but enters from the opposite angle.

Third, evolutionary economic theory is particularly concerned with the role and functioning of for-profit organizations in the economic system. Overall profitability and cash flow are distinctive forms of environmental feedback that powerfully shape the behavior of such organizations. The study of the functioning of this feedback mechanism is a distinctive subject matter that naturally draws the attention of economists. How this relates to survival, selection, and inheritance among economic organizations is an issue of particular interest.

From these three focal concerns, others are derived. For example, although large corporations are certainly not the most convenient objects of evolutionary study, they must remain high on the research agenda because of the centrality of their role in key respects. Productive performances of large scale and high complexity are typically their province; consider aircraft production, or telecommunications. Relatedly, they provide the most vivid examples of organizations, in contradistinction to individuals, serving as repositories of productive knowledge over extended periods of time. Whereas a local restaurant may prosper for the lifetime of its founder or the tenure of its chef and then disappear or be fundamentally transformed, many large corporations having been doing what is recognizably the same thing over periods that are long relative to human productive lifetimes — consider Boeing and AT&T.

Further, although there is an understandable sense in which these organizations have been doing "the same thing" over an extended period, there is equally clearly a sense in which their productive competencies have changed radically. Concern with major and cumulative innovation, illustrated again by aircraft and telecommunications, likewise directs attention to large corporations. Organized research and development activity is largely their province — at least as measured by R&D inputs.[3]

Finally, although large corporations are vastly outnumbered by small corporations and other business forms, they account for a large share of total activity in manufacturing and their relative importance is on the rise in other sectors. A rough criterion for distinguishing between "large" and "small" businesses, and one that is helpful in guiding thinking about the theoretical issues involved here, is to classify as "large" a business that operates at more than one geographic location. In 1982, single-establishment companies accounted for about 77% of all manufacturing establishments, but only about 18% of manufacturing value added.[4] In retail trade, the percentage of sales accounted for by establishments that are part of multiestablishment firms rose from 30.1% in 1954 to 53.2% in 1982 (U.S. Department of Commerce, 1989, Tables 1264, 1324).

For these several reasons, large corporations deserve an important place in the subject matter of economic evolutionary theory, and indeed of economics generally. Undeniably, they present a number of research challenges that smaller organizations do not; some of these challenges are noted below. A research strategy of focusing on small organizations has its advantages, but the foundations of a theory that is supposed to elucidate the many forces of economic change cannot involve concepts that are applicable *only* to the study of small organizations.

A second derived concern, closely related to the first, is the problem of organizational boundaries. Depending on the purpose at hand, a number of different definitions of the boundaries of an organization may be useful. Here, the purpose at hand is understanding the evolution of methods of doing things, and it is assumed that organizations are usefully regarded as consisting of packages of competence. In some cases, the organization as a whole (with its boundaries delineated by some standard other than competence) may be thought of as one single, coherent package. Such cases are particularly convenient from an empirical point of view, since data on organizations (variously defined) are more prevalent than data on packages of competence. These convenient conjunctions happen most frequently for single-establishment business firms, where data on the organization *qua* productive locale, *qua* business enterprise and *qua* package of competence, may provide complementary perspectives on essentially the same activities. Even the competencies of small firms, however, are often seen to be complex when scrutinized in detail.

ROUTINES AS UNITS OF ANALYSIS

As has just been suggested, the assumption that each organization possesses a unitary competence does not have sufficiently broad applicability to provide a general foundation for an evolutionary approach to organization. It oversimplifies the activities even of small organizations (when those are scrutinized in detail), becomes increasingly strained as one moves along the continuum toward larger, more complex and diversified organizations, and is plainly inappropriate in application to the large conglomerate corporation. Some fundamentally different way of thinking about the relation between organizations and their competencies is needed.

In our contribution to economic evolutionary theory, Nelson and I have proposed that organizational *routines* should have a prominent place in the lexicon of evolutionary theories of organization.[5] The proposal has a number of advantages. For example, the biological analogy evoked by the phrase *routines as genes* serves immediately to suggest two important points related to the discussion above. The first is that the entity on which the environment acts and that generally lives or dies as a unit — the organism or organization — is a complex entity with numerous traits. Theoretical or empirical inquiry

TABLE 12.1: Some Examples of Routines

Airline reservation systems
Fast-food fried chicken
Assembly lines
Markup pricing
M-form corporation
LIFO inventory accounting

focused on a single trait may well be useful, but useful primarily because the assumption makes things easy for the analyst and not because reality frequently exemplifies competition among organisms/organizations differing in a single trait. The second point is the genotype-phenotype distinction: Observed variations among individual organisms/organizations are partly a reflection of the different environments they have encountered, and not entirely of the inherited portion of their characteristics.

To develop the routines as genes approach fully, the problem of inheritance mechanisms needs to be dealt with convincingly. Here, the biological analogy provides little help; the argument must be grounded directly on the specifics of the subject matter. Before I proceed in the following section to discuss inheritance mechanisms and some related problems involving the growth and survival of individual organizations, the basic idea of a "routine" requires some further explication.

Table 12.1 names some illustrative examples of routines. The examples are diverse in the dimension "hard" (technological) versus "soft" (organizational). They are also diverse in the level of detail involved: Assembly lines might be roughly at the taxonomic level of fast food, while "fast-food fried chicken" is like "automobile assembly lines."

Among the features that the examples have in common are the following: First, they all involve repetitive patterns of activity, though literal repetition is not necessarily a major feature of the repetitive pattern. (For example, a large part of the point of airplane reservation systems or fast-food chicken service is that these routines cope quickly and efficiently with customers who express different specific demands, though they are asking for the same sort of thing.) Also, they all require, to varying degrees, investment in routine-specific human and physical capital. People have to know their jobs, they need appropriate equipment, and neither the skills nor the equipment is costlessly transferable to another way of doing things.

Finally, they all have the property that different instances are easily recognized as belonging to a class denoted by a concise label of the sort used in Table 12.1. If more precision is needed to deal with ambiguous examples, it can generally be supplied by developing (with only a few arbitrary judgments) a list of traits that are common to all examples of the routine, and perhaps noting the distinctions that set apart related routines.

It should be emphasized that it is the pattern of activity, the process, the *organizational performance* that is the routine—not the diagram, device, plan, or recipe. For example, "M-form corporation" denotes particularly the periodic process of developing performance reports for divisions organized along particular lines, and the forwarding of those reports to headquarters for review in characteristic ways.

In our 1982 book, Nelson and I pushed the idea of routine rather far, stating for example that

> most of what is *regular and predictable* about business behavior is plausibly subsumed under the heading "routine," especially if we understand that term to include the relatively constant dispositions and strategic heuristics that shape the approach of a firm to the nonroutine problems it faces. (p. 15, see also p. 133)

I now believe that we went too far. By blurring the distinction between routines on the one hand and heuristics or dispositions on the other, we underemphasized the advantages of a narrower concept that is more easily operationalized. These advantages derive from the features of routines emphasized above: repetitiveness, embodiment in human and physical assets, and ease of identification. The conjunction of these features will serve as a working definition of *routine*.

To the extent that routines remain constant, careful description of prevailing routines can provide a basis for predicting the future behavior of the organization. Some work of this sort has been done.[6] In my view, a good deal more of it could usefully be done, and the theoretical guidance available from evolutionary theory could enhance its fruitfulness. Veblen's mission statement does not, however, enjoin us to describe methods of doing things, but to understand *change* in methods of doing things. Although short-run predictive power is an important collateral benefit from the description of prevailing routines, the principal benefit is the contribution to understanding change.

That benefit arises for two reasons. First, much change is incremental and produces new routines that closely resemble the old. The course of incremental change reflects the differential strength of the various sources of continuity in the routine, and understanding of those sources may therefore aid prediction (Winter, 1986). Close scrutiny of prevailing routines may also aid in the difficult task of predicting radical innovations — but in this case it is contrast rather than similarity that is the key. Incremental change gradually defines and enhances the stress points and coverage gaps to which radical innovation often responds — semiconductor devices are notably *un*like vacuum tubes in power requirements and heat production; railroad systems are notably more adaptable to a variety of terrains than are canal and river boats.

The effect of prevailing routines on the channeling of change is an area where evolutionary economics makes contact with the substantial social science literature on organizational innovation and the diffusion of innovations among organizations.[7] In that literature, the "innovation" is the unit of analysis, and an "innovation" is ordinarily understood more narrowly than we would understand "new routine." An automatic teller machine, for example, would typically be regarded from the diffusion of innovations perspective as an innovation consisting essentially of a piece of hardware. In a routines-based evolutionary analysis, the machine itself is a routine-specific physical asset, and useful as one identifying trait for the ATM routine, but the ATM is not itself the routine. The diffusion of innovations perspective is historically associated with a presumption that the innovation is a "good thing" and the puzzle is why it is not more rapidly or widely adopted.

Similarly, in the organizational innovation literature, innovativeness is generally a good thing. Kimberly (1981) identifies and criticizes this bias and notes that it may be adaptive for an organization to know when to give up on a previously adopted innovation ("exnovation"). In evolutionary theory, it is recognized that maintenance of routines is an activity that organizations must perform, and resistance to change is functional, at least in part. The puzzle, as noted above, is to understand how the various (functional and dysfunctional) sources of continuity in behavior affect the rate and character of change. In spite of these differences in approach, both theoretical and empirical work in these other literatures has addressed many of the same issues featured in the economic evolutionary theory. Downs and Mohr (1976) persuasively argue that studies of innovation in complex organizations should treat "the innovation" and "the organization" symmetrically; both have multiple attributes that are relevant to explaining what happens where the history of the innovation overlaps the history of the organization (see also Kimberly, 1986; Zaltman, Duncan, & Holbek, 1973). They propose that "an organization in relation to an innovation" should be the unit of analysis in organizational innovation studies. Although evolutionary (and other) economists might suggest different attributes for consideration than have been explored in most organizational innovation studies, the general idea of a "mating" approach to a theory of organizational innovation is a perspective shared by evolutionary economics. More recently, Tushman and Anderson (1986) have explored the distinction between "competence-enhancing" and "competence-destroying" innovations. This distinction provides a particularly helpful way of thinking about "an organization in relation to an innovation" (or perhaps the reverse).

Understanding of innovation has been advanced through research guided from a variety of disciplinary perspectives. The work mentioned above is particularly noteworthy for its close relationship to studies of organizations, but a number of other branches of scholarship—economic history above all—have made major contributions to our understanding of "change in the methods of doing things." In economics at least, a major appeal of evolutionary thinking is its potential to be enriched by contact with other disciplines and perspectives—and perhaps to provide, ultimately, a unifying view. Evolutionary theories of organization can offer something more than a repetition of the familiar academic routine of erecting new isolated pinnacles of specialized understanding in the immense plain of general ignorance.

SURVIVAL, INHERITANCE, AND SELECTION

Survival

It is a commonplace that organizations are open systems; they survive through interactions with their environment. A familiar example of an open system is a candle flame: The flame melts the wax of the candle, which permits it to be drawn into the wick, where it undergoes combustion to produce more heat and permits the process to continue. With candle flames, and with all but the simplest biological organisms, there is ordinarily not much ambiguity about the phenomenon of death. Death may be produced because the environment no longer contains enough of a vital resource (oxygen, for example) or because something (a puff of wind) intrudes to break the self-sustaining dynamics of the process: Once the flame is snuffed out, a spontaneous restart does not occur even if all the requisite resources are available.

On further consideration, the apparently unambiguous character of death in these cases turns out to depend on an underlying assumption identifying the "individual" whose survival is at issue. Suppose that when there is an inch of candle left, the better burning candle is placed on top of another (not burning), with the result that the bottom candle ignites as the top one is exhausted. Has the original flame survived or has a new one taken its place? In simple organisms that reproduce by cell division, there is similarly an ambiguity about what the individual is, and the ambiguity carries over to the definition of survival. After the cell divides, is the original individual present twice, once, or not at all?

In the realm of organizational life and death, these semantic puzzles have counterparts that can pose serious conceptual and measurement challenges. The challenges are least severe in the case of a small organization that disappears through liquidation, its members and physical assets going their various separate ways. The disappearance of the organization as a legal entity then means that the organization "really" dies in the sense relevant for economic evolutionary theory — the particular package of productive competencies that constituted the firm exists no more. Data analyzed by Pakes and Ericson (1990, Table 12.1) suggest that when business firms disappear, it is usually through liquidation, and the smaller the business the more likely it is that liquidation is involved. Of 44,272 firms with one or more employees that were active in Wisconsin in 1978, 45% had liquidated or undergone an ownership change by 1986. Of these, 81% were liquidated. Of the firms with more then 50 employees in 1978, 25% disappeared by 1986; of those, 58% were liquidated.

For this reason and others, small businesses (or, more generally, small organizations) are promising territory for evolutionary inquiries that emphasize the adaptive fitness of the organization as a unit; the typical alternative to survival as a legal entity is a relatively unambiguous form of death. Of course, it should be recognized that liquidation may represent the voluntary termination of a successful but time-bound enterprise; the inference of a negative verdict by the environment may not be warranted. (Business *failures* that result in liquidation, however, are quite reliably interpretable as disappearances that reflect a negative verdict by the environment.) Finally, liquidation itself is a matter of degree in the sense that the assets of the business can be separated into chunks of various sizes. For moderate-sized and large firms, even liquidation does not necessarily imply that *no* part of the firm survives as a functioning entity with its routines intact.

Acquisition by another firm is also a common mode of disappearance for both small and large firms. Unfortunately, the proposition that a business has "disappeared" through acquisition by another has — in the absence of other information — virtually no useful meaning for the purposes of evolutionary theory. Acquisition may be a close kin of liquidation, perhaps reflecting the fact that efficiently liquidating the firm is a process involving challenges that the acquirer feels well qualified to meet. It may represent, from the acquirer's viewpoint, a cheap alternative to construction of new facilities. Or it may reflect the success and maturation of an entrepreneurial start-up that reaches a point where full exploitation of its profit opportunities requires a major infusion of capital or more specific assets that the acquirer is able to provide. The acquired firm in this case may or may not survive as an identifiable entity within the acquiring organization. And if it does so survive, its operations may or may not be substantially affected by the fact that it is now part of a larger organization.

When the events under examination are mergers, acquisitions and divestitures of large or medium-sized firms by other large or medium-sized firms, it becomes quite problematic to discern in these events the survival, demise, or perhaps resurrection of productive organizations. All of the ambiguities noted in the case of small organizations are present in greater degree. Death by acquisition is much more likely to be followed by some sort of reincarnation as a different but recognizable entity, and even ultimate resurrection as a free-standing firm is a common outcome.[8] The situation is further complicated by the fact that parts of an acquired firm may have quite different fates in the hands of the acquirer — a part may be liquidated, another fully consolidated with the acquirer's operations, another established as a division or subsidiary of the acquirer, and yet another spun off as an independent firm. A major challenge to understanding is obviously posed by this sort of complexity; to avoid being overwhelmed by it, one must keep fundamental theoretical objectives continuously in view.

In economic evolutionary theory, organizations are viewed as packages of routinized competence; as such, they are important among society's repositories of productive knowledge and arrangements for advancing such knowledge. From this perspective, the fates of routines are of more fundamental interest than the fates of organizations. Considered as a repository of knowledge of the sort that is "remembered by doing," an organization (*qua* package of competence) survives if its repertoire of routines remains intact, does not survive if it suffers total amnesia regarding its routines, and passes through some sort of intermediate transition when only a portion of its routines are changed (even if for the better). To distinguish survival from nonsurvival in a way that is not influenced by superficial institutional distinctions, and to sort out the complex intermediate cases, it is necessary to identify the key routines and ask what has happened to them.

Institutionally defined business failures that take the form of bankruptcy followed by reorganization may, for example, represent little or no break in the continuity of routine operation. Railroad bankruptcies of the nineteenth century are classic examples of this phenomenon; contemporary reorganizations under Chapter 11 of the Bankruptcy Reform Act of 1978 illustrate continuity through failure even more clearly. On the other hand, the acquisition of an entrepreneurial firm by a larger corporation may result in the destruction or loss of key routines of the acquired firm, even when that firm is plainly successful at the time of the acquisition and major efforts are made to maintain continuity. Recently, for example, the acquisition by GM of Ross Perot's Electronic Data Systems and the acquisition by IBM of Rolm were prominent instances in which intentions to preserve the special character of the acquired firms were publicly pronounced and supported by structural arrangements to that end — but these intentions have not been fully realized. While it might be premature to pronounce EDS and Rolm totally "dead" by virtue of complete digestion by their parents, it is clear that they are not nearly as "alive" as was forecast when the acquisitions were made.

Inheritance

Like the issues of life and death, issues relating to the scale and scope of the business firm are interpreted in economic evolutionary theory in a way that reflects its emphasis on organizational routines. At least since the era around the turn of the century when the great trusts were created, large firms have rarely been created *de novo*. The large firms of today typically became large through internal growth and incremental acquisitions, punctuated by occasional large acquisitions and mergers. Evolutionary theory focuses on the processes of internal growth and incremental acquisition. It interprets these processes as a reflection of the past success of the firm's routines and of the reinvestment of some of the monetary rewards of that success in additional productive capacity. The additional capacity is operated according to routines that, though they may differ from those that gave rise to the previous success, represent the application of the firm's basic competence on a larger scale — a step motivated, at least in part, by the hope of deriving larger profits from that basic competence. In economic evolutionary theory, inheritance is first of all a matter of replication of successful routines by the individual organization.

In simple theoretical models of evolutionary processes, it is assumed that routines can be replicated perfectly and, in the jargon of economic theory, there are (long-run) constant returns to scale in production. If routines have not changed in the interim, the successful firm that has grown up to producing 1,000 units per period is, so far as production is concerned, precisely ten times what it was when it produced 100 units per period. The overall scale of the firm matters to investment decisions (e.g., in avoiding excess capacity in a limited market); it also matters to the financing and exploitation of research and development efforts. But so far as production routines are concerned, the activities of a large firm with a given set of routines are simply a multiple of those of a small firm with the same routines.

With only modest further elaboration, these simple models capture a number of salient features of industrial structure and behavior. They are consistent with the observed fact that firms that differ quite dramatically in size participate with approximately equal success in many markets; if there were marked net advantages to size per se, or a single efficient firm size, one would not expect this to occur.[9] They are consistent with the fact that market share is a significant predictor of individual firm profitability (Schmalensee, 1985); the interpretation is that market share is an indicator of competitive strength and as such bodes well for the firm in question and ill for rival firms. Given the individual firm's share, on the other hand, market concentration may be an indicator both of the competitive strength of rivals and of their ability collectively to enhance profitability by restraining total output; on balance there is no clear theoretical implication for the profitability of the individual firm. Empirically, it seems that the "strength of rivals" effect is generally more important (Ravenscraft, 1983). The output restraint effect is more likely to be significant, however, when concentration is high absolutely and certain other identifiable circumstances prevail in the market (Scherer, 1980, chaps. 6, 7).

The dynamic assumptions of evolutionary theory are further corroborated by observed correlations between profitability and growth, and by the tendency of firms that display profitability and growth that are above or below average in a particular period to "regress to the mean" fairly slowly over time — a pattern that suggests the existence of persistent idiosyncratic features of firms that affect profitability and growth. There is also evidence that firms that have recently made major innovations tend to experience a period of enhanced profitability and growth (Mansfield, 1962; Singh & Whittington, 1975). These regularities are all consistent with the simple models that acknowledge the idiosyncratic features of individual firms and represent firm growth primarily as spatial replication of production — a second similar machine standing beside the first, a new but similar factory in another region of the country.[10]

Although it correctly predicts a number of the significant patterns in firm growth and market structure, the simple theoretical story of firm growth as spatial replication is clearly inadequate as an account of the scope of the large corporation. The first step toward a more adequate account is to recognize that the basic technological and organizational competencies of a firm can be profitably brought to bear in more than one product market. As Teece (1982) has remarked, "A firm's capability lies upstream from the end product—it lies in a generalizable capability which might find a variety of final product applications" (p. 45). Similarly, a firm may integrate upstream or downstream, motivated at least in part by recognition that it already possesses part of the relevant competencies in these related areas. Analysis along these lines is fully consistent with evolutionary theory's general emphasis on the firm's role as a repository of productive competence. As diversification reaches the levels displayed in some giant conglomerates, however, the evolutionary interpretation becomes more problematic. A discussion of the issues involved here is beyond the scope of this chapter.[11]

Selection

As the discussion above makes clear, a number of significant difficulties must be overcome to apply the basic concept of replication of routines to empirical arenas involving the survival and demise of large organizations. The concept itself has, however, important theoretical implications regarding the role and functioning of selection in organizational evolution. These mark a major structural distinction between economic evolutionary theory and theories of biological evolution. If, for example, an analogy is drawn between the individual organism and the individual organization — as is clearly appropriate for some purposes — then inheritance through spatial replication, within the framework of a single organization, is a process with no biological counterpart. *Populations* of organisms spread spatially, and a subpopulation consisting of a particular genotype may display other subpopulations. But single organisms do not grow spatially to the point where they account for significant fractions of the total biomass of the population; their growth takes place within the constraints of genetically determined morphology. Similarly, life span is limited by mechanisms that have a major genetic component. "Fitness" is a matter of representation in the next generation of individuals. By contrast, it is not unusual for a single organization to grow to become a major factor in the ecological equilibrium in which it participates, and there seems to be nothing intrinsic to organizations that assures their mortality. "Fitness" can be understood to be reflected in the growth of the individual organizations as well as in the growth of the number of like types.

Given that the objective is to inform understanding of economic processes, and not to spin out elaborate analogies with biology, there seems to be no point in trying to blur or bridge these differences between the theoretical schemes. For some significant purposes, including in particular the understanding of innovation, large organizations must be understood as unitary: they are not the simple sum of the results of a set of routines replicated many times. For other purposes, particularly the understanding of production and market transactions over a short period, the "simple sum" view is a good approximation. The theory must, and does, have it both ways.

In brief, the general evolutionary ideas of survival, selection, and inheritance are reflected in concepts with specialized and related meanings in economic evolutionary theory. These meanings are adapted to the subject matter in ways that seem to be helpful in addressing the particular puzzles that the subject matter poses. Organizational survival is a matter of continuity of routines, inheritance is a phenomenon reflecting the special advantages that an organization has in spatially replicating its routines, and growth of individual organizations through such replication is a prominent feature of selection processes.

Although it remains the case that biological analogies are easily drawn, these specialized meanings open up a substantial conceptual gap between economic and biological evolutionary theory. For example, the "fundamental theorem of natural selection," proved in biological theory by R. A. Fisher (1929/1958, p. 37), has an interesting analogue in economic evolutionary theory (see Iwai, 1984a, 1984b; Nelson & Winter, 1982, p. 243). The interpretive distinction between the two results is significant, however, since the economic result involves immortal firms growing by replication and the biological result involves mortal organisms and genetic inheritance; also, the fact that selection destroys variance is featured more prominently in the economic result. Even the formal mathematical analogy is far from exact.

In this regard, the population ecology approach seems to stand on the biologists' side of the gap. Some of the implications of this difference are explored below.

CONTRASTS, QUESTIONS, AND CONCLUSIONS

A number of the issues discussed above are part of the common terrain of evolutionary economics and the organizational ecology approach to the sociology of organizations. Since its founding by Hannan and Freeman (1977) and Aldrich (1979), the organizational ecology school has developed a major empirical research tradition with a number of significant achievements to its credit—some of them reported in this volume. An impressive feature of this tradition is its emphasis on the development of data sets for the testing of theory. Carroll and Hannan's contribution to this volume (Chapter 5) is a notable illustration of the payoff that sustained investment of this sort can yield. To encounter something about "an empirical test" in a subtitle is fairly commonplace—but "five empirical tests" signals a tour de force. This is all particularly impressive to an observer from a discipline often and legitimately criticized for its indifference to original data collection.

Under the general rubric of organizational ecology, it is useful to single out the *population ecology* viewpoint as involving some particularly significant contrasts with economic evolutionary theory. Perhaps it would even be appropriate to identify, under the "population ecology" heading, a particularly distinctive outlook that deals with the population level of analysis and might be dubbed "early Hannan and Freeman." This view has clearly been highly influential in shaping recent work in organizational ecology generally, but it is less clear how many adherents it now has. It is not my purpose here to censure or census the present adherents of this view (whatever their names or number), but to address some of the significant theoretical problems it presents. In what follows, the term *population ecology* references, in particular, the "early Hannan and Freeman" viewpoint, whereas *organizational ecology* refers to the broader and more eclectic school of thought that combines work at the organization, population, and community levels of analysis.

There are both significant similarities and important differences between the theoretical perspective of evolutionary economics and organizational ecology. Certainly the most fundamental similarity is a deep skepticism toward highly rationalistic or intentionalistic explanations of organizational phenomena, and a corresponding emphasis on the actual (not merely anticipated or conjectured) environmental feedback that shapes organizational change. Among the differences, there are some that clearly derive from the difference between the concerns of economics and sociology. Interestingly, there are also some that can be linked to the contrast between "evolution" and "ecology"—the former connoting a relatively greater emphasis on the driving forces of long-term change and the latter suggesting more attention to the relationship between a particular type and its environment (including competing types). Both of these broad-brush characterizations are illustrated in the following discussion of specific contrasts between the two approaches.

Some of the work of the population ecologists of organizations is particularly illustrative of the evolution/ecology distinction. Scant attention is given to the possibility that some members of the organizational populations under study may simply be better than others at making a living in the particular way characteristic of the population. The theoretical discussion is at the population level, and the intrapopulation variance in (genotypic) fitness is not among the variables considered. At the level of the individual organization, age matters (liability of newness), age cohort may matter (as in Carroll and Hannan's treatment of density delay), type distinctions matter, and a variety of other variables of marginal theoretical significance may be identified as determinants of mortality. In general, however, different organizations are treated as if they were all accurately cast from the same type-specific mold. In the theoretical equations, different organizations are interchangeable in their key roles of competing for resources and conferring legitimacy upon the type.

Differences in fitness at the organization level are, by contrast, central to the evolutionary view in economics — as, correspondingly, variation in genotypic fitness among individuals is central in evolutionary biology. It is the variation in fitness within the population that provides the lever without which natural selection could not do its work of improving the average fitness of the population.

While it is in general a fallacy to interpret "more fit" as "better," part of the interest in studying evolutionary struggles among different business firms does derive from the belief that such struggles may yield benefits for society at large. This is most clearly the case if (as in the simplest theoretical models) fitness differences derive from differences in cost of production and the struggle eventuates in lower prices for consumers.[12] The basic concern with the sources of economic progress is in this instance reflected in the theoretical emphasis on fitness at the individual firm and industry (population) levels.

A related but more specific contrast between the population ecology and evolutionary economics perspectives is the difference in interpretation of the "liability of newness" and of the initial decline of mortality with rising population numbers. Both the evolution/ecology difference just discussed and the economics/sociology difference are reflected here. Following Stinchcombe (1965), population ecologists place strong emphasis on the concept of *legitimacy* in explaining these phenomena. An individual organization faces the problem of building its relationships with resource providers; its path is smoothed to the extent that other organizations of the same type have previously succeeded in doing so and thus built social acceptance of the type.

By contrast, the primary explanation offered for these phenomena by evolutionary economics features *competence*, not legitimacy. New organizations may be regarded as a sample from some distribution of potential new organizations, and not all of them are equally fit. Although organization founders undoubtedly attempt to found viable organizations, not all of them succeed. Seriously maladapted organizations will tend to fail early; moderately maladapted ones, with some delay.[13] As time passes, five effects combine to decrease mortality as the number of organizations of the type increases: (a) the culling of less fit organizations that is reflected in the liability of newness; (b) the growth of more fit organizations, which tends to give them larger resources as buffers against adversity than they had at birth; (c) the improvement of skills and routines through learning at both individual and organizational levels; (d) the availability as models for imitation of successful representatives of the type; and (e) the historical trend of the environment in a direction favorable to the type (which trend ordinarily must be presumed to exist, since otherwise it is difficult to explain why the type should appear at that time at all).

To some extent, perhaps, the concept of legitimacy can be subsumed under that of competence. An organization that is ineffective in establishing basic relations of trust with its transacting partners lacks an important dimension of competence that is closely akin to legitimacy. Relatedly, in the sphere of external relations, the imitation of successful representatives of the type is both a way of acquiring competence and a way of "free riding" on the reputational capital of those successful firms (the latter is the legitimacy benefit freely translated into economic jargon). But there are certainly dimensions of competence other than those that can reasonably be associated with legitimacy, and in the line of argument sketched above it is not necessary to stipulate in advance which dimensions might be the key to the phenomena in a particular case.

There is no disagreement regarding the point that new organizations may bear higher costs because of the effort that goes into the development and improvement of their routines. Neither is there disagreement on the point that the limits of the "carrying capacity" of the environment will eventually be reached, and that a period of heightened stress and mortality risks will then ensue.

A second area of important contrasts between the two approaches involves the very different degrees of emphasis on organization size. Most population ecology models focus on the number of organizations, frequently do not discuss size variation at all, and, when they do discuss it, cast it in a supporting role. For example, Freeman (Chapter 3, this volume) introduces number of employees as a regressor in his equations explaining exits, but considers this variable only as a proxy for size considered as an indicator of ability to withstand temporary adversity. In the basic interplay of competition and legitimation that drives his model, a small firm apparently confers the same legitimation on the type as its larger fellows, and places the same burden on the carrying capacity of the environment. This is consistent with the general tendency of the population ecology school noted above, of thinking of individual organizations of a given type as being cast from the same mold, apart from a few secondary characteristics represented by control variables. Organization size and its relation to fitness have been largely ignored.

The tendency of the population ecology tradition to focus on vital rates and neglect organizational size is in fact noted by Hannan, Ranger-Moore, and Banaszak-Holl (Chapter 11, this volume), who report on efforts to correct the situation. Their contribution to the multidisciplinary literature on size distributions and organizational growth rates emphasizes in particular the notion of *localized competition*; in contrast to the simple evolutionary models, the assumption is that organizations of different sizes do not compete in a uniform way for the same resources. Rather, there is stronger competition among organizations that are "close" to each other in the niche space. This general idea has considerable appeal, and in fact establishes an interesting link between uses of the niche concept in ecological and strategic analysis. Hannan et al. adopt, however, the special assumption that "closeness" is a matter of similarity in *size*. In many economic contexts this formulation will conflict significantly with a more straightforward notion of "closeness," geographical proximity. To the extent that firm growth takes the form of spatial replication of routines, and assuming transportation costs are a factor, the large, multiestablishment firms will compete not only with each other but with most of the small firms, whereas the small firms compete only with those few of their small fellows that are geographically nearby.[14]

The question of the role of organizational size in ecological models is central to Barnett and Amburgey (Chapter 4, this volume), and their discussion of this question is notably clear. The special characteristics of the telephone industry — which are *not* consistent with the assumptions of a standard evolutionary model — make it a particularly interesting arena in which to study the interplay of size, numbers, and geography. Even allowing for these special characteristics, their empirical finding of a "diffuse mutualism" generated by large organizations comes as a surprise. To an economist, however, this result seems suspect because the "mass" variable used is arguably a measure of the *demand* served by other firms rather than of the supply (capacity). When both supply and demand are varying over time, it is the demand at typical unit cost levels that determines the carrying capacity and the productive capacity installed that measures the burden on the carrying capacity and hence the intensity of competition.

Apart from these current examples of attention to organizational size, the theoretical formulations of the population ecology school have dealt simply with the number of organizations in existence and the sources of change in that number. The most straightforward rationale for this approach is that organizations are homogeneous within type, but there are undoubtedly weaker assumptions under which the number of organizations would provide an adequate proxy for the aggregate effects of the population on legitimation and (especially) competition. An effort to describe these weaker conditions should be a high priority for population ecology theorists.

Whatever success may be encountered in this endeavor, the results are unlikely to be reassuring as to the applicability of the models to many populations of business firms. Across populations defined by a wide variety of criteria, it is a good generalization that the largest firms tend to be quite a lot larger than the many small firms, and to have correspondingly disproportionate impact in shaping the environment of the population.[15] Another good generalization is that entry and exit activity, as measured by numbers of firms, is concentrated in the smaller size categories (Dunne, Roberts, & Samuelson, 1988). It would be surprising, therefore, if a mere count of the number of firms proved to be a good indicator of the degree of pressure on the carrying capacity of the environment or other consequences of population size.

This same issue arises in Carroll and Hannan's treatment of "density delay" (Chapter 5, this volume). While impressive empirical support for the density delay hypothesis is found in the developmental histories of a variety of organizational populations, the basic puzzle that motivates the inquiry is a familiar and unpuzzling feature of evolutionary models that take organization size into account. It may be, also, that organization size is the key to understanding how density delay operates.

The puzzle that Carroll and Hannan discuss is why the number of organizations should typically turn down as the population matures, instead of monotonically approaching a stable equilibrium. Such a downturn is entirely characteristic of a large class of evolutionary models in which the growth of an individual organization is linked to its profitability. All one needs to generate the full pattern observed in the population ecology literature is a limited but initially empty market, an entry process that generates heterogeneous firms that seize the latent opportunity, growth related to profitability at the firm level, and profitability ultimately adversely affected by total output via declining price. The phase involving numbers decline even appears in disguised form in the behavior of the "numbers equivalent" in models that do not allow for actual exit but permit firms to waste away to arbitrarily small size.[16]

The mechanism here is that the more successful and hence larger firms are crowding the smaller ones out. The smaller ones are smaller (ultimately) *because* that are less successful: Whatever prosperity and growth they may enjoy in the early years, when aggregate output is small, gives way to decline and possible exit as the competitive pressure rises. This is the familiar story of the "shakeout," a feature of industry life-cycle patterns that was noted in the literature long before there were analytical or simulation models that captured it.

Two questions arise in this connection that deserve more careful examination than I can provide here. One is whether "density at time of founding" would turn out to play a role consistent with Carroll and Hannan's findings in an evolutionary model of the type sketched above. A good way to determine the answer would be to subject simulation output from such a model to the sort of statistical analysis carried out by Carroll and Hannan. I conjecture that the effect they identify as "density delay" would in fact show up in such an analysis, but that a substantial asymmetry would be found in the effect of density at founding depending on whether the cohort in question was founded before or after the population peak. The reason is that, following the argument above, the number of organizations in the population has quite a different significance before and after the peak. The number is a better proxy for the degree of pressure on carrying capacity early in the population's history than it is late, given the tendency for successful organizations to grow (Dunne et al., 1988). A related conjecture is that organization size is the mediating variable in the delayed density effect. Organizations founded early, when density is low, have the opportunity to grow before adversity sets in, and are thus subject to less risk of failure. These same conjectures, particularly the prepeak/postpeak asymmetry, should be testable on some of the data sets used by Carroll and Freeman.

The second of the two questions is, How far is it appropriate to treat evolutionary models of industries as potential substitutes for ecological models of populations of organizations in general? In the evolutionary models, an "industry" is typically a collection of firms producing a single homogeneous product, and the demand curve for that product defines the carrying capacity of the environment. Such models obviously do not approximate well the situation in many populations of nonbusiness organizations — or, for that matter, in many populations of business organizations. They are likely to be at their best when the obstacles to spatial replication of successful routines are low and the incentives for such replication are large. These conditions are likely to be well satisfied by a population of semiconductor firms, but not by populations of labor unions or voluntary social service organizations. The telephone companies of Barnett and Amburgey are an intermediate case.

By contrast, the basic population ecology models may be particularly relevant when opportunities or incentives for organizational growth are absent. In such cases one would not expect to see the highly skewed size distributions characteristic of business firms, and numbers of organizations should be a good proxy for the burden placed on the carrying capacity of the environment. The environment itself would be conceived as an array of different niches, with little or no resource competition among organizations in different niches. Competence would matter only in terms of ability to exploit a given niche, and it would be hard to distinguish empirically between the effects of high competence and a munificent niche. Legitimacy, on the other hand, might be an effect that travels easily among niches. Rising "density" might be interpreted primarily in terms of recourse to more marginal niches. As argued by Carroll and Hannan, a delayed density effect on mortality would then appear due to "tight niche packing."

Under these conditions, however, it is not obvious that total population numbers should be expected to fall substantially after the peak is reached.[17] One might expect, instead, a stochastic equilibrium at an average level not much below the peak, with high birthrates and mortality rates in marginal niches coexisting with low rates in the more munificent niches. Also, this scheme of quasi-independent heterogeneous niches does not naturally accommodate interesting models of competition among types — since the equilibrium distribution of organizational types is implicit *ab initio* in the distribution of niche types.

For a final point of comparison between the population ecology and evolutionary economics viewpoints, consider the important question of the ability of organizations to learn from and adapt to change. Both schools concur with common observation in noting that organizations often display behavioral rigidities that are in sharp conflict with theories that treat organizations as "unitary rational actors" (Allison, 1971). Both agree that while such rigidities can obviously be dysfunctional in particular circumstances, they are in large measure and for a variety of reasons intrinsic to organization itself. They can be entirely avoided only at the cost of being disorganized (Hannan & Freeman, 1984). Finally, there seems to be agreement on the point that adaptability is not an all-or-nothing proposition, that the pace of adaptation relative to environment change is key, and that differing degrees of adaptability can characterize different activities or characteristics of an organization.

All of this said, there remain some significant contrasts. These seem to derive in large part from the population ecologists' emphasis on populations of small organizations as a convenient field for empirical work on organizations, versus the concern of evolutionary economics with the sources and patterns of change in industries and the economy as a whole.

In some of their earlier statements, Hannan and Freeman have argued that adaptation to environmental changes typically occurs at the population level — that is, through replacement of one organization form by another (e.g., see Hannan & Freeman, 1977). If it is correct to interpret this statement on the assumption that individual organizations either cannot change form or do so only at high risks of death — an interpretation consistent with both the theoretical argument of the population ecologists and their empirical concern with vital statistics of organizations — then this is an extremely strong claim. It gives no weight to the fact that organizations may have effective routinized capabilities for coping not only with the high-frequency portion of the environmental change spectrum, but also with change occurring over the span of a few years and posing, absent adaptation, moderately serious hazards to survival.

Of greater importance to industrial organization economists, the claim simply cannot be squared with the histories of most industries. When the same firms persist among the industry leaders over decades of tumultuous economic and social change, it is hard to believe that those firms are not adapting successfully to change, and correspondingly hard to accept the dominance of replacement as a mode of adaptation. They may, of course, be adapting less quickly than they should according to some normative standard.

More recent statements of the population ecology view have given more attention to the respects in which organizations can change, and contrasted these with "structure":

> Population ecology theory holds that most of the variability in organizational structure comes about through the creation of new organizations and organizational forms and the replacement of old ones. (Hannan & Freeman, 1984, p. 150)

To assess this proposition fully, it would be necessary to amplify and refine it in several respects. Rather than pursue this detailed exegesis, it seems important to emphasize that the statement may represent one milestone in what seems to be a process of convergence of views on the question of organizational adaptability. This process should, and I think will, continue. The emerging consensus is not on a particular sweeping generalization about the levels of adaptability/rationality or inertia/irrationality that organizations display, but an emerging agreement that arguing about the generalizations is less interesting than sorting out the cases and testing the strength of competing interpretations (Singh, House, & Tucker, 1986).

For the guidance of the latter undertaking, I offer the following summary of a common position from which population ecologists, evolutionary economists, and other students of organizations might bring their diverse inquiries. (a) In any individual case, the degree and nature of the adaptability displayed by an organization is an empirical question, not one settled by a priori theorizing. (b) Foresight reflected in conjectures and plans plays a different and less powerful role in shaping organizational change than actual experience. (c) From the population-level or societal point of view, the appearance of new organizations with new forms, structures, or routines is a substitute for adaptation by existing organizations, and often plays an important role. (d) Because population-level adaptation may occur through replacement rather than adaptation at the organization level, evolutionary forces do not always, or generally, favor highly adaptable types. (e) Different time scales of environmental change pose very different challenges to organizations: The responses to these challenges involve widely varying mixtures of routinization, learning, adaptation, search, and other decision modes.

In considering evolution and adaptation on long time scales, it is important to note that even very routinized or "inertial" organizational performances can be the source of powerful and perhaps unsustainable dynamics in a wider system. Thus, for example, the burning of fossil fuels is an activity that is carried on in a variety of now familiar, routinized ways in vehicles, homes, factories, and power plants. The resulting atmospheric accumulation of carbon dioxide is expected to produce a greenhouse effect that will present unprecedented challenges to many organizations and perhaps to humankind itself. Evolutionary economics emphasizes that organizations do not just adapt to change, they cause it — rapidly through innovation, but also gradually through adherence to established routine.

NOTES

1. Similarly, Boyd and Richerson (1985) acknowledge that "our definition of culture is not at all specific about the nature of the information that affects phenotypes" (p. 37). They explicitly disavow any commitment to a theory of "particulate inheritance" — warning, in effect, against the propensity to load a concept like "meme" or "culturgen" with the same conceptual baggage carried by "gene" in genetics.

2. Lest we become discouraged about this vagueness on a key issue, we should recall that Darwin himself, not having the benefits of the insights of Mendelian genetics, hedged his bets on the question of how traits are transmitted.

3. The results reported by Cohen, Levin, and Mowery (1987) imply work imply that R&D spending is somewhat more concentrated among large firms than sales — which is quite concentrated. The greater concentration is, however, accounted for by the fact that large firms are more likely to do R&D, and not by an increase of R&D intensity with sales among firms that do R&D.

4. Note the corroboration of the validity of "multiunit company" as an indicator of size. The value added *in a single establishment* of a multiunit company averages about 15 times that of a single-unit company.

5. Our concept of routines has a long genealogy and a correspondingly long list of synonyms or near synonyms in both organization theory and everyday language (see Winter, 1986, p. 165).

6. The work of Cyert and March (1963) is the *locus classicus* for this sort of work. Although behavioralism is not part of the mainstream in economics (any more than evolutionary theory is), it is at least alive and may be getting a new lease on life. (See, for example, the handbooks recently published by Gilad & Kaish, 1986a, 1986b.) Also, mainstream economists have done some significant work in the empirical description of behavioral rules.

7. What I refer to as a "literature" is the union of the innovation subset of the literature on organizations and the organizations subset of the literature on diffusion of innovation. There are, in general, important differences of orientation and approach between the two components; on the other hand, there are also some specific contributions that point toward unification (e.g., Downs & Mohr, 1976).

8. Ravenscraft and Scherer (1987, chap. 5) explored the details of 15 cases of sell-offs of business units previously acquired by a conglomerate or in a diversifying move. Among these 15 sell-off cases, 8 resulted in the creation of one or more free-standing enterprises, and only 3 passed into the hands of other conglomerate acquirers.

9. Even within the ranks of the largest firms, size disparities are striking. Among Fortune 500 companies the sales of the largest firm in an industrial category typically exceed those of the smallest by a large factor. Some examples include chemicals (51 Fortune 500 companies), 64.9; food (48 Fortune 500 companies), 38.4; forest products (33 Fortune 500 companies), 19.4; and petroleum refining (29 Fortune 500 companies), 132.6 ("Fortune 500," 1989).

10. The relative importance of these two replication modes varies from industry to industry in a manner that depends on production economies of scale, transportation costs, and other considerations. See Scherer, Beckenstein, Kaufer, and Murphy (1975) for a thorough theoretical and empirical investigation of this problem.

11. Joint work is currently under way by Giovanni Dosi, Richard Rumelt, David Teece, and myself that is directed to understanding the nature and importance of the "coherence" (or lack of same) in the competencies of large corporations.

12. As orthodox economics teaches, there is an important caveat here: The costs that the firms are struggling to minimize must be the social costs of production — not, for example, costs that can be reduced at the individual firm level by transferring them to some third party.

13. See Lippman and Rumelt (1982), and Jovanovic (1982) for models that incorporate these features in various ways. Although entry and exit mechanisms are not featured in the analytical and simulation models in Nelson and Winter (1982), the logic of interfirm differences explored in those models generates the phenomena in question as soon as the entry and exit features are introduced (as is illustrated in Winter, 1984).

14. The formulation of the Hannan et al. "second scenario" is broadly consistent with this last implication.

15. Among the 31 top "four-digit" manufacturing industries as ranked by value of shipments, the top eight firms account for an average of over 50% of total shipments (U.S. Department of Commerce, 1989, Table 1266).

16. All the simulations reported in Nelson and Winter (1982, chaps. 12-14) display this pattern except those in which the initial number of firms is very small. The same pattern appears in simple analytical models akin to that in Chapter 10, since output concentration is increased by the selection process.

17. In the data collected by Klepper and Graddy (1990), the average over 22 product markets of percentage decline from the peak number of participants is 52%, and there is wide variation from case to case. This is broadly consistent with what is shown in the five cases examined by Carroll and Hannan.

REFERENCES

Alchian, A. (1950). Uncertainty, evolution and economic theory. *Journal of Political Economy, 58*, 211-222.

Aldrich, H. E. (1979). *Organizations and environments.* Englewood Cliffs, NJ: Prentice-Hall.

Allison, G. (1971). *Essence of decision: Explaining the Cuban missile crisis.* Boston: Little, Brown.

Boyd, R., & Richerson, P. J. (1985). *Culture and the evolutionary process.* Chicago: University of Chicago Press.

Cohen, W., Levin, R., & Mowery, D. (1987). Firm size and R&D intensity: A re-examination. *Journal of Industrial Economics, 35*, 543-565.

Cyert, R., & March, J. (1963). *A behavioral theory of the firm.* Englewood Cliffs, NJ: Prentice-Hall.

Dawkins, R. (1976). *The selfish gene.* New York: Oxford University Press.

Downs, G., & Mohr, L. (1976). Conceptual issues in the study of innovation. *Administrative Science Quarterly, 21.*

Dunne, T., Roberts, M. J., & Samuelson, L. (1988). Patterns of firm exit and entry in manufacturing industries. *RAND Journal of Economics, 19*, 495-515.

Fisher, R. A. (1958). *The genetical theory of natural selection.* New York: Dover. (Original work published 1929)

The Fortune 500. (1989, April 24). *Fortune,* pp. 345-395.

Gilad, B., & Kaish, S. (Eds.). (1986a). *Handbook of behavioral economics: Vol. A. Behavioral microeconomics.* Greenwich, CT: JAI.

Gilad, B., & Kaish, S. (Eds.). (1986b). *Handbook of behavioral economics: Vol. B. Behavioral macroeconomics.* Greenwich, CT: JAI.

Hall, B. H. (1987). The relationship between firm size and firm growth in the U.S. manufacturing sector. *Journal of Industrial Economics, 35*, 583-606.

Hannan, M. T., & Freeman, J. (1977). The population ecology of organizations. *American Journal of Sociology, 82*, 929-964.

Hannan, M. T., & Freeman, J. (1984). Structural inertia and organizational change. *American Sociological Review, 49*, 149-164.

Iwai, K. (1984a). Schumpeterian dynamics: An evolutionary model of innovation and imitation. *Journal of Economic Behavior and Organization, 5*, 159-190.

Iwai, K. (1984b). Schumpeterian dynamics, part II: Technological progress, firm growth and "economic selection." *Journal of Economic Behavior and Organization, 5,* 321-352.

Jovanovic, B. (1982). Selection and the evolution of industry. *Econometrica, 50,* 649-670.

Kimberly, J. R. (1981). Managerial innovation. In P. C. Nystrom & W. H. Starbuck (Eds.), *Handbook of organizational design* (Vol. 1). New York: Oxford University Press.

Kimberly, J. R. (1986). The organizational context of technological innovation. In D. D. Davis & Associates, *Managing technological innovation.* San Francisco: Jossey-Bass.

Klepper, S., & Grady, E. (In press). The evolution of new industries and the determinants of market structure. RAND *Journal of Economics.*

Lippman, S. A., & Rumelt, R. P. (1982). Uncertain imitability: An analysis of interfirm differences in efficiency under competition, *Bell Journal of Economics, 13,* 418-438.

Lumsden, C. J., & Wilson, E. O. (1981). *Genes, mind and culture: The coevolutionary process.* Cambridge, MA: Harvard University Press.

Mansfield, E. (1962). Entry, innovation and the growth of firms. *American Economic Review, 52,* 1023-1051.

Nelson, R. R., & Winter, S. G. (1982). *An evolutionary theory of economic change.* Cambridge, MA: Harvard University Press.

Pakes, A., & Ericson, R. (1990). *Empirical implications of alternative models of firm dynamics* (Working paper). Yale University Economic Growth Center.

Penrose, E. (1952). Biological analogies in the theory of the firm. *American Economic Review, 42,* 804-819.

Ravenscraft, D. (1983). Structure-profit relationships at the line of business and industry level. *Review of Economics and Statistics, 65,* 22-31.

Ravenscraft, D., & Scherer, F. M. (1987). *Mergers, sell-offs and economic efficiency.* Washington, DC: Brookings Institution.

Scherer, F. M. (1980). *Industrial market structure and economic performance* (2nd ed.). Chicago: Rand McNally.

Scherer, F. M., Beckenstein, A., Kaufer, E., & Murphy, R. D. (with F. Bougeon-Maassen). (1975). *The economics of multi-plant operation: An international comparisons study.* Cambridge, MA: Harvard University Press.

Schmalensee, R. (1985). Do markets differ much? *American Economic Review, 75,* 341-351.

Schumpeter, J. A. (1934). *Theory of economic development.* Cambridge, MA: Harvard University Press. (Original work published 1911)

Singh, A., & Whittington, G. (1975). The size and growth of firms. *Review of Economic Studies, 42,* 15-26.

Singh, J. V., House, R. J., & Tucker, D. J. (1986). Organizational change and organizational mortality. *Administrative Science Quarterly, 31,* 587-611.

Stinchcombe, A. L. (1965). Social structure and organizations. In J. G. March (Ed.), *Handbook of organizations* (pp. 142-193). Chicago: Rand McNally.

Teece, D. J. (1982). Towards an economic theory of the multiproduct firm. *Journal of Economic Behavior and Organization, 3,* 39-63.

Tushman, M. L., & Anderson, P. (1986). Technological discontinuities and organizational environments. *Administrative Science Quarterly, 31,* 439-465.

U.S. Department of Commerce. (1989). *Statistical abstract of the United States, 1989.* Washington, DC: Government Printing Office.

Veblen, T. (1961). Why is economics not an evolutionary science? In T. Veblen, *The place of science in modern civilization.* New York: Russell & Russell. (Original work published 1898)

Winter, S. G. (1971). Satisficing, selection and the innovating remnant. *Quarterly Journal of Economics, 85*, 237-261.

Winter, S. G. (1984). Schumpeterian competition in alternative technological regimes. *Journal of Economic Behavior and Organization, 5*, 287-320.

Winter, S. G. (1986). The research program of the behavioral theory of the firm: Orthodox critique and evolutionary perspective. In B. Gilad & S. Kaish (Eds.), *Handbook of behavioral economics: Vol. A. Behavioral microeconomics*. Greenwich, CT: JAI.

Zaltman, G., Duncan, R., & Holbek, J. (1973). *Innovations and organizations*. New York: John Wiley.

Commentary

Notes of a Skeptic:
From Organizational Ecology
to Organizational Evolution

MARSHALL W. MEYER

The purpose of this essay, of course, is to review and provoke thought concerning the seven preceding chapters. A further purpose is to stimulate thought about the distinction between organizational evolution and organizational ecology, the latter possibly a subset of the former, and to suggest that the premises of ecology are too restrictive to accommodate recent developments in theory as well as research results that have surfaced over the last ten years.

Alongside organizational ecology, I believe that we must have an evolutionary perspective on organizations, one that focuses on change within organizations as well as on turnover in organizational populations. The juxtaposition of ecological and evolutionary perspectives raises, in turn, a set of theoretical questions that we have barely begun to address. These questions ask, broadly, under what circumstances are organizations incapable of internal change yet susceptible to extinction consistent with the premises of organizational ecology, under what circumstances are organizations capable of continuous incremental adjustments that permit them to survive over long intervals, and under what conditions does neither pattern obtain? One pattern fitting neither ecological nor evolutionary thinking is that of the short-lived organization whose structure changes with great rapidity. I know of no theoretical work on such types, partly because the combination of rapid internal change and rapid demographic turnover yields units that are barely recognizable as organized. Another pattern departing from both the ecological and evolutionary models is the stable long-lived organization, which never changes yet never dies. Some of my colleagues label such fixed organizations — fixed in structure, fixed over time — as "institutionalized" and have developed some interesting theories of institutionalization, but I prefer to call them "permanent failures" (Meyer & Zucker, 1989) since, once frozen into established patterns, they can succeed only at reproducing themselves.

This essay is organized as follows: To begin, I express some skepticism about ecology and then ask whether empirical studies of organizational mortality, which are highly developed, tend to support the ecological or the evolutionary view. I find the results at hand more supportive of evolution than of ecology, even though the ecologists have produced most of these findings and believe these findings to support their position. I then review the preceding chapters, drawing attention to their distinctive contributions to thinking about organizations. In conclusion, I develop some preliminary ideas suggesting where the ecological models are likely to operate on organizations and where evolutionary processes are likely to operate within organizations.

SOME PRELIMINARY OBSERVATIONS

I have always admired the work of organizational ecologists, but have been somewhat skeptical of some of the premises of ecology. Let me sketch some of the sources of my concern. Ecology, to begin, asserts the primacy of environments in shaping organizations. Environmental primacy falls somewhat short of determinism in that mutations and mistakes appear, but causality clearly lies very much on the side of the environment. Ecology argues that organisms and organizations alike are exceedingly vulnerable to shifts in the environment, so much so that deliberate adaptation to change is either impossible or so limited as to be inconsequential.[1] This assertion of strong environmental primacy places ecology at odds with organizational design (the choice of organizational structures given technological and environmental constraints) and organizational strategy (the choice of business lines and markets), which are practice oriented and seek to expand the range of choices available to organizations as well as to account for choices already made. Strong environmental primacy also removes ecology from most other organizational theories. Virtually all theories save for ecology permit organizations to make choices that are consequential, although the latitude for choice does vary somewhat — standard bureaucratic theory, for example, allows organizations somewhat more latitude or power than resource-dependence theory.

TABLE 1: Organizational Change, Environmental Change, and Mortality

| | Organizational Change | |
	(−)	(+)
(−) Environmental Change	Cell I	Cell III
(+)	Cell II	Cell IV

Organizational ecology is nearly unique in enunciating strong environmental primacy that excludes volition or choice from organizations.

Organizational ecology is distinctive in another respect. Not only does it posit strong environmental primacy, but it also ignores or discounts change within organizations due to the strength of inertial or conserving forces. Ecology focuses instead on "vital events" such as births and deaths. Since neither causality nor change capacity lies within organizations, the fundamental syllogism of organizational ecology becomes this: Given that environments have causal primacy over organizations, and given that organizations, once formed, are incapable of significant internal change, change in organizational populations occurs almost entirely through differential rates of organizational birth and death.

The distinctive premises of organizational ecology — environmental primacy, inertia within organizations — can be tested by comparing actual with expected rates of mortality under different conditions. Consider Table 1, where mortality patterns are treated as functions of change in environments and change in individual organizations themselves. Two of the four cells in Table 1 are consistent with the premises of organizational ecology: cell I, where neither environmental nor organizational change occurs, and cell II, where there is environmental but not organizational change. Two cells, however, are not consistent with the ecological perspective: cell III, where there is organizational but not environmental change, and cell IV, where change in both organizations and environments occurs.

Consider now the expected relation of organizational age to mortality, which has been studied extensively.[2] Given constancy in both environments and organizations, organizations falling in cell I will be expected to exhibit fairly low death rates that are age invariant: The likelihood that an individual unit will vanish will neither increase nor decrease with age. But given inconstancy in all environments and stability within organizations, as in cell II, expected patterns of organizational mortality will be somewhat different: Death rates will actually increase with age as the initial fit between environments and organizations deteriorates. In sum, cells I and II, which are admissible under the premises of organizational ecology, yield either flat organizational mortality rates or rates that increase with age.

Let us turn now to cells III and IV, where organizational change or adaptation is possible, inconsistent with the premises of ecology. Cell III corresponds to settings where there is constancy in the environment but not in organizations. Organizations, of course, are now free to make choices, including foolish choices. But assuming that they do not do so, or at least do not do so intentionally, one would expect the initial fit of organizations to their environments to improve somewhat over time with learning. Declining organizational mortality with age is thus expected. Outcomes in cell IV, where change occurs in both environments and organizations, are less predictable. Intendedly rational action in organizations can yield disastrous outcomes in the face of uncertain and uncontrollable environmental change. Most likely, mortality rates for organizations will be age-independent but somewhat higher than in cell I.

Clearly, a formal modeling apparatus is needed to anticipate the full consequences of environmental and organizational change for time dependence of mortality in organizations. The intuitive results suggested by Table 1 do indicate, however, that observed mortality patterns can be used to validate the premises of organizational ecology, particularly the assertion that organizations are incapable of change. To the extent that there is positive age dependence of mortality, as in cell II, the premises of organizational ecology would be supported — environments change but organizations cannot. But to the extent that there is negative age dependence, that is, declining mortality with age, a different set of premises may be in order, one that admits the possibility of organizational adaptation to environmental conditions. *What evidence exists indicates that organizational mortality either declines with age or, less often, is curvilinear or age invariant.* Positive age dependence of death rates is rare. The most parsimonious interpretation of these results, to my mind, is that much learning, adaptation, and change take place within organizations. My reading of the seven preceding chapters suggests the same conclusion.

THE PRECEDING ARTICLES

Let me now turn to the preceding chapters. My ordering of them is not random: I focus, first, on papers closest to the ecological tradition (Levinthal; Hannan, Ranger-Moore, & Banaszak-Holl; McPherson). I then turn to papers amending the evolutionary model, ordered roughly by their degree of departure from orthodox ecology (Burgelman; Tucker, Singh, & Meinhard; Lumsden & Singh; Winter). I do not pretend that these chapters are in any sense unified, but I do indicate points of convergence as well as major differences among them.

Levinthal on Selection and Random Walks

Let me comment first upon Daniel Levinthal's "Organizational Adaptation, Environmental Selection, and Random Walks." Levinthal uses a simulation procedure to explore the consequences of three distinct models of organizations: an adaptation model, a selection model, and a model of random change in which organizations experience neither adaptation nor differential selection. In all three models, organizational wealth varies with performance. "Correct" choices yield increments in wealth, "incorrect" choices yield decrements. A common performance constraint is specified in all three models: When an organization's wealth falls to zero, it dies. Other constraints differ. The adaptation model permits organizations to learn from their mistakes. (It turns out, interestingly, that the rate of learning, so long as it is nonzero, makes little difference.) The selection model does not permit learning but does assume that decision rules vary across organizations. (Given no learning, these decision rules are fixed even if flawed.) The random model eliminates both learning and differences in decision rules. Survival, that is, retention of positive wealth, is entirely a matter of chance in this model. Chance processes, however, give rise to a random walk outcome whereby organizations that survive the early stages of the simulation accumulate wealth and are subsequently protected from dying. Somewhat surprisingly, the random model yields negative age dependence in mortality rates. Older organizations are less likely to die than the young, mainly because they have accumulated substantial wealth, through the random walk process, over time. The adaptation and selection models also yield negative age dependence in mortality. Levinthal labels this an unfortunate case of equifinality and introduces the notion of a "refined risk set" as a way out of the conundrum.

I do have some comments on Levinthal's results, as they are apparently inconsistent with the qualitative model sketched above. Most importantly, Levinthal's model takes no account of variation in the environment, assuming by default constancy in the environment as in cells I and III in Table 1. Levinthal's results for the adaptation model and my intuition about organizations falling into cell III (environmental constancy, organizational change) correspond exactly — there is negative age dependence in mortality. His results for the selection model are, in my view, potentially misleading in two respects. First, there is no variability in the environment. Second, absent variability in the environment, Levinthal has to introduce heterogeneity into his population in order to simulate selection processes. Some organizations, it will be remembered, had good decision rules, while others did not. In terms of the categories used to construct Table 1, Levinthal's selection model falls into cell I, but his population of organizations is heterogeneous. Given that population heterogeneity almost always gives rise to negative age dependence in mortality, Levinthal's result, in this instance, is predictable.

The most interesting feature of Levinthal's model, however, is the postulate that good decisions (which may be random events) at time 1 augment capital stock, which in turn reduces the likelihood that bad decisions at time 2 will reduce capital stock to zero. An organization making a series of good decisions, even if for no good reason, is thus better buffered against failure than a new organization in this model. This insight is important, and it has some very interesting substantive implications, which are almost wholly overlooked by Levinthal because he seeks to remain within the ecological framework by directing attention to "refined risk sets."

The most important implication is this: Mortality patterns will depend upon the capacity to build capital stock. Negative age dependence in mortality is expected for organizations that are able to build capital or endowments, whereas little or no age dependence can be expected where gains are distributed as dividends, "rents" of office, and the like. Not all for-profit organizations are able to build capital stock. For example, closely held firms and subchapter-S corporations are less likely to accumulate capital than are widely held firms. And capital accumulation does occur in the nonprofessional sector. While public agencies normally do not accumulate capital or even maintain capital accounts, nonprofit organizations frequently have permanent endowments and use operating surpluses to augment them. More generally, Levinthal's model suggests that the presence or absence of mechanisms allowing resource accumulation affects long-term survival prospects. Researchers ought to identify these mechanisms and determine whether or not their hypothesized effects hold.

Hannan, Ranger-Moore, and Banaszak-Holl
on Size Distributions

I have few comments on the Hannan et al. chapter, largely because it accomplishes its purposes so well. The first portion of the chapter provides an exemplary review of the literature on size distributions, adding to the classical models of Gibrat and Simon a set of ecological models in which environmental carrying capacity, exits, and entries are considered explicitly. Competition on the size axis is then introduced as an additional constraint. In one version of this model, each organization competes with every other organization in inverse proportion to size differences. In a second version, competition is restricted, in Hannan et al.'s terms, to size "windows" of specified width. This second version yields size distributions departing significantly from the lognormal, due to a depression at the center of the distribution, and this effect is exaggerated when growth rates are modeled as declining functions of size.

The empirical side of the chapter displays actual size distributions of New York City banks and insurance firms operating in New York State over the 1830-1980 and 1860-1980 intervals, respectively. In both cases, size distributions evolve away from the lognormal and toward bimodal distributions, which the earlier modeling exercise showed to be characteristic of size-localized competition. The empirical results do differ from the simulation results in that they show gaps (or dips) to occur to the left-center of the distribution, rather than to the right-center as anticipated in the modeling exercise. Even so, there is some support for the notion that organizations of different sizes do not compete with one another. Why this is so is not explained. One hypothesis derived from Carroll's (1985) work on resource partitioning is that large organizations capture the advantages of generalism and small organizations the advantages of specialism, leaving organizations in the middle range of size with the liabilities of both. One hopes that hypotheses like these can be tested with the data sets amassed by Hannan and his colleagues.

McPherson on Voluntary Associations

J. Miller McPherson's chapter, "Evolution in Communities of Voluntary Organizations," extends ecological thinking in a wholly different direction. McPherson has consistently focused on voluntary organizations rather than on work organizations, a feature that has enabled him to develop rather crisp models describing connections between organizations and their environments, but, at least in the present work, has also limited the generalizability of his results. Almost a decade ago, McPherson pioneered hypernetwork sampling, which allows researchers to infer characteristics of organizational populations from sample surveys of individual respondents. The hypernetwork method is an exemplar of elegance: Given a large but bounded population and assuming a similarly bounded set of organizations available for individuals to join, the characteristics of this set of organizations can be determined from affiliation patterns of individuals. The hypernetwork sampling technique is standard procedure in large-scale organizational surveys nowadays. A variant of the hypernetwork technique is now used in the NSF-sponsored organizational data base initiative.

While it is relatively easy to draw representative samples of organizations from data provided by samples of individual respondents, I think it is more difficult to link the ecological dynamics of organizations to population characteristics of individuals, except in special cases. McPherson's chapter demonstrates why, possibly inadvertently. McPherson argues that membership is the principal resource needed by organizations. Since, he argues, new members are likely to resemble current members, both the character of the organization and its fit to the environment derive from membership characteristics. Comparison of membership characteristics with population characteristics, in turn, yields exploitation curves indicating underexploited populations available for membership and overexploited populations, which are relatively unavailable. Organizations, McPherson argues, will move from over- to underexploited regions on the curve, but not all can move with equal facility. Those closest to the underexploited regions are most likely to take advantage of available populations; those furthest away are least able to attract newcomers. Exploitation curves can also be used to anticipate growth and decline as well as organizational movement toward generalism and specialism. McPherson argues, based on his analysis, that "the appropriate unit of selection in organizational evolution . . . *at least for voluntary organizations* . . . is the individual member" (emphasis added).

Some observations are in order. To begin, despite some fairly arcane language (homophily/heterophily, Blau space, and the like), McPherson's model is in fact one of organizational adaptation. None of the propositions developed toward the end of the chapter concerns organizational birth and death. To be sure, selection processes operate. Individual members are included in or excluded from membership in individual organizations. Members are, in the language just used, the unit of selection, and selection of members, in turn, drives niche movement, the migration of organizations, as it were, from one niche to another. A further observation is that McPherson's model is generalizable to nonvoluntary organizations only to the extent that the unit of selection is shifted also. Consider, for example, the case of conglomerate firms. Here, exploitation curves might help predict which businesses are added and shed. The ease with which business lines are changed as a function of both external variables (heterophily in the social networks of existing business units) and internal variables (generalism versus specialism across current businesses). The usefulness of exploitation curves for determining personnel shifts is questionable, since membership per se is only slightly related to the viability of a conglomerate firm. For McPherson's model to apply to conglomerates, then, the unit of selection is clearly the business unit rather than the individual member. McPherson's hypotheses, then, may be generalizable to many types of organizations other than voluntary associations, but only when the unit of selection varies with organizational type. Basically, this unit of selection must be the same as the basic "building blocks" of the larger organization: for voluntary associations, members; for conglomerates, businesses; for universities, departments and programs. It turns out, then, that the units we use to sample organizations — individual people — may not also be the units most appropriate for evaluating propositions about organizational evolution. This is an unfortunate outcome for research. The apparent implication of McPherson's piece is that we could both sample organizations and gauge environments and hence test propositions about organizational niche movement using data selected from individual respondents. This turns out not to be the case more generally.

Burgelman on Ecology and Strategy

The notion that the unit of selection may be something other than whole organizations is also the essence of Burgelman's essay on intraorganizational ecology of strategy making. Burgelman distinguishes induced from autonomous strategic processes. Induced strategic processes correspond to strategy as conventionally conceived: Top management articulates long-term objectives, identifies distinctive competencies, and delineates action domains, and administrative as well as cultural mechanisms are put in place to ensure that action remains consistent with these top management perspectives. As Burgelman notes, induced strategies are intended to reduce variation within organizations. Autonomous strategic processes, by contrast, arise from below. Autonomous strategies reflect the experience of operating businesses with technologies and market conditions. They reflect the actual competencies of organizations rather than management's perception of these competencies.

Autonomous strategic processes are thus variation-enhancing rather than variation-reducing. Burgelman's argument, stated succinctly, is that autonomous processes allow selection processes to operate within organizations, allowing fundamental renewals and reorientations to take place. By implication, then, to the extent that the unit of selection is shifted downward from the organization as a whole to subunits whose strategies arise autonomously, the survival prospects for the larger organization are enhanced.

I have no quarrel with Burgelman. But I do wish that he had pursued his intuition further. Consider the following: The multiunit/conglomerate model of organizations, which reserves to top management responsibility for overall strategy, is claimed to maximize efficiency in assignment of cash flows to operating units (Williamson, 1975, chap. 8). Where strategic decisions are less centralized, it is argued, this advantage is lost, and multiunits/conglomerates devolve into holding companies offering no particular advantages over separate firms. What Burgelman must reconcile are the apparent advantages of allowing strategies to arise bottom-up in an evolutionary fashion with the apparent advantages of centralizing the allocation of cash flows to individual units. Burgelman, of course, recognizes that autonomous strategic processes sometimes trade survivability for efficiency, just as generalism sometimes sacrifices efficiency. But he does not address the issue of how one best reconciles these autonomous processes with the management of overall firm assets.

Tucker, Singh, and Meinhard on
Voluntary Social Service Organizations

Tucker et al.'s chapter represents a novel approach to the problem of imprinting in organizations. Imprinting, or inertia, is the obverse of change. Inertia *of* organizations themselves is indicated by organizational persistence, and, in Hannan and Freeman's (1984) formulation, by death rates declining with age. Imprinting or inertia *within* organizations is indicated by the persistence of certain organizational features and, possibly, by declining rates of change in these features with age. Most evidence suggesting imprinting or inertia *within* organizations is anecdotal. Tucker et al.'s chapter, by contrast, attempts to model rates of change of organizational features as functions of conditions at the time of founding, taking advantage of the longitudinal nature of their data set.

These data, which describe some 389 voluntary social service organizations in the metropolitan Toronto area, were collected for the purpose of studying organizational mortality and present some limitations for research on change. One limitation is the low frequency of change in many organizational features. The data span a 13-year interval, 1970 through 1982. During this time, about half of the VSSOs shifted location, structure, and chief executive. But less than 20% changed other and perhaps more significant features, including name, sponsorship, service area, goals, clients, and conditions of service to clients. (The last two changed among 2% and 4% of VSSOs, respectively.) Another limitation, more subtle but perhaps more serious, is that the short study interval renders it difficult to theorize about this data set. Let me explain. The imprinting hypothesis postulates that founding conditions affect founding characteristics of organizations, and that these founding characteristics remain essentially unchanged over time despite changes in the environment and hence in founding conditions for later generations of organizations. The longer the study interval, the greater the changes in founding conditions and, by implication, the greater the likelihood of differences appearing between newer and older generations of organizations. The imprinting hypothesis does *not* argue that founding conditions will affect propensity to change; it argues, rather, that change rates in organizations are somewhat lower than in environments.

Tucker et al.'s general hypothesis is that organizations founded in favorable environments will experience lower rates of change throughout their lifetimes than organizations founded in less auspicious circumstances, but the opposite argument could be made plausibly (only stable organizational forms can be founded in periods of adversity). Given that the hypothesis is tentative at best, it is not surprising that the study of VSSOs yields mixed results. The simplest models in which rates of change in name, sponsor, location, and so on are modeled as functions of founding conditions yield no significant results at all. More complex models do attain statistical significance, but the overall pattern of results is mixed. To illustrate: Generalism at the time of formation promotes change in goals and administrative structure, but so does specialism. (Apparently, these changes occur least frequently in VSSOs that were neither generalists nor specialists when founded.) Density at time of formation as well as contemporaneous density do promote change in several respects, but it is difficult to gauge whether density indicates favorable conditions due to institutionalization or unfavorable conditions due to competition. On balance, the Tucker et al. study is best understood, to use the authors' description, as exploratory research. As such, it points to the need for more studies that permit the organizational imprinting hypothesis to be tested more rigorously.

Lumsden and Singh on Speciation and Entrepreneurship

The Lumsden and Singh chapter on the dynamics of speciation represents a departure from conventional thinking about organizations, for it asks how new organizational forms appear rather than how existing forms are shaped by various internal and external pressures. Two basic premises of the Lumsden and Singh model of entrepreneurship through speciation are of note. One concerns the creative potential of entrepreneurs. Speciation — development of a new organizational form — occurs when a new organizational schema is produced in the mind of the entrepreneur. New schemata arise when connections are made among existing ideas. The implication, demonstrated formally, is that new schemata arise in proportion to the *density* of connections among existing ideas rather than the strength of these connections. A second result, which is of some interest from the perspective of conventional organizational theory, concerns conditions affecting the timing of entrepreneurial innovations. The result is this: The expected time to entrepreneurial innovation increases exponentially with the parameter N, which is the number of dimensions of the speciation space needed to describe the relevant parameters of organizations. Stated somewhat differently: As the capacity to simplify the environment through "chunking" diminishes, entrepreneurial potential suffers.

Both results, I believe, carry implications for the relationship of existing organizations to entrepreneurial activity. Assuming entrepreneurs to suffer normal bounded rationality limits, the strength of connections among existing ideas is likely to be an inverse function of the variety of ideas in the environment. There is a trade-off: Variety in the environment potentially yields segmentation or compartmentalization that inhibits entrepreneurial thought. Thus, just as large size potentially induces distortions in markets, a highly variegated environment may weaken or segment internodal connections essential to the speciation process. Perceived complexity in organizational alternatives, it appears, also inhibits entrepreneurial innovation, indeed, dramatically so. Almost all research studies show required complexity in organizations to have increased over time — indeed, this development is the cornerstone of the institutional school of organizational theory (Meyer & Scott, 1983). The Lumsden and Singh chapter, then, suggests that entrepreneurial and institutional processes are somewhat antagonistic. It also suggests that the established organizations have an interest in perpetuating variety and complexity as barriers to market entry. But its most important contribution is in introducing the notion of speciation to thinking about organizations.

Winter on Evolutionary Economics

Sidney Winter's essay on survival, selection, and inheritance is a major statement of the precepts of evolutionary economics and is in some respects a significant advance over the Nelson and Winter volume, *An Evolutionary Theory of Economic Change* (1982). No summary can do justice to this carefully crafted chapter, which, in my judgment, stands out among the excellent chapters in the second part of this volume. It is nonetheless possible to sketch Winter's key propositions, which are as follows: The most appropriate unit of analysis when studying organizations is the routine or competence. Environmental feedback tells organizations whether or not their routines and competencies are successful. Successful routines are replicated, leading to growth, while unsuccessful routines die off. Because success yields replication, large size is associated with profitability (in firms) as well as with enhanced survival chances. The same association of large size with survival and prosperity indicates that literal biological analogies do not fit firms well; organisms, whose growth is limited due to genetic inheritance, and organizations, which grow through inheritance and hence spatial replication of routines, follow different laws. Diversification is often an outcome of adding activities requiring more of the same competencies already possessed by firms. Vertical integration occurs after firms possess the competence needed to move either upstream or downstream. Large conglomerates operating vastly unrelated businesses, however, are evolutionary aberrations, "hopeful monsters" likely to be eliminated because headquarters cannot pay their way.

Winter's views place him at odds with orthodox economists. But they also set him apart from both transaction-cost economics, which offers an affirmative interpretation of large size and diversity in firms, and organizational ecology, which largely overlooks the possibility of variation and hence improvement within organizations. The contrast with organizational ecology is especially pertinent to this volume. In this regard, let me quote Winter directly: "Scant attention is given [in population ecology] to the possibility that some members of the organizational populations under study may simply be better than others at making a living. . . . the growth of more fit organizations . . . tends to give them larger resources as buffers against adversity than they had at birth." These statements reproduce Levinthal's argument, albeit in different language. The parallel between Levinthal and Winter becomes exact once one substitutes the notion that some firms are, perhaps for accidental reasons, more fit than others for the random walk process, and the notion of organizational growth for the accumulation of capital stock.

What weaknesses, if any, are there in Winter's position? I see two. One is the notion of routine. Conceptually, it is appealing. But, operationally, bounding and measuring routines may prove controversial and, probably, elusive. To illustrate: Is fast food or fast-food fried chicken a routine? (Burgers do differ from Kentucky Fried.) Winter's best defense is that organizations, as understood by ecologists, also have fuzzy boundaries. (When Consolidated Foods owned Fundimensions, which, in turn, owned Lionel Trains, which was the organization?) However, organizations often have legal standing and membership criteria, whereas routines have neither of these properties. Another weakness lies in Winter's appeal for a "common position" from which evolutionists, economists, and other students might operate. The gist of this common position is that data are better than conjecture, even highly formalized conjecture; from a societal point of view, organizational births and deaths often serve the same function as adaptation but not always so; and the only useful generalizations about organizations are highly qualified ones. I cannot help but wonder whether this common position is but another hopeful monster, which seeks to unite theories that are too diverse to be reconciled because they operate in different domains. Might it not be more useful to seek knowledge aggressively as to where the precepts of ecology apply and where the metaphors of evolutionary economics are more apt than to seek a premature theoretical consensus?

SUMMARY REMARKS

With some effort, it would be possible to classify the chapters in Part II on several dimensions, including the unit of analysis (routines in Winter, people in McPherson, and so on), ecological versus evolutionary perspective (the former position maintained most consistently by Hannan and his colleagues, the latter by Winter, and the like). But such classification, I believe, would serve to obscure rather than to illuminate the central issue raised here, namely, whether we must begin to theorize about where the laws of organizational ecology apply and where the laws of organizational evolution, which permit considerable latitude for adaptation and change within organizations, take precedence over the laws of population ecology. Quite frankly, I think that we have not even begun to think about the implications of these contrasting views. To illustrate: Some advocates of ecology argue that it is a science of small organizations (which, after all, are numerically the majority).[3] The advocates of evolution might not agree. Winter's chapter, for example, argues that evolutionary economics is centrally concerned with large firms. But Winter also argues that organizations remaining small do not grow because the environment selects against them. By implication, then, the evolutionary perspective stereotypes population ecology as the science of failing and failed organizations.

An empirical question, then, is whether successful but nonadaptive organizations are possible, and, if so, where we may expect to find them. Some possibilities come to mind: highly specialized small business enterprises and industrial firms having highly specialized capital assets, which cannot be redeployed cheaply. A further empirical question concerns whether second-order evolution is possible, that is, whether large firms shape their own evolution by structuring subunits that are highly vulnerable to the laws of ecology. Burgelman's chapter points in this direction but does not go far enough: While autonomy probably enhances the likelihood that any particular strategy and hence the subunit attached to it will fail, restricting capital accumulation and growth within subunits will in all likelihood accelerate failure rates even more dramatically. Other questions should be pursued. The issue of imprinting remains central to the ecology/evolution debate. Imprinting might be understood merely as stasis, as nonadaptation within organizations. But imprinting may represent the perfection of organizational routines and competencies, in which case it would be understood as adaptive. I very much doubt that large-scale macroscopic research will be able to address questions like these effectively. I believe, rather, that we are going to have to enter into the world of functioning organizations and observe them closely over time in order to develop even suggestive answers.

Toward this end, let me advance some tentative hypotheses. Size is a crucial causal variable: Small organizations are subject to the laws of ecology, whereas large organizations tend to follow the rules of evolution. But size is also an outcome: Firms not defeated by ecological processes evolve and hence grow. Institutional processes play a role in the choice between ecology and evolution. Organizations seek institutional supports for protection against ecological forces. Indeed, the largest organizations, national governments, are usually called institutions and are surrounded by mechanisms aimed at promoting orderly change (elections, courts) that preserves the continuity of the larger system. Finally, we need to know whether ecological processes can be managed and hence directed toward the evolution of larger corporate systems operating in truly competitive environments. Competition is normally unforgiving of error, yet improvement cannot occur if errors prove fatal. It may be that a richer understanding of market structures will be possible if we can bring both ecological and evolutionary perspectives to bear on them.

Organizational ecology is at a turning point. There is a choice between further studies of births and deaths, either by extending the populations studied or by extending current studies further over time, and taking our ideas about ecology and evolution within organizations and developing the kinds of thick knowledge necessary to make fine discriminations and interpretations. I am not arguing that we should return to the era when organizational studies were exclusively case studies. But I do believe that theory building and theory testing require greater variety in our observations than we now have, and that arguments for and against particular theoretical propositions should hinge upon the results of both extensive and intensive studies.

NOTES

1. This statement reflects the position taken initially by Hannan and Freeman (1977) but modified since (1984).

2. Table 1 assumes homogeneity among the organizations studied, as it is well known that population heterogeneity will produce artifactual age dependence in mortality rates. See Barnett and Carroll (1987, pp. 407-408) for data showing age dependence to disappear as sources of heterogeneity are controlled. Table 1 also assumes the fit of organizations to environments to be relatively good at the time of formation. This assumption seems reasonable, as it is well known that organizations reflect environmental conditions existing at their time of formation throughout their lifetimes (Meyer & Brown, 1977; Stinchcombe, 1965).

3. See Aldrich (1979) for a full statement of this view.

REFERENCES

Aldrich, H. E. (1979). *Organizations and environments.* Englewood Cliffs, NJ: Prentice-Hall.

Barnett, W., & Carroll G. (1987). Competition and mutualism among early telephone companies. *Administrative Science Quarterly, 32,* 400-421.

Carroll, G. R. (1985). Concentration and specialization: Dynamics of niche width in populations. *American Journal of Sociology, 90,* 1262-1283.

Hannan, M. T., & Freeman, J. (1977). The population ecology of organizations. *American Journal of Sociology, 82,* 929-964.

Hannan, M., & Freeman, J. H. (1984). Structural inertia and organizational change. *American Sociological Review, 49,* 149-164.

Meyer, J. W., & Scott, W. R. (1983). *Organizational environments: Ritual and rationality.* Beverly Hills, CA: Sage.

Meyer, M. W., & Brown, M. C. (1977). The process of bureaucratization. *American Journal of Sociology, 83,* 364-385.

Meyer, M. W., & Zucker, L. G. (1989). *Permanently failing organizations.* Newbury Park, CA: Sage.

Nelson, R. R., & Winter, S. G. (1982). *An evolutionary theory of economic change.* Cambridge, MA: Harvard University Press.

Stinchcombe, A. L. (1965). Social structure and organizations. In J. G. March (Ed.), *Handbook of organizations* (pp. 142-193). Chicago: Rand McNally.

Williamson, O. E. (1975). *Markets and hierarchies: Analysis and antitrust implications.* New York: Free Press.

13

Future Directions in
Organizational Evolution

JITENDRA V. SINGH

The rich diversity of the preceding chapters bears testimony to the current intellectual excitement among organizational evolution researchers. In addition, however, the various chapters help to highlight some important questions that are outstanding and need to be addressed in the future. This chapter outlines some of these issues.

First, competition in organizational populations needs to be explored further. The usual approach to modeling competition has been the investigation of density dependence of founding and mortality rates (see the chapters by Aldrich, Staber, Zimmer, & Beggs; Freeman, this volume) although McPherson's chapter focuses more on how competition for members drives niche movement, and the Hannan, Ranger-Moore, and Banaszak-Holl chapter emphasizes the effects of size-localized competition on size distributions in populations. The Barnett and Amburgey chapter takes an important step forward by modeling mass dependence of founding and mortality rates simultaneously with density dependence. This permits an examination of the robustness of density dependence. Ruling out alternative interpretations of the density dependence findings in the context of specific populations is a question of more general significance. Whereas the underlying processes of legitimation and competition may be more descriptive of the population of labor unions, in the semiconductor industry the early range of density probably reflects more the learning and copying of technological skills, and it may be difficult to distinguish the two. As discussed below, testing competing theoretical models for density dependence of founding and mortality rates holds considerable promise.

Second, although there already exists some work on how founding conditions imprint the character of an organization, the nature of imprinting itself and what processes underlie it need further elaboration. How, for example, is imprinting best studied? Should it be studied by examining the effects of founding conditions on organizational mortality? Such an approach is related to the Carroll and Hannan chapter, which shows how density at founding influences mortality rates in five populations. Or is another appropriate approach to examine how founding conditions influence organizational processes themselves? The Tucker, Singh, and Meinhard chapter takes this latter approach by exploring how founding conditions influence rates of change in organizational features themselves. It may be that the effects of changing environmental conditions work over time to erode the persistence of imprinting effects on change processes.

Third, an area of crucial importance deals with individual organizational change, an issue frequently seized upon by critics (Astley & Van de Ven, 1983; Perrow, 1986; Young, 1988). Most work in organizational ecology has hitherto focused on demographic processes of organizational founding and disbanding. This was premised mainly on the assumption that organizational forms, once created, are relatively inert. This was a quite sensible initial modeling strategy, but it is now time to examine empirically under what conditions this assumption is valid. This is particularly significant because some empirical evidence suggests systematic relationships between organizational changes and mortality (Carroll, 1984a; Singh, House, & Tucker, 1986). Such work on intraorganizational change (also see the Burgelman, Tucker et al., and Winter chapters in this volume), when taken together with research on foundings and mortality, promises a significant beginning to an evolutionary approach to strategy and organization in the future (Burgelman & Singh, 1988). An added advantage of this view is that it demonstrates the fundamental complementarity of adaptation and selection views of organization, offering a partial resolution to the often-debated issue.

Fourth, the continuing convergence of ecological and institutional ideas (Singh & Lumsden, 1990) holds significant promise for future progress. Two specific ways in which this convergence has occurred are already well established in the literature. The first explores the effects of institutional changes, particularly related to the role of the state, on vital rates in organizational populations. The second approach examines the role of legitimacy in population dynamics, either through how the acquisition of institutional support reduces selection pressures on organizations (Singh, Tucker, & House, 1986) or through the density dependence of founding and mortality rates. Less explored, however, is how ecological dynamics culminate in institutional changes, an important question still open.

Fifth, work on community ecology can add significantly to organizational evolution research. Although the community level has long been acknowledged as important (Astley, 1985; Carroll, 1984b), researchers have only recently attended to it more seriously (see, for example, Barnett & Carroll, 1987; Beard & Dess, 1988). In their chapter in this volume, Barnett and Amburgey demonstrate how increasing population mass increases foundings and reduces mortality of early telephone companies, contrary to their expectations. They interpret their results to support mutualism among the community of telephone companies. In his chapter, McPherson examines the evolution of communities of voluntary organizations over time by focusing on changes in organizational niches. Among others, the question of what processes drive change and stability in the structure of organizational communities is likely to yield rich dividends.

Sixth, an important but underexplored area relates to systematics (Baum, 1989; McKelvey, 1982). Until now, most researchers have defined populations as aggregates of fundamentally similar organizations. Although this was itself a major step forward, a more thoroughly grounded evolutionary approach demands more work. What is needed is a theory of differences that enables classification and taxonomy research. It has also been argued that such work would render research findings more applicable (McKelvey & Aldrich, 1983).

Seventh, critics of organizational ecology research have pointed to its inattention to how organizational forms are created (Astley, 1985; Young, 1988). This is an important, though thorny, problem. It seems evident that the dynamics of such speciation events (see Lumsden & Singh's chapter) may be different from the founding of new organizations of the same form. The first of a new form of organization encounters more severe legitimacy problems and cannot readily access the mimetic opportunities available to following organizations. Modeling speciation and linking it to founding processes promises significant potential for progress. Analogously, another question in need of greater exploration is that of population extinction, the disbanding of the last of an organizational form. An interesting question is whether, like speciation, this is a different class of event from disbanding or if it should be treated as another form of disbanding.

Eighth, an arguable weakness of much of the work on organizational ecology has been the lack of strong inference (Platt, 1964). This consists of explicitly developing and testing equally plausible competing theoretical models. An advantage of such an approach is that progress can be dramatically enhanced by using data to rule out competing views. Arguments in this spirit are already appearing (see Carroll & Hannan, 1989a, 1989b; Zucker, 1989), and suggest that researchers may resort to strong inference more frequently in the future.

Finally, a critical examination of the nature of organizational evolution is one fundamental question that requires more attention. Current research approaches range from Darwinian (Hannan & Freeman, 1989) to more Lamarckian views (Nelson & Winter, 1982; Winter, this volume). Whereas, for biological organisms, evolution is primarily based on propagation of genes, and is, therefore, genealogical, organizational evolution is different. Organizational evolution begins with the appearance of a new form, a product of entrepreneurial thinking, and ends with the extinction of the last organization of a specific form. Thus organizational evolution incorporates speciation, founding, failure, transformation, and extinction, and it is sensible to talk of selection, adaptation, learning, populations, and communities. The critical question that needs answering is how organizational evolution resembles biotic evolution, and the ways in which it is uniquely different. A fundamental challenge for organizational evolution researchers is to develop an approach with a preponderance of Lamarckian rather than Mendelian inheritance mechanisms. Such social learning-related inheritance mechanisms have the added advantage of easily admitting change in individual organizations and attending to the hierarchical nature of organizational evolution (Singh & Lumsden, 1990).

REFERENCES

Astley, W. G. (1985). The two ecologies: Population and community perspectives on organizational evolution. *Administrative Science Quarterly, 30*, 224-241.

Astley, W. G., & Van de Ven, A. H. (1983). Central perspectives and debates in organization theory. *Administrative Science Quarterly, 28*, 245-273.

Barnett, W., & Carroll, G. (1987). Competition and mutualism among early telephone companies. *Administrative Science Quarterly, 32*, 400-421.

Baum, J. A. C. (1989). *A population perspective on organizations: A study of diversity and transformation in child care service organizations.* Unpublished doctoral dissertation, University of Toronto, Faculty of Management Studies.

Beard, D. W., & Dess, G. G. (1988). Modeling organizational species' interdependence in an organizational community: An input-output approach. *Academy of Management Review, 13*(3), 362-373.

Burgelman, R. A., & Singh, J. V. (1988). *Strategy and organization: An evolutionary approach* (Working Paper 89-04). Philadelphia: University of Pennsylvania, Wharton School, Reginald H. Jones Center for Management Policy, Strategy and Organization.

Carroll, G. R. (1984a). Dynamics of publisher succession in newspaper organizations. *Administrative Science Quarterly, 29*(1), 93-113.

Carroll, G. R. (1984b). Organizational ecology. *Annual Review of Sociology, 10,* 71-93.

Carroll, G. R., & Hannan, M. T. (1989a). Density dependence in the evolution of populations of newspaper organizations. *American Sociological Review, 54,* 524-541.

Carroll, G. R., & Hannan, M. T. (1989b). On using institutional theory in studying organizational populations. *American Sociological Review, 54,* 545-548.

Hannan, M. T., & Freeman, J. (1989). *Organizational ecology.* Cambridge, MA: Harvard University Press.

McKelvey, B. (1982). *Organizational systematics: Taxonomy, evolution, classification.* Berkeley: University of California Press.

McKelvey, B., & Aldrich, H. E. (1983). Populations, organizations and applied organizational science. *Administrative Science Quarterly, 28,* 101-128.

Nelson, R. R., & Winter, S. G. (1982). *An evolutionary theory of economic change.* Cambridge, MA: Harvard University Press.

Perrow, C. (1986). *Complex organizations: A critical essay* (3rd ed.). New York: Random House.

Platt, J. R. (1964). Strong inference. *Science, 146*(3642), 347-353.

Singh, J. V., House, R. J., & Tucker, D. J. (1986). Organizational change and organizational mortality. *Administrative Science Quarterly, 31,* 587-611.

Singh, J. V., & Lumsden, C. J. (1990). Theory and research in organizational ecology. *Annual Review of Sociology, 16:* 161-195.

Singh, J. V., Tucker, D. J., & House, R. J. (1986). Organizational legitimacy and the liability of newness. *Administrative Science Quarterly, 31,* 171-193.

Young, R. C. (1988). Is population ecology a useful paradigm for the study of organizations? *American Journal of Sociology, 94*(1), 1-24.

Zucker, L. G. (1989). Combining institutional theory and population ecology: No legitimacy, no history. *American Sociological Review, 54,* 542-545.

Author Index

Subject Index

About the Editor

Jitendra V. Singh is Joseph Wharton Term Associate Professor of Management, The Wharton School, University of Pennsylvania. His research interests center around models of ecological and evolutionary processes in organizations and populations. His research has appeared in *Administrative Science Quarterly, Academy of Management Journal, Annual Review of Psychology, American Sociological Review,* and *Annual Review of Sociology,* among others. He currently serves on the editorial boards of *Administrative Science Quarterly, Academy of Management Journal,* and *Organization Science.* He received his MBA at the Indian Institute of Management, Ahmedabad, India, and his Ph.D. in organization theory and behavior from the Graduate School of Business, Stanford University.

About the Contributors

Howard Aldrich is Professor of Sociology, Director of the Industrial Relations Curriculum, and Adjunct Professor of Business Administration at the University of North Carolina, Chapel Hill. His book, *Organizations and Environments*, was one of the first major statements in organizational ecology. With his collaborators, he is currently working on patterns of organizational founding and merger in the American trade association population. He is also conducting a cross-national study of social networks and entrepreneurship.

Terry L. Amburgey received his Ph.D. in sociology from Stanford University in 1984. He is an Assistant Professor of Management at the University of Wisconsin – Madison. His research interests include organizational ecology, institutional theory, and corporate strategy.

Jane Banaszak-Holl is a graduate student in sociology at Cornell University. Her recent work focuses on the effects of legitimation and competition on the founding and failure rates and size distributions of organizational populations. Her current research includes a study of the evolution of commercial and savings banks in Manhattan from 1791 through 1980.

William P. Barnett is an Assistant Professor of Management at the School of Business, University of Wisconsin – Madison. His research on the organizational ecology of the American telephone industry has appeared in *Administrative Science Quarterly*. He is now concluding his investigation of that industry with a study of the effects of deregulation, and is beginning a study of multiestablishment competition among American banks. He received his Ph.D. in business administration from the University of California, Berkeley.

Joel A. C. Baum is an Assistant Professor of Management at the Stern School of Business, New York University. He received his Ph.D. in 1989 from the University of Toronto. His current research is focused on the development of a population perspective on organizations. His specific areas of inquiry include organizational taxonomy and classification, age dependence in change and persistence in organizational populations, the complementarity

332

of adaptation and selection processes in organizational populations, and the roles of organizational founding, failure, and change in the transformation of organizational populations.

John J. Beggs is an Assistant Professor in the Department of Sociology at Louisiana State University. His dissertation research at the University of Illinois at Chicago examined the effects on labor market outcomes of equal opportunity attitudes and public sector presence in the industrial environment. His published work includes research on the effects of Black entrepreneurship on the urban Black community. His current research projects include a study of the organizational ecology of trade associations and a project examining the ecology and measurement of the urban underclass.

Robert A. Burgelman is Associate Professor of Management at the Graduate School of Business, Stanford University. He was the BP America Faculty Fellow for 1988-1989. He received a licenciate in applied economics degree from Antwerp University, Belgium, an M.A. degree in sociology, and a Ph.D. degree in management of organizations from Columbia University. He has published articles in *Administrative Science Quarterly, Management Science, Academy of Management Review, Strategic Management Journal, Sloan Management Review,* and other journals. He is coauthor of *Inside Corporate Innovation: Strategy, Structure and Managerial Skills* (Free Press, 1986) and *Strategic Management of Technology and Innovation* (Irwin, 1988). In 1984 he won the Outstanding Paper Award, Division of Business Policy and Planning, Academy of Management. He has been a speaker at academic conferences and executive education programs in the United States, Europe, Asia, and Australia, and has been a consultant with several major companies.

Glenn R. Carroll is Professor of Business Administration at the University of California at Berkeley. He is also an affiliated faculty member in the university's Sociology Department and an Associate of the Institute of Industrial Relations. His recent books include *Publish and Perish: The Organizational Ecology of Newspaper Industries* (JAI) and *Ecological Models of Organizations* (Ballinger), for which he served as editor.

John Freeman received his Ph.D. in sociology from the University of North Carolina at Chapel Hill in 1972. After spending five years in the Department of Sociology at the University of California at Riverside, he moved to the School of Business Administration at the University of California at Berkeley. Ten years later he moved to Cornell University, where he is jointly appointed in the Johnson Graduate School of Management and the Sociology Department. He also serves as Editor of *Administrative Science Quarterly*. With Michael T. Hannan, he published *Organizational Ecology* in 1989. This monograph reports 15 years of collaborative research on population ecology of organizations. His current work focuses on the process by which changing technology affects the dynamics of organizational populations.

Michael T. Hannan is Henry Scarborough Professor of Social Sciences and a member of the Sociology Department at Cornell University. His research focuses on organizational ecology and evolution. His recent books include *Social Dynamics: Models and Methods* (with Nancy Brandon Tuma), *Organizational Ecology* (with John Freeman), and the forthcoming *Legitimation and Competition in the Evolution of Organizational Populations* (with Glenn R. Carroll).

Robert J. House (Ph.D., Ohio State University, 1960) is the Joseph Frank Bernstein Professor of Organizational Studies at the Wharton School of Management. He has served as a consultant to several of the largest U.S. and Canadian corporations and is the author of four books and seventy articles in professional and learned journals. He is a fellow of the Academy of Management and the American Psychological Association. His research on population ecology, with Jitendra V. Singh and David M. Tucker, has been recognized by awards of excellence from the Academy of Management and the Canadian Association of Administrative Sciences. His current research concerns the distribution and exercise of power in complex organizations and the behavior and effects of charismatic leadership in complex organizations.

Daniel A. Levinthal is May Department Stores Term Associate Professor of Management at the Wharton School, University of Pennsylvania. His current research interests are interorganizational relationships, organizational learning, and industry evolution. His recent publications include "Dynamics of Interorganizational Attachments: Auditor-Client Relationships" (with Mark Fichman; *Administrative Science Quarterly*, September 1988), "Innovation and Learning: The Two Faces of R&D" (with Wesley Cohen; *Economic Journal*, September 1989), and "Durable Goods and Product Obsolescence" (with Davavrat Purohit; *Marketing Science*, Winter 1989). He received his Ph.D. in 1985 from the Graduate School of Business, Stanford University.

Charles J. Lumsden is Associate Professor and Medical Research Council Career Scientist, Department of medicine, at the University of Toronto. His undergraduate and graduate degrees, all in theoretical physics, are from Toronto. He is interested in evolution of mind and the relations between biological and cultural history. He is coauthor of *Genes, Mind, and Culture: The Coevolutionary Process*; *Promethean Fire: Reflections on the Origins of Mind*; and *The Creative Mind*. He has published extensively on mathematical theories of gene-culture coevolution.

J. Miller McPherson is Professor of Sociology at Cornell University. He is gathering new data on voluntary associations to test the theory outlined in this volume under a grant from the National Science Foundation. He is also testing some aspects of this theory using data from the General Social Survey. He has collaborative projects under way on social networks, church memberships, the dynamics of organizational memberships, and other related issues.

Agnes G. Meinhard is Assistant Professor, Faculty of Management, University of Toronto, Toronto, Ontario. Her research interests include organizational ecology, women in organizations, group processes and intergroup relations, and the use of advanced multivariate statistical procedures in the analysis of longitudinal social data. Her publications have appeared as chapters in books as well as in *Academy of Management Journal, International Journal of Communications Research, Social Review,* and *Journal of Welfare and Social Security.* She received her Ph.D. in social psychology from the University of Tel Aviv.

Marshall W. Meyer is Professor of Management and Anheuser-Busch Term Professor in the Wharton School and Professor of Sociology at the University of Pennsylvania. He has taught at Harvard, Cornell, and the University of California, Riverside, and has been a Visiting Professor at UCLA and the Yale School of Organization and Management. Some of his books include *Environments and Organizations* (with several coauthors), *Change in Public Bureaucracies, Limits to Bureaucratic Growth* and *Bureaucracy in Modern Society* (with Peter M. Blau), and *Permanently Failing Organizations* (with Lynne Zucker). He is President of Research Committee 17, Sociology of Organizations, of the International Sociological Association. He has served on the editorial boards of *Administrative Science Quarterly, American Sociological Review, Computational Statistics and Data Analysis, Contemporary Sociology, Social Forces,* and *Social Science Quarterly,* and is currently Associate Editor of *Administrative Science Quarterly.*

James Ranger-Moore is a National Science Foundation Fellow at Cornell University. His recent works have focused on the use of simulation techniques to model size distributions in organizational populations. His current research interests include the evolution of the life insurance industry in New

York State and changes in the composition of voluntary associations over time.

Udo Staber received his Ph.D. in organization theory from the New York State School of Industrial and Labor Relations at Cornell University. He is currently an Associate Professor in the Faculty of Administration at the University of New Brunswick, Canada. He has published primarily on trade associations and cooperatives, and is currently involved (with D. Boegenhold) in an international comparative study of trends in self-employment.

David J. Tucker is Professor, School of Social Work, McMaster University, Hamilton, Ontario and from fall 1990 will be a Professor at the School of Social Work, University of Michigan, Ann Arbor. His research interests include the structural analysis of interorganizational service delivery systems, the ecology of human service organizations, and the critical analysis of selected public policy issues. His publications have appeared in a variety of journals, including *Academy of Management Journal, Administrative Science Quarterly, Social Service Review,* and *Canadian Public Policy,* and as chapters in several books. He received his Ph.D. in social work from the University of Toronto.

Sidney G. Winter is a graduate of Swarthmore College and received his Ph.D. in economics from Yale University in 1964. His most recent academic post was at Yale, where he was Professor of Economics and Management from 1976 to June 1989. He had previously served on the faculties of the University of California, Berkeley, and the University of Michigan. Early in his career he was a staff member of the RAND Corporation and of the Council of Economic Advisers, and he has since served as a consultant for a variety of public, private, and nonprofit organizations. His primary research interests have been in the area of firm behavior and technological change. While at Yale he coauthored *An Evolutionary Theory of Economic Change* (1982), and was founding Coeditor of the *Journal of Economic Behavior and Organization* (1980). He is currently the Chief Economist of the U.S. General Accounting Office in Washington, D.C.

Catherine Zimmer is an Assistant Professor of Sociology at North Carolina State University, Raleigh. Her current research focuses generally on organization-environment links, with specific projects on the environmental causes of organizational misconduct and, with Howard Aldrich and Udo Staber, the organizational demography of trade associations. She received her Ph.D. in sociology from the University of North Carolina at Chapel Hill.